LEARNING POLITICS FROM SIVARAM

Anthropology, Culture and Society

Series Editor:
Dr Jon P. Mitchell, University of Sussex

RECENT TITLES:

LEARNING POLITICS FROM SIVARAM

The Life and Death of a Revolutionary Tamil Journalist in Sri Lanka

Mark P. Whitaker

Pluto  Press

LONDON • ANN ARBOR, MI

First published 2007 by Pluto Press
345 Archway Road, London N6 5AA
and 839 Greene Street, Ann Arbor, MI 48106

www.plutobooks.com

British Library Cataloguing in Publication Data
A catalogue record for this book is available from the British Library

Hardback
ISBN-10   0 7453 2354 5
ISBN-13   978 0 7453 2354 1
Paperback
ISBN-10   0 7453 2353 7
ISBN-13   978 0 7453 2353 4

Library of Congress Cataloging in Publication Data applied for

10   9   8   7   6   5   4   3   2   1

Designed and produced for Pluto Press by
Chase Publishing Services Ltd, Fortescue, Sidmouth, EX10 9QG, England
Typeset from disk by Stanford DTP Services, Northampton, England
Printed and bound in the European Union by
Antony Rowe Ltd, Chippenham and Eastbourne, England

CONTENTS

ACKNOWLEDGEMENTS

Sivaram often used to say '*My* riches are my people. I collect people.' The truth of this became more generally apparent to me as I was trying to remember all of the people – most, like me, members of Sivaram's 'collection' – who helped create this book.

Research for this project was funded by three research grants from the University of South Carolina and by an American Institute of Sri Lankan Studies Fellowship. Jeanne Merecek, John Rogers and other AISLS members helped make my time as a fellow in 2003–04 rewarding. The University of South Carolina, Aiken, graciously granted me leave for the 2003–04 school year so that I could complete my research. I want to express my gratitude to the Anthropology Department at Sussex University for making me a visiting research fellow for the fall of 2003. In Sri Lanka, the International Centre for Ethnic Studies, Kandy, kindly allowed me access to their well-stocked and thankfully cool library, as well as some much needed cups of tea. For this I want to thank S.W.R de A. Samurasinghe, the Institute's director, and Kanthi Gamage, the centre's supremely helpful Librarian and Documentation Officer, who often pointed me toward resources that later proved invaluable. I also want to thank K.M. DeSilva for setting set me straight about several events at Peradeniya University during the 1983 riots. My thanks to Neelan Thiruchelvam of the International Centre for Ethnic Studies, Colombo, for answering many questions when he was so busy in 1997 must be, sadly, posthumous. S. Nadarajah, Chief Editor of *Viirakeesari*, was extremely generous in making available to me copies of all of Sivaram Dharmeratnam's 2003–04 columns. I want to thank the editors of TamilNet.com for answering so many questions about their operation.

At Pluto Press I want to thank Anne Beech, the Managing Director, for her early and continuing interest in this project. David Castle, Robert Webb and Sophie Richmond edited my manuscript with admirable dispatch and tolerance for my various foibles. Ray Addicott and Chase Publishing Services have also been most helpful with the production. Back on my side of the Atlantic, Diane Cochrane deserves special thanks for helping me wrestle American spellings and usages into compliance with Pluto Press's British style sheet. I am also in debt to two anonymous reviewers of my original book proposal. Their comments were brilliant, and helped me reshape the book to address audiences I might otherwise have neglected.

My larger intellectual and social debts are too many to completely enumerate. First of all, of course, is what I owe Sivaram Dharmeratnam. For 24 years he was my friend and intellectual jousting partner; I do not – I never shall – quite believe it is over. Years ago Gananath Obeyesekere, as my academic mentor, provided a wonderful introduction to Sri Lanka. This project was also inspired, in various ways, by the works of Kevin Dwyer, Kumari Jayawardene, Newton Gunasinghe, S.J. Tambiah, Susan Harding, David Anthony, and E. Valentine Daniel. Conversations, in turn, with both K. Sivathamby and the late K. Kailasapathy, though separated by sixteen years, helped convince me of the importance of studying the *intellectual* history of Tamil Sri Lanka. Michael Roberts encouragingly edited my first essay on Sivaram. A brief outline of this project was read to a South Asian work group at the University of California, Santa Cruz. I want to thank Triloki Pandey, Annapurna Pandey, Kristy Bright, and Dina Siddiqi for their encouragement and helpful comments. Anne Blackburn and Laura Ahearn, members of my South Asia study group at the University of South Carolina, read and helpfully commented upon other parts of this project. I also presented bits of this book at colloquia for the Anthropology Department at the University of South Carolina, and am grateful for the many useful comments I found there. R.L Stirrat, Elizabeth Nissen, Dennis McGilvray, Patricia Lawrence and Jude Fernando have all granted me not only the benefit of their superior expertise but also their congenial hospitality. Jonathan Spencer, in addition to being a kind and humorous host, also shared keen critical insight into some of the trickier issues involved in doing a biography such as this. I also want to thank Michele Ruth Gamburd, Margaret Trawick, Yuvaraj Thangaraj, Ram Alegan, Seela Aleduwaka, Ramani Hettiarachchi, and Laxman Kumara Keerthi for sharing, at various times, their professional insights about Sri Lanka. R. Cheran and D.B.S. Jeyaraj amiably answered some last minute questions. Rajes Kandiah, Bhamini Jayaraman, David Buck, Balasundaram Elayathamby, and S. Punchchalingam all helped me cope with my weak Tamil. Many journalists were generous with their advice and ideas, often in difficult circumstances. J.S. Tissainayagam, Gamini Weerakon, Marwaan Macan-markar, V.S.Sambadan, Chandana Keerthi Bandara and Rajpal Abeynayake must all be thanked.

My friends and family, thankfully, have sustained me through this long and sometimes difficult project. To have parents like Burt and Hilda Whitaker, a brother like Jeff Whitaker, and a sister like Gail Wright is to be rich indeed. Ann Kingsolver, my wife, not only loyally supported my many years of work on this biography but also, as a fellow anthropologist and researcher, shaped it for the better. David, my son, put up with all our travel and loved his uncle Sivaram.

It almost goes without saying that I could not have completed this book without the kind forbearance of all the Sri Lankan people I interviewed. I thank you all from the bottom of my heart. But it is to Sivaram's far-flung family, I think, that I owe my deepest thanks. They not only put up with my presence and my probing questions, but also added their own insights and ideas – so much so that this book clearly became a collective enterprise. Meena Dharmeratnam and S. Dharmavasan both took time to read and correct the manuscript; and I must thank S. Dharmavasan and his father, Somasundaram, further, for allowing my family to stay in their lovely house in Batticaloa, and for other kindnesses while we were in Sri Lanka. In Suriyakumaran Dharmeratnam and K.O.Pillai I found gracious hospitality, intellectual companionship, and new-found kin. Lee Karu made my visit to London in 2001 truly memorable. Surendaran and Seevaratnam Vellupillai were also most kind. I must thank all the other family members in Colombo, Batticaloa, London and Toronto who have received me with such kindness. Daniel and David Poopalipillai, Bavani's brothers, have been yet more brothers to me. Bavani, Vaishnavi, Vaitheki, and Seralaathan have become a part of our family now, and we a part of theirs.

Finally, I would like to dedicate this book to the Sri Lankan journalists of all ethnicities who, like Sivaram, risk their lives every day, or have already lost them, to keep the stories coming.

NOTE ON TRANSLITERATION, TRANSLATION, NAMES, AND NEUTRALITY

The Sri Lankan Tamil words and phrases in this book are transliterated according to the scheme used in David McAlpin's *A Core Vocabulary for Tamil* (1976: xix–xxc). Tamil's long vowels are signaled by doubling letters, and retroflex consonants by capitalization. Readers of English can get a feel for long-vowel Tamil sounds if they hold doubled vowels (aa, ee, ii, oo, uu) for an extra beat. Retroflex consonants, transliterated here as 'L,' 'N,' and 'T,' can be approximated by rolling back one's tongue and touching the roof of one's mouth (which sounds more difficult than it is) while pronouncing the English sounds 'l,' 'n,' or 't.' The letter transliterated here as 't' sounds a bit like the 'th' sound in 'thespian.' The Tamil letter transliterated here as 'R' represents a lightly trilled 'tr' sound. The letter transliterated as 'c' can sometimes sound like an English 's' and sometimes, especially when doubled in the middle of words, like the 'ch' sound in 'church' or 'chug.' The letter transliterated as 'k' can sound like either the English 'k' at the beginning of words, and a 'g' or 'h' elsewhere. There is also a letter in Tamil, here rendered as 'ng,' which sounds like the 'ng' sound in the English word 'sing.' I have generally refrained from transliterating place names and people's personal names, preferring to allow them to appear as they generally do in English maps and newspapers.

I have had, and certainly required, a lot of help understanding written Tamil. Sivaram Dharmeratnam translated most of the Tamil words and texts discussed in the earlier chapters of this book. V.B. Jeyaraman of Kandy helped me read twelve of Sivaram's later *Viirakeesari* articles, and translated many more. David Buck, a translator and Tamil scholar, gave me the benefit of his insights into Sivaram's Tamil prose style. And Dennis McGilvray of the University of Colorado frequently supplied me with the meanings of words and phrases. I thank them all. Any mistakes, however, are all mine.

This is a hybrid book: an intellectual biography written by an ethnographer. Because this is an intellectual biography, and thus a form of history, I have used people's names whenever people gave me permission to use them, or whenever the person in question was a public figure. Because some of the background of this book is ethnographic, however, I have mostly avoided using names altogether when discussing things in general or, of course, whenever people wished to remain anonymous. Ex-Tamil militants who appear in this book are generally identified only by their 'party names' or aliases. This, generally, was how Sivaram told me about them, and I have made no effort to go beyond what he told me to find out or use their real names, nor did he want me to. I have made an exception, however, for those militants or ex-militants who became public figures. I should add that Batticaloa Tamil names do not work the same way British or American ones do. Generally, the father's name is placed first, followed by the child's name. Hence, Sivaram P. Dharmeratnam in Tamil was Dharmeratnam P. Sivaram. In this book, so as not to be confusing, I have followed the English convention.

Finally, although this book is concerned with Sri Lanka's ethnic struggle, it does not pretend to be a neutral account. If I were writing this as an ethnography of Sri Lanka's crisis as a whole I would have been careful to include a balance of views. But as this is an intellectual biography of Sivaram Dharmeratnam, Sri Lankan events are presented largely as they appeared to him, and Sivaram was anything but neutral. At the same time, Sivaram was a subtle man. Partisans looking either for a straw man or an easy ally likely will be disappointed. Also, I should note that Sivaram was checking for errors as I wrote, but he was killed before I had completed Chapter 5 or had written Chapters 6 and 8. I am responsible, ultimately, for all the errors in this book, but I especially want to apologize in advance for any errors in those chapters.

THREE PROLOGUES

First, it was 1982. Aside from its spectacular heat, I found Sri Lanka's easternmost Batticaloa district before the war a wonderful place in which to live and do anthropological fieldwork. A splash of tawny, alluvial sand between hazy western mountains and the eastern sea of Bengal, the district near harvest time always glistened like burnished gold beneath an exaggerated sun – beckoning, I thought. So, on days when I was bored with fieldwork and in need of some senseless motion, I would allow myself to be called by it. I would climb onto my tiny blue Honda 90, drive out of the Hindu temple village of Mandur, where I was working, and head either south toward the largely Muslim town of Kalmunai, with its busy roadside bazaars and prayer-singing, green- striped mosques, or north to the district capital, Batticaloa, with its sleepier colonial residues, following either way the bumpy road that ran beside the district's long and sluggish, warm, and semi-saline lagoon. Sometimes, if going south, I would stop on the concrete causeway between the two Karaiyar caste villages that people called the Kallars, and watch ungainly young palm trees wave luxuriantly on the sea dike, near where the Portuguese once tried to build a fort in the early seventeenth century; and near, also, where British Methodist missionaries built a school and had rather more success implanting Christianity. Or, on other days, with the excuse of some message for its temple elites, I would dip down toward the rice or 'paddy' fields of Turaineelavanai, an ancient, ciirpaatar caste, Hindu town of sandy paths and *cajan* (mud and straw) walls, established sometime in the distant sixteenth or perhaps seventeenth century by royal fiat of the Buddhist Kandyan kingdom. There, if it was planting time, the new paddy would glow like backlit jade, a color so unrestrainedly iridescent I could never quite take it seriously, and I would have to pause a moment on my bike to stifle my wonder, and a vague hysteria, as hallucinogenic blue and green kingfisher birds wound down low over my head to feast on the new-sown fields. Or, going north, I would run to this bend in the road I liked, closer to Batticaloa town, where the cactuses always seemed to be in bloom. The air would be thick with a syrupy perfume, and the monkeys would come out to play and throw rocks at passing trucks, though never, oddly enough, at me. From there, of course, I would have to drive on into Batticaloa town to carry out whatever task I had invented to give me leave to go. Often this 'task' would be merely a cold beer and a rest in a wicker chair under the fans at the rest house. But it was on one such trip that I first met Sivaram.

As I remember it, I was coming out of the Batticaloa public library at the time. The library was an odd building, curved and slightly crumbly, like a stale cake, and frosted in festive pink and white. With its somewhat colonial gothic overtones, the library seemed to me a kind of colonial spoor. And so it was, for it was built by the British during the waning days of their dominion over Sri Lanka – or, as they called it then, Ceylon – which began in 1796 when they, as part of the European dance for power, cut in to replace the Dutch, who themselves had pushed out the Portuguese little more than a hundred years before that in 1668. When the British left 'Ceylon' in 1948, they ended roughly 400 years of direct colonial control over the Island, traces of which in 1982 could still be seen in Batticaloa's library, with its shelves of mildewed Dickens and Walpole, Russell and Kant, Bertie and Jeeves. But these leavings were, I must admit, a guilty comfort to an often homesick fieldworker, especially one as geeky as me: really better fitted for reading novels in a quiet room than playing the anthropological hero out and about among people busily engaged in life's more serious (and dangerous) pursuits.

In any case, upstairs was the library's more scholarly Batticaloa room which, along with some time-worn wooden tables and chairs, burnished smooth and fragile by many years of use, contained a worthy collection of locally produced monographs. There, Batticaloa intellectuals and historians, pundits and poets, could often be found arguing, in passionate whispers, over details of Batticaloa history or Sri Lankan politics. For my part, I had made a deal with myself that each hour spent downstairs wallowing in nostalgia should be earned upstairs by an hour of diligent scholarship in the Batticaloa room. Yet I think Sivaram probably spotted me downstairs, reading the library's well-worn paperback copy of Gilbert Ryle's *The Concept of Mind*; cheating, that is, on fieldwork by indulging in my old hobby of reading philosophy. However it happened, he was waiting for me when I stepped out of the dark of the library.

'Excuse me. You must be Mark Whitaker, the anthropologist?'

'What? Who?' I fumbled for my sunglasses, almost dropping Ryle.

'But I see you read Mr Ryle too?' He laughed, somewhat sourly. 'Isn't that unusual for a social scientist?'

I finally got my sunglasses on and saw, to my surprise, a very young man, extremely thin and with a face, like mine, largely eclipsed by massive black spectacles. He was dressed in threadbare brown, polyester pants, a dirty white shirt, and disintegrating leather sandals, the whole ensemble seeming to bespeak a genteel but dire poverty. Not a farmer or a 'peon,'[1] then, he looked like a thousand other young Batticaloa men. Perhaps, I thought, he is some low-level clerk, or maybe an undergraduate arts student come to bend my ear about a local caste controversy – although he was, by this time, neither. And how to explain his remark about Ryle? He appeared to be about 18 (he was actually 23); his demeanor, however, was completely, somewhat offensively, assured. He tapped the book I had in my hand.

'If you like this kind of thing, perhaps you should come to lunch at my house. I have started a reading group that discusses philosophy, and other things. And I would like to talk to you about your research.'

He did not smile.

Then it was July 2001. The Sri Lankan civil war was 18 years old. That July day, the summer before the bombing of the Twin Towers and American's war on terror, London was brightly lit by an evanescent sun and somewhat chilly, but peaceful, while Sri Lanka, thousands of miles away, was still burning after a devastating attack upon its central military and commercial airport by the much feared Liberation Tigers of Tamil Eelam (LTTE). Sivaram and I had met up that morning, carrying our bags, to attend his BBC interview, scheduled for that afternoon, and had hurtled about London on the tube beforehand so he could carry out his hectic schedule of other meetings and interviews. We ended by cooling our heels and continuing our argument, in a little triangular park near the BBC building, a park dedicated to the British dead of, I believe, World War I. There was a relatively small, soot-blackened granite plinth at its center on which stood a bronze Tommy gesturing, somewhat anxiously, for help, apparently to a nearby oak tree. There were many names written on the plinth's side.

'I don't suppose,' said Sivaram, morosely, 'that I'll get my name on a memorial.'

'Don't be ridiculous!' I snapped. 'If you think you are in that much danger, don't go back.'

'Young man,' he said, patronizingly, for he often called me 'young man' or, sometimes, *tampi*, younger brother, though I was several years his elder, 'Young man, not going back would be ridiculous.'

I gritted my teeth. We had been arguing about this for weeks, ever since I had met up with him in New York, soon after his arrival from Sri Lanka, to accompany him on a month-long trip to Toronto and London. As, a lot of that time, he had been quite happily partying, the arguments had never seemed to get very far. Nevertheless, he knew my position. It seemed to me that as he had been, several times by then, directly threatened by the Sri Lankan government, it was time to pull himself and his family permanently out of the country. It had seemed to him that this was not even a possibility. And so we argued.

'But now,' he said, holding up a hand, 'it's time for the BBC.'

We collected our bags and tramped to the BBC building. At the reception desk, however, there was a problem. A sallow-eyed, rather Mr Bean-like guard looked at our passports and then looked troubled.

'Mr Sivaram, you are expected, sir, and so may go up. But who,' he eyed me suspiciously, 'are you?'

'I'm his biographer.'

'Entourage,' he sniffed. 'You can certainly wait here.'

'But ... I need to see the interview ...'

'Don't worry,' said Sivaram, somewhat magisterially, and openly laughing, 'I'll send someone down to get you.'

Then it was April, 2005.

Journalist Sivaram murdered

[TamilNet, 29 April 2005, 02:37 GMT] The body of abducted journalist Mr Dharmaretnam [sic] Sivaram was found with severe head injuries in Himbulala, a Sinhala suburb between Jayawardhenapura hospital and the Parliament building in Colombo Friday morning. The location is about 500 meters behind the parliamentary complex and lies inside a high security zone. Mr Sivaram, a senior editorial board member of TamilNet, was abducted Thursday evening around 10:30 pm by unidentified persons in front of the Bambalapitya Police Station in Colombo.

Family members visited the scene and have identified the body ...

1 INTRODUCTION: WHY AN INTELLECTUAL BIOGRAPHY OF SIVARAM DHARMERATNAM?

On the field of truth, on the battle-field of life
What came to pass, Sanjaya, when my sons and their
Warriors faced those of my brother Pandu?
(*Bhagavad Gita* 1962: 43)

A Lotus blossoms in the mud! (A frequent saying of Mahesvari, Sivaram's mother)

You made me realize the fecundity of Being, which you have completely misunderstood! (Sivaram Dharmeratnam, personal communication about an earlier draft of this book)

This is how it was supposed to happen. When the book came out, I would stick it in my bags and travel to Sri Lanka. Once there, I would go to his house in Mt Lavinia, near Colombo, and invent a reason why we had to go to Batticaloa, his beloved hometown. He would complain at first but ultimately comply; for, if pressed hard enough, he could not refuse a maccaang. *So we would travel east by van, most likely at night, as we had done so many times before, first north, to Habarana, then east through Polonnaruwa, one of Sri Lanka's ancient cities. Somewhere east of Welikanda some subtle line would be crossed, and the ubiquitous sand, the alluvial flatness, and the many army checkpoints would tell us we were in the east. Then it would be a matter of crossing the much battered, bullet-riddled Valaichennai bridge, passing the ruins of Muslim Eruvar, and driving south along the lagoon road into Batticaloa, most likely as dawn was breaking. But even after arriving at his cousin's house, I still would not tell him about the book, not yet. Sivaram would hurry off somewhere – for he had a thousand reportorial things to do in Batticaloa. That night, however, after we had traveled south of Batticaloa to the house he was always dreaming of building, it would be as he once imagined it in an email. 'Batti is cool,' he wrote. So:*

I am planning to buy a small plot of land by the lagoon's estuary in Koddaikallar – the village in which we stayed the night over when I took you south to Thirukovil etc. Plan is to build a terrace into the lagoon where we can relax over a drink at dusk, with the sound of the sea waves ... coming over the rippled waters of the lagoon. Small cottage – with office, bedroom and living area with French windows. I have had a full life. What more should I look forward to?

There, several drinks in, I would pull out this book and he would laugh. He would say, dismissively, 'Mark, you bugger, I knew about this weeks ago,' and then we would drink to it, and argue about it, and it would have been great.

He never got to build the house.

Sivaram Dharmeratnam was a man of many names. Once 'Kunchie' to his family, and 'Siva' to his class or 'batch-mates' at the University of Peradeniya, he was perhaps best known to the English- and Tamil-reading Sri Lankan public as the mysterious 'Taraki,' a famous and, to some, infamous military and political columnist for, successively, *The Island*, the *Sunday Times*, and, finally, the *Daily Mirror* – all major Sri Lankan national dailies. To the cognoscenti among Sri Lanka's intellectual elite, however, Sivaram was also recognized by his own name, Sivaram Dharmeratnam, as the editor of the well-known and controversial news agency and website, TamilNet.com, arguably the most powerful and influential news source on Sri Lankan Tamil affairs in the world; a voice so well heeded, indeed, that it was frequently cited, while Sivaram was alive, even by those who detested it out of an inaccurate belief that it was simply a front publication for the the Liberation Tigers of Tamil Eelam (the LTTE or, simply, the 'Tigers'), Sri Lanka's ruthless and single-minded Tamil, separatist army.[1] And, let there be no mistake, plenty of people of various political sorts did detest both TamilNet.com and, more particularly, its editor. In the month of January 2004 alone, for example, Sivaram (as Taraki) was denounced in the Sri Lankan government-controlled press as an LTTE agent, and by the LTTE's chief theoretician, Anton Balasingham, as, at once, a CIA and an Indian secret agent!

But more of this anon.

For there were other names as well: 'SR,' which was Sivaram's underground, PLOTE name during the first of the so-called Eelam wars, in which he was an active combatant – PLOTE being the People's Liberation Organization of Tamil Eelam, one of the many armed Tamil separatist groups fighting in Sri Lanka in the 1980s to create a separate Tamil state, an Eelam; 'D. Sivaram,' which was the name Sivaram used since he was 20 to write for Tamil-language journals and the Tamil press ('D. Sivaram,' for example, wrote a weekly column for *Viirakeesari*, the Tamil national daily with the largest circulation, from 2003 to 2005); 'Ponambalam,' 'Gnanasothy,' and 'Joseph,' all names Sivaram adopted for nefarious business reasons during one of Sri Lanka's vague periods of peace. Beyond these incarnations, Sivaram had also been 'Mr Dharmeratnam the security consultant' to various governments interested in his views about terrorism and counter-terrorism. But to me, for over 20 years, Sivaram was either, simply, Sivaram, which is what I shall call him in this book or *maccaang* – cousin or brother-in-law, those terms being interchangeable in Tamil – which is what Tamil male friends tend to call each other when they are of a similar age and status. We were *maccaang* to each other mostly when we had been drinking together, or were in danger. 'I have many names, Mark,' he said to me one night in 1996, waving a glass of scotch toward a rumpled early draft of this book that he had just got done savaging, 'and they are all equally my essence. Be sure you make note of that in this book you are writing about me. It was you, after all, who made me realize in 1982 that it was imperative not to be caught, or, as Wittgenstein says, "bewitched" by the language games of identity, by bringing Narayan's novel, *The Guide*, to my attention when we first met.'

'I did?'
'Yes you did. Of course, you don't remember it. You don't remember anything.'
'I remember whose bottle of scotch you are drinking!'
And at this he laughed, as always.

Sivaram's many names bespeak an interesting life. A life lived dangerously, yet deliberately, during a period of Sri Lankan history (from 1983 to the near present) that has often been painful and chaotic beyond all description. For Sri Lanka's 18-year-long inter-ethnic civil war has been a study in national disintegration. During this war, Sri Lanka's predominantly Sinhalese, largely Buddhist majority has fought its largest minority, the generally Hindu Tamils – and to a lesser extent has fought also its own periodically revolutionary Sinhala youth – to a bloody standstill. The conflict has shattered Sri Lanka's economy, distorted its democracy and legal system, modified its sovereignty, and filled (if we count *all* its various wars) well over 100,000 official and (perhaps as many) unofficial graves.[2] Even now, as I write, in 2004, Sri Lanka teeters, however unwillingly, on the brink of renewed conflict. So the traces of that awful past left in the trail of identities Sivaram has littered about his own personal history suggest, perhaps, reason enough why his life might be one worth chronicling by a biographer, simply as an exercise in history or ethnography. Indeed, perhaps everyone who managed to survive this terrible period of Sri Lankan history deserves to have their story told. But this biography is less intended as an addendum to the already vast social documentation of Sri Lanka's national disaster – though (inevitably) it is part of that as well – than as an *intellectual* history *per se*; as, in other words, the chronicle of a mind achieving its particular thoughts in the midst of a ruthless period in history. But why must this be an intellectual biography? And why should such a biography be written by me: an American, and, for that matter, by an anthropologist?

Of these three questions, the initial one – why this must be an *intellectual* history rather than a straightforward biography or 'life history' – will be perhaps easiest to answer for a Sri Lankan audience. Since those from outside Sri Lanka or those without any specialized interest in its affairs will require a bit more explanation, however, I hope Sri Lankans will forgive me for appearing, in what follows, sometimes to rehearse the obvious. There have been, as is well-known there, many Sri Lankan public intellectuals of various political stripes at work during Sri Lanka's long ethnic crisis who need and deserve to have their intellectual histories told. Indeed, one of the most unexamined facts of the Sri Lankan conflict has been the complicated role played in it by a rich allotment of intellectuals, for good and ill; and, in this respect, Sivaram

Dharmeratnam's biography must be seen as an attempt to take on one small part of that much larger issue. Among Sri Lankan Tamils, for example, there is the central position occupied by the LTTE's 'chief theoretician' (and ex-South Bank University DPhil student; see Balasingham 2003: 30), Anton Balasingham; and, at the opposite extreme for Tamils, there is the tragic Neelan Thiruchelvam, the constitutional theorist and former leader of the moderate, Tamil United Liberation Front (or TULF), who was murdered by the LTTE in 1998. Also relevant here are the various *Jathika Chinthanaya* intellectuals (like Gunadasa Amarasekera) who, according to Chandraprema (1991: 112–17), provided the intellectual justification for the JVP's (Janatha Vimukthi Peramuna or People's Liberation Front) revolutionary impulse in the late 1980s.[3] But even leaving aside intellectuals so indelibly party-linked (the United National Party's G.L. Peiris[4] and A. Jeyaratnam Wilson are two other examples), a host of other names present themselves for future explication: the senior, expatriate professors Gananath Obeyesekere, Stanley Tambiah, and Michael Roberts, for example, who have done so much to probe the tender historical roots and sensitive cultural politics of the crisis; the prescient (now dead) Marxist sociologist, Newton Gunasinghe, whose various analyses presaged so accurately Sri Lanka's future; the journalist, poet, and expatriate Professor Cheran, whose vigorous observations about the North American Tamil diaspora have revealed the inner workings of a new kind of refugee community in Toronto; the various, long-suffering members of the University Teachers for Human Rights (Jaffna) who, even now (those that remain alive) must hide from the LTTE; such senior political and military commentators (respectively) as Professor Jayadeva Uyangoda and Iqbal Athas, who have long been astute analysts of Sri Lankan affairs; and the many intellectuals, such as the United Nations (UN) Human Rights commissioner and anthropologist Radhika Coomaraswamy and the eminent historian K.M. De Silva, who are associated with the International Centers for Ethnic Studies in Colombo and Kandy; and so forth, and so on ... and on. Any list of names that truly did justice to all of Sri Lanka's important public intellectuals – or, even better, that included also Sri Lanka's many (as we shall see) not so public, but also very important, *local* intellectuals – would be longer than this book; for it is one of the peculiarities of Sri Lanka that a nation so lacking in effective political solutions has been, nevertheless, so replete with subtle, heartfelt, and often accurate analyses of its own failures. It is, I imagine, courting no real refutation to assert that the journalist, editor, and now nationalist martyr, Sivaram Dharmeratnam, belongs at least somewhere on this long, long list.

But, more than this, Sivaram Dharmeratnam, as Taraki, arrived on the public scene in such a form, stemmed from so unusual a background (for what other nationally recognized journalistic voice hailed from Sri Lanka's deeply rural east, *and actually fought in the war?*), came at so confusing a time, and had almost immediately such a dramatic effect on public knowledge that, I think, his story stands out among the others as truly unique. Sivaram, it must be remembered, first came to prominence as Taraki in 1989. This was a particularly dark and complex period in Sri Lanka's recent history: for the Indian Peace Keeping Force (the IPKF), brought into Sri Lanka's north and east with so much hope under the 1987 Indo-Lankan accord, was preparing, warily, to pull itself out after having been fought to a bloody standstill by the LTTE. The Sri Lankan United National Party (UNP) government of R. Premadasa, meanwhile, was still locked in savage conflict in the south with a newly radicalized, nationalist, ruthless, and resurgent JVP, while also secretly funneling weapons north to their former enemies (according to Balasingham, 2003: 244), the LTTE, to help complete the Indian army's humiliation. So the fog of not one but two wars (linked in sometimes inscrutable ways) was considerable, and it was into this murk that Sivaram's column threw so valuable a light. For what was so distinctive about the Taraki columns was, first of all, their cool clarity of purpose. Focusing on the north and east, and generally eschewing all rhetoric except for a rather understated irony, Taraki concentrated on analysing the military and political strategies of the various Indian, Tamil, Sinhalese, and international participants in the conflict. His analyses, which combined uncannily accurate 'inside' knowledge of the intentions of all the participants with pellucid, often ethnographic, descriptions of their strategic discourses, tactical aims, and socio-political preconditions, not only made sense of what otherwise often appeared mysterious, irrational, and scary geopolitical and military moves, but, eventually, seemed even to anticipate them. For example, Taraki was one of the first columnists to speculate about a convergence of interest in the late 1980s between the Sri Lankan government and the LTTE with regard to India, as well as one of the first to anticipate that their (publicly) unspoken cooperation would also soon break down (Taraki 1991: 3–4, 39–40). Moreover, as military analysis *per se*, the columns showed a shrewd awareness of modern military theorizing about 'counter-terrorism' and 'low-intensity warfare' at the highest level – so much so that, as we shall see, they attracted the attention of military leaders and strategists in South Asia and, eventually, the world at large. Perhaps the Taraki column's real value, though, to people at large, was as a public tutorial on the hitherto private, specialist, and hidden culture of geo-military strategy: the very cultural logic that now dominated every endangered Sri Lankan's fear-laden life. And although the exact popularity of Sivaram's Taraki columns in the early 1990s is hard to gage accurately, Gamini Weerakon, the former editor of the *The Island* and Sivaram's first editor, told me that he reckoned Sivaram, at the time, the most-read of all his columnists writing in English; and Neelan Thiruchelvam (though he was less happy about this) thought Taraki's initial readership almost as large and enthusiastic when I interviewed him about Sivaram in 1997, shortly before his death. But Taraki's fame was not limited to the (actually quite small) English-reading public of Sri Lanka. For the large expatriate Tamil community, hungry for news and understanding, quickly made Taraki a household name throughout the extensive, perhaps

700,000-strong Sri Lankan Tamil diaspora (Fugelrud 1999). They did so at first by passing his articles around by hand; but soon, as though anticipating Sivaram's next move, they began posting them on websites and chat-rooms throughout the rapidly expanding Sri Lankan Tamil corner of the World Wide Web. It therefore became a relatively common concern, not only for people in Sri Lanka but also for Sri Lankan Tamils in the diaspora, to find out something more about the mind that wrote the Taraki columns. Who, after all, was this Taraki?

But there was more to come. In 1996 Sivaram also became involved in revitalizing a moribund Tamil website called TamilNet.com. His achievements there were remarkable for a number of reasons. First, until his involvement, TamilNet.com had been a relatively conventional, and largely ignored, Sri Lankan Tamil expatriate website concentrating on clichéd Tamil nationalist rhetoric, translations of LTTE patriotic announcements, and on clipping relevant news stories from the Sri Lankan and international media. Under Sivaram's guidance, and in accordance with his theories, however, TamilNet. com was quickly transformed into a working news agency, with its own independent reporters and editors, its own physical plant (in the cyber-real form of a web page brilliantly designed by an ingenious Norwegian-Tamil computer scientist named K. Jeyachandran), and its own editorial style: a tone, basically, as dry and authoritarian as that of Reuters or the Associated Press, and with an even more passionate emphasis on the need for all reporting to be backed up by tape-recordings, double sourcing, and documents in hand. The real key to TamilNet.com's success here, though, was not only that it collected and edited its own news in a professional manner, but that it collected this news from indigenous reporters living in the most rural parts of Tamil Sri Lanka, rather than from (as was the case with the other news services) reporters in the twin 'capitals' of the crisis, Colombo and Jaffna. Moreover, TamilNet.com did all its work incredibly cheaply: for only US $2000 a month.[5] For all these reasons, and this is the second quite remarkable thing about it, TamilNet.com soon became a kind of world template, for it was one of the first (if not actually *the first*) strictly web-based, indigenously created, news agencies in the world; and as such its design has since been widely copied. (Indeed, on 18 February 2004 the Sri Lankan government briefly launched its own imitation: www.newswire.IK – see Jaimon 2004). Moreover, third, deeply controversial though TamilNet.com remains for Sri Lankans, there can be little doubt that it has had, and continues to have, a dramatic effect on how news about Sri Lankan Tamil affairs is reported both in Sri Lanka and abroad. Domestically, for example, all the independent Sri Lankan dailies regularly run TamilNet.com reports in their papers – even if only, sometimes, to try to dispute them in their editorial pages. Internationally, the Associated Press, Reuters, and the BBC, who between them control most of the flow of news about Sri Lanka to the rest of the world, often cite or must otherwise reflect TamilNet.com reports. And as if all this is not enough, there is one last, more subjective aspect of TamilNet.com worthy of note: again, as with the

Taraki columns, there is sometimes a rather uncanny element of *anticipation* to TamilNet.com's reports, as if they are not just models *of* but also *for* the events they, with at least formal neutrality, report; or, to put it another way, as if there is an intention behind TamilNet.com's reporting to both convey and, somehow, participate in history. For, as in the Taraki columns, there is often a clearly discernible strategy operating behind TamilNet.com.

But a strategy of what sort? Nationalist? Pro-LTTE? Socialist? Or something more (or much less) cynical? All of these interpretations were offered about both Taraki and TamilNet.com. On the one hand, in 2003, a good friend of mine, Jonathan Spencer, a distinguished English anthropologist with years of experience in Sri Lanka, once confidently averred to me that TamilNet.com (and thus Sivaram Dharmeratnam) must have some kind of 'understanding' with the LTTE: otherwise, how could it report as it does? Were this claim true, then obviously TamilNet.com and, by extension, the Taraki columns would have been little but veiled (and sometimes not so veiled) parts of the LTTE's own propaganda machine. This view was a popular one among Sri Lankan leftists and anti-LTTE Tamil expatriates, and made a kind of *prima facie* sense. The LTTE's fascist intolerance of divergent views and inconvenient reporting was and is well-known, and its victims many; so perhaps TamilNet.com *was* an LTTE pawn. But, on the other hand, as I noted earlier, there was Anton Balasingham, the closest associate and confidant of LTTE leader Prabaharan, vehemently accusing Sivaram Dharmeratnam of being a double agent for the US and India. Further, there were Sivaram's columns being published by Sinhalese editors, sometimes in Sinhalese nationalist newspapers; and there were these same editors and newspapers running TamilNet.com reports, often without editorial comment or rebuttal – something they never did, for example, with stories drawn from any of the LTTE's official publications. What could explain this inconsistency?

Obviously, for Sri Lankans and anyone interested in Sri Lankan Tamil affairs, such a wide range of interpretations and actions (often contradicting each other) about one man's work bespeak a need for some kind of explication. Of course, since the connection between Taraki's columns and TamilNet.com was unknown or only dimly perceived by many, part of that explication can be supplied by simply noting that behind both was the inventive mind and complex personal political and philosophical beliefs of one man. But noting this is not enough. Indeed, it opens up rather more questions than it answers: for how *can* one man's works have engendered such mixed interest and condemnation? More to the point, given Sri Lanka's dangerous history, how could one man have aroused such divergent views – sometimes within the same camp, sometimes even within the same person – and yet have continued writing? For Jonathan Spencer's point is well taken: Sri Lanka's recent past is littered with the dead and mangled bodies of outspoken intellectuals. And in this regard, the various Sri Lankan governments and the LTTE are almost equally culpable. That Sivaram Dharmeratnam was for so long pervasively and, for some, perversely, *still writing* is a puzzle. Even his death has left open the question of who hated-loved him most. So here I would argue that understanding his continued effectiveness, his long survival, and his eventual murder alike require understanding the political beliefs and personal philosophies, both ethical and epistemological, that animated his actions.

'In the end, Mark,' he said to me one night, 'I believe only two things and two things only: As Mario Puzo says, *Only fools die*; and, as *I* say, never a dull day!' And then he laughed, and waved another glass of arrack and ginger. 'Of course, there is also the little problem of Rorty and his stupid true and false relativism ...' There is indeed. Clearly, there was always a puzzle about Sivaram that argues the need for a specifically *intellectual* history of Sivaram Dharmeratnam.

But why am I, an American, doing this work? I do not want to belabor this second question too much. Thankfully, the fashion in anthropology, and scholarship in general, for reflexivity of the most embarrassingly revelatory sort seems to be waning. And besides, my deeply suburban, American life, with its malls and mild tribulations of career and home, would make extremely boring (and, for some Sri Lankans, teeth-grindingly annoying) reading. But the issues behind such revelations, however sleep-inducing, are nonetheless serious, especially in this case. The relevant issues here are two: first, specific to Sivaram's case, why is an American writing this biography rather than a Sri Lankan who, after all, might be reckoned to understand better both the true meaning and existential sources of Sivaram's work? For we have already established that there is no shortage of able and eloquent Sri Lankan intellectuals; and, in fact, that they are obviously rather thicker on the ground there than in my own, deeply anti-intellectual, America. Second, and this is applicable to all scholarship about people, in what way does my specific background, and the many differences in geopolitical status and position between myself and my subject, condition (or, perhaps, distort) my account? For, clearly, a white, suburban American with a Ford Taurus wagon and a mortgage is living in a different universe of striving from a Tamil ex-militant journalist who survived, despite his renown, on little more than 30,000 rupees ($300) a month.[6]

The answers to both these question, it turns out, are rather more accidental and autobiographical than theoretical – though there is a bit of theory here too – so I must be forgiven for talking a little about myself. As the prologue hints, I met Sivaram long before he became famous, while I was still doing my PhD research in Batticaloa between 1981 and 1983. And although I was indeed doing ethnographic research, he was never an informant or involved (except as an acerbic critic) in my early work on Hindu temple politics in any way. Instead, because he and I shared an interest in philosophy, because he was so well read on the subject (to my initial, rather arrogant, surprise), and, frankly, because his house was cool and his mother made amazing food, I used to enjoy visiting there and talking to him as a kind of refuge from doing research. After a time, it did occur to us that we might try to write some things together, and so I began to take notes on what we were talking about; but then the war came, and chaos reigned, and I went home. I did write one long account of a strange – strange to me, anyway – conversation we had had just before he and I both left Batticaloa: he to the war; me to finish my PhD. I wrote it, frankly, as a kind of memorial, because I thought he would soon be dead. It was never published then, however, because the various American journals I sent it to found the notion of a 23-year-old Sri Lankan Tamil, university dropout conversing knowledgeably about Wittgenstein, Gramsci, Blake and Marx unbelievable (Whitaker 1998: 247–70). So that, I thought, was that.

But Sivaram did not die, not then; and when I next saw him, ten years later, battle-scarred but still loquacious, he was already Taraki. As both his fame and questions about his writing grew, and as no one else stepped forward who knew him in his youth, or who knew Batticaloa, I began to realize that I had accidentally become his natural biographer. Of course I knew there were many other Sri Lankan Tamils, intellectuals like Sivaram, who could in many ways, and for obvious existential reasons, do a better job than I of talking about Sivaram's work. And Sivaram himself was quite capable of writing an autobiography on his own; I always thought, eventually, he would, and in it tell me how I had done my work all wrong. Still, the project, as I saw it, chose me rather than I it. For, in fact, while many knew him better in various periods of his life, no one else knew him, as I did, at the very crux of it: that is, both before and after it was bifurcated by his participation in the first Eelam war, *and* at his moment of decision about doing so. For it was at that crucial moment, as the savage tide of war was rising about him, that Sivaram worked out before my eyes – his accidental visitor – his own (as he put it) 'ironic' compromise between a need for action that drove him towards the fray and a love of analysis that counseled the messy inadequacy of all such politics. And while I never fully shared his particular convictions, I knew that knowledge of his 'ironic' compromise was the key to understanding what he did and continued doing. So if anyone was going to write about him, it had to be me.

This accident did nothing, of course, to lessen the importance of the differences between us. Indeed, right from the beginning (as we shall see) those differences – my privileges and safety, his oppression and danger; my professional career, his political goals – were the friction that lit up our interactions with all the sparks and flames one might expect. For, of course, I did not understand him easily, and perhaps continued to misunderstand him in many ways, not so much because we were from 'different cultures' (for, in some crucial ways, having often read and thought of the same things, we were not) but because what was desperately concrete and of mortal importance for him in his world of palpable terrors could only, most of the time, be of academic, theoretical, or, worse, professional importance to me in my world of softened suburban sensibilities.

Why? I think back to 11 September 2001, when the Twin Towers came down. To a few of my South Carolina students who caught a glimpse of that gruesome catastrophe on the hall TV as they breezed late and uncomprehending into class, it seemed, in their understandable American innocence, as if they were looking at a movie advertisement. I cannot imagine any Sri Lankan, let alone Sivaram Dharmeratnam, given what the last 20 years have put them through, making such a mistake. The gulf between those who live mostly in the world of safety and those who live mostly in the world of terror is vast. And although, recently, Americans and, even more recently, the British, have experienced terrible periodic bursts of political violence, the cultural consequences of being *continually* under the gun is, I suspect, largely unimaginable to middle-class people like me in both places. This gulf between the mostly safe and the mostly endangered was the first that had to be bridged before I could begin to understand Sivaram's arguments; and, while many Americans received an awakening dose of cold water in this regard when the Twin Towers came down, mine came much earlier, in July 1983, during the anti-Tamil riots in Colombo, as I traversed a suddenly deadly landscape with Tamil friends who were targets. I remember thinking at the time, as I hurried past one burnt-out car and its casually calcified former driver, 'Oh, so *this* is history.'

'No,' Sivaram later told me, 'this is politics.'

One task of this book, therefore, is to convey, in palpable terms, the context of terror in which Sivaram and others of his generation – Tamil and Sinhalese – came of age. For that was what *I* had to understand, not just intellectually but (as it were) in my belly, to be able to write about Sivaram's life.[7]

Beyond this, however, and perhaps even less comprehensible to me, is that Sivaram was, for a time, one of 'them.' That is, he took up arms, ran around in the jungle, planned and carried out 'operations,' and thus could be considered from a conventional American or British point of view (though here I would strongly disagree) as having been himself a 'terrorist.' Of course, as an anthropologist interested in the culture of transnational politics, I am intellectually aware in a way that my undergraduate students are not that all nation-states, proto-national groups, and global political powers, including my own, use and thus incite political violence and even terrorism as a matter of conventional practice. Violence, I know, is an intrinsic part of the transnational cultural discourse of world politics as it is currently enacted: and, as Noam Chomsky has so consistently (and embarrassingly) reminded Americans, the bigger and more powerful the state, the greater its violence (see, e.g. Chomsky 2004: 217–23). So Sri Lanka's 100,000 or so dead pale in comparison, for example, to the millions directly and indirectly killed by America and the Soviet Union in their various 'proxy' conflicts during the Cold War. And I am well aware that the 'coercion and enforcement' theories of 'low-intensity conflict' favored by, for example, American military theorists among others – applied so unsuccessfully in Vietnam (Stubbs, 1989: 7), and being reapplied now, I fear, in central Iraq – are only *formally* rather than concretely distinguishable from terrorism as defined by the US Department of Defense in 1990: that is, '*the unlawful use of, or threatened use, of force or violence against individuals or property to coerce and intimidate governments or societies, often to achieve political, religious, or ideological objectives*' (cited in Laqueur 1999: 5). Thus, even the Twin Towers horror – and, make no mistake, like most Americans I will forever have the CNN tape playing in my head of that Golgotha – must be seen, upon reasoned analysis, as an extension of, rather than a real departure from, current modern practices.

No, my problem with understanding Sivaram and his writings was not that I found the use of political violence and even 'terrorism' in modern politics *intellectually* incomprehensible; it was that I found, and still find, the modern politics it presupposes inherently (emotionally, ethically, but also practically) objectionable. Not that Sivaram ever practiced or advocated 'terrorism' in the above sense. It is important to be quite clear about this. During the first Eelam war, from 1983 to 1987, before leaving the PLOTE, Sivaram was a guerrilla fighter and carried out operations aimed at the Sri Lankan army. He never carried out operations against civilians, however (although PLOTE, like almost all of the other separatist groups, sometimes did). And from 1987 Sivaram was a journalist; and in his writing he consistently, sometimes passionately, argued against the use of terror tactics, albeit more often on strategic grounds than moral ones.

But even leaving 'terrorism' aside here, as we must given Sivaram's actions and views, I always had a problem coming to grips with Sivaram's active participation in PLOTE during the first Eelam war. My problem with understanding this stemmed from two things: first, an emotional and existential point, or perhaps confession, *I simply could not quite imagine myself ever actively participating in such political violence*; second, I had a deep intellectual suspicion – which age and experience has actually hardened – that *modern political violence is, in the long run, and in all its forms, part of an inevitably self-defeating cultural practice*. That is, although Sri Lanka's war can be viewed in one way as a very local, and very Sri Lankan, inter-ethnic struggle, lots of recent ethnography (and Sivaram's own writings) suggests it was also a conflict firmly connected, by various historical and direct concat-enations, to similar 'low-intensity' war-making and 'containment' practices occurring around the world (and throughout the history of late modernity), all involving military techniques whose sanguinary application (by all sides) has generally produced results that are ambiguous at best and wholly ruinous at worst (see Ferguson 2004; Scheper-Hughes and Bourgois 2004: 12–13, 16–17; Whitaker 1996). Here the key to grasping one aspect of Sri Lanka's war is found not so much in the *communal* nature of its conflict (although that is obviously important too) but in understanding the modern forms of military life that have been imported and enacted there by all sides. Yet, though deeply aware of this very point – indeed, it is precisely his understanding of the deadly transnational nature of military technique that made Sivaram's work as a military analyst so unique – and though Sivaram partly understood this point even before the war began, he nevertheless persisted in participating in PLOTE and argued then, and since, that historical circumstances left him no other choice but to do so. Moreover, Sivaram continually suggested in his journalistic work that political violence in certain circumstances, correctly deployed, is not only inevitable but also, potentially, productive – a point of view shared, of course, by the majority of modern scholars of warfare (Keegan 1993: 385), and, less publicly, but firmly, by almost all modern politicians, as the American Bush administration's 'pre-emptive warfare' doctrine makes clear.

These, then, were two points of essential, even existential, disagreement between Sivaram and me. First, firmly and safely middle class, I could not easily imagine engaging in political violence while Sivaram (who is, as we shall see, a kind of *declassé* refugee from Sri Lanka's declining rural elite) actually did so. And, second, I suspected that modern political-military violence generally destroys what it purports to save (or create) while Sivaram believed that there are historical circumstances where there is no alternative but to use it (or, perhaps more accurately, put up with its use). These are, obviously, not so much cultural differences as emotional and philosophical ones, albeit emotional and philosophical differences that were held by each of us for reasons that are somewhat rooted in cultural, class, and geopolitical differences. Moreover, insofar as there are philosophical issues involved here, they are issues that offer no easy solutions. Most people, whether Sri Lankan or Euro-American, for example, would claim that violence is bad; but most people would also argue that, in certain circumstances, self-defense say, violence is justified. (I certainly believe this.) But can this same justification be used at the 'communal' level, as both Sinhalese and Tamil ideologues generally claim? That is, is a 'community,' however defined, justified in defending itself against another 'community'? Again, most international legal theorists (somewhat uncritically) certainly believe this would be justified if the communities were legally constituted states;[8] but the issue becomes less clear for them when we are talking about communities *within* states. After all, by what measure is a community determined to be a legitimate actor here? On the other hand, by what authority can a state determine that some community within it is *not* a legitimate actor? Sivaram's answers to these questions were both extensive and complex. But. whatever the answer to these quandaries, a greater difficulty for me was that there seemed to be a kind of 'category mistake' involved in all this talk, at whatever level, about communities attacking and defending themselves. For does not viewing communities as actors this way lead to both the self-destroying 'misrecognition' and other-hating depersonalization that make up such a large part of modern warfare (whether communal or geopolitical)?[9] I thought and continue to think so. Indeed, that this 'category mistake' seems to entail a depersonalizing collectivization of blame (and, thus, collective *targeting*) is, in part, what leads me to object to modern warfare in all its current forms. But Sivaram made the salient point here that where one comes down on this issue of whether a community can be thought of as an entity (and therefore as something that can 'attack' or 'defend') is often, really, determined by how concretely fixed one is within often terrifying local circumstances – a point chillingly driven home for me by the billowing smoke of the 1983 riots. Certainly, for example, Jews in Europe were right to think that their community *per se* was under attack by the Nazis, and thus entitled to do anything to attack Nazis in turn. But ... and so on.

Clearly, there are no easy answers here. In what follows, therefore, these issues will come up again and again in various arguments between Sivaram and me – for, to a certain extent, and for reasons that will be explained at greater length below, this intellectual biography is also a record of our continual bickering. I do not view this as a weakness, however; for it is out of the continual efforts by each of us to explain and defend our beliefs to the other that this account grew, and grew clearer, as will be seen soon enough. Anthropologists, by the way, often refer to this kind of interpersonal parry and thrust as 'achieving intersubjective agreement.' In some ways, to be sure, this is nonsense: agreement has nothing necessarily to do with learning another person's views (rather than the 'Others' views), as anyone who has hoisted a few with Sivaram while debating a testy political or philosophical issue would certainly know. Rather, as Wittgenstein and Marx alike would argue (now there's a pair!), it is out of disagreement that real understanding grows. And so I hope it does in this book too.

But, all this said, our last question remains: why is an anthropologist writing this intellectual biography? Or, rather, to put it another way, why should a biography of Sivaram Dharmeratnam (or anyone, for that matter) be in any way ethnographic or anthropological? Sivaram's decidedly acerbic view of professional socio-cultural anthropologists like me, after all, was the largely Gramscian one that we are, for the most part, 'organic' intellectuals of the hegemonic powers that pay for us. As such our job, he argued, is partly to mute or suppress the views of people like him by 'translating' them into complex theoretical languages of our own that are irrelevant to local concerns but helpful for career-building. Sivaram's own politicized intellectual practice, therefore, was quite self-consciously *in opposition* to professional scholarship of all sorts, including anthropology. Or, as he put it to me once, more pithily, 'For God's sake, don't make this book fucking anthropology!'

But the issue here was more complex, even for Sivaram, than this summary condemnation of anthropology would suggest, since much of what he himself wrote, as a journalist, was basically, a kind of ethnography; and much of his own independent scholarship relied on the methods and prior research of a variety of professional scholarly work that included Anglo-American and continental philosophy, military history, and, of course, anthropology. So, although Sivaram condemned the scholarly professions, he willingly used their tools and, when he found it useful, their work. Similarly, with regard to this biography, the question of whether and to what degree it should be 'anthropological' is equally Janus-faced since an answer vectors off in two diametrically opposed directions. That is, on the one hand, I would argue that this intellectual biography *should* be anthropological, or at least ethnographic, because of some signal and, these days, little recognized, virtues that anthropological ethnography can bring to such a project.[10] On the other hand, I would claim that writing Sivaram's story as a specifically *intellectual* biography is also intended to subvert and, ultimately, escape anthropology (and related forms of social or cultural analysis such as cultural studies, subaltern studies, etc.) – a destabilizing strategy, I should add, that Sivaram and I cooked up together.

Let me pick up on this last point by briefly discussing the role biography has played in anthropological writing. Basically, to make a very long story rather shorter, biographical writing in anthropology has gone through two phases. Early in the history of the field anthropologists tended to write what they called 'life histories.' I am thinking here of such works as Paul Radin's editing and translation of Sam Blowsnake's *The Autobiography of a Winnebago Indian* (1963), Theodora Kroeber's (1964) *Ishi in Two Worlds: A Biography of the Last Wild Indian in North America*, and James Freeman's (1979) *Untouchable: An Indian Life History*. Such books, despite often proceeding out of genuinely warm relationships between the writers and their subjects, were accounts of the lives of 'informants' that were given to *exemplify* the life of a 'typical' person of the society under consideration. Such life histories were, hence, less about the person whose life they were supposed to be recounting than they were a means to the end of describing a particular society's culture. And as such they could be properly characterized as 'project-driven' biographies. Now one obvious flaw of such project-driven works is that they tended, in one way, to reduce the individuals being described in a procrustean way to their role as exemplars. And if typicality or a presupposed kind of 'exoticism' was what you were looking for, then inconvenient personal quirks and heretical opinions had to fall by the wayside. Moreover, since the purposes of such accounts were so manifestly those of the anthropologists writing them, the goals, if any, of the life-history subjects themselves tended to be lost. The aims of Kroeber's famous Ishi, for example, are difficult to find, though some find them less difficult to guess, when submerged beneath their designation of him as 'the last wild Indian.' As Scheper-Hughes (Scheper-Hughes and Bourgois 2004: 61–8) points out, who knows how (or if) Ishi would have wanted his story told?

After the 1970s however, and the reflexive self-questioning that followed the collapse of the old colonial empires (and the more momentary doubts felt by American intellectuals about their own country's international ambitions during the Vietnam War), anthropologists became uncomfortable with what suddenly seemed an arrogant use of others for one's own enlightenment, and began to work on methods to redress some of the inequities they now perceived to be built into the fieldwork situation. One method involved using biography and autobiography to place some control over ethnographic description in the hands of informants. Hence, in the 1980s and early 1990s, works like Marjorie Shostak's *Nisa: The Life and Words of a !Kung Woman*, Kiran Narayan's (1986) *Storytellers, Saints and Scoundrels*, and Ruth Behar's (1993) *Translated Woman: Crossing the Border with Esperanza's Story*, tried to rely to a larger degree on the actual words and stated motivations of their subjects. Such works also tried to be 'reflexive' by allowing readers enough biographical details about the ethnographers' own lives so that the political and personal context of their writing would be transparent. These kind of reflexive biographies and autobiographies were a great advance and produced some enduring classics – the above three books being particularly valuable examples – but also created their own set of problems. Foremost among these, I think, is that in the hands of less skilled practitioners 'reflexive' biographies often became exercises in anthropological narcissism. Moreover, the original problem of the motivation underlying the biographical impulse had still not been solved. Subjects were still selected because of the exemplary role they could be made to play by an anthropologist within her anthropologically (or politically) defined project. The power imbalance was, hence, still all on the anthropologist's side, regardless of how deconstructive and intellectually subversive the original intent. In the end, even the best of these works, however 'reflexive,' remained as 'project driven' as the most traditional, early life-histories; though the greatest of these biographies – again, Narayan's work springs to mind – also openly acknowledged this paradox, and agonized over it.

This paradoxical and inadvertent absorbing of people by anthropological projects was, of course, not limited to ethnographic biographies. It became particularly acute in the 1990s whenever anthropologists tried to give accounts of people actually *thinking* about their world (and, hence, of local intellectuals) – for however willing most anthropologists were to give up their (already badly damaged) epistemological privileges, the idea that anyone outside Western-style academia could have a viable, critical analysis of the world as such turned out to be rather harder to grasp. Hence, even in anthropology's powerful, thoughtful, and important literature on resistance – I am thinking here of James Scott's hidden transcripts (1990), Smadar Lavie's allegories and poetics of rejection (1990), and even the revelatory and ingenious studies of outright violence by Feldman (1991) and Zulaika (1988) – people's practices were generally treated, as per interpretive anthropological convention, as *texts* that required deconstruction by professionals to free the unspoken, semi-conscious, and disarticulate reactions of non-anthropological people to the world. What was found, thereby, was usually a *habitus* of resistance rather than a local analysis *per se*. Of course, there was often no real alternative to doing this kind of work. Not every moment (or location) of historical danger offered up, as Sri Lanka's conflict has and does, a veritable legion of local intellectuals, girded about with their own sets of well-articulated counter-analyses, ready to debate with wandering Western-style social scientists (whether home-grown or foreign) about the meaning of their crisis. Nor would the mere presence of such local thinkers really overcome, as we shall see, that bleak tension between ignoring the voices of the powerless and reinscribing power upon them that complicates any witnessing of such moments. But, necessary or not, it must be admitted that non-elite convictions, when presented as passive text, all too easily became demoted to a kind of semi-conscious, subaltern rejection of abhorred conditions that burned weakly, like the smoldering of some lost wreck, just beyond the ridge of history. So distanced, subaltern musings were rendered visible only to the most intrepid anthro-critical-pioneers, who alone (in their seminar rooms) could envision how such *lumpen* thoughts were connected to the vaster world-historical patters from which they sprang. Here, again, people's utterances, imprisoned within sophisticated anthropological projects, were not really events in themselves at all, but merely symptoms of events. So the paradox of 'reflexive' anthropological biography – that the project captures just what it is trying to set free – remained here too.

But coming back to biography, it is interesting that *conventional, nonanthropological* biographies have always avoided this paradox. They have avoided it because conventional biographies have always presupposed the prior importance of the people being written about and the lesser importance of the biographer. And this is true at all levels of non-anthropological biography, from Boswell's *Life of Johnson* to the sketchy articles in America's up-scale gossip glossy, *People Magazine*. For even the crudest trashy exposé assumes (or, in some cases, asserts) that its subject is already important and thus proclaims its own parasitic subservience. In conventional, non-anthropological biography, thus, the power imbalance is precisely the opposite of what it is in anthropological biography. Indeed, it is our knowledge of this fact that provides a certain subversive pleasure to the spectacle of some nonentity of a biographer exposing a VIP's dirty linen in public. Let us call this kind of biography, then, 'subject-led biography.'

Have anthropologists ever written biographies of this latter, subject-led sort? Rarely. There have been, of course, some instances of biographical writing in this sense by anthropologists. Anthropologists, for example, have sometimes written biographies of each other. But the only two examples of explicitly anthropological biography that presupposed the prior importance of their subjects that I am aware of are Richard G. Fox's fascinating *Gandhian Utopia: Experiments with Culture* (1989), and Susan Harding's rather terrifying book on Jerry Falwell (2001). Both are works to which this one is manifestly indebted. Still, my biography of Sivaram Dharmeratnam will be different in some rather important ways from both of these books. For while the prior importance of Ghandhi and Falwell was obvious, Sivaram Dharmeratnam – because of his many aliases, because Sri Lanka is far from Britain and the US, because Sri Lanka's conflict is so obscure to Americans, and because (even in Sri Lanka) Sivaram was famous and important mostly to the forgotten and the 'unimportant' – is a subject who will start out looking like an informant in a 'project-driven' biography, but who will, I hope, explode out of that category to become, by the end of this book, a biographical subject of the second sort: one whose work, writings, and life are obviously more important than the fact that some anthropologist is writing about them. Of course, ultimately, any person's life is more important than what any social scientist might write about them, and it is precisely to illustrate that very, informant-busting, irony – for we discussed this at great length, Sivaram and I – that Sivaram Dharmeratnam urged me to write this book. 'But perhaps you should really call it,' he laughed at me one night, 'the informant who got away.'

2 LEARNING POLITICS FROM SIVARAM

EAST COAST SRI LANKA, 1984 (AS WRITTEN IN 1987)

EMPEDOCLES, a philosopher of Agrigentum, in Sicily, flourished about B.C. 444. He was learned and eloquent; and, on account of his success in curing diseases, was reckoned a magician. His death is said to have been as miraculous as his life. One tradition related that he threw himself into the flames of Mount Aetna, that by his sudden disappearance he might be believed to be a god; but it was added that the volcano threw up one of his sandals, and thus revealed the manner of his death ... (Blakeney 1910: 206)

The conversation took place in the summer of 1984. Sri Lanka's Sinhalese majority and Tamil minority had, by then, arrived at a point where each seemed to believe that only violence against the other made any sense. Indeed, as we talked, the largely Sinhalese Sri Lankan army was occupying Batticaloa town, the provincial capital of the district where I was living, while, all about the Tamil areas, signs of an increasing guerrilla and political mobilization were taking place. As an anthropologist with friends on both sides, the nationalist rhetoric of each group – the historicist fantasies and 'racial' stereotypes – seemed abhorrent, surreal. Yet the burnt-out houses and dazed refugees that I had seen the year before, the sheer ferocity of the island-wide anti-Tamil rioting of 1983, made it obvious, even to me, that, at least for the Tamils of the east coast, the time for words had passed.

Yet I was determined to remain, somehow, neutral. And an official stance of tolerant but firm neutrality was exactly what I attempted to effect. I felt I had good reason on my side. It was not my country, and not, therefore, my fight. I could see, of course, why Tamil people no longer felt that a regular political solution to their problems was possible. Thirty years of such attempts had merely spawned ever more vitriolic forms of Sinhalese nationalism. At the same time, I could also understand the queer sense of mingled inferiority and chauvinism that seemed to animate Sinhalese politics, the sense of frustration that close to 400 years of colonial domination had engendered. Still, when I confronted Sinhalese claims, to me disturbing, that their command over all Sri Lanka was mandated by the Buddha, as laid down in their sixth-century historical chronicle, *The Mahavamsa* (1934); or Tamil claims, to me equally strange, that freedom from the Sinahalese would allow a return to the glories of a sixteenth-century Tamil kingdom, I wanted to be able to place both in a bin marked 'other,' for analysis later. For neither seemed to me politics of a sort with which I could, or should, get involved. It was all real; I knew people were dying from it; but it could not be real, as ideology or as politics, to me.

Of course, Sri Lanka's political groups and parties were hardly so unitary as the above would make them seem. There were many forms of Tamil and Sinhalese nationalism to choose from; within each camp, in fact, the ideologies, though all nationalist, spanned the gamut from utopian left to practically fascist right.[1] My feeling, however, was that even this range seemed to turn on an axis alien to my ability to judge. Hence, while I could, like a good liberal intellectual, deplore the actions of the UNP government then in power, and denounce, in my way, all the atrocities being committed on both sides, I felt that it was not only impossible for me to take sides, but even improper to get involved. As an anthropologist – no, even as a human being – I felt my only hope of seeing the situation clearly was to remain, as it were, poised between perspectives, taking little peeks through all offered views, but declining ultimately to accept the clarifying and limiting lens of any. And I fancied that this, somehow, was in itself a kind of contribution: the preservation of a vantage point above the fray, so that either side, in a cooler moment, might have available an alternative, more 'balanced,' vision of the conflict.[2]

So I was thinking, anyway, when Sivaram came to visit.

It was late July, roughly twelve months after the anti-Tamil riots of 1983. Like the rest of the east coast, the Tamil village where I had spent two years doing fieldwork was in the hot and sleepy time before the harvest. All the land around the village not directly fed by canals was burnt brown, even yellow, and the hot winds off the central highlands spiraled dust-devils high up into the sky. For a month, the large, black buffalo, for lack of their wallows, had roved the streets of the village complaining. Everyone else, all the people, had abandoned the streets to them by ten, withdrawing into the shade. On this particular day, I had withdrawn as well, into the verandah of the little dowry-house that my host, Mr M, had loaned me, his daughters as yet being young; and there I was alternatively reading, or typing, or playing with Mr M's children.

Indeed, as I remember, Parvati and Sita, Mr M's 10-year-old twin daughters, were giggling together over one of my field notebooks. They had acquired a pen from my desk, and my Tamil–English dictionary from the shelf, and were busy copying out a list of words, in Tamil and then in English, ostensibly to practice writing English letters. They wrote: 'Lecturer, enemies, madman, lawbreakers, nurse, rioters ...' and then, further on, 'politician, thugs, classmates, soldiers, clever boy, rich man, my pet, neighbors, tourists, headwaiters, poor farmers, own lorry.' A history, so it seemed to me, of Sri Lanka. After a while, ever the anthropologist, I got them to draw a picture of a *kumpam*, a little pot with a coconut resting on its fluted top, which is a representation of deity. I had never received an adequate account of how the thing was actually made, and their playful drawing exactly fit the bill. They had just finished this when Muttusvami,[3] their mother's younger brother, looking rather worried, stepped up onto the verandah.

'Uncle,' he said, 'you have a visitor.'[4]

'Who is it? Do you know?'

'I think it is that *paTicca aal* [learned person] from Batticaloa. That Sivaram.'

Sivaram was right behind him, dressed, oddly for him, in trousers and a new shirt. Perhaps all of 25 then, he looked older, as he always did, though whether because he possessed an older man's experience, or despair, it was hard to say. Muttusvami gave a worried look, of which I knew the meaning.

'Is Mr M around?'

'Attan is not happy. He went to the fields.' Mr M was Muttusvami's *attaan*, his eldest sister's husband, and, to put it shortly, the butter on his bread. Mr M did not like Sivaram, who was standing, somewhat sunblind, just inside my door, because he thought him a radical, and perhaps because Mr M felt them to be from competing castes (*kulam*). It was going to be Muttusvami's sad task to calm Mr M down, something I was only going to be able to help him with later. So we exchanged a look of pained resignation and then, after muttering a comical 'Uncle!' he swept out the door, hitching up his sarong as he did so, for the long walk to the fields.

Sivaram chuckled as we watched him go.[5]

'Your Mr M is upset with me, and that poor cousin has to take the burden, eh? By the way, how about a cigarette?'

I gave him one, took one myself, and while we were lighting up, said, 'You always despise Mr M. Are you really surprised he returns your contempt? And anyway, where have you been for the last six months? I tried to find out, but nobody seemed to know. I thought you might be, well, in prison.'

'Or dead?'

'Or dead. What's going on?'

He smiled his wry smile, and settled himself on a bench, smoking in his careful way, looking at the cigarette after each considered puff.[6]

'I've been all over – up to Jaffna, over to Peradeniya, to Colombo, across to Trincomalee. Things are heating up. Even here, things are happening.'[7]

'Yes, I know,' I said, 'many of the village boys have gone off – some say to India, some say to the jungle to fight. I hear there are lots of groups now, not just the Tigers. It seems crazy to me, just crazy.'

'That's why I came to see you. I may not get the chance again. As I said, things are happening.'

'I'm sure I don't want to know. I will say, however, I think you'd be out of your mind to get involved in all this. I mean, look, you know as well as I do how absurd the movements are. Do they really think the proper response to loony Sinhalese Buddhist nationalism is loony Tamil Hindu nationalism? It reminds me of a movie I saw in Colombo, a Monty Python movie called the *Life of Brian*. Ever see it?'

'No. I was a little short of rupees that month.'

'Well, it was a satire about the passion of Christ, with Brian being mistakenly taken for the son of God. Anyway, one of the clever things in it was that Brian, the inadvertent messiah, was surrounded by all these wacky little revolutionary groups, each with its own precisely defined ideological axe to grind. They were all, of course, ostensibly fighting the Romans; but they were really far more interested in fighting each other. Well that's what's happening here, I think. If there was some sort of sane, coherent, response to the Sinhalese, that would be one thing. But the Tigers, and a lot of the other groups, are just cowboys, more interested in carving out ideological territory than in doing anything about the real situation. Hell, you know this as well as I do. It's just crazy.'

Sivaram, appearing completely unfazed, rolled his eyes, and said, pointedly,

'Maybe it seems so crazy only to people like you, who like to remain neutral? Perhaps if you got involved, it would seem a little more sane?'

'Oh no,' I said, waving my hand at an imaginary enemy, 'I've got my work to do. Besides, I just hope, somehow, that by remaining above the fray, I can spy out something that might eventually, I don't know, transcend all this craziness. And it seems to me that is what you ought to be doing too. I mean, frankly, if you get too involved with "the boys", you're going to get yourself killed, which would be a terrible waste.'

Sivaram shook his head, looking, for the first time, somewhat angry.

'You talk about *Life of Brian* to illustrate the absurdity of little revolutionary groups going round shooting each other. So let me advance a Marxist notion, that the ethical discourse in which you are caught is really an ideology derogatory of revolutionaries. And let me ask that you think about the equal madness of fellows like the US government, who would destroy everyone in a nuclear war to preserve their own ideology. Surely that is madness too?'

'I am aware of that other madness,' I said. 'If my "technical discourse" were really so obscuring, I wouldn't be.[8] So you're wrong about that. More to the point, if I took a side as an anthropologist, either about this mess in Sri Lanka, or about the "other madness", I wouldn't be doing anthropology. I might be doing something else, and I'm not saying that it's bad to be doing something political, but it's not anthropology. So you are wrong about that too.'

'No I'm not. Look,' he said, gesturing at the two of us, 'we intellectuals tend to locate these two madnesses in disconnected spheres, all the time remaining in a sort of ironic isolation from within which we can, uninvolvedly, simply, judge. But if these two spheres were seen to be organically linked, or even simply juxtaposed, the intellectual would have to make a choice in the actual world – would, that is, have to provide a new course of action.

'I'm thinking, here, of Gramsci's notion of an organic intellectual.[9] For me, the social scientist has become an organic intellectual in the sense, and the way, he has become domesticated by the ideology he has followed about in his role as social scientist. That is, by the notion that each field of study is separate from all the rest, and that a social scientist's function should be limited to his own intellectual specialty, lest he be perceived as "unprofessional".

'Let's take an example. You once said, when we were arguing about this before, that one must write one kind of thing in a paper on religion in [this village] and another kind of thing on the ethics of a particular system of power. You separated political rhetoric – or even your opinions and your values about what specifically should be changed – from so-called social-scientific analysis. This is precisely the ideological block which keeps you harmless. In this way, you become organic – in the sense of a vegetable growing quietly in the garden. In fact, you remind me of the low-caste *paraiyar* [drummer] man who once explained to me that it was quite natural, since it was god-given, for him to be low caste.[10] That this was simply the way things should be. This fellow, by the way, asked permission to come near me! Now you, like him, are a low-caste fellow. That is, just as the low-caste man is organically included within a particular, exploitative social formation by what he believes – I use this word because I don't want to be called an Althusserian – so you also are a harmless part of a social organization which wants you to keep quiet. This kind of domination – like that of the low-caste man and of the social scientist – is one and the same, which is perfectly natural since each system requires this kind of self-suppression in order to maintain its existence – that is, to preserve its own social equilibrium. Now since a fellow like me – a revolutionary – is possible, we have to believe that such balances are not inevitable.

'But let me use an example from your own culture: Noam Chomsky. Now I have accused you, sarcastically, of being a low-caste man, and that you never realized that you were low caste while you were engaged in all your bombastic social scientific "descriptions". You never realized your functional equivalence to this low-caste fellow – your ethical and moral similarity. Here I use the word "low caste" the way a Velalar[11] fellow would – pejoratively. Now if Noam Chomsky had simply accepted this ideology and quietly been a linguist, he would never have written books like *The Washington Connection and Third World Fascism*.'[12]

I pointed out that, just as Chomsky was often dismissed by professional political scientists in the US as a linguist who had strayed from his field, so he was often dismissed by Americans in general as just another intellectual. As I would be, should I attempt to write ideological polemics. Moreover, it seemed to me, Sivaram was, as a 'revolutionary,' dismissing me and my work in the same way.

Sivaram looked pained.

'You mistake my position. I'm saying this ideology has a double function. First, the individual believes it and domesticates himself. Second, when there is questioning on the part of the individual, be that individual a low-caste fellow or a social scientist, people could dismiss him as irrelevant on the basis of the same ideology. That is, just as the low-caste man can be dismissed by the ideology of hierarchy, so the intellectual may be disregarded by the ideology of atomization of intellectual activity – stranded, as I like to put it, on his own magic carpet of discourse – and by his institutionalization as a social scientist.'

By this time it was late in the afternoon. I could tell Mr M was back from the field, for I could hear his somewhat reedy voice through the gate that linked our compounds. Fairly soon, it would be necessary for me to ask Sivaram to leave. And yet I knew he wanted to talk more, and somehow it did not seem that we had reached the core of what he wanted to say. His attacks on my attempts at anthropological neutrality were, between us, old hat. He had been haranguing me about my 'objectivity,' my claim that only by remaining neutral to all sides could I render a sensible account of what was going on in Sri Lanka, for as long as I had known him. But he had never called himself a 'revolutionary' before, especially since he knew, as I did, that the ideology of the powerful groups in both the Sinhalese and Tamil camps were, for the most part, straightforwardly nationalist and only rhetorically 'revolutionary.' Nor had he been, nor was he so far as I knew, now, a member of any of the groups. Indeed, actually becoming a member of a group of almost any kind was something I thought he had hitherto avoided. It seemed to me that he had crossed some great divide, and that possibly much of his argument against me was also an argument with himself. I wanted to hear more.

As if reading my thoughts, Sivaram suggested I give him a ride back into Batticaloa and spend the night at his mother's house. I agreed and, after explaining what we were going to do to a disapproving Mr M, we set off on my Honda motorcycle. While riding along, enveloped in the noise of the road, I thought about how odd it was that I'd come thousands of miles to be called an organic intellectual by this strange man.

By the time we reached his mother's old house outside Batticaloa, it was growing dark. As we got off the bike, I could see, framed against the candlelight inside – for obviously there had been another power failure – several young men, *paTicca aal* friends of Sivaram's, waiting for him on the verandah.

While they spoke with Sivaram about some books they had borrowed, I went inside and said hello to his mother, a nervous, hard-used woman who nevertheless carried herself like the aristocrat she had once been. She was glad to see me – someone, after all, with whom she could practice her beautifully accented, though now rather antique, English. But listening to her old-fashioned speech, I was reminded, by the contrast between her manner and her threadbare sari, of what she had told me of their family's fortunes. I remembered that Sivaram's great-grandfather and grandfather had been powerful Vanniyars, one of the small number of large landowners who had once owned an overwhelming percentage of the land in the eastern province.[13] His great-grandfather, indeed, had been one of the first native elected officials under the British colonial reforms of the 1920s. Sivaram's own father, like Sivaram an intellectual, had taken an economics tripos at Cambridge, where had had also attended Bertrand Russell's lectures and read a lot of the early works of Wittgenstein. Sivaram's uncle (his mother's

brother) had a law degree from the Inns of Court, London, and had gone on
to become a judge in Fiji. Other relations had been lawyers, high bureaucrats,
and parliamentarians. But the land reforms of the 1950s, 1960s, and
1970s, and the decline of the abseentee landlord system in Batticaloa and
the Amparai District, had reduced their power and increased their enemies.
When Sivaram was 13, and a private school boy, his father had died, an
embittered man, leaving the family almost destitute. Their remaining land
and money were tied up in an endless lawsuit – a lawsuit Sivaram's mother
had been pursuing, alone, for eight years. The final blow had been delivered
by the cyclone that had blown through Batticaloa in 1978, leaving their once-
proud home a gutted shell. 'The large Dutch-period verandah was blown off.
Tile roof. Grecian pillars.' All gone.

Despite their new poverty, however, Sivaram's mother would have left him
in school had he himself not begun to act up. 'I failed my O-levels, mainly
due to chasing a girl and being a general truant. So she packed me off to
Colombo to go to a Tutory to sit for O-levels again. That is where I discovered
the beginnings of my intellectual adventures – in the Colombo Public Library.
Frazer's *The Golden Bough*, Das Gupta's *History of Indian Philosophy*, and things
like that. Then I passed my O-levels.'

As if all this were not, as Sivaram once put it, Dickensian enough, it was on
a bus ride home from Colombo, where he had continued to study on his own
for his A-levels, that he had had to face not only his family's shattered home
and fortunes but his own internal cyclone. He told me that while the bus rolled
along, he had kept remembering having once gone with his maternal uncle,
the old judge, to watch him receive *kai visheesham* (also called *kai mulutham*) at
one of the remaining family estates in a large paddy town a number of miles
down the coast. *Kai visheesham*, or 'distinction by hand,' was the ceremony
in which landless laborers and their *potiyar* employers gave gifts to one
another as a mark of their mutual bond. On this occasion, as one very old,
very thin, laborer had obsequiously advanced toward his uncle's verandah to
ask permission to bestow his gift, Sivaram's uncle, according to local legend
a man both massive and intimidating, had leaned over Sivaram, then a boy
of 6, and said, 'This is power, boy. Power. Don't you forget it. If you ever do,
you'll be the one asking permission to come up on the verandah.'[14]

Sivaram didn't. He arrived home thoughtful. Thought, very carefully, for
several years. And then, buying a cheap sarong, he laid his trousers aside,
put his postal savings account pass book in his shirt pocket – it had about
500 rupees in it – and set off on a bus to see, as he put it to me, what being an
'average' Sri Lankan might be like.[15] Somewhere along the line, he decided
to become a *paTicca aal*.[16]

After leaving Sivaram's mother, I retreated into what Sivaram called his
study. It once may have actually been his father's study, although now, with
the old roof gone and replaced by thatch, it was hard to say. Inside was a
clutter of books and papers: philosophy and literature in Tamil and English,

cheap magazines from Jaffna, the remains of an article Sivaram was trying to write on Althusser. I settled in a chair by the one table with an oil lamp, pushed aside a copy of the *maTTakaLappu maanmiyam*, the eastern province's historical chronicle (McGilvray 1982: 59; Nadarajah 1962), and started leafing through Sivaram's photocopy of Foucault's *Discipline and Punish* (1979), which was heavily annotated in Sivaram's somewhat spidery hand. On a piece of paper, jammed in the book, was a list that looked to be notes for something Sivaram was writing, or thinking about. It read: 'Four Things: (1) Observations on French Perspectivism; (2) Intellectuals and power/Foucault; (3) Gramsci's writings on the intellectual; (4) Derrida's idea of strategy and stratagems.'[17] While I was holding this up to the light, Sivaram entered with another lamp, a bottle of VSOA (arrack), and two glasses.

He poured me a glass.

'As I've been insulting you all day, the least I can do is get you drunk.'

Contemplating my glass, I said, 'I take it you have arrived at some sort of decision. You're jumping in.'

He stopped pouring his own glass, and looked at me. Then he smiled his wry smile, 'I'm already "in" a little. Enough so that I can't back out. That's the thing.'

He finished pouring his glass, took a long draught, and looked about with a grimace of momentary satisfaction. His mother bustled in, complaining that she had no proper food, and set down a tray with dinner. After setting the plates out and serving the rice, she looked from him to me.

'Perhaps you can talk to him,' she said, disgusted. 'Tell the little genius he can't argue with a bullet.'

'She knows?' I asked, after she left.

'She's frightened. She's my *Amma*.[18] And she would like things to be the way they were.'

We ate quickly, and in silence. I realized, only then, that Sivaram had missed his lunch by coming to speak with me, and that I, being so engrossed in our conversation, had offered him nothing to eat in the village. When we were finished, Sivaram picked up the Foucault I had been leafing through, and staring at it, said:

'It is only when you try to do things within actual conditions that you feel the real texture of those formerly intangible things which you had been debating.'

Then he put the book down.

'Why am I going off tomorrow to get my hands dirty, when a normal anthropologist, equally (or assumed to be equally) a repository of knowledge about, for example, the ideology of caste or about the ins and outs of various forms of ethnic chauvinism, would simply go back to his desk and write articles for university press publication? I think it is all a question of the ethics of intellectual production.'

And so Sivaram began his lecture. Let me say, before I go on, that my notes from here on are rather sketchy. I was tired, the bottle of arrack was there, and I had stopped doing fieldwork – it seemed, really, the wrong time to even try. What survives are my memories and a number of quick notes, some in his hand, some in mine, of conclusions or points of importance touched on in the course of the argument. Nevertheless, Sivaram had his views clearly thought out; and the notes provided a pretty good frame for holding his argument. I have, therefore, tried to summarize his argument as best I can.

Sivaram saw himself as trying to answer three big questions. First, what were the ethics of, as he called it, 'intellectual production'? Then, why was his tradition – the tradition of being a *paTicca aal* – driving him to 'get his hands dirty,' while the tradition of being a university intellectual drove one to keep 'clean'? Finally, what were the dangers of getting involved or of remaining uninvolved?

Sivaram saw the first question – that of the ethics of intellectual production – as revealed in the kind of intellectual production that 'university intellectuals' as opposed to *paTicca aals* engage in. University intellectuals, for Sivaram, resembled the philosopher in the famous example from Wittgenstein's *On Certainty* (1969: 61e), who, engaged in a philosophical conversation with a fellow thinker, shocks a passerby by asking, repeatedly, while gesturing at a tree plainly there for all eyes to see, 'But how do I know this tree is here?' The epistemological conversation between the two philosophers is so at odds with normal discourse, so much a cog turning without reference to the rest of the machine, that the passerby must be assured that the philosopher is not mad. This, according to Sivaram, is the sort of 'magic carpet discourse' that university intellectuals not only most often engage in, but which their place in the (by now) almost universal social formation of late capitalism makes necessary.[19]

Two very sad examples of classic university intellectualism typified his case, as far as Sivaram was concerned: that of the so-called 'critical' theorist, and that of the anthropologist. According to Sivaram, cultural critics such as Habermas and Derrida had taken essentially sound insights, in Habermas's case about political legitimization, in Derrida's case about the impossibility of using discourse to investigate itself, and turned them into intellectual products.[20] 'When intellectual production becomes merely the construction of locally marketable, because marketably obscure, jargon,' Sivaram had me write, 'then we can say that the writing, and the circumstances it aims to service, have usurped the initial motivation for engaging in intellectual production. In short, intellectual production becomes the manufacturing of products that sell because they package what is common in a false uniqueness.' In other words – for, I must say, Sivaram was not himself averse to obscurely packaging a common insight – such university critics, driven by the need to keep coming out with something new to secure tenure or reputation, often pushed their work beyond a legitimate insight or, more often, the reiteration of an old insight, to a new jargon, even a whole new technical vocabulary.

But herein lay a very special danger. For while it is bad enough when their jargons are needlessly obscure, it is even worse when such jargons, as it were, transcend their authors, perhaps actually becoming new forms of what Sivaram called 'social pathology'; that is, discourses, unmoored from intention, invented for no real reason, but now taken up to generate new hierarchies, new forms of power-knowledge, which 'assume their own power-generating independence. This is when Satan loses control over Satanism, and becomes its creature, consolidated by it, and, as it were, bewitched.'

I shall come back to Sivaram's use of the figure of Satan – for he was thinking of Milton's Satan here, not, say, Billy Graham's. Nonetheless, it is well to mention that what Sivaram called 'bewitchment,' can happen, according to him, to the *paTicca aal* as well, and so the issue of the Satan being swept away in his own out-of-control Satanism is actually part of a larger question. More normally, however, the 'critical' university intellectual simply markets his falsely unique product, and thereby becomes a symptom of the very pathology his writing was often started in order to address – hence Sivaram's view of Habermas's work on communicative competence as, itself, in his opinion, an example of a distortion in communication.

This is also the normal fate of the university anthropologist, who, in Sivaram's eyes, is special only in how close he or she comes to escaping university intellectual production only to be drawn back into it, willy-nilly, by the writing of ethnography. For Sivaram, anthropologists come to the field, and, if they are smart, discover that culture and society do not really exist there. What exists, according to him, are 'knowledges' (he was partial to Foucault's terms) held by certain people, whom Sivaram called 'repositories.' Just who these local repositories of knowledge are is not mysterious, for almost everyone anywhere is one – they are old mothers well aware of who belongs to what caste, old politicians wryly cognizant of who belongs to what group, or anybody who decided, or was forced, or who just happened to take up magic, or astrology, or Marxism, or, well, anything. Repositories of knowledge, then, are simply the people to whom others go when they are unsure of how to proceed in a given thing, or when they just want to learn about it. Eventually, anthropologists, for lack of anything better to do, go to them too. And if they and the anthropologist are industrious enough, they can themselves become repositories of these local knowledges. At this point, the anthropologist is very close to the *paTicca aal*, whose task it is, in Sivaram's eyes, to become a repository for as many different kinds of knowledge, local and otherwise, as there are available to get to know.

But anthropologists, unlike *paTicca aals*, must write ethnographies; and ethnographies, like all intellectual products, must at least make some pretense of uniqueness, or at least of knowledge production. Otherwise the anthropologist will not get hired. In other words, the knowledges the anthropologist acquired in the field cannot simply be passed on – even assuming this were possible given the problem of translation. Rather, they must be worked on, made more of (or, as likely, less of). As an example, Sivaram picked up a copy of a well-known ethnography and read me a 'description' of the town of Akkaraipattu. It was all 'true.' What the anthropologist said about the town was indeed the case. But, according to Sivaram, its technical descriptions of matrilineality, hypergamy, and matriclans captured the town of Akkaraipattu, or, for that matter, even its caste realities, about as well as a report on its chemical composition might have done. 'You know what this says to me,' said Sivaram, gesturing at the page, 'it says, "How do I know this is a tree?" It's just another magic carpet ride; that's the thing. When I translate it to my friends, I have to assure them the man who wrote it was not mad. Just doing – anthropology!'[21]

Hence, in Sivaram's view, both the critical university intellectual and the university anthropologist are forced by their need to get hired into specialized discourses, or magic carpets, that carry them away from everyday knowledges and activities, rendering them harmless or worse. The *paTicca aal* stands in contrast to all this.

Sivaram recounted to me a story, told to him by a boatman, to illustrate the difference between a *paTicca aal* and Sri Lanka's own home-grown university intellectuals – whom the boatman called *longs potta akkal*, or 'trousered scholars.' One day, at Akkaraipattu, some tourists got on a bus in which Sivaram's boatman friend was traveling. There was a small boy on the bus who was trying to sell peanuts. Because the tourists did not understand his Tamil sales pitch, and because the boy understood no English, he filled a bag with the peanuts and gestured to the tourists that they should take them, believing, no doubt, that no one could be silly enough not to know what this meant. Either because they actually thought it was a gift, or because, as the boatman believed, they wanted to punish the child for his hard sell, the tourists took the peanuts and ate them, and then went on chatting merrily among themselves, quite oblivious to the politely irate demand of the little boy that they owed him money. Now on the bus, as well, was a *longs potta akkal*, a university lecturer from Peradeniya, whom the boatman knew to be fluent in English, and whom he thought would interfere. Instead of intervening, perhaps by explaining to the tourists that the boy had meant to sell the peanuts rather than give them away, he had said nothing. And the boy had had to get down from the bus without his money. The boatman had finished the story, angrily according to Sivaram, by quoting a well-known Batticaloa folk saying: 'If the learned men sit quietly by, who then will ask?'[22]

For Sivaram, this story illustrated precisely the difference between the traditional expectation of how a learned man should act – as contained in the saying – and what university intellectuals had become. What was missing, first of all, was a kind of elemental moral indignation. But this lack was consequent, Sivaram thought, upon the role played by knowledge in the university. With his knowledge of English locked into its classroom role, it was even possible it never occurred to the *longs potta akkal* to use it on a bus to save a boy's 2 rupees. His English, rather, was part of his magic carpet, circling in a parking orbit high overhead. He might have been able to ask if the peanuts were a tree; he could not ask for the boy's money.

In the same way, Sivaram argued, since the arrival of 'the Troubles' – which was what people in Sri Lanka then called the civil war – the university intellectuals, even when attempting to comment on the crisis, have circled high above events, while the *paTicca aals* have felt constrained to get in among them, to 'get their hands dirty.' And that, to make a long story short, was why Sivaram now felt it imperative to get involved, even if he was not convinced that any of the groups were completely 'right.'

To my objection that, however right his argument might be, it did not necessarily imply participating in what might well end up being gratuitous violence, Sivaram pointed out that things had now gone much too far for peace to be very likely, whatever he might think about it.

'The situation is such that a peaceful kind of solution has become impossible,' he said. 'Things on the Tamil side have taken a course or logic of their own. There are now about 18 groups. Each is running to outdistance the others toward the goal of separation. If any group attempts to negotiate a solution, they can be accused of opportunism – just in the way the TULF [the Tamil United Liberation Front – once the only legal Tamil separatist party] was accused – and the others will simply run faster to maintain their legitimacy. It is, as Habermas might say, a legitimization crisis.' As a *paTicca aal*, Sivaram concluded, he had to deal with what was, not with what he would like things to be. His duty was plainly to put his knowledge into play where it could be used, whether he personally liked the consequences or not, and be damned.

By this time in the conversation it was three or three-thirty in the morning. One of the oil lamps had burned out and the other was wavering, and the room was thick with the smell of kerosene fumes, cigarette smoke, congealed dinner, and the two of us. We lumbered about, numb, trying to find kerosene for the lamps and my spare pack of Bristol cigarettes. When we finally got the lamp burning, and rescued the cigarettes from under a copy of the *18th Brumaire of Louis Bonaparte* (Marx 1963), Sivaram suggested we move out to the verandah and look for the dawn.

Outside, we set the lamp on a crumbling pediment and sat down on what had once been the house's outer wall. Everything was dark, and the stars still blazed with dazzling clarity, but I heard a cock crow, and, high overhead, I could see busy little black bodies hurrying through the sky – giant fruitbats bustling back sated from grazing the paddy fields for insects, looking now for their own special place under a palm to sleep for the day. I was beginning to glaze over when I was jerked back by Sivaram's voice.

'Sado-masochism,' he said.

'What?'

'Sadomasochism. You said, inside, that throwing yourself into a cause knowing that there is no fundamental sense in which it can be true is intellectual sado-masochism.'

'I did. Golly, how clever of me. I don't remember.'

'You're falling asleep. So am I, that's the thing. But it is an interesting idea. It is sado-masochistic. I have read the French Perspectivists, read Nietzsche. I don't believe in the will to power, but I believe I have to do something within what is going on. Still, it is sado-masochistic.'[23]

Sivaram sat quietly for a time, watching the darkness turn by imperceptible degrees toward the inclarity of light. Finally, after passing his hand tiredly over his face, he asked me if I had ever read Milton. I said I had, and quoted the line 'he for god, she for god in him,' which I said I thought was the most eloquent and blatant male chauvinism in English. Milton is not one of my favourites. Sivaram laughed, openly for once, like the young man he was. And then he closed his eyes and quoted Satan's address to Pandemonium:

> Hail Horrors, hail
> Infernal world, and though profoundest Hell
> Receive thy new Possessor: One who brings
> A mind not to be changed by Place or Time
> The mind is its own Place, and in its self
> Can't make a Heaven of hell, a Hell of Heaven
> And what I should be, all but less than he
> Whom Thunder both made greater? Here at least
> We shall be free.[24]

'Note especially that last line: "Here at least we shall be free,"' said Sivaram, somewhat tensely. Sivaram said he had never very much believed in Blake's theory that Milton wrote better about Hell than Heaven because he identified with the evil in Satan, or even those who held merely that Hell made for a better story than bland Paradise. He believed that Milton wrote better about Hell because Hell was life, we were all in Pandemonium; and *paTicca aal* and especially university intellectuals sometimes knew this, and therefore could only choose between unthinking action, to do something for something, even if you knew it was just another dream; or the epistemological arrogance, the Empedoclean folly, of Satan's freedom.[25]

He said that was the final delusion of the intellectual. 'The fellow might think, satanically,' he said, slowly, 'that he actually can subsist in a region between paradigms, manipulating and creating them, but not being swallowed up by any position. This is Feyerabend's thesis in his *On Method*.[26] In it lies the danger of the re-introduction of the transcendental self, the *sub specie aeterni* self, which, independent of space and time, watches the watching. It's like Derrida thinking you can have strategy and stratagems without a strategist. He doesn't realize he just becomes pathological, captured by his own escape. But we are all, all the time, ontologically confined and escaping, only to be confined by our next escape. And like Satan, we are always thinking we are free.'

I do not remember anything else. I fell asleep in the coolness of the dawn and awoke, hours later, in the hot sun. Sivaram was up already, putting his things in order to leave. I put my notebook, which I had found under my head on the verandah, in my pack, said good-bye to Sivaram with a handshake, and went out to my motorbike. Sivaram's mother, looking older than I'd ever seen her, was waiting for me.

'You couldn't convince him?' It was only formed as a question.

'No,' I said. Then, knowing it was small comfort. 'If things turn really bad, and you need my help to get him out ...'

'No. He'll never leave. I know that all too well.'

And she watched while I climbed on my bike, and on my plane, and on my magic carpet.

3   THE FAMILY ELEPHANT

Before bed read the book on Sabu, the elephant boy. Much taken up with thoughts about my own elephant. (Diary of Puvirajakirthi Dharmeratnam, 29 Dec. 1945)

Twenty-one years later, in 2005, I found myself in a *Daily Mirror* news van, at 12 o'clock at night, barreling across the Sri Lankan countryside, headed back to Batticaloa. The arrangements had been made by Sivaram. The normally traffic-filled roads were now quiet; the *Daily Mirror* people accompanying us, a political reporter and a photographer, were already nodding somnolently to the rhythm of the road. Journalists tend to travel at night, at least Sri Lankan ones do, because to travel by day is to lose the chance to gather news. But the consequence of this was already becoming apparent to me as a stray spring adrift within the back of my seat began to bang insistently at my spine at every passing pothole. Sivaram, having been up late the night before to meet several deadlines, was lapsing into snores as well – no small thing, for he snores like an asthmatic elephant – when I jostled him awake with my elbow.

'This is unbearable. You're doing this to punish me, admit it.'

'Ha, ha. *Maccaan*, I am just returning once again to the land of my youth. Anyway, it could be worse. Sleep. Sleep.'

And so he did, uproariously. I, meanwhile, pondered the possibility of seeing Batticaloa at peace, something I had not witnessed since first I left it, all those years ago, with Sivaram's words clashing discordantly in my skull. Of course, I had been back since: in 1984, with Sivaram absent, to watch (seemingly) an entire generation of Batticaloa youths heading off to war; in 1993, to see the scars of that war drearily etched into the landscape in the form of bunkers, burnt-out buildings, army checkpoints, and the other 'secret' places where the bodies were buried; and in 1997, when the noose of war had tightened even further, to find everyone now afraid of everyone else, even more secret horrors and more toasted wreckage, and to discover that just getting to Batticaloa, for years a convoluted process, suddenly involved passing through the ongoing, deadly, war of attrition itself. For by then everything was so slow and dangerous. What had been a one-day trip had, by that time, become a two- or even three-day journey, where every checkpoint might mean an arrest, every choke-point a stray bullet or shell. In this way modern war, I realized, had widened what modernity otherwise is said to shrink. Batticaloa, already (emotionally, at least) as far from the rest of Sri Lanka as anything can be and still be on the island, had retreated even further by 1997, beyond far borders of fear, inconvenience, army and police inspection, gunfire, mines, and bad roads. Indeed, you could see the fresh remnants of this even 'at peace' as we made our way into the Batticaloa district in 2004. Where once the road had run straight and true, following the train line into Batticaloa, now it detoured around huge, fortified army and police camps on lumpy dirt roads that brought – and were, perhaps, designed to bring – driving to a crawl. Nevertheless, as we ran down to Batticaloa at dawn along the road from Chenkaladi, and beside lagoon waters suddenly blue-gray in the new light, I was overwhelmed by how much this place – its sights and smells, its now visible sand and paddy fields – was so central to the mystery of my snoring companion. Later in the day, as we drove about looking for news stories, crossing through the places he had fought for 15 years before, Sivaram would occasionally gesture at a passing house or field and say: 'There. We used to own that. My family used to run this whole place. Long ago, though.'

And so it was.

Batticaloa, in Tamil, is called *maTTakkaLappu*, which is generally and, I think, unfairly, translated as 'muddy swamp.' The name refers to the region's most signal characteristic: a 30-mile-long inland waterway or 'lagoon' (which never struck me as particularly muddy) that runs along Sri Lanka's east coast from Chenkaladi, just north of Batticaloa town – where the fighting would often be very heavy during the war – to just south of Kalmanai, a large, mostly Muslim town that stands at the halfway point of the Eastern Province (of which the Batticaloa District is but one part), which then trails on south, through increasingly Muslim villages, for a further 50 miles. The lagoon marks a social divide in the district as well as a physical one. The thickly populated villages on the sandy sea side of the lagoon, called the 'land of the rising sun,' tend to be richer and more urban in tone; the widely scattered villages on the landward side of the lagoon, the 'land of the setting sun,' more rural and impoverished. Everywhere, however, everyone grows rice – 'paddy' – the signal crop of the east. In the main the whole area, alluvial and sandy, looks rather like the outer banks of North Carolina or the rice-growing lowlands of South Carolina – so much so, indeed, that when Sivaram came to visit me in South Carolina in 1996 on his first trip to the US he stopped beside one of the old irrigation bunds of a pre-Civil War plantation and laughed: 'Mark, this could be Batticaloa. I should watch out for landmines.'

The Batticaloa that Sivaram was born into, the Batticaloa of the 1950s and 1960s, was still, for the most part, in thrall to its colonial past. For although Ceylon had achieved independence in 1948, the structures and forms of an old colonial order hung on there with the tenacity of a climbing vine. Indeed, you could still see them plainly twining about in the Batticaloa of the 1980s, when I arrived to do my fieldwork. There were, of course, the physical reminders in the old colonial schools: the Methodist girls' and boys' schools, St Vincent's and Central College, with their tidy hint of old British nonconformist rectitude; or the castellated massiveness of the Catholic St Michael's, built in 1914, a boys' school created and still run by American missionary Jesuits. There was the old Batticaloa library, first established in 1855, outside of which I was eventually to meet Sivaram. There was the ancient seventeenth-century Dutch fort, made out of coral concrete, and as thick, dour, and dark as a giant's old washtub; by the nineteenth century, as the 'Kachcherie,' it housed the offices of the province's administrative head or Government Agent (GA). But the colonial past also hung on, as it were, sociologically and even (though most anthropologists would never use this word) spiritually. You could see it in the old colonial titles that people still proudly bore, or, later, reported that their parents and grandparents bore: Vanniyar, Mudaliyar, Udaiyar, these being the old colonial 'chieftain' positions that served as the undergirding of British administration in the province. You could trace it in the odd *modus vivendi* that had sprung up between the district's largest Hindu temples, its so-called *teecatta kkoovil*, and the provincial representatives of colonial and state government: arrangements whereby the officials attached to each institution – temple priests and 'owners' on the one hand, government officials on the other – studiously misunderstood each other in ways that, nevertheless, served to confirm one another's authority (see Whitaker 1999). And you could see it in the ways people generally still treated authority with a kind of exaggerated respect and wariness. In the 1980s, landless laborers still brought gifts each year to the landlords who employed them, as the Muslim workers did whom Sivaram's family employed when he was a child on its 1000 or so acres of coconut and rice plantations in Akkaraipattu and Tirukkovil, villages about 40 miles south of Batticaloa. You could see it in the beatings that were still meted out in the 1950s and 1960s by landlords to their laborers, generally without any recourse for the latter. You could see it in the exaggerated regard with which white people like myself were still treated. Though the roots had been pulled out, the vine still clung.

It could hardly be otherwise for a district that was among the most rural, impoverished, and obscure (to other Ceylonese) in the whole island. And the psychological *gravitas* of its past colonial order was indeed deep. Sivaram's maternal great uncle, Seevaratnam Velupillai, then 81 years old, once described for me what it was like to live as a child of one of the District's elite 'native' families, in the colonial Batticaloa of the 1930s, the Batticaloa of Sivaram's parents. He did this over tea and biscuits at his modest, detached villa in Oakwood, London, where I had traveled to see him in July 2001 with Sivaram and Oppi, Sivaram's irrepressibly intellectual cousin, and where we were all received with the old man's vast calm kindness. Seevaratnam Velupillai was a courtly man, small and precise. Though long retired, he still dressed in the conservative, gray business suit that he had worn for so many years at the accounting firm in the City for which he had worked since leaving Ceylon in the late 1950s, around the time of Sivaram's birth, and after the first anti-Tamil riots.[1] A hint of sadness clung to him, for he was still very much in mourning for his wife, Evelyn, dead years before. But his memories were very clear. He talked about the bullock cart that used to take him to school in Batticaloa town, about how his first schooling had been at a traditional temple school where you learned your letters from a priest by writing in the sand, and about how bemused he had been when, a little later, he had moved on into the more Europeanizing arena of the missionary colleges.

'I went to school there,' he said, 'and the set-up at the time was that the American missionaries did Catholicism; the Protestants were all British. The principal of St Vincent's school, where both boys and girls went for the early grades, was one Miss Croft. She stayed there about 50 years. I mean,' he laughed, 'she came and she stayed and she stayed. She saw generations of people go through her. And they all liked her. And then later on another lady came to assist her named Miss Champness. She used to take music and art. She was very good at drawing and she used to teach that. They introduced – this is where British culture was first introduced. The first rule was: you cannot speak in Tamil in school time. Second, we were all taught in English. Tamil was a second language. Then they taught more English music, not oriental music ... And of course, like in every country, the better class or the upper class joined up with the British because this gave them a privileged position. And that is how society evolved then.'

'And when you went to Central College, the boys' school ...?'

'Well, the principal was a European. His name was Holtom. He was a Methodist missionary. He was a reverend and he was a graduate. I don't know what university he came from, but he was a graduate.'

'What was he like?'

'Oh, he was good in the sense that he was ...' he paused a moment, considering, obviously trying to speak kindly. 'Well, they had a job to do. And they did it. They were professional missionaries as opposed to people who are occasional missionaries. But they were all Europeans. And they had a tennis club in front of the GA's house called the Gymkhana Club. Only the Europeans were allowed to play tennis there.'

'Hey,' said Oppi, *sotto vocce*, nudging Sivaram with his elbow, 'isn't that old GA's house occupied by ordinary people now?'

The old man, ignoring this, went on: 'So, of course, the locals formed their own club. The old sports club. That is later on. So I am only stating facts; I am not criticizing. That is how life was at that time. You had the GA, his assistant, and so on and so on. They lived in their own world. The missionaries did their work. They conducted their service. We had to go to the church and do our prayers and every year on Armistice day, on 11 November, the schools people all had to go to the church – whether you liked it or not – for a service.'

Suddenly, quietly, he started laughing.

'I can still remember, we were there and there was a Muslim boy who hadn't a clue about what was happening.'

'Everyone had to go to church, even Hindus and Muslims?'

'Oh yes, and I didn't have a clue. They would say, kneel down, and I would do it. But the Muslim boys were the worst. We used to have a real giggle. Because they didn't know what the heck was happening. They had their fezzes and it was so funny to see a fez cap in a church. I am looking at the comic side of it.'

He laughed again, and then paused as if to drink a little tea – then gestured, gently, with the cup instead.

'You see, normally they wouldn't step in. The Christian won't go to the mosque and the Muslim won't go to church. And here they were in this church. And among them we had a boy who was an absolute terror. You know he would giggle like mad. And it was a very serious service but to us it was great fun.'

He shook his head, smiling to himself. And then whispered.

'Once a year. Oh well.'

Sivaram was born a little over 20 years later, in 1959, to his mother, Mahesvariammal ('Mahesvari') Tharmalingam, and to his father, Puvirajakirthi Dharmeratnam – whom everyone called 'Keerthi' – and into a large and important Batticaloa family. Both his mother and his father were well educated and English-speaking, his mother having attended St Vincent's in Batticaloa, and his father having gone to St Thomas's College in Colombo, one of Sri Lanka's oldest and most prestigious schools – in tone like a British public school – and then on to Cambridge for a brief undergraduate career. They lived on Lady Manning Drive in Stanley House, a large, whitewashed, terracotta-roofed, colonial bungalow, with a vast colonnaded verandah, surrounded by high, bougainvillea-dappled concrete walls, in the very center of Batticaloa town.

Being in the center of town meant, effectively, being enisled. For Batticaloa is a town that is surrounded – indeed, almost overwhelmed, by water – composed as it is of two islands, Puliyantivu ('Tamarind Island') and Buffalo Island, caught between two opposing promontories, like two fat pebbles between a thumb and a forefinger, and thinly lashed to each by bridges. In the 1910s a colonial surgeon, Dr C.A. Kriekenbeek, in an excess of exotic rhetoric over reality, once called Batticaloa 'the Venice of Ceylon,' no doubt in the same spirit of colonial romanticism that caused another colonial scholar to seriously consider whether the lagoon's dark, semi-saline waters might be harboring fish that sing to the moon – doing so, somehow, through their gills (Canagaratnam 1921: 15).[2] In 1845, the inveterate Victorian naturalist Sir George Tennent, in a bustle of investigative zeal, traveled to Batticaloa and, hiring some no doubt bemused local fisherman, boated out into the lagoon on a moonlit night to investigate this mystery. His conclusion? There were no fish involved. Instead, while it was true that Batticaloa was indeed being serenaded – 'not one continuous note but a multitude of tiny sounds, each clear and distinct in itself, the sweetest treble mingling with the lowest bass …' – shellfish were clearly providing the submarine chorale (Tennent 1861:

381). In any case, Stanley House was situated very near where Tennent took his night-time boat ride, and just across the thin sliver of the Batticaloa lagoon that separates Lady Manning Drive from the colonial-gothic law courts and the brooding Fort Kachcherie which were, collectively, the center of town, and the legal and spiritual heart of the old colonial order. Since the early 1990s, unsurprisingly, this area has been occupied – and massively refortified – by the Sri Lankan army.

In colonial times, however, these were offices well known to the men in Sivaram's family, which ran heavily to lawyers and colonial officials. For many years, since the late nineteenth century, many of these men had been accustomed to taking the small outrigger canoe they stored on their bank of the lagoon, and having it paddled (for they hired boatman for the actual labor) in the half-dark across the dawn waters to work. Those making this journey had included Sivaram's mother's maternal grandfather, Charles Velupillai, the Mudaliyar, translator, and court reporter, who bought Stanley House from its former owner, a British coconut planter and businessman named, of course, Stanley, sometime in the late nineteenth century; as well as Sivaram's mother's own father, Tharmumar Tharmalingam, a lawyer, originally from Point Pedro, Jaffna, who was 20 years dead when Sivaram was born. They also included Sivaram's maternal uncle, Samuel 'Barrister' Nallaratnam Vellupillai, a graduate of Cambridge who owned the equally imposing bungalow, Highbury just down Lady Manning Drive from Stanley House; and, whenever he was up from Akkaraipattu, Sivaram's paternal grandfather, Andrew Sabapathipillai Dharmeratnam, Vanniyar, who, in 1938, became the second elected Member of the State Council for Batticaloa.

But the eminence of Sivaram's family in the district, despite the aristocratic air of Stanley House, and the professional prominence of its men, was relatively new in the first half of the nineteenth century – 'relatively' being an important qualifier when speaking of a region that is mentioned fairly often in the sixth-century Pali chronicle, the *Mahavamsa*. Actually, firm documentary evidence about Batticaloa itself runs back only to the thirteenth century, when an obscure terror called the Magha of Kalinga, a realm-hungry younger son of a South Indian monarch, utilized Mukkuvar (*mukkuvaR*) caste mercenaries from Kerala (on India's Dravidian and famously matrilineal west coast) to invade Ceylon and, subsequently, Batticaloa, supposedly to protect his own Vira Saivism sect from various opposing heresies – if his own inscriptions and the regional folk chronicle, the *maTTakkaLappu maanmiyam*, are to be believed (De Silva 1981: 64; Pathmanathan 1979). According to this chronicle, the Magha was a conqueror very fond of stomping about, laying waste to Buddhist shrines, smashing non-Saivite temples and plucking the eyes out of opposing heretics (Pathmanathan 1979: 5). Eventually, in the wake of his Batticaloa depredations, the Magha left behind seven or eight Mukkuvar chiefdomships or *pattus* – each ruled by its own Vanniyar (or 'chief') – and these entities evolved under various subsequent Kandyan, Portuguese, and Dutch forms of indirect rule over the east coast into a firmly conservative social order in which landowning Mukkuvar *poTiyar* (or 'Podis') dominated the local social scene. This the Podis did not only through their control of land, but also by asserting their 'rights' (*urumai*) over the garish, status-displaying rituals (*tiruvila*) of various 'regional' (*teecatta*) temples. These Podis, in turn, paid tribute (in the case of the Kandyans) or taxes of one sort or another to their successive and various colonial overlords. Of course, there were other castes and peoples in Batticaloa too: Velalar, Timilar, Seerpathar, and Karaiyar[3] (like Sivaram's ancestors), all of whom later became landowning castes; and goldsmiths, temple workers (*koovilar*) and, later, Muslims, who largely worked for the landowners or became traders; and then the various servant or 'service' castes – barbers, washermen, lime-burners, and drummers – all brought, according to the local folk poems, called *kalvettu* ('stone carvings'), to serve the landowners and their temples. Indeed, north of Vakarai there were even some Tamil-speaking 'Vedda' people, supposedly ancestors of the island's aboriginal inhabitants, and once famously studied by the Seligmans. Regardless, all of these people were, in theory, situated somewhere below the Mukkuvar in Batticaloa's ritual-political order (McGilvray 1982). But the really key thing to remember about this local Mukkuvar hegemony is that it all began to unravel when the British arrived at the end of the eighteenth century.

Hence, according to Sivaram and his cousins, and Sivaram's own historical research, the family's fortunes actually stem back to just this time, and the rise of a rich Karaiyar trader, Panakkara Pathiniyar (Sivaram 1993: 13–24). Pathiniyar was a rich, but landless, coastal trader whose fortunes rose with the arrival of the British in the region. Pathiniyar apparently worked for the British in the 1790s and fought beside them when the province's Mukkuvar Podis rebelled in 1803. The British crushing of that rebellion, and the erosion of the Mukkuvar's near monopoly ownership of Batticaloa's rice-growing lands, set the stage for Pathiniyar's own rise, accomplished initially by his funding of the 'Thavalam' (*tavaLam*) or bullock-cart trade in lowland goods (such as salt and dried fish) with the Kandyan kingdom. Pathiniyar grew so rich from this trade that his wealth became legendary locally: indeed, he was named after it, 'Panakkara' meaning, basically, 'Rich Man.' Pathiniyar's marriage of his daughter to Sambunatha Vanniyanar of Araipathai, another Karaiyar enriched by the region's altered colonial circumstances, and the wealth he passed on to them as her dowry, established what Sivaram and his cousins call, in English, 'the clan.'[4]

Of course Sivaram and his cousins always used the word 'clan' ironically. They never used the Tamil word for clan: *kuTi*. Indeed, none of the men in Sivaram's family, right back to Sivaram's grandfather, appear to have taken seriously Batticaloa's matrilineal caste or clan system. And this skepticism points to another characteristic of the clan worth mentioning: an inherent struggle, especially in Sivaram's parents' generation, between their sense of themselves as Batticaloa Tamils and an equally strong belief that they were (as Sivaram's father frequently put it in his diary) more 'civilized' than the 'peasants' who worked for and lived around them. This ambivalence, born of their role as agents and beneficiaries of British rule, can be seen in an interesting contradiction between the way family members named themselves and yet managed their inheritances. For, as converts to Christianity during Charles Velupillai's time, and then as either Bertrand Russell style rationalists or only nominal Hindus thereafter, the men of the family took to identifying themselves the British Christian way, with paternal surnames: Velupillai and later Dharmalingam and, in Sivaram's case, Dharmeratnam. Moreover, in family recountings of family history a distinct patriarchal bias is discernible: it is always of men and their public exploits that one is told. And, of course, when Sivaram's paternal grandfather died intestate, his father sued for control of the estate as 'the eldest son and heir of the deceased.'[5] Yet, if one traces the path of Pathiniyar's wealth, the outlines of Batticaloa's old matrilineal practices become clearly apparent, revealing Sivaram's family as – structurally speaking – a Batticaloa 'clan' (or lineage) indeed.

Why? Because of the way Batticaloa's marriage system has traditionally worked – according to the Batticaloa chronicles – since the Magha's thirteenth-century invasion. Leaving aside some of their more Byzantine characteristics, Batticaloa's castes have generally contained intermarrying clans or *kuTi* (and, within these *kuTi*, lineages or *vamisam* – that is, 'wombs') through which inherited wealth and lands, following the mother's line, were generally passed at the time of marriage as 'woman's wealth' or *ceetanam*. Sivaram's *kuTi*, by this reckoning, was his mother's (and *her* mother's, and *her* mother's mother's) *Veeramanikkan kudi*, which is one of the old Karaiyar caste *kuTi* of Batticaloa, rather than the *kuTi* of his father, which the men of the family, perhaps unsurprisingly, seem to have forgotten completely. Further, by this system, women continued to have some rights over the wealth that passed through them – for example, if there was a divorce or a separation, the *ceetanam* property stayed with the woman.

So perhaps it should occasion no surprise that Pathiniyar's bags of gold were given, as dower, to Charles Velupillai, by way of Pathiniyar's daughter's daughter, Ponnammah; and that it was this wealth that allowed Charles Velupillai and Ponnammah to begin acquiring, a generation later, the thousands of acres of paddy land and coconut plantations that would eventually constitute the family's visible wealth. Those lands and wealth, including the little house (the *cinna veedu*) that lay behind Stanley House, were eventually passed, in turn, to Ponnammah's daughter, Kanakammah, and, in the latter case, from her to Mahesvari, Sivaram's mother. Though Tharmalingam bought Stanley House outright, its deed was somewhat in dispute thereafter, but it is noteworthy that it was the woman of the 'clan' – Mahesvari, 'Baby,' and Mahesvari's daughter – who continued (and continue) to live in it. But just how important Pathiniyar's wealth really was to the family, and to the 'clan,' is best signaled, perhaps, by the battered old wooden trunk that sits gathering dust in Stanley House, which is now (of course) owned by Mahesvari's daughter, Suriyakumari. It is Pathiniyar's old money box – the very same in which, according to long-held rumor, he kept his many bags of gold. It was into this ambiguity – this by turns colonial, matrilineal, patrilineal, Christian, Hindu, rationalist, conservative, nationalist, class-conscious, caste-semi-conscious Stanley House – that Sivaram was born to Mahesvari and Keerthi.

Stanley House was crowded in 1959. Crowded and, frankly, both complicated and rather gothic in its internal dynamics. In addition to housing Sivaram's mother and his brother, Suriyakumar, and his sister Suriyakumari, the house provided permanent and temporary shelter to many other maternal kin. First, there was his maternal grandmother, the redoubtable Kanakammah. Redoubtable because she, along with Sivaram's still living maternal great-grandmother Ponnammah, and his father's mother, Alagamma (who lived in Akkaraipattu), so dominated family affairs with their wisdom, intrigues, decisiveness, mutual suspicions, and their continued rights over the founding fortune, that they were called, collectively, especially by Sivaram's father, 'the living stones.' Kanakammah was also literate – something relatively rare for her generation of Batticaloa Tamil women – and, even more unusual, well read in the Tamil classics. The sight of her sitting by the doorway of Stanley House, deep in the *sangam* classics, was something that awed and inspired Sivaram as a child.

Then there was his mother's rather fearsome brother, Karunairatnam, a lawyer who later became a judge in Africa and, later, Fiji. Although gentle with children, Karunairatnam was well known for his toughness and fiery temper. To the cousins he was the embodiment of macho, of danger: a real 'man's man.' For this was the very same uncle who first taught Sivaram, so graphically, about provincial political power while sitting imperiously on the verandah of Stanley House receiving requests from hopeful and desperate petitioners. He lived, somewhat restively, in Stanley House, along with his young wife, Malar, formerly a teacher at St Vincent's, and his son, Lee Karu, whom the other cousins simply called '*maccaan*,' or cousin.[6] Lee later became an Old Bailey barrister in England, and would be greatly admired by Sivaram for his ambition, ferocious confidence and cool disregard for authority. I could certainly see all these qualities on display when I eventually interviewed him, one night in August 2001, after he had just returned, flawlessly dressed and recently victorious, from court. He insisted on taking me out to an expensive Italian restaurant in London where the wine alone cost more than my airfare; regaled me there, for hours, with elegantly spun tales of legal malfeasance and derring-do; and later, over coffee and Italian pastries in his posh four-story house, grilled me like a witness till my eyes stung.

There were also many frequent visitors to the house, including various cousins, aunts, and uncles, but mostly children of Sivaram's mother's many sisters and brothers. Among the most important was Pillai Kanapathipillai Oppilamani, or 'Oppi,' who always came down from Colombo on his school holidays. Oppi, who was 11 in 1959, was an intellectually curious child who would eventually became an intellectually driven surgeon in England.

So driven, indeed, that once, bemused by a philosophical quandary, he walked one night all the way from his suburban home to central London, completely absorbed in this thoughts, and oblivious to time, until the dawn's cold light alerted him of the need to hurry to his hospital for the surgery he was scheduled to perform that morning. 'And you know, Mark, when I got to the hospital I performed it flawlessly – better than I otherwise might have done. Thinking really helps clear the system.'

Oppi was the son of Sivaram's mother's beloved sister Manomani and her husband, Professor Kandasamy Kanapathipillai, the famous Tamil scholar, playwright, and early nationalist, who, educated in London and Paris, eventually went on to found the department of Tamil studies at the University of Ceylon, which later became the University of Colombo. When Sivaram was older, and trying to bone up for his A-level exams in Colombo, he would often stop by Oppi's house for a meal and find himself amazed by the thousands of Tamil books that lined the professor's walls. As Sivaram said to me later: 'He had an amazing array of Tamil books. And it was left to me to rediscover them. My awakening into Tamil classics and into a sort of Tamil scholar had a lot to do with this library.' So, in various ways, Oppi and his family brought a hint of their more cosmopolitan world to Stanley House. Yet it was Sivaram's young father, with his talk of Bertrand Russell and Ludwig Wittgenstein, and his general air of singular philosophical concern, who inspired Oppi to read philosophy seriously. He would throw books to him and, occasionally, ask him, mischievously, 'But Oppi, how do you know a road is a road?' Oppi remembers this question once torturing him all through his school holidays and, later, even when he had returned to Colombo from his vacation rambles with 'the gang.'

'The gang' was Oppi, Lee, and 'Kuttan,' which is what everyone called Sivaram's elder brother Suriyakumaran; and they were and remain, in many ways, the center of 'the clan.' They were together every holiday, a bumptious pack of equals, always running around or hunting the Akkaraipattu estates, or meeting up for junkets in Kandy or Colombo, and talking, always talking – talking in a way so unique to themselves that Sivaram's brother once told me he believed their jargon constituted a kind of separate language. But 'the clan' had divisions within itself that rather embarrassed 'the gang.' For from a completely different direction, both in terms of class and orientation came their fellow cousins: Shanthikumar, Ravivarman, Yogesvaran, Surendran and Sathyendra, the sons of Mahesvari's popular but disruptively principled brother, Mylvaganam.

Mylvaganam's 'crime,' at least in the eyes of his sisters, mother, and grandmother, was his love-marriage, as they put it (with doubtful accuracy), to a Mukkuvar caste 'country' girl (actually a fellow teacher) he met while teaching in a distant village. This was a marriage entered into out of genuine emotional and political conviction – a genuineness Mylvaganam, who once idealistically joined the Trotskyist LSSP (Lanka Sama Samaja or 'equal society' party) in the 1930s out of a concern for union politics, successfully communicated to his sons – but which aroused much consternation on Lady Manning Drive. Mahesvari's sisters and mother were displeased by the match not only because the bride's family were from a different caste, but also (they believed) from an inland 'country' (*naaTu*) village and, therefore, in their opinion, mere peasants: they would not speak to the bride, found it difficult to be civil to their brother's children, and never spoke to Mylvaganam again. And in Akkaraipattu, Sivaram's father's sister, Ranjani, and her mother, Alagamma, were also shocked because they had always assumed, along with most of 'the clan,' that it was Ranjani who was destined one day to be Mylvaganam's bride. Keerthi, newly married to Mahesvari at the time, was so angry he actually threatened to shoot Mylvaganam for, as he saw it, having deceived his sister by frequenting their house in Akkaraipattu in his role as her suitor. Only Mahesvari was inclined to give Mylvaganam's actions the benefit of the doubt, something for which Keerthi's mother, Alagamma, and Ranjani as well, never forgave her.

This expectation of marriage bespoke, by the way, another aspect of Batticaloa's marriage practices that continued to operate within 'the clan,' despite its anglicized ways. In Batticaloa at that time (and, for the most part, today as well) an ideal marriage was reckoned to be one that took place between maternal cousins whose parents were of opposite sexes: that is, in anthropological terms, 'cross-cousins.' Since Keerthi's mother, Alagamma, was also the daughter of Sivaram's maternal great-grandmother Ponnammah's brother Thevanayagampillai, Mahesvari and Keerthi were also cross-cousins, albeit somewhat distant ones. So the hope – forlorn as it turned out – that their marriage would be complemented by a parallel marriage between Keerthi's sister and Mahesvari's brother had been very great indeed. Hence the bitterness and the distain, painful for 'the gang' to witness, with which their cousins were treated by the women of Stanley House whenever circumstances forced Mylvaganam's sons to come to Lady Manning Drive.

So wheels within wheels were spinning in Stanley House when Sivaram was born. The house was a rich familial crossroads, full of love and feuds, food and fights, land and money, as it had been since it was bought over a half-century earlier. This was especially true, obviously, for Sivaram's matrilineal kin; but some of his maternal grandfather's kin, such as his beloved fraternal 'uncles' – Grandfather Tharuvar's, strong and kindly brothers – also passed through Stanley House and added their share of love and drama.

Of course, it was also a house of great opulence, at least by Sri Lankan standards of the day. There were the polished wooden pillars holding up its terracotta roofed verandah; there was the teak furniture and china dishes; the pictures on the walls from Cargills and from the shops his father had frequented as a student in Cambridge; the gramophone that played his father's beloved symphonies and, later, Frank Sinatra and Kuttan's Beatles records; and the European food Mahesvari had learned to cook to satisfy Keerthi's sophisticated tastes. There were the many books – and not just the many Keerthi brought back from Cambridge – but Kanakammah's Tamil texts, and the Chicago Great Books series that Keerthi eventually purchased by mail from America. There were the cars they owned, such as the huge Rover that Kuttan especially remembered being parked in the circular drive at Stanley House, and that took the children to school and to Colombo and Kandy for holidays. There were the play things: the roller skates, comic books, and the big toy car that Kuttan drove back and forth on the veranda. And Stanley House was itself merely a bead on a string of other houses: the beach bungalow at Tirukkovil, where the estates were, with its rose garden, grass lawn, French windows, cane furniture, and cut glass vases; and the rented holiday houses in Mt Lavenia, Colombo – where Kuttan attended St Thomas's as a day student – and in Kandy, where the 'gang' would gather for holidays.[7]

And then there was the elephant. Its exact history is rather hazy, but before Sivaram was born, and before his own marriage, Keerthi one day came back from a hunting trip with an orphan baby elephant, which he established, initially, at his father's Tirukkovil house, and which was accorded there, according to Lee Karu, full house privileges. Lee claims that the baby elephant would rush right through the house like a child, crashing over vases and tables, causing pleasant havoc. The other cousins are not so sure. However it really was, the elephant grew up, and was eventually packed away to the estates, where it was put under the charge of a mahout and set to work. Even so, the elephant, called 'Raja' – 'King' – remained important to Sivaram's father, a symbol, perhaps, of the special place he felt the family occupied in the scheme of things. Keerthi felt that Raja actually knew him when he looked into his eyes, and occasionally he would think of it while homesick, studying late into a cold night, in his digs in far-off Cambridge. For Sivaram's father – always remembered by everyone as gentle, kind, and philosophical – was, by all accounts, something of a dreamer, an idealist.

'What was your husband like?' I once idly asked Sivaram's mother, Mahesvari, as I sat on a chair, feverish and indifferent, outside Stanley House on one particularly hot day in 1993. I remember it was during the war, and I had come without appointment to see Sivaram, who was not there, so we were having tea. The sun had already done its job on me, and I could feel everything bending and twisting in the light. She had laughed, and pushed back a lock of her bright, white hair that had been blown free by the wind. 'My husband? Well ... he was a dreamer.'

All about us tropical crows cawed in the bright, repressive sun. Beneath my feet the huge, rectangular, concrete slab that had once been part of the house's verandah rippled in the heat, the sumptuous colonnades and terracotta roof long blown away by a cyclone in 1978. Behind us, Stanley House's whitewashed walls, somewhat in need of repainting, radiated heat and light like a burnished shield. I noticed that part of the terracotta roof had been re-covered with thatch, now itself in need of re-covering. I noticed that high brown grass and tangles of brush had grown everywhere throughout the yard. I noticed fear in the eyes of an old man in a brown sarong who just then passed the gate, hurrying on, glancing uneasily toward an army checkpoint that was just up ahead. I noticed that Mahesvari's green sari was rather tattered, and her hands shook. Her eyes followed the man as he skulked quickly by.

'Things haven't been going well here, have they?'

'He was a dreamer.' She nodded her head, more to herself than to me. 'And this place, Mark, is not for dreamers.'

When Keerthi went to Cambridge, he kept a diary to record his thoughts for his father, Andrew Sabapathipillai Dharmeratnam, whom he revered. He had already agreed to marry Mahesvari, and left for England, on 15 September 1945, deeply in love with her. Passing through the Suez Canal, he read Plato, Bertrand Russell, and the *Bhagavad Gita*, and tried to keep his thoughts in proper order to meet the coming task. He marveled at the superficiality of his fellow passengers. 'How empty of greatness most of the students traveling with me are' (3 Oct. 1945). He was repeatedly seasick on the open ocean, though generally only in the afternoons. In England he settled quickly into an academic routine: going to lectures, tutorials, browsing the bookshops (buying too many books), meeting fellow Ceylonese students for tea and discussions, and studying in his room. His ambition was a first. He frequently wondered at the 'efficiency' of the British and the corresponding faults of the 'Ceylonese': '9th October Tuesday. What a third rate crib Ceylonese industrialization is of that of the West ...' Occasionally he spotted pretty English women, and sometimes went out just to see them; but he found them, generally, wanting next to his memory of Mahesvari.[8] He loved his first sight of snow, staying out one night as it floated down just to walk in it. He dreamed of Akkaraipattu, of his sister and his father, of warm sunshine and green rice paddies, and of his elephant. He dreamed of things he could do for the 'peasants' of Akkaraipattu – of doing things, as he put it, from the 'heart' rather than from the head, as he imagined a fascist or a communist would do. 'Politics,' he wrote, 'is a dangerous game. Yes, a dangerous game to those who are dishonest and think politics is of dirty tricks. But to those who are honest, able, deep & far & broad sighted, & have the welfare of the country at heart politics are a most noble & valuable game & is not in the least dangerous' (2 Dec. 1945). He saw himself building his 'peasants' a bridge, a theater for their country dramas, a toddy tavern in which they might happily drink, a cooperative house in Colombo. He imagined introducing new, more efficient paddy cultivation techniques. 'I must not get a swelled head,' he wrote, on 3 November 1945, but there was the 'Idea of service to my birthplace from Akkaraipattu as centre, to Ceylon in its councils, to the world from Cambridge.' By December, he had passed gently from an ardent Hinduism to a mild skepticism. At the end of December, he sent the diary home to his father in Tirukkovil, begging him to allow his sister to read it also.[9] Then, before he had completed his first year, his revered father, Andrew S. Dharmeratnam, the old State Council Member, got sick, and Keerthi was called home by his mother to take over the estates, his university career over.

The cause of his father's 'sickness,' as it turned out, was really an excess of love – though not for his public family. Keerthi's father had been long estranged from Keerthi's strong-willed mother, Alagamma, whom he apparently used to beat, and so had become involved in a series of infidelities culminating in a locally well-known affair with two young sisters in Akkaraipattu. So well known, indeed, that in the 1960s this and Dharmeratnam's many other dalliances were the subject of a number of generally admiring local folksongs. In any case, after the first Akkaraipattu sister tragically died in childbirth bearing his child, the second sister came to obsess him more and more. Eventually, driven by unknown despairs, and distressed by the disdain with which his passion was being treated by those who knew him, Dharmeratnam, a Vanniyar since the age of 17, and once the State Council Member for Batticaloa, slit his wrists with a knife and wandered off into the jungle, cursing everyone. He did not die, but when he was found, many days later, delirious in a jungle clearing, his health and, apparently, his mind were shattered. He lingered on, sick and helpless, for seven more years before dying in 1952 in a hospital in Colombo.

After this precipitous return from Cambridge, and his marriage to Mahesvari, Keerthi found it difficult to get interested in the running of the estates. He read his philosophy books and listened to his symphonies – often playing Jules Massenet's *Meditations* continuously for endless listless hours – and gazed, day after day, at the sea through the big French windows of the Tirukkovil bungalow; or he hunted in the forest, sometimes all night, sometimes for days, quietly flowing through the lands he knew so well. He was thin and wiry but 'very leisurely,' according to Mahesvari's Uncle Seevaratnam. He seemed to find it almost painful to set to work. So it was Mahesvari, with her dominating personality and cool efficiency, in so many ways like the still 'living stones' of the preceding generation, who actually ran the estates – which, in combining her share of her own family's fortune with Keerthi's, were now huge – and so determined affairs within Stanley House. But her efforts were viewed with increasing disfavor, as 'unfeminine' and 'calculating,' within the ever more anglicized ambiance of 'the clan.' When Keerthi did get involved one time, he made a terrible mistake. Once – uncharacteristically – he violently chastised a boy for stealing coconuts on the estate, only to discover later that another servant had manipulated him into doing so. The boy's enraged mother picked up a handful of sand and threw it at his feet: 'I curse you all!'

And then his elephant had to be killed. It was Oppi who told me the story at his crowded, rather modest house in High Barnet while Sivaram and I, plates on our knees, had a late dinner, tired after a day's work in London. Across the hall, Oppi's daughter was tapping away at the computer in his study, preparing a school essay. Oppi closed the door, settled back in his sofa, and swirled whisky thoughtfully in his glass. He suddenly laughed.

'You know the story about the elephant there? No? Well, they had an elephant. As I remember ... there was a bit of a coconut plantation at the back, and the elephant used to pluck coconuts for them. So he was a working elephant. Did he have a name? I can't remember, probably had.'

Sivaram looked up from his plate, 'For a long time the very big wheel of the elephant cart was on the estate, put on the side – but it was massive.'

'Anyway,' said Oppi, waving his big, expressive, hands, 'I remember vaguely the chap who looked after him. Ah yes. One holiday we went and there was the elephant; and the next we went and he was gone – and there was this story of how this mahout had got drunk, and had not fed him for one day, and the elephant got restless and suddenly the mahout ... started mistreating the elephant, and the elephant got so cross it just killed him ... just smashed him on the ground. And after that the elephant got distressed and started shouting and this shook everybody; and when it ran away they wanted it killed straight away. So they all ran – all of his relations because the mahout had died – they ran to the house and they said to Sivaram's father: "This elephant must be killed straight away." Well, the elephant was so distressed that it ran away right through the village. And so they decided, reluctantly, to kill it because the villagers were so up in arms. So they went in a tractor, I think, and started running behind it. I believe they had a professional chap to kill it, and his father went, and in the end, I think, it was one shot through the head. Raja was the elephant's name, I think. And it dropped dead.'

Sivaram shook his head. 'But the rest of the story,' he said, looking up from his dinner, 'is that it looked very sadly at my father before it died.'

'Definitely,' said Oppi, swirling his whisky, 'it was an unnecessary death. It was the fault of the mahout. But it was shot and it died. And it, sort of ... it was a disaster.'

There was more 'disaster' to come, though things went smoothly for a time. Sivaram was born in 1959, the third of his mother's four children; Mahesvari went on to have his brother, Sheshakumaran or 'Anthony,' in 1961. But Sheshakumaran was by no means the last of his *father's* children. For soon after Sivaram's birth, Keerthi, to the great shock of Sivaram's mother, took her younger sister, Nagesvari, as his second wife, and settled down to live with her and his new, gradually increasing family in the 'small house' directly across a back street from Stanley House. Either because of the old feud between Mahesvari and Keerthi's sister and mother, or because Mahesvari's tough running of the estates inspired the suspicion and jealousy of the men – or perhaps because the feelings between the two were so palpably authentic – the move was, for the most part, accepted without comment by the rest of the family. And so, in short order, between 1960 and 1966, Sivaram acquired three sisters and a brother: Meenambikai (whom I was introduced to as Meena, and who became his playmate), Parvathi, Arunthathi, and Neelakandan. This business of establishing so publicly a second household, while not as unusual in Batticaloa's rural hinterlands and among its landowning *poTiyar* elites as it might be elsewhere – since taking on a second wife or 'bed' was relatively common there until the middle of the twentieth century—was nevertheless becoming unusual (or, at least, unfashionable) for the anglicized, provincial, now neocolonial bourgeoisie of whom Sivaram's family were still a part. The men of such families ran more toward unacknowledged mistresses than openly held second homes. And so its outrageousness was fully felt by Sivaram's elder sister, Suriyakumari and by Kuttan, only 10 at the time. Normally a soft-spoken, circumspect, and rather gentle man, Kuttan, now a medical doctor in England, recalled the inarticulate, burning anger that seethed within him in his youth. He said to me that although he could speak to no one of what he felt at the time –'for what *could* one say?'– nevertheless the whole 'disaster' had made him so frustrated that he had sent an angry, though anonymous, letter to his father. For his was a sentiment that had to be more felt than said.

This dramatic break between Mahesvari and Keerthi seems, in retrospect, a part of a more general unraveling for 'the clan' and, perhaps, more widely still, of postcolonial Ceylon – or, as it was soon to be known – of Sri Lanka as a whole. For Andrew S. Dharmeratnam, it turned out, had died intestate, leaving an estate eventually valued 438,439 rupees (in 1972 money, and mostly in land) up for legal grabs. The Bleak House legal production that, to Mahesvari's mind, then unfolded – in which Keerthi's claim as 'eldest son and heir' was balanced by his sister, Ranjani's, and his mother, Alagamma's, 'traditional' matrilineal claims – was not settled (as she saw it) until 1972, 20 years later, just in time for whatever was left of old Dharmeratnam's roughly 800 acres of paddy and plantations lands to be redistributed under the Land Reform Law of 1972 – and just in time too for Keerthi's own death, at age 48, from a heart attack and, I suppose, sickness of heart, that same year. There was then a further 20 years or so of dispute as Mahesvari argued with the Land Reform Commission over who should receive posthumous compensation – and so the money slowly leaked away.[10]

Meanwhile, between Keerthi's return from England and his death in 1972, Sri Lanka began its own journey toward civil disunion and bankruptcy. Independence came peacefully in 1948, two years after his return from Cambridge; but the British left behind a Westminster-style, first-past-the-post parliamentary government within which the inexorable logic of majoritarian, increasingly ethnic politics soon began to play themselves out. Although Ceylon, as part of a colonial experiment in limited colonial self-government, had had a kind of universal franchise operating since the early 1930s, its colonial councils were always exclusively elite gatherings and largely devoted, therefore, to elite concerns and affairs. For the most part, thus, Ceylon's elites, whether Sinhalese or Tamil, were, like 'the clan,' far too anglicized and detached from the gritty realities of people's daily lives to govern them with any real finesse or understanding. Many elites, indeed, were only minimally fluent in Sinhala or Tamil. Most barely stirred, socially, from 'Cinnamon Gardens,' the posh, tree-lined, Colombo neighborhood where they tended to live. Moreover, to govern in a statesmanlike, unified manner, a postcolonial state like Ceylon that had been left by the British burdened with a single-resource, plantation economy and high levels of landlessness, poverty, and pent-up rural frustration – especially in Sri Lanka's overpopulated and deeply poor southern provinces – was a trick perhaps beyond anyone's ken. In the end, they found they simply could not communicate with such rural masses with any effectiveness by means of unifying appeals to the nation as a whole. But they quickly discovered they *could* do so by using divisive ethnic rhetoric to energize languishing postcolonial disappointments and mutual suspicions.[11] So in 1949 the new, Sinhalese dominated Parliament swiftly voted to disenfranchise plantation Tamils – those Tamils, that is, who were originally brought from South India by British planters as cheap labor for Sri Lanka's tea-producing highlands in the nineteenth century.[12] And in 1949 Tamil political leaders, mostly from Jaffna, now worried about the erosion of their political rights, formed the Tamil Federal Party, and began advocating the formation of a federal state in which Tamils might have some measure of independent governance.[13]

And so it began. In 1950 S.W.R.D. Bandaranaike, a lapsed Anglican with political ambitions, broke from the moderate, colonially flavored, United National Party (UNP), that the British had also left in their wake, and formed the Sri Lankan Freedom Party (SLFP) to advocate a more assertively pro-Sinhalese set of policies. In 1955, in reaction to a stated UNP intention to amend the Constitution to give 'parity of status' to Sinhala and Tamil languages, Bandaranaike began to advocate passing laws giving Sinhala legal pride of place while allowing merely 'reasonable use of Tamil' – a policy that was quickly seized upon by hungry Sinhalese enthusiasts as 'Sinhala Only.' In 1956, pushed by this groundswell of Sinhalese feeling, Bandaranaike's newly elected SLFP government enacted the 'Sinhala Only Act,' and jubilant mobs attacked Tamil leaders who tried to stage a *Satyagraha*[14] demonstration against the Act on Galle Face Green, the colonial sea-wall promenade in Colombo near the old Parliament building. Eventually, anti-Tamil rioting flared up in numerous places all across the island. Alarmed by the violence, Bandaranaike and S.JV. Chelvanayakam, the leader of the Federal Party, signed a pact to settle the language issue and devolve power peacefully through regional councils and along ethnic lines; but massively popular anti-pact demonstrations, some led by future UNP leader and eventual first Sri Lankan executive president, J.R. Jayawardena, ensured that this pact was only honored in the breach (De Silva 1981: 514, 530–1; Wilson 2000: 85). Ultimately, island-wide anti-Tamil rioting in 1958 meant the Act had to be abrogated, and in 1959 S.W.R.D. Bandaranaike was assassinated by a Buddhist monk and his party reorganized along more socialist lines under his widow, Sirimavo Bandaranaike, in the hope (forlorn as it turned out) of addressing some of the foundational economic grievances of which Sri Lankan communalism was obviously, at least partly, the symptom. In 1965 a new UNP government under Dudley Senanayake, desperate to keep a voting majority in Parliament, signed a new pact with the Federal Party, and eventually passed the Tamil Regulations in 1966, which allowed Tamil to be used as the language of administration in the north and east; but although the regulations stood, the pact was again canceled due to its unpopularity, vociferously voiced, among the Sinhala masses. Before leaving office, Senanayake presided over the inauguration of the huge Mahaweli Ganga (river) diversion project, a massive irrigation scheme, partly inspired by Sinhala-nationalist hopes of restoring the dry northern regions which once boasted Ceylon's ancient Buddhist civilizations. This project would eventually bring many thousands of Sinhalese colonists up from the south into the eastern Trincomalee and Batticaloa Districts, and become a major bone of contention between Sinhalese and Tamil politicians in the 1980s, especially for Tamils from the east. In 1970 Mrs Bandaranaike's SLFP-led United Front government, espousing a mixture of socialist and ethnic ideals, took power with a huge majority. After violently suppressing in 1971 a brief insurrection in the Sinhala south by the JVP (*Janatha Vimukthi Peramuna* or 'People's Liberation Front'), a neo-Marxist and nationalist group led by educated but unemployed rural youths (Chandraprema 1991: 33–8), the United Front solidified their power by constructing and passing, in 1972, a new Constitution in which the Senate was abolished, and power was greatly centralized and placed at the disposal of the prime minister. In 1970 and 1971 laws were passed effectively limiting admissions of Tamils from Jaffna into the university system. In 1972 the new Constitution changed the name of the country to the Buddhist-Pali 'Sri Lanka,' or 'Holy Island,' and gave Buddhism the 'foremost place' among the religions of the country (Tambiah 1992: 63). Further, Section 29(2) of the old Constitution, the one guaranteeing minority rights, was eliminated. In the same year, in reaction, on 14 May 1972, most of the Tamil parties, including the Federal Party, gathered in Trincomalee and formed the Tamil United Front, the nucleus of what would become later, though not until 1977, the explicitly separatist Tamil United Liberation Front (Nesiah 2001: 16).[15] But perhaps more important: in 1972, the year of Keerthi's death, and of the dispersal of the family fortunes, Velupillai Pirabakaran in Jaffna was forming a small group of disaffected Tamil youths – many of whom had been denied admission to university under the new 'standardization' regulations – into the Tamil New Tigers, the proto-guerrilla group that would eventually become the ruthless Liberation Tigers of Tamil Eelam.[16]

But in the 1960s and early 1970s, Sivaram, or 'Kunchie' ('chick'), as the others all called him, was aware of none of this, neither of the gathering familial storm nor of the equally impending national one. Meena was his playmate; the others were his sisters and brothers. And he was tiny, curly haired, curious, a bundle of energy, and everyone, in both families, thought he was a beautiful child and doted on him. He ran about naked; he stole food; he grabbed at his cousins' clothes and hid in the bushes; he refused, categorically, to go to school for a whole year, and no one insisted. He had a ball. There was for him no hint of distant guns, not yet.

For the next 13 years Sivaram lived the life of a provincial elite, privileged in all that he did. As often as he could, he played on the estate in Akkaraipattu. But, of course, he had to go to school too. So, in 1966, like members of the clan before him, he was placed at St Vincent's, which in its lower grades was a coeducational school. St Vincent's in 1966 was not like the Vincent's of Sivaram's mother's day. Among the nationalist reforms of Mrs Bandaranaike's first government (1960–5) were laws that nationalized mission schools, a policy 'implicitly' aimed, according to the historian K.M. De Silva, at increasing Buddhist power over education (1981: 527), and at defusing the influence of both Ceylon's Roman Catholic and Protestant schools over the civil service – for such schools, particularly the ones in Tamil Jaffna, were famous for having turned out English-speaking civil servants for the former British, colonial administration. Regardless of these concerns, Sivaram was at first an indifferent student and even flatly refused to go to school at all for his entire second year. In 1968, however, the family finally cajoled him into returning to school, this time to St Michael's, which at that point was limping along, independent but under-funded, as a 'private non-fee-paying' institution (Miller 1974: 20–5). The principal, Emmanuel Kamalanathan, remembered Kunchie well: 'At that time he was very obedient, very quiet in the classroom. Only he *would* ask questions – even when I was teaching!' By the time Kunchie was 12, Kamalanathan remembers seeing him finally come alive to knowledge and fall in love with books. 'I didn't see any friends. He was always with his books.'

But then, in 1972, when Kunchie was 13, his father died. Sivaram stoutly maintained that his father's death had little emotional impact on him. Surrounded by his mother, aunts, grandmothers, and a horde of other children, perhaps the effect was muffled. But whether he was greatly affected or not, two consequences were indisputable. First, with Keerthi dead, the money Mahesvari had to keep the family going trickled away to almost nothing. She managed to keep Kuttan at St Thomas's till he finished, but for the others the well had run almost dry – hence her years of bitterness against Alagamma and Ranjani, who she felt had kept Keerthi's compensation money. Second, in 1975, three years after his father's death, Sivaram, already bookish and obviously intelligent in the eyes of his teachers, completely failed his O-levels, every one of them. Mahesvari, desperate, somehow scraped money together to send him to Colombo to live with her sister, Oppi's mother, and to attend Pembroke College, a secular 'private tuition school' – basically an O-level crammer – that had once been attended by his great uncle Seevaratnam Velupillai.[17]

There, after a year, Kunchie was prodded somewhat unwillingly into enough O-level passes to go on. In 1977, still in Colombo, Kunchie – or, rather, Sivaram now, was placed in Aquinas College, in the Borella neighborhood of Colombo – a school very near the cemetery where, six years later, there would erupt the 1983 anti-Tamil riots that would help begin Sri Lanka's civil war. Again, despite being briefly stimulated by an old English teacher,

Kuruwila, Sivaram's learning was indifferent. After a year and a half of it, in 1977, he returned to Batticaloa and Stanley House to sit about his father's library reading books, to pace up and down under its big verandah roof, and, apparently, to brood. When he took his A-levels in Batticaloa he failed them.

So he was sent back to Aquinas's again. Not wanting to stay with his aunt and (recently deceased) uncle, within the too rarefied air of their academic house, Sivaram choose to move instead into a boarding house on Flower Road, where his brother had once stayed before him. There, according to a diary he began keeping around this time, he settled into a peripatetic life of wandering, reading, musing, visiting friends, flirting with politics, and day dreaming. He spent a lot of time thinking and began to drink. He was 19 and a lot of his thinking was, unsurprisingly, about sex. And then, on 23 November 1978, a cyclone hit Batticaloa.

'I came home as soon as I could,' he told me, later, 'but I couldn't get transport any further than Ampara,' which was about 60, muddy kilometers from Batticaloa. 'So I had to walk most of the rest of the way. The roads were littered with downed trees and dead cows, but no dead people. I think almost no one died in that cyclone. Everyone in my family was OK. But when I got home to Stanley House I had a shock.'

For the great terracotta verandah of Stanley House was down, flat on the ground, the roof and pillars all shattered, the windows all blown in. Amidst its rubble-strewn walls and wind-twisted gate, the great family house – the pride of the clan – had been reduced to an eviscerated shell of its former magnificence. The glory of 'the clan' was gone, and suddenly, for Sivaram, everything was different.

4 ANANTHAN AND THE READERS' CIRCLE

The first National Convention of the Tamil United Liberation Front meeting ... on the 14th day of May 1976, hereby declare that the Tamils of Ceylon by virtue of their great language, their religions, their separate culture and heritage ... are a nation distinct and apart ... (Vaddukoddai Resolution, 14 May 1976)

The purpose of my birth
Is to evoke joy in others' minds
At the sight of me ...
(Ananthan 1997: 4)

How does knowledge become power? Or how does knowledge directly or indirectly become associated with domination or even tyranny? ... Through the Empedoclean motive. Through language. Through knowledge. Through the creation of languages ... (Sivaram's Diary, 7 Dec. 1979)

On broken butterfly wing, your crippled mind
Fluttered into my schoolroom. Failed. And Died.
I couldn't do a thing to stir its organs of poor
Maimed sense to life again.
(Richard de Zoysa, 'Lepidoptera,' in Wijesinha 2003: 77)

It was 1977 and the Tamil United Liberation Front (TULF) was suddenly campaigning very hard in Batticaloa. It set up large grandstands near the lagoon, festooned with DMK-like rising-sun symbols, from which its candidates harangued the assembled crowds in their best, DMK-style rhetoric – the DMK being the *Dravida Munneetra Kazhagam* or the Dravidian Progressive Front, the South Indian Tamil nationalist movement of the 1950s and 1960s that so influenced Sri Lankan Tamil political style in the 1970s (see Palanithurai and Mohanasundaram 1993; Wilson 2000: 37). Loudspeaker trucks wound round the streets blaring out the party's message, sometimes deep into the night. And the TULF's fiery youth leader, Kasi Anandan, dressed in a white *versti*, kept arranging huge, blatantly emotional rallies, stoking the enthusiasm of the young. 'Rise up O Tamil Youth!' he would say. 'We were once a great warrior race; we must reclaim our Motherland!' At some point, someone might quote the party's official platform, calling 'upon the Tamil Nation in general and the Tamil youth in particular to come forward to throw themselves fully into the sacred fight for freedom and to flinch not till the goal of a sovereign state of Tamil Eelam is reached' (Vaddukoddai

Resolution 1976: 7). Then young men, mostly in their teens, would often indeed surge forward. Rally after rally they would prick their thumbs, and use their own blood to put a promise-sealing *rattam poTTu* (or blood mark) on Kasi Anandan's forehead – a *poTTu* being a tiny, round, dedicatory thumb-print, more usually made of sandalwood paste, and more often placed upon the forehead of devotees after a visit to a temple. And among these fired-up youths, sometimes with them, was an 18-year-old Sivaram, overwhelmed with excitement.

'Did you really do this?' I asked Sivaram, curiously, somewhat shocked.

'I think I did it once. I can't remember. I vaguely remember doing that but I can't remember the exact ...' he wound to a stop, rather put off, I suspect, by his youthful enthusiasm. In fact, he looked a little embarrassed, quite an odd emotion to see flitting (even fleetingly) across his otherwise blithe, battlefield face. But then he started up again, more enthusiastically: 'But this was all in Batticaloa, for the elections. The elections were the big thing for us youth – and not just in Batticaloa. Back in Colombo I used to go for campaign meetings at a TULF MP's house on Laurie's Road. And there I was promised that soon after elections the struggle for Eelam would begin and that I must be prepared to go to the jungle for training; that I would be given weapons and training.'

'Really? In 1977?'

'Yes.'

'But ... the TULF ... why?'

Because less than a year earlier, in May 1976, the TULF had held their 'First National Convention' at Vaddukoddai and declared that secession from the Sri Lankan state would henceforth be its stated goal. It was a move that was little noted at the time in the Sinhala south. But in retrospect it was clearly this declaration that pushed mainstream Tamil politics, as Wilson has noted (2000: 109), across a Rubicon that hitherto only its most radical fringe had crossed; for henceforth secession, utter separation, Eelam, as the new Tamil state they envisioned was to be called, would be seen, especially by middle-class Tamil youths of the 1970s and 1980s, as the *only* acceptable political ambition worth working toward.

The TULF at Vaddukoddai, of course, had given reasons for this declaration. Chief among them was the nearly 30 years of failed attempts to make the Sri Lankan state, as it then was, sufficiently protective of minority – or, at least, of Sri Lankan Tamil – rights. Even the aging and ailing S.J.V. Chelvanayakam, former leader of the Federal Party, had declared in a speech two years earlier in Batticalao that all his efforts to bring a federal solution to Sri Lanka's ethnic crises had come to nothing, and that now 'there is no alternative for the Tamils to live with self-respect other than fight to the end for a Tamil Nadu (that is, a Tamil state)' (Wilson 2000: 108). The Vaddukoddai Resolution had also laid out the specific Sri Lankan government actions that most Tamil leaders saw as their main justifications for separatism. Hence, the Resolution mentioned, in order: the disenfranchisement of the so-called 'up-country' Tamils, which occurred in 1948, soon after independence – 'up-country Tamils' being the population of indentured tea plantation laborers that were brought to Sri Lanka from South India by British planters in the late nineteenth and early twentieth centuries; the government-sponsored Sinhalese colonization of formerly Tamil areas under the aegis of huge, internationally funded development schemes such as the Mahavelli Dam project (of particular concern, this, to east-coast people like Sivaram, for the bulk of such colonies were in the east); the enactment in 1956 of the law that made Sinhala the only official language of Sri Lanka (a 'stamp of inferiority,' as the document put it, which, however modified since, still rankled with Tamils); the granting of a 'foremost place' to Buddhism by Sri Lanka's 1972 'Republican' Constitution (a constitution that also, more seriously, eliminated Section 29(2) regarding the protection of minority rights, from the old 1948 Constitution, something the Vaddukoddai Resolution interestingly declines to note); the 'denying to the Tamils,' as the document put it, 'of equality of opportunity' in the economy and in education (this last in reference to the 'selective standardization system' laws passed in 1972 that effectively limited the number of Jaffna Tamils who could enter university, and hence was particularly infuriating there); the various statutes banning the import of 'cultural materials' (mostly films and books) from Tamil Nadu, which the document describes as the Sri Lankan state 'working inexorably towards the cultural genocide of the Tamils'; and, finally, the various anti-Tamil riots and police attacks that had occurred in Sri Lanka in 1956, 1958, 1961, 1974, and 1976 . It was this last, long history of fairly continual anti-Tamil violence (with some notable gaps) by the Sri Lankan state that was perhaps the most emotively telling point for Tamil Sri Lankan people as a whole – although there would be new anti-Tamil riots in 1977 to freshen people's anger further. For there had been two recent outrages that Tamil people in 1977 found particularly galling: the violent (and in several cases fatal) attacks by state police on Tamil scholars attending the Fourth International Conference of Tamil Research in Jaffna in 1974; and the burning 'by a security unit' of the venerable Jaffna library with its irreplaceable 97,000 books and ancient manuscripts (Wilson 2000: 125). People were still voicing their horror about these events when I arrived, utterly unaware of all of this, to do my fieldwork in 1981.

But, as any number of commentators have pointed out, at least as important as all these listable grievances to the firming up of the TULF's separatist resolve was the growing, frustrated, and insatiable impatience of Tamil youths. This impatience had, by the middle 1970s, begun to take firm institutional form, for by 1975 the Liberation Tigers of Tamil Eelam (formed first, significantly, as the Tamil *Students'* Federation in 1970, and then reformed, inspired by a Kasi Anandan poem, as the Tamil New *Tigers* as early as 1972) and the TULF's own youth wing, the Tamil Youth Front (TYF) were both on the scene, and agitating for a 'holy war' (*punitha yutham*) against the Sri Lankan state (Swamy 2003: 24;Wilson 2000: 124).[1] In a sense, then, the

TULF had no choice but to pass the Vaddukoddai Resolution, and to campaign in 1977 on a platform that proclaimed the elections a referendum on Eelam; for the secessionist tide was already rising. When the TULF subsequently won almost every Tamil majority seat, they could indeed claim that Eelam had received a mandate from the people. Yet, having chosen to ride this tide, the TULF quickly found that it had drifted itself into a difficult, and ultimately self-destructive course for, as Wilson argues:

The passing of the Vaddukoddai Resolution had one serious implication for Tamil politics. Parliament would soon be replaced by the gun in the freedom struggle. This meant that the moderates and constitutionalists would be displaced by a militant movement of Tamil youth, who had no faith in Parliament. But there was an interval before the militants emerged ... (2000: 122)

It was in this 'interval' that Sivaram lived from 1978 to 1983, newly impoverished but anxious for involvement, and moving haphazardly back and forth between Colombo and Batticaloa, continuously taking on board the explosive mixture of revolutionary Tamil nationalism and strategically racist Sri Lankan state repression that was the political fuel of that time. In retrospect, his own fate seemed less settled than his country's sad future course. For with the cyclone, the family's fortunes had taken another turn for the worse. And despite the increasingly dire familial circumstances, Sivaram's dedication to passing his A-levels did not, could not, increase. He returned to Aquinas College for another try, however, between late 1978 and early 1979, living in a boarding house in Borella that his brother had once used before him – for he was 19 suddenly, and no longer a child. There he shared a room with two other students, both older and more experienced than him, and again reveled in the peripatetic life: eating quick *dosai* lunches at Greenlands, a well-known Indian restaurant; slipping out for movies and clandestine drinks at all-night bars; arranging late-night, roving, drunken conversations with other students; and conducting various, now quite serious, and rather emotionally cruel, liaisons with women, many of them married, and with whom he behaved, as he himself put it, 'disgracefully.' (As if, it seems, he was actively remembering his father, or his grandfather.) And, of course, there were the more normal, student-like, pranks, albeit with a political tint: one day, in a fury of remodeling, Sivaram and his roommates painted the top of their room completely black, and shocked their straight-laced landlady by writing fiery Tamil nationalist slogans – 'Eelam or die!' – all over the walls in indelible ink.

But it was now, also, that Sivaram began to experience a personal intellectual explosion. He began to read voraciously, almost indiscriminately, haunting Colombo's libraries and the Lake House bookstore, in Fort, like a young ghost. The names of an eclectic list of his favorite authors were faithfully recorded in his diaries, frequently accompanied by extensive quotations and commentaries: Hegel, Kojève, Bradley, Plato, Shakespeare, Arthur Miller, Asimov, Conrad ('Mr Kurtz – he dead' was one of his favorite tags), the early

Wittgenstein, Freud, Ayer, Spinoza, William James, Darwin, Blake, Milton, Heine, and T.S. Eliot. He also gave himself a quick tour through the world's religions and mythologies, reading, in English translation, Buddhist, Muslim, Shinto, Confucian, and Christian writings. And he began to train himself seriously in logic, argument, and analysis, writing short, carefully composed arguments in his diaries, and evolving rules for himself to use in his own reading such as the rather portentous one he wrote down on 13 February:

Edifices of thought are built on the frail foundations of a certain set of axioms. In some works [these are] formally stated as in the 'Ethics' of Spinoza and the 'Elements' of Euclid, and in some works – these are more numerous than the former – the axioms are not definitely stated but are assumed intuitively ... When the analyzing mind reads such works it should extract the unconscious assumptions of the author and see whether they are historically, logically and contextually acceptable, and then see whether the superstructure of the work can stand on those foundations.

At the same time, he faithfully continued to go every Friday, as he always had done before in Colombo, to the Hindu temple in Wellawatta, at first to worship and then, as his faith began to wane through the year in favor of a 'rationalism' very much like his father's, more to attend its cultural events and literary seminars. By 1978 he was regularly attending a seminar on Tamil language and literature conducted by a number of university students in a house near the temple. Indeed, it was there that he met a short, gentle-voiced, scholarly young man from Batticaloa, Mahadeva, who, though training to be a statistician, shared Sivaram's growing love of Tamil literature. Gradually, as Sivaram later put it, he began to 'fall in love with the beauties of the Tamil language.' But at the same time he began to seriously think about, and dabble in, politics. 'I just didn't want to be left out,' he said. 'It was the excitement of my time.' But once more he found it hard to concentrate on his official subjects, and once again he fell short of the grades he would need to go on to university – his mother's dream – when he failed his economics A-level.

Perhaps it was the politics that did it. Although Sivaram was briefly courted in 1977 in Batticaloa by a man he later learned was an early LTTE recruiter, Sivaram's involvement in politics really took a serious turn in 1978 when he joined a short-lived group called the Tamil People's Democratic Movement, a Maoist organization led by a young engineering student, Visvanandathevan, himself a follower of the Ceylon Communist Party (Peking wing) leader and intellectual, N. Shanmugathasan,[2] whose other, more famous 'student' was Rohana Wejeweera, the founder of the JVP (Chandraprema 1991: 23).[3] Sivaram admits that he did not know precisely what kind of group this was when he joined it. He was fired up by the general expectancy of the times and, more particularly, by his politically enthusiastic roommates. One of his roommates, after all, claimed to be a member of some, unnamed, militant group that had already set off bombs. 'He was a mad bugger,' Sivaram said to me later. 'He really inspired us.' It was this roommate who, in an excess of zeal, had dictated the Eelam-ist slogans that Sivaram had written 'in my good English' on the walls of their room. His other roommate, a student from Jaffna, had added his own special air to the spicy separatist atmosphere that Sivaram was breathing. Returning home one night with Sivaram, tipsy after a movie and several late drinks, he had staggered to the center of Borella junction and screamed out, defiantly, 'Eelam or death!'

'And I was fallen on my knees, *maccaan*, begging him to stop!'

'My god,' I said. 'What an idiot. You could have all been killed.'

Sivaram laughed, 'So it was like that. Luckily, it was the middle of the night and no one heard or paid any attention to us. But it was all like that. So when I joined the TPDF I didn't really know what I'd joined. Because the fellow said: "There is a need to launch an armed struggle to establish the democratic rights of the Tamils!" – but he very carefully avoided the words "to establish a separate state".'

'Why?'

Because, Sivaram explained, there was a serious debate going on at the time within the Tamil 'revolutionary' community about the exact nature and value of nationalism. On the one hand, there were the out-and-out nationalists, like the shadowy LTTE, 'whom we knew about, vaguely, as being out there, but who were so underground we never saw them,' who simply, instinctively, took the need for a separate state for granted. Their nationalism, Sivaram quickly realized, was comprised of a set of beliefs undergirded by the same sort of unstated presuppositions that he had warned against so strongly, earlier, in his note to himself. That is, those dangerously unexamined 'axioms that are not definitely stated but are assumed intuitively.' On the other hand, there were the Marxists whose reasoning was much more explicit. Many post-1977 Tamil Marxists believed, together with many Sinhala Marxists, that a struggle focused on achieving a separate state was a mistake, for they saw class struggle as conceptually and politically prior to – or, in the popular, Althusserian language of the day, as 'overdetermining' – ethnicity; and they believed that the obsession with ethnicity was a petit-bourgeois concern and a form of false consciousness (Balasingham 2003: 35). They argued, therefore, that the 'democratic rights' of Sri Lankan Tamils would be best looked after in a revolutionary state following an island-wide revolution; and hence that it was really an all-Lanka revolution for which Tamil youths ought to be struggling. Sivaram noted that it was to argue against this very position that the LTTE began to draw, at the time, on the services of Anton Balasingham, then a PhD candidate trying to complete a dissertation on the psychology of Marxism for London's South Bank Polytechnic (Gunaratna 1997: 9). But, in Sivaram's opinion, it was difficult for intuitive nationalists to make much intellectual headway against such Marxist arguments because the only languages (or 'tools,' as he later put it) that nationalists had available to argue about the nature of nationalism were, again, Marxist. That is, nationalists had to formulate their arguments using what concepts they could glean from either Lenin's discussions of national self-determination and/or from Marx's relatively few journalistic pieces on the 'Irish question.' At the time, Sivaram believed, there were simply no other useful texts on nationalism available in Tamil floating around the revolutionary community – aside from the emotive, DMK-inspired rhetoric that animated TULF speeches. Hence, as Sivaram began to read more Marx – something he did with great thoroughness, starting with the early, philosophical, neo-Hegelian Marx and proceeding, in a workman-like fashion, right up through *Das Kapital* – and as he began to re-examine Sri Lanka using the tools of class analysis, he became more and more convinced that the Marxists were right, and that only an all-island peasant–proletarian revolution, in concert with the Sinhala left, would secure the rights of the Tamil people – a belief that he would continue to hold until the end of his association with PLOTE in the early 1990s. Intellectually, then, he was convinced that the Marxists were right.[4]

Not that Sivaram ever became a *conventional* Marxist. Even in 1979, Sivaram's background reading in Western philosophy had made him, as he put it, a 'critical Marxist.' And he quickly became convinced that the quasi-religious dogmatism plaguing the Marxism that was being invoked by various Tamil groups at the time would eventually become an impediment to their practical success. 'People,' he complained, wearily, 'used to stand up to read Mao's words, as if they were reciting a *religious* text. It was ridiculous!' Sivaram, on the other hand, felt distant from this sort of unquestioning fidelity. For, as he later said to me:

... I was one of the few Marxists in Sri Lanka [involved in the Tamil movements of the time] that had a background in Western philosophy. Therefore I could look at Marxism from a critical point of view. I could discuss Hegel, its history – I mean I was one who could discuss its background. Now since 1976, when I first came to Colombo, I had been reading a lot of traditional Western philosophy. This has always been my argument with Marxists. You have to place Marx in his context, that is: in his philosophical milieu.

And so, of course, he was ambitious to see whether he could not bring his critical understanding of Marxism to bear on the Marxist-flavored Tamil separatist groups that were just beginning to surface at the time.

The larger debate about nationalism, however, posed a kind of paradox for Sivaram between his heart and his head. For if he increasingly *thought* that the Marxists were right, he increasingly *felt* that the nationalists were too. Or as he put it: 'I was increasingly influenced by the Marxist arguments. Intellectually. But *socially* I think I was a nationalist because my interactions were with people who were in the separatist nationalist movement.' So 'I was neither here nor there.' And this contradiction just did not seem right to him. Perhaps his feelings of intellectual unease had something to do with his failing his A-levels again – or, at least, his economics A-level– and then falling, perhaps in reaction, quite sick. For he returned to Batticaloa, and to Stanley House, still ill, fully tired of Colombo, and ready to divorce himself from that part of his life. For months thereafter he buried himself alone in his father's library, where he proceeded to read all of Gibbon's *The History of the Decline and Fall of the Roman Empire* in one extended reading. That done, he moved on, rather obsessively, through all the philosophers in the Chicago Great Books series, the long line of books that his father had bought, at great expense, just before he died. Ironically, it was also at this point in his life that he began to tutor other A-level students. Then one day he ran into Mahadeva again, now a graduate and firmly ensconced as a clerk in the statistical investigation department of the Batticaloa Kachcharie. Mahadeva, ever the amateur scholar, had begun to attend classes held by two famous Batticaloa *paTicca aal*, or 'learned men,' F.X.C. Nadarajah and Sivasubramaniyam, and, knowing how interested Sivaram had been in the Tamil-language seminars back in Colombo, suggested Sivaram come along. He did.

But just what is a *paTicca aal*? In Tamil the word *paTicca aal*, as I said, means 'learned man' and has no exact translation into English; for a learned man in Batticaloa is more than just a graduate (as, indeed, he may not be) or an intellectual. In the traditional intellectual hierarchy of the Batticaloa District, astrologers, temple priests, and Ayurvedic physicians all played important roles. But poets (*pulavar*) and *paTicca aal* – which is to say, anyone who possesses formal learning of any kind, but especially those who have taken those exams in Tamil literature and language which qualify one to be called *panTiTar* or *vittuvaan* – in some ways held the pivotal position. Indeed, Sivaram in his diaries used to refer to such people for this reason as the district's 'repositories of local knowledge.' This was because *pulavar* and *paTicca aal* were the primary recorders and interpreters of the region's folk songs, temple histories (*kaveTTu* or 'stone engravings'), and caste chronicles, the documents generally found in or compiled from the District's many locally written palm-leaf manuscripts. F.X.C. Nadarajah, who was a *vittuvaan*, for example, was famous in Batticaloa as the compiler and editor of the *maTTakkaLappu maanmiyam*, a historical chronicle of the Batticaloa District (the bulk of which was probably originally written in the seventeenth century at the instigation of the Dutch). In any case, producing and interpreting such documents required a *paTicca aal*'s expertise because they were generally written in the meter, style, and archaic language of late medieval, Tamil literature, and were therefore beyond the ken of most Batticaloa Tamils, however otherwise well educated. And interpreting and, at a pinch, producing such palm-leaf documents (and the books derived from them) was very important in Batticaloa for two reasons. First, historically, for the past several hundred years at least, rural power in Batticaloa's villages had been partially managed through a conservative, local caste hierarchy, firmly backed by colonial courts, that partly derived its ideological and legal justification from the 'official' *kaveTTu* histories of the District's large, regional temples, called *tecattakkoovil*. (It was, indeed, one of these *tecattakkoovil* – the *Sri Kantucuvaami* temple, in the village of Mandur – that I, rather rumpled and confused, would shortly be arriving to document.) Beyond this, Batticaloa's small but growing 'middle class' of white-collar government workers also needed *pulavar* and *paTicca aal* to help them pursue the local inter- and intra-caste conflicts in which they were now, so often, eagerly engaged. For Batticaloa, in the post-independence period, and particularly during the 1960s, 1970s, and early 1980s, boasted a number of caste-based organizations or *cangkam* formed to do literary battle over perceived slurs to the honor (*kauravam*) of various caste groups – a sign, perhaps, that the conservative caste hierarchy, petrified by colonial rule, was already eroding even before the coming revolutionary nationalist solvent. In any case, a good example of this was provided in 1980 by the *Ciirpaatar* Caste Social and Cultural Union (*ciirpaatakula camuka kalaaccar onRRiyaam*), a group of middle-class, Batticaloa-area *Ciirpaatar* caste enthusiasts formed from temple officials, high-school teachers, Kachcherie clerks, and some district irrigation officials to fund a *paTicca aal*-written reply to a book edited by F.X.C Nadarajah, Sivaram's chosen teacher, which they believed slandered their caste (Whitaker 1999: 111). *PaTicca aal*, of course, were key to such disputes because only they could knowledgeably wield the archaic evidence that constituted the weapons of choice in such honor battles (*kauravam caNTai*).

Sivaram had always cast scorn upon what he termed 'petit-bourgeois' concerns with caste status and temple-centered history. His family's peculiar history had kept him socially isolated from the caste politics of both Batticaloa's *teecatta* temples and its middle-class caste *cangkam*. Moreover, in the early 1980s, his Marxist revolutionary beliefs would have had him seeing both as evidence of a kind of local false consciousness. Nonetheless, it was this milieu of middle-class caste and temple politics that produced Sivaram and Mahadeva's Tamil teachers; or, rather, supported Nadarajah and Sivasubramaniyam by giving them the time and the interest required to delve, as they eventually did, not only into local manuscripts, but also deep into classical, *cangkam*-period, Tamil literature as a whole. Eventually, they began to turn their attention to the new research and writing about Tamil literature that was burgeoning in South India's universities and literary magazines (*ciRu pattirikaikal*).[5] And it was their knowledge and enthusiasm for this larger, pan-Tamil, intellectual world that they communicated to a small, but enthusiastic, younger generation of Batticaloa intellectuals that included Sivaram. Sivaram, indeed, credits their teachings with making him, as he puts it, 'an experiential nationalist.' For, as he said to me one day:

... there it was: my interest in classical Tamil was making me a nationalist without my knowledge. I was thinking: 'this was a nice thing, a good language, why should we allow this to be bloody erased by the state?' The more I delved into Tamil the more of an experiential nationalist I became. Nationalism in this sense: I started loving the richness of the Tamil language and became a romantic lover of its poetic beauties. The more of a student of classical Tamil I became, the more I became a lover of ancient Tamil culture.

But Sivaram's first impulse this time was not political; it was scholarly, or at least pedagogical. First, he and his friends began asking the district's most important writers and scholars how they might bring the literary knowledge they had learned to love to a wider Batticaloa audience. They spoke with

Sivaram's old St Michael's headmaster, Kamalanathan; with S. Poonadurai, a local author famous for his award-winning novel *Ritual (caTanku)*; and, of course, with their two *pulavar* teachers. All were encouraging. Nadarajah eventually mentioned that he had been exchanging correspondence with a literary society in Madras called the Readers' Circle (*vaacakar vaaTTam cennai*); perhaps, he suggested, they could start something like that in Batticaloa? So with a small group of like-minded young intellectuals that included P. Mahadeva and a new friend, Thevakuthan, an accountant with a new degree from Jaffna University, Sivaram formed the Batticaloa Readers' Circle (*maTTakkaLappu vaacakar vaTal cennai*).

I remember visiting the Batticaloa Readers' Circle 17 years later in 1997. It was during a period of fairly intense fighting in the east and our conversations were periodically punctuated by the sound of heavy artillery firing from the army camp near the old Kachcherie. We met at Mahadeva's house: a small, neat home situated down a twisty Batticaloa side street so narrow that my elbows nearly rubbed houses on both sides as I wound my way to it, for I was riding pillion on the back of the hard-used, wheezing, once-green, Honda 90 of one of the members. 'Don't worry,' he kept saying, soothingly, 'the street is wide enough. It's really very wide.'

'Your mirrors just scraped the walls!'

'Oh that. Well that happens.'

The whole group, six in all, were there to meet me when I arrived, although of the original six members only Mahadeva and Thevakuthan remained, the rest of the old group having been scattered by time, politics, death, and war.[6] Seeing them waiting there – so serious, so thoughtful – I suddenly felt as if I were meeting a group of intellectuals from a nineteenth-century Russian novel. (And with their interested faces and twinkling eyes, I was very much afraid that they were waiting for an André, whereas they would be getting – at best – a rather pathetic Pierre.) What I remember most intensely about the subsequent conversation, though, was the lively intellectual bonhomie of the group, despite the background thrum of war, and the fact that they were still in mourning for Ananthan, one of their original members. Mahadeva and Thevakuthan did most of the talking. Thevakuthan was an intense, contemplative, bespectacled man, carefully dressed in creased jeans, every inch the accountant, but quick to laugh; Mahadeva was similarly intellectual, if a bit more voluble, his prominent teeth occasionally lighting up a surprisingly sly smile. I asked them if they remembered their first meeting.

'Oh yes,' said Thevakuthan, 'We held our first meeting at Sivaram's house and asked people interested in these matters to come.'

'Actually,' added Mahadeva, pensively, 'the founder of this association was Sivaram. He was the founder, really. Anyway, after the first meeting most of the people who participated ... went off, but a few of us remained. We were about 40 people.'

There was a distant rumble of artillery.

'And,' he went on, 'we soon began to organize things. We asked the District Council, then under the administration of the special commissioner, Anthony Muttu – he was killed in a land mine explosion in 87, after the IPKF came – anyway, we asked him to recommend us to the library advisory committee. And we sent Sivaram as our representative. We wanted to suggest that they should buy new books with new ideas. Earlier they would just send employees from the library to buy the books. But we suggested that we should go to bookshops in Colombo or Jaffna and select new books for the library. So once or twice this happened, and Sivaram went to select the books. In the meantime we held several literary meetings. We held them on full moon days [which are monthly state holidays].'

'Then we shocked everyone,' Thevakuthan laughed: 'We allowed people to *criticize* the meetings!'

'What?'

'Well, you know,' said Mahadeva, 'earlier, of course, other associations held meetings like ours. But they never allowed people, the audience, to voice *their* views – and criticize even us, the people who organized the meetings. So views from the audience were accepted, and this was revolutionary – to have open discussions at a meeting! So some of the older literary people boycotted our meetings, saying this was a useless thing. Fortunately, we had backing from S. Poonadurai and some other people.'

'Then, in 1981,' said Thevakuthan, 'there was an international Tamil research conference in Madurai. And four people from Batticaloa went, including Mr F.X.C. Nadarajah. So we asked them to deliver speeches on their experience at that conference when they returned to Batticaloa.'

'There was a massive crowd for that meeting,' said Mahadeva, enthusiastically. 'Two or three hundred people – the most that had ever come to such an event in the history of Batticaloa. Because, as you know, these type of literary meetings are generally not attended by a lot of people.'

Everyone laughed knowingly. Overhead, several heavy helicopters passed, their engines rattling the teacups.

'And so, because it was successful, we became well known in Batticaloa.

'Anyway, in this same period, Mr Ananthan also started coming to our meetings and became a member of our association. And it was after Mr Ananthan joined that we seriously thought about having a constitution and bylaws and such. So one day we got together and talked about all this, wrote one up, it was accepted, and we became a formal organization.'

It was V. Ananthan who thereafter dominated the group, and blazed much of its future path. A heavy set, sad-eyed man with a big moustache, always notoriously rumpled in appearance, he could, his friends claimed, light up a room with his lively talk, and then warm it gently with his genuinely kind demeanor. In debate he crackled with wit and new ideas (Ananthan 1997: 4). The only person who, at first, could keep up with him was Sivaram; but even Sivaram, 'Well, you know,' said Mahadeva, 'he was still young. We all were then.' Ananthan, on the other hand, was at least ten years older than most of the rest of the group – ten years he had filled with diverse experiences.

Ananthan had been born into a poor family in the largely *veLLaaLar* village of Samanthurai, at the far end of the lagoon – or 'lake,' as people there say – from Batticaloa. As an innately curious boy, he had done his A-levels in the Bible and Islam, an unusual step for a Hindu child. After graduating, he had worked for the Jehovah's Witnesses for several years, canvassing door to door, handing out leaflets, and selling books.

'Was he a convert?'

'Did he believe?' said Mahadeva, 'Not a word of it. No, he didn't believe but he found the ideas interesting and started to write a series of poems about them. He compared ideas from the Bible to ideas from Hinduism, and with the Tamil's current situation. He even wrote a book of them: *The Injustice of Imbalance.*'

Ananthan then became interested in Marxism and eventually, in 1969, joined the Ceylon Communist Party (Peking wing), still led then by N. Shan-mugathasan. He worked for them full time for several years, and assiduously read all the books they provided, but gradually became disillusioned – for it seemed to him that the party was not doing anything concrete for poor Tamil people in Batticaloa. So he left the party and turned instead, perhaps in reaction, to the study of Malayalam, a Dravidian language closely related to Tamil that is spoken in the South Indian state of Kerala, the state most famous both for its Communist Party government and its high rates of literacy and education. For a time he traveled frequently to Colombo to the office of the Kerala state-funded *malaiyala kalaalayam*, where his enthusiasm quickly won him both friends and teachers, and within a short time he was fluent. Anxious to take his knowledge back home to Batticaloa, he applied to become a teacher, something his good A-levels in the early 1970s qualified him to do, but he was turned down (he was convinced) because of his membership in the Communist Party. It was this last, bitter experience with the after-effects of political involvement, perhaps, that made him insist that the Readers' Circle should place in its new bylaws a special rule forbidding active membership in any named political party.

In any case, after working for several years as a laborer in a sugar factory and getting married, Ananthan took a job as a postal 'peon' back in his home village of Samanturai. To his mind the job was merely a support for his reading, which had by then become truly voracious. For, as Mr Thevakuthan put it: 'He was *always* reading, reading, reading' – and reading, generally, in Malayalam. Malayalam had not only opened up a whole new literature to Ananthan, but also access to literary magazines, published in Kerala, that were full of translations unavailable in Tamil. It was in these that he read stories and essays by Camus, Sartre, Gorky, Merleau-Ponty, and Maupassant. He also read the Bible in Malayalam, arguing, to Mahadeva, that its translation into that language was far superior to its Tamil and English versions (although he did not read much English, and remained largely indifferent to the language). And he began to collect and read serious Indian critical writing about cinema. All this he began, also, to translate and bring to the attention of the Batticaloa Readers' Circle – and to Sivaram.

Eventually, with Ananthan on board, the Batticaloa Readers' Circle began to branch out. They invited writers and scholars – and *pulavar* –from around the area and from Tamil Nadu to come to Batticaloa to address the group, including Ragunathan, a member of the Progressive Writers Front of Tamil Nadu who had recently written a book on Tamil literary criticism; and Kovindan, a prominent leftist also from South India who had compiled a book of early Saivite saints' songs (*Cittar paaTalkal*). They organized a three-day seminar in Batticaloa on the new journals being written in imitation of the literary magazines of Tamil Nadu – journals such as the Jaffna magazines *Now!* (*putucu*) and *People's Literature* (*makkal ilakkiyam*), and the Colombo magazine *Young Man* (*kumaran*). As Mahadeva said, 'Before 1982 there was nothing like them in Batticaloa. So we introduced them to the public and only then did some local journals begin.' They also organized a seminar on the history of Tamil literature to help out the District's A-level students. And, inspired by Ananthan, they started holding seminars on folklore, modern South Asian cinema, and on Malayalam literature (translations supplied by the ever industrious Ananthan). Eventually, they organized a story-writing competition in concert with the editors of Tamil journals all over Sri Lanka and gave out prizes. It was a heady, busy, productive time, and Sivaram was in the thick of it. Perhaps that was why, in 1980, when he sat down for his A-levels once again, he passed them with flying colors and earned himself a place at the University of Paradiniya, at that time one of Sri Lanka's most selective universities. The members of the Readers' Circle were overjoyed; Sivaram's mother was too. Sivaram, however, was not so sure.

But in September 1981 he went to university anyway. He would last there a little over two years.

It was also in September 1981 that I arrived in Sri Lanka. Around the time Sivaram was leaving for university, in fact, I was moving into a YWCA on Union Place in Colombo. I arrived incredibly sick, however, for the day before my departure from America a distant, elder cousin, visiting from the Midwest, had thundered at me that my journey to 'the land of idol worship' would put my immortal soul in peril. This opinion was spoken with such religious force that it efficiently conveyed my distant uncle's flu, which matured enough by the time I arrived in Colombo, after a 24-hour flight, to make my first few weeks there a fevered dream. A large, friendly faced woman with vast, steel-gray hair, dressed in a magnificent white sari – the YWCA's owner, I learned later – looked at me skeptically and shook her head as I stood, wheezing, sweating, and swaying, in the doorway of the hostel.

'You need a bed.'

'Yes,' I said, weakly, 'I'd like to rent ... something.'

'I mean you need a bed right now.'

I suddenly sat down, on the floor.

'Sashi!'

'I'm an anthropology graduate student from Princeton University,' I managed, weakly, from below. 'I'm here to do research.' I seemed to be addressing a ceiling fan. A worried-looking young man dressed in a blindingly white *verti* suddenly interposed himself.

'Pick him up and put him in bed.'

When I became mobile again, several days later, I found myself in an E.M. Forster novel. The YWCA seemed to be populated by an eclectic mixture of down-market tourists and displaced Sri Lankans. There were several boisterous Australian surfers (who seemed to dress solely in bathing thongs), a Muslim gem merchant, a trio of secretive English teachers, a Tamil nun who prayed alone in whispered Latin late at night in the garden, an American doctor and an expat Canadian engineer on holiday from his project somewhere in India. The American doctor was of indeterminate gender. I knew this because, on the first day that I was well enough to sit on the veranda, she/he had sat down next to me and said, 'I imagine you find yourself troubled about my gender?'

'Yes? What?' I said, doubtfully. Actually, stuffed up and still feverish, I was having trouble registering anybody. I tried to focus on my speaker. Short, thick-bodied, with close-cropped brown hair, a stern pug-face, and dressed in a brown safari suit buttoned up to the neck. Purple socks, too, I realized.

'Um ...'

'Do not try to guess. You can't. I have traveled beyond gender. And do you know why?'

'Why?'

'Ananda Comaresvamy.'

'Who?'

'Ananda Comaresvamy. The scholar, art critic, and mystic. He took the wisdom of the East and merged it with the scholarship of the West. He died in Connecticut, but he came from here. I am on a pilgrimage to absorb his soul.'

'Is that ... wise?'

I was told, at great length, that it was.

Several days later, on my first venture out into the city to procure cough drops, I found myself walking next to the Canadian engineer. He told me a bit about his engineering work and the special expat community in which he lived. Special because, he said, 'You can't be too careful.'

'About what?'

'You just can't.'

He was a peculiar-looking man. Dressed entirely in black, and nearly spherical, with a floppy thatch of white-blond hair over his perpetually anxious face, he looked rather like a worried eight-ball. This impression was heightened by the way he kept twisting and turning, bouncing really, to avoid even incidental contact with other people on the crowed streets. Finally, at a junction, a tall man with a briefcase, jostled by people getting down from a bus, tripped and fell against me. I touched his arm, briefly, to steady him while he regained his feet. I thought he muttered, 'Thank you,' but then:

'DON'T TOUCH THEM!' screamed the Canadian, his face now beet red.

I stared at him. I thought he was having some sort of attack. The tall man hustled away.

'Don't you know,' he said, through clenched teeth, 'about skin diseases?'

'Skin diseases?'

'You touch them like that and the next thing you know you'll have balls the size of basketballs. Oh, I can't walk with you any more. You're just not safe enough.'

And he stalked away, his round body spinning, bouncing, and jerking to avoid the crowd, a very white little man surrounded by a balloon of paranoia so palpable that people seemed pushed aside by it as he progressed.

I stared after him, mesmerized, suddenly convinced that my coming to Sri Lanka was a big mistake. It was certainly an accident. I was supposed to have done a study of religious behavior in communist Romania, and had even learned some of the language in preparation, but my funding had fallen through. Professor Gananath Obeyesekere, one of the giants of Sri Lankan anthropology, the chair of my department at Princeton and himself Sinhalese, had taken pity on me and suggested that I work in Sri Lanka, specifically in Batticaloa. 'You're interested in large-scale religious ritual. Well, Mark, they certainly have that in Batticaloa in their big regional temples. Take a chance. Borrow the money, go there, and work up a project.'

'But I don't know anything about South Asia!'

'Fresh eyes can be a virtue. Anyway, what else have you to do?'

Lacking anything better to do, I quickly read through the extraordinarily long list of books he suggested, took out another school loan, and came. But Colombo was a shock. It was hot, smelly, too busy, and too full (apparently) of demented white tourists. And it was also, of course, incredibly alien to my white, suburban, middle-class American sensibilities. There were thousands of tiny shops all selling the same things, piles of garbage that nobody ever appeared to collect, little suicidal three-wheeler taxis with engines that squealed like giant mosquitoes, and battered buses crammed with people so closely packed they seemed to be solid rather than particulate. Everywhere coconut oil smoke seemed to merge with diesel fumes to coat my tongue and clothes alike in a thick oleaginous sludge.

And I had never been out of my country before, except for a brief trip to Romania with my high-school folk-singing group. Until my arrival at Union Place, indeed, my interest in anthropology had been philosophical rather than practical or ethnographic. Despite being an anthropology graduate student, I was not all that interested in travel; I was more fascinated by the quirky puzzles of moral and epistemological relativism that the field tended to generate. Hence, I was interested in religions because religions seemed to me to be the most intensely various things about which people were absolutely convinced that they are right. But confronting real people in this really (as opposed to a philosophically) different place appeared suddenly beyond my psychological strength. Was this just culture shock? Much of it, of course, certainly was. But somehow the image of the paranoid Canadian rolling down the street in his sterile balloon suggested something more complex to me; something far more upsetting, and self-implicating, that was beyond both my ken and my simple models of cultural difference. Fortunately, that night, I discovered that arrack and ginger is a very cheering drink.

Four months later, after some Tamil language training at the University of Colombo, which graciously agreed to take me on as a 'casual student' in sociology, I departed for the Batticaloa District, and the relatively large temple village of Mandur. (My departure was blessed by no less an eminence than Newton Gunasinghe, my nominal advisor at Colombo University, who said, blithely: 'Go forth, young man. You can't do too much harm.') There I was to remain, for the most part, for the next two years. I was, of course, hot and lonely and socially inept. Once, trying to eat with my hands in the correct manner, I inadvertently propelled a sloppy chunk of jak-fruit curry half way across the room. My hosts kindly pretended that nothing messy had happened to their clean wall. My recently acquired Tamil inspired giggles in the children of the house. My questions to older people were generally greeted with puzzlement or exasperation. My sarong tended to slip at inopportune times. And, as a child of America's antiseptic suburbs, I found the presence of wallowing water buffalo, scurrying chickens, meandering goats, and the occasional suspiciously inert crocodile unnerving. I was a mess.

But having presented myself to people there as a scholar, they gradually took me in hand and made me behave like one. They had me hire a research assistant – a mild-mannered, highly competent, retired Kachcherie clerk named S. Panjalingam, to whom I owe most of my understanding of Batticaloa. Then the officials of Mandur's famous *Sri Kantisvami* temple made me turn my attentions toward their temple – its officers, myths, histories, documents, disputes, and festivals – in a way that made me realize, gradually, that I was dealing with a very complicated socio-political system as much as a religious institution. Mandur's temple, in fact, was 'owned' by four other villages – the *Karaiyar* caste villages of Kotte Kallar and Periya Kallar, and the *Ciirpaatar* caste villages of Turaineelavanai and Kurumanvelli – whose own local customary socio-political systems were simultaneously legitimized by their 'rights' (*urimaiyal*) in the Mandur temple. Indeed, in a manner that I eventually found to be roughly similar for all of Batticaloa's 'regional temples,' the elites at the top of the conservative local social hierarchies that dominated the temple's five towns tended to legitimize themselves by using a temple-centered ideology. An ideology, that is, in which their contemporary elite status was generally presented as a natural consequence of the temple's distant divine origins. I also began to realize that this arrangement was by no means age-old; rather, it had been arrived at in colonial times by the temple elite's effective, strategic use of colonial law in a series of late nineteenth- and early twentieth-century legal disputes.

In fact, the whole thing reminded me, in a curious way, of something I'd read in a book: Ludwig Wittgenstein's *Philosophical Investigations* (1958). I had long been fascinated by Wittgenstein's later 'common language' philosophy. Even reading him as an undergraduate, I had felt there was an interesting similarity between the philosophically puzzling realities of ethnographic fieldwork (at least insofar as I had read about them) and Wittgenstein's investigative philosophical method. For this method, in his later work, involved building intermediary, inevitably incomplete, 'primitive language games' to contrastively illustrate the enacted social practices, or 'forms of life,' within which he believed all meanings occurred (and could only occur). This was how Wittgenstein hoped to escape the danger of decontextualization (due to meta-theoretical redescription) that he felt was pathologizing the philosophy of language. And, of course, the resemblance between this problem and the problems faced by any anthropologist (or social scientist, for that matter) trying to describe local forms of life without reducing them to mere fodder for professional seminars is obvious. Years later I even wrote a small paper about this similarity (Whitaker 1996). But it was a further implication of Wittgenstein's method that struck me here.

For I had been impressed by what one might call Wittgenstein's 'multidimensionality' of meaning (something that, unknown to me, Sivaram was also just then hearing about from Professor Kalansuriya, his philosophy professor at the University of Paredeniya, and an expert on Wittgenstein). By multidimensionality I mean Wittgenstein's observation that since actions and utterances are meaningful only within enacted forms of life, there is no reason why, at any given moment, particular actions or utterances should not mean various, different, and even contradictory, things by virtue of their simultaneous presence within multiple, overlapping forms of life. That is, there is no reason, say, why a professional cricketer should not be, at one and the same time, lifting a ball for a critical, match-winning six (meaning number one) *and* increasing his personal and team's market value (meaning number two). For although cricket and sport capitalism are quite different 'forms of life,' they coexist, most of the time – unless a killjoy cultural critic is lurking somewhere – without noticeable friction. One might even say that capitalism mostly works by well-lubricated envelopments of this sort (see Kingsolver 2001: 40); and, as we shall see, Sivaram would add that nationalism does too.

In any case, Mandur and its Sri Kantucuvaami temple seemed a perfect example of multidimensionality as well. That is, on the one hand, Mandur was a village presided over by a government appointed *gramasevaka* (headman), in an electoral subdivision represented by a Member of Parliament, and in a district of the republic of Sri Lanka ruled over, in 1981, by an executive President. On the other hand, Mandur was also the royal seat of a paradigmatic divine sovereign, Murukan, and at the center of his 'nation' (*teecam*) and its caste-conscious social system. (And on yet *another* hand, although I was rather unaware of it at the time, Mandur was also a part of the potential nation-state of Eelam. And eventually, in 2004, the LTTE's eastern commander, Karuna, would claim Batticaloa as yet another potential entity: South-Eelam!) Moreover, the more I looked into the legal history of the arrangements that underlay the way the Sri Lankan state officially (though rather unconsciously) backed the temple's local system, I found a similar multidimensionality: for, there, colonial era, agnostically utilitarian, public Trust laws quietly existed in unacknowledged coexistence with Mandur's god-saturated temple ideology in a largely frictionless relationship that I began to think of as a kind of 'amiable incoherence' (Whitaker 1999). In the end, struck by *this* multidimensional thought, I suddenly, almost hallucinogenically, envisioned the whole landscape of Batticaloa – the whole of everywhere else too – bubbling, whirling, and seething with ghostly, overlapping, indifferently intermingling, but sometimes subtly and even violently interacting forms of life. It reminded me of the way the many fruit bats that inhabited the coconut palm in our compound sometimes played at twilight in a whirling ball of flowing fur.

This multidimensionality of social life, by the way, is what Sivaram, writing in his diaries at roughly the same time, started to call the 'fecundity of being.'

Still, the infinite complexities of this vision seemed, to me, rather impossible. Perhaps, I thought, I have misread this aspect of Wittgenstein's work? I decided I had better go and see if I could reread the relevant passages. So one day I pulled out my blue Honda 90, put on my helmet, and drove the 25 or so miles to Batticaloa to try to look up Wittgenstein in the town library, though why I thought I would find the book there I do not know. I also wanted a cool beer and a bit of a rest under the ceiling fans of the Rest House. Anyway, when I got to the library, I did not find anything by Wittgenstein; I did find Gilbert Ryle's *The Concept of Mind*. Of course, that was the afternoon I met Sivaram.

We had a very pleasant conversation at his house – very pleasant for me, especially, because his mother made a lunch of chicken and mashed potatoes covered in a savory gravy, the first food I'd had other than rice and curry for close to a year. After discovering that Sivaram was an undergraduate, I was at first dubious when he expressed an interest in Wittgenstein. Gradually it dawned on me, however, that he knew Wittgenstein's philosophy at least as well as I did. And I found discussing epistemology with him in his father's disheveled library, despite its leaky roof, a convivial respite from doing fieldwork. I was tired of having to view every person I met as an 'informant'; here, finally, was a casual acquaintance with whom I could drink a few beers and pass the time spinning my mental wheels. So I wrote the address of the room I sometimes rented in Borella, Colombo, in his diary – for anybody could find me, the lone white man, in Mandur – and left. Over the next year, whenever I happened to be in Batticaloa, I would check his house to see if he was in. Generally he was not but, when he was, we had more such amiable conversations. I was slightly disturbed, however, by one thing he said during our first conversation.

'The problem with Wittgenstein, Mark, is that he leaves the politics out.'
I wondered what that meant.

Sivaram arrived at the university as a student of English literature and began to lead two lives. On the one hand, there was Sivaram the dedicated student; on the other hand, there was Sivaram the neophyte Tamil militant. As a student Sivaram attended lectures and tutorials; watched (but generally avoided) ragging; lived with other students in a typically messy rented room; stayed up late reading, writing, talking, and drinking; and soaked up hundreds of books. As a potential militant, Sivaram periodically traveled to Jaffna and made contact with the LTTE. But Sivaram never jointed the LTTE and, later, in 1982, frustrated that the LTTE did not work in Batticaloa, and perhaps also by its non-Marxist nationalism, he entered the Gandhian Movement, which was a front for PLOTE (or the Peoples Liberation Organization of Tamil Eelam).[7] Although Sivaram eventually allowed this membership to lapse for a time, lulled perhaps by the relative political quiet of late 1982, he remained an inactive member of PLOTE. And he waited.

And at first, despite what he now claims, Sivaram was a very serious student indeed. For there is almost nothing in Sivaram's 1982 university diary about political interests or actions, and while this may have been due to caution, it was also, I think, a reflection of his very real initial absorption in university life. But he was an unusual student; everyone noticed it. His batch mate, Jude Fernando, for example, remembers Sivaram as an overwhelming presence in the classroom. Over lunch one day, in June 2004, Jude reminisced: 'Frankly, Mark, there were simply no lecturers who knew as much as Siva did, especially about philosophy. His knowledge of Western philosophy at the time was simply amazing. When he came to class, he would hold forth and the professors would just kind of fade to the side. It was quite something.' Then Jude looked thoughtful, and added: 'Of course fairly soon he largely stopped coming. But whenever he *did* come, he still always knew more and had read more than all of us, the lecturers included, put together. Fantastic.'

Nevertheless, intellectually, Sivaram did discover a few scholars equal to his inquisitiveness, especially his philosophy professor, Kalansuriya. They argued from his first day in class – Sivaram thought he had rather 'made a fool of myself' – but Kalansuriya quickly recognized the quality of his mind, and Sivaram took to dropping by his house to continue their discussions. He also began to read serious literary criticism, including F.R. Leavis, Northrop Frye, and structuralists such as Roland Barthes, as well as a much wider array of English and modern Tamil literature, all in preparation for taking his General Arts Qualifying (GAQ) exam, which he was supposed to sit in 1982. Indeed, if Sivaram's journals are to be believed, this GAQ reading so inspired him that he began to seriously consider a future career as either an academic or, as be began to write more Tamil poetry, as a poet. At the same time, socially, at least in the beginning, Sivaram fully tasted the life of a 1980s undergraduate

– though adding to it, perhaps, some peculiar flavors of his own. So: Sivaram got drunk on a trip with batch mates to Hunas Falls; attended a lighthearted trip to Adam's Peak with his roommates; pursued various female undergraduates romantically (or, rather, sexually); and wandered about Kandy with his friends one *poya* day – in fact, the day of the Perahera – trying to discover where one could purchase cheap illegal beer (for 'full moon days' like Perahera are public holidays and alcohol sales are banned). He was incredibly poor. At one point, he was so short of money he had to secure a loan from a friend to buy soap for a bath, and he frequently skipped meals. He was also given to intense bouts of depression and an almost hallucinogenic, dark nostalgia for his earlier life in Colombo. (He vividly remembers that day; he was in his room, suffering from fever, and was in delirium – 'I also think I may have been taking some medicine.') But, for the most part, he seemed to be enjoying himself.

Nevertheless, as 1981 wore into 1982, Sivaram began to spend less time at the university and more time in Jaffna and Batticaloa. Partly politics was becoming more absorbing; partly he was simply bored. For Sivaram, ultimately an autodidact, was used to working on his own. In 1981, for example, while waiting to find out if he would be even admitted to university, and for his own amusement, he wrote a highly technical paper entitled 'Syntactic Functions and Some Semantic Features of the Adjectival Relative Participle in Early Tamil.' In it he not only addressed the semantic peculiarities of the adjectival relative participle as a part of speech found and used in Tamil in *cangkam* poetry (BC 300–200 AD), but also the wider issue of which research methodologies properly should be used to address linguistic puzzles likely to arise in the study of ancient Tamil. Then, not knowing what to do with the paper, he sent it off to one of his intellectual heroes: K. Sivathamby, at that time professor of Tamil studies at Jaffna university and a well-respected scholar.

Professor Sivathamby still remembers opening the letter as he was descending the stairs of the Arts building at Jaffna University and being completely taken aback by what he was reading. 'Mark, here was a letter, written by someone completely unknown to me, anticipating things in Tamil studies my colleagues and I were only then beginning to think about.' Seeing his colleague, K. Kailasapathy, coming up the stairs, Sivathamby hailed him and, for a time, they stood together on the middle landing reading the paper together over each other's shoulders. 'Who *is* this?' Sivathamby kept asking. Finally Kailasapathy looked carefully at the name.[8]

'Why this is old Professor Kanapathipillai's nephew,' said Kailasapathy, referring to Sivaram's cousin Oppi's father. 'But, my goodness, he isn't even at the university yet.'

Nor, by 1982, for the most part, was Sivaram in the university any more. Though nominally still a student, Sivaram never sat for his General Arts Qualifying exam, without which further work at the university was impossible. Why did he avoid the exam? Partly, of course, it was politics taking up more and more of his time; and he claims, now, it was indifference. But one has to wonder whether all those A-level failures, plus his prickly relationships with some of his tutors at Peradeniya, did not dim his hopes that he could actually pass the exam, regardless of how much knowledge he had acquired on his own. Or perhaps it was his arrest in Jaffna. For at around this time Sivaram was picked up by the army, and regular beatings accompanied his two days in custody – before the camp's commander recognized him as a the nephew of his well-respected Jaffna uncles and let him loose, certain, ironically, that no one connected with them could be involved in anything so nefarious to the Sri Lankan state as militant separatism. Certainly that brief trauma must have firmed up his belief in the unavoidable hostility of the Sri Lankan state. In any case, increasingly, Sivaram simply stayed away from classes and the campus altogether.

Not that Sivaram's touchy, more out than in, relationship with the university was unique in the early 1980s. In 1997, shortly before I visited the Readers' Circle, I happened to have a long conversation with Professor K. Sivathamby about Tamil youths and the universities in the early 1980s. A large, friendly-faced man, with unruly salt-and-pepper hair and a deep, naturally expressive, and rather soulful voice, Sivathamby happened to be guest lecturing at Batticaloa's Eastern University that year. I found him in his quarters – a rented room – changing into his sarong, as he had just returned that moment from campus. In 1997, by the way, returning home from campus was no small feat. Eastern University's campus is north of Batticaloa, and that July the front lines between the Sri Lankan army and the LTTE had collapsed upon the very Trincomalee road everyone had to use to get to it (or, for that matter, to get out of town). Firefights were frequent and, as a result: 'We lose two or three a week on the bus to campus, Mark. It is quite a shame.'

'But you continue to go?'

'Well, I have classes you see.'

I remember digesting this and trying to imagine American or British academics risking death every day to deliver lectures, or American or British students risking death to attend them. But I was there to talk about Sri Lanka's student militants, and Sivathamby's experiences had allowed him to know them well. A fixture on Sri Lanka's leftist intellectual scene since the mid-1950s, when he and the well-known Tamil scholar, K. Kailasapathy, had formed the Progressive Writers Association, Sivathamby had been a lecturer at Sri Jayawardenepura University during the 1971, mostly Sinhalese, JVP insurrection, and had known and been liked by many of the militants. Then he had moved to Jaffna in 1978, just in time, he noted somewhat wistfully, to witness the rise of the separatist movements. It first came to his notice, he told me, as a kind of intellectual movement, often led by young men who had been excluded from the university by the quota system.

'At that time,' he said, 'there were groups of young men, Mark, most of whom were outside the university. Blocked, in fact, from getting into the university, many of them, by the laws. And their problem was they wanted a break away from the past. They were not getting what they needed from outside the university, and even *in* the university our mode of education was such that they were not getting it here either. We were teaching *classical* economics, *classical* political economy and so forth – and they believed our forms of knowledge were not, uh, *diversified* enough to address the times. So they felt they had to go out on their own and find out something, and when they did that, we found that they wanted Marxism but not the Marxism that was prevalent in Sri Lanka.'

He shook his head and laughed, somewhat ruefully. 'You know, they called us the "old Marxists". Because the old Marxism in Sri Lanka believed in national unity ... a national unity of Sinhala and Tamils.'

'And they did not.'

He smiled.

'You see our society was a society in which, as I said somewhere, everything was planned for a person, from birth to marriage to death – even naming the child was the prerogative of the grandfather. The family decided who he should marry, who she should marry, how they should live, where they should live and so on. But suddenly their future was blocked. You see, *my* father could guarantee *my* future. At least, he believed, if you have a degree, you can become a teacher. And I *did* become a teacher. But when the older generation could not guarantee that, and with the younger generation being exposed to these new ideas, then ...' (see Sivathamby 1995: 61–73).[9]

'They rebelled?'

'*That* is number one. Number two: this communal discrimination has been going on for a long time. It did not start in the 1960s and 1970s; it was there in the 1950s and the 1940s. But these people who were at the helm of affairs then were helpless; they could not do anything.'

'And the boys noticed this?'

'Right, and it manifested itself in two or three ways. One way was that they started discussing in groups. They had readers' groups and they started these little journals. For example, there was the EROS group: the Eelam Revolutionary Organization of Students. Actually, a number of the preliminary groups that grew into militant groups were student groups.'

'And then,' he said, 'they started showing up in my seminars. You see, I remember these young men coming and sitting in my seminars that I never expected. Sometimes they would want to discuss things with me; sometimes they would come and ask, "Can you help us with this?" There were one or two other teachers whose knowledge was tapped for this type of purpose. And to a certain extent, because of my interest in Marxism, there were a few students who used to come to me.'

'And what did they want to know?'

He laughed. 'They wanted to know how you start a revolution! Not theoretically but practically, and right now. No, the question they were asking was about how to organize themselves for the establishment of a Tamil Eelam. And I would even say that, at that time, they were more interested in how they could launch a liberation struggle. They were quite sure about their targets. They knew whom they were aiming at.'

Nor, Sivathamby observed, were they particularly interested in the kinds of Sinhalese leftists that Sivathamby himself had been working with for years and for whom he had, and continued to have, the deepest respect: people such as Kumari Jayawardena, Charles Abeyesekere, Dayan Jayatilake, and Newton Gunasingha who, he knew, had a good grasp of the Tamil problem and a profound sympathy for their plight.[10] 'And they really suffered for this at the hands of the Sinhala chauvinists in the 1980s and early 1990s, Mark.' But the sights of 'the boys' were already set on separatism, on Eelam, in complete contradiction to Sivathamby's long-held dream of a union of Sinhala and Tamil leftist politics. Nonetheless, he found himself admiring them. For, despite the fact that many of these young would-be militants were not, in fact, actual students, they had developed a kind of critical intelligence – a way of reading texts very closely and cleverly – that he wished he and his university were able to teach their actual students.

'I find it very astounding ... and perhaps we can understand it [in Sivaram's case] because he reads English and so forth. But in that period there were some young fellows who could only read Tamil and yet somehow they developed also this critical tradition – and it did *not* come from the university.'

And where was Sivaram all this time? Partly he was in Jaffna, participating in those very seminars, discussion groups, and journals that Sivathamby describes. One of Sivathamby's clever young men, Sivakumar,[11] remembers Sivaram showing up at their impromptu seminars in 1982 and dazzling everyone present with his grasp of the issues – 'even though,' Sivakumar noted, darkly, 'he was from a landowning family.' But mostly Sivaram was in Batticaloa, involved in another project: producing an issue of a local intellectual journal: *KeeRRu* (Slice). By late 1982, the Readers' Circle's seminar on the intellectual and literary journals of Jaffna and Madras had borne much fruit. Imitation journals had begun to sprout in Batticaloa, and Sivaram was asked to edit one of the first issues of one of these. This he did, assiduously, not only writing the lead article and editing all the others, but actually pushing the foot pedal of the tired old printing press they used to print the thing. This all took place, rather ironically, in the town of Akkaraipattu, near the family's old estate – by that time subdivided, owned, and run by the people who used to work on it. Perhaps he was thinking of them as he wrote. For in his article (1982: 1–9), 'The weakness of an intellectual milieu,'[12] Sivaram sarcastically castigated South Asian Marxists for using Marx without being aware of his proper historical and philosophical context, an observation he was to continue to make with equal vehemence even during his time in the movement. The article caused a stir – of a sort. One Indian Marxist still refused to talk to Sivaram years later, when they ran into each other at a conference; at the time, he had merely contented himself by sending a reply to Sivaram's article so extensive that, had they published it, it would have been longer than the entire original issue of the journal!

Beyond this, Sivaram was back to reading and thinking on his own. According to his 1982 and early 1983 diaries, Sivaram was frustrated by what he felt was the inelastic, unresponsive, epistemologically unconvincing kind of Marxism generally followed in Sri Lanka, but convinced, nonetheless, of the intrinsic value of class analysis. At the same time, Sivaram was impressed by the 'fecundity of being' he saw illustrated in Wittgenstein's account of meaning – his term for the seething mix of 'language games' that I had suddenly perceived from my verandah in Mandur – which he saw as an effective reply to the epistemological woolgathering of much Western philosophy.[13] He was also impressed by the 'new' histories of science being written by Kuhn (1962) and Feyeraband (1975), which he saw as partially inspired by a similar epistemological view. But Sivaram also saw the epistemological 'therapy' advocated by Wittgenstein, and Wittgenstein's investigative method as explicated by Western philosophers such as Rorty (1979), as inherently, and *naïvely*, apolitical. And Sivaram was particularly worried by this naïveté because of his reading, at this time, of Noam Chomsky's various critiques of American foreign policy, which convinced him that the political field that Sri Lankan Tamils needed to worry about was not just local and Sri Lankan, but also transnational and very dangerous. So, as an antidote to all this, he began seriously reading post-structuralists such as Foucault and Derrida, hoping by this means to discover some kind of bridge between his political-revolutionary and epistemological interests. He also began reviewing the history of other social revolutions, particularly those in China, Nicaragua and Vietnam.

Gradually, feeling he needed to know *what* exactly he was trying to change, and what his role in changing it could be, Sivaram began to build a model in his mind of how he believed societies actually worked. He began to envision societies as 'techno-social organisms' – though he worried somewhat about the biological metaphor implied here – composed of 'fecund' bundles of language games and 'gadgets' (by which he meant small technical language games), generally chaotic but loosely organized internally into a hegemonic 'web' by class interests and strategies in the dialectical ways Marx and Gramsci had described (relations of production, hegemony, and so forth). For Sivaram, such a web was 'a field of subjectivities with a multiplicity of overlapping fields' (Sivaram's diary 13 August 1983). And, within such webs, 'overlapping language games exist with their own rules but these are subject to the dominant processing influence of the epoch' (ibid). He began thinking about doing a 'case study' of the rise of Islamic fundamentalism in Batticaloa's Muslim community to demonstrate this, and began gathering statistics, attending mosque lectures, and doing impromptu interviews to that end. At the same time, he saw such 'webs' in poor 'paddy-dependent' countries like Sri Lanka as beset from without by repressive, and state-supportive, 'imperialistic language games' such as 'development,' 'Westernization,' 'English education,' and 'neoclassical capitalism'; and to this he also began to envision counter-strategies – that is, ways of subverting what he called

the local and international 'language games of social control.' He began
to think, here, of local intellectuals such as the *pulavar* and of his friends
in the Readers' Circle, as keys to this side of the struggle. That is, he began
to argue that if one viewed such intellectuals as 'folk repositories' of local
knowledge, then it was obvious that they had a dual potential. *Dual* because,
on the one hand, such intellectuals could be (and mostly were) co-opted
by the hegemonic 'web' as teachers, graduate students, journalists, and so
forth, in which case they merely, 'organically,' reproduced the overmastering
'web'; yet, on the other hand, they *could* become (to their peril and inherent
risk) the central sources of inspiration and knowledge for the production
of a counter-hegemonic revolution. He began to imagine this duality as a
singular, existential *choice* open to such intellectuals, to all intellectuals, and
to himself. And he began to chafe ever more at the apolitical rules Ananthan
had imposed on the Readers' Circle.

But about none of this did he speak to me, except in the vaguest terms,
during our periodic meetings in late 1982 and early 1983. Rather, he was
content to pass the time engaging in philosophical chitchat, although he
did ask to borrow my copy of Rorty's *Philosophy and the Mirror of Nature*
(1979). So 1982 passed into 1983, with Sivaram still occasionally passing
by Peradeniya for brief visits but, for all intents and purposes, no longer really
a student there.

And then it was July 1983.

I remember July 1983. The story, of course, has been much told in
many accounts: how an ambush led by the leader of the LTTE, Velupillai
Pirabhakaran, killed 13 members of the Sri Lankan army; how rioting broke
out in Borella cemetery in Colombo – near my rented room – as the soldiers'
bodies were being buried; how mobs of thugs on government buses roamed
the streets of Colombo guided by election lists and burned down most Tamil
homes and businesses; how this may suggest some degree of government
involvement, though how much is hard to say; how, in any case, several
hundred thousand Tamils were made refugees, and several thousand killed;
and how the rioting spread all over the island, and was particularly vicious
and sanguinary in the up-country, where the targets were mostly plantation
Tamils.[14] It was all a grisly mess.

At the time, I was stuck by the curfew down south, near Yala, where I
had been visiting some British anthropologists, and saw none of this. But
on the third day after the start of the rioting, I found a ride to Colombo and
took refuge with Colin Kirk, another British anthropologist, in the suburb
of Ratmalana, on the outskirts of Colombo. The next day I rode with him
on his motorcycle into town, to Wellawatta, a section of Colombo mostly
occupied by Tamils. I was looking for the house of my Tamil instructor at the
University of Colombo, a kind man who had once taken me to dinner at his
tiny house. When we got to where his street and home should have been we
found only a field of rubble, punctuated, here and there, by burnt-out cars,

one with a twisted black thing inside that might once have been a person. Eventually, in the distance, I noticed a dirty white cube: it was a refrigerator, and all that was left of my teacher's house. We retreated in confusion to the Mt Lavinia Hotel where we sat down for a rather shaky cup of tea. We did not say much of anything; mostly we just looked out over the ocean. After a few days, I returned to Mandur, which I found full of terrified refugees from Colombo and the up-country. The roads all around Batticaloa, however, were covered with chalk-written, pro-Eelam messages signed with peculiar initials: LTTE, EROS, EPDP (Eelam People's Democratic Party), TELO (Tamil Eelam Liberation Organization), and so forth. Shortly after this, in August, the Sri Lankan government passed the 6th Amendment to the Constitution, making it a crime to advocate a separate state, and effectively banning the TULF and, thus, all Tamil representation, from Parliament. The civil war had begun.

It was about a month after this, as I was back in Colombo preparing to go home, that I learned my first lesson in politics from Sivaram. He came to visit me unexpectedly, showing up at my rented room in Borella, and shocking me by even being out and about. The curfew had only just been lifted, but we decided, anyway, to hop on a bus and go to a movie. I think we both wanted a respite from the palpable tension gripping the city. Still, all the way to the theater we argued about whether it was possible for a Western academic like me to really understand politics. I maintained that I knew full well what politics were. He maintained that I could not know, because real politics involved personal stakes that I simply could not comprehend. I gestured at the burnt-out rubble around us and said I thought I had a pretty good idea of what the stakes were. And so we argued.

The movie was some forgettable bit of American escapist trash, and we both enjoyed it immensely. Afterwards we had coffee and egg *rotis* at the Majestic Hotel, across the Galle Road from the Majestic Theater, and talked about philosophy. Then we hailed a trishaw, one of those little three-wheeled, beetle-like vehicles that are the taxi-cabs of South Asia. As we were bumping down the road toward my rented room, however, we were hailed, and an armed soldier stepped out before the beam of the trishaw's single headlight.

It was a roadblock, manned by an officer and several other soldiers. Sivaram and the trishaw driver were ordered out of the vehicle, and I was told to stay where I was. The soldiers held their rifles aimed and ready as the officer interrogated the trishaw driver, a Muslim man, who fumbled out his documents. He was soon allowed to get back in his trishaw. When it was Sivaram's turn, he just stood there, completely quiet. After several questions, the officer started screaming at him. Then he ordered his soldiers to take him, and gestured for the trishaw driver to go on. Without thinking, I jumped out of the trishaw. I was a visiting professor at Colombo University and he was one of my students, I lied, approaching them. I threatened to call the American Embassy if they arrested my 'student.' The officer yelled, in English, for me to come no closer, to get back in the trishaw. Then he barked an order, and one of the soldiers lifted his rifle and aimed it directly at my head. I kept babbling on about the embassy, but even I did not hear myself. All I could see was that hole at the end of the rifle and, above it, the sweaty face and very frightened eyes of the soldier. He looked very young, maybe 18. I thought, *I'm going to die right now*. And then we grew very quiet.

The officer barked another order, the soldier lowered his gun, and the other soldiers pushed Sivaram back toward the trishaw. We got in and took off. I do not believe we said anything on the way back to my rented room. I remember giving the trishaw driver a big tip. Once inside, I sat down in one of the two big rattan chairs in my room and tried to light a cigarette. But I had the shakes and kept missing the end. Sivaram lit it for me, and then sat staring at me in the other chair.

'My God,' I said, 'that was horrible. He could have killed us.'

'He wanted to kill us both.'

'My God.'

'But, one good thing *maccaan*, at last you begin to understand politics now.'

A year later, in 1984, when I had returned to Sri Lanka for a conference and some further research in Mandur, Sivaram walked up onto the verandah where I was sitting and suggested we have a serious talk.

5   FROM SR TO TARAKI – A 'SERIOUS UNSERIOUS' JOURNEY

My dissatisfaction with the scheme of things: I won't be doing justice to this dissatis-faction if I do not inscribe it forcefully on the web of humanity. (Sivaram's diary, 24 Aug. 1983)

Critics like Clausewitz, who doubted the validity of any theory of war, failed to distinguish between a theory of systems and a theory of principles. Principles were guides to action, not infallible mathematical calculations. The specific application of principles would vary with the thousand changing physical and psychological factors that made war a great drama. (John Shy 1986, quoted in Taraki 1991)

If I'm there on Tuesday, you'll know that Batticaloa is safe. If I am not there on Tuesday, then you'll know that Batticaloa is not safe. (Sivaram, phone conversation, 9 July 2004)

After the summer of 1984 I did not see Sivaram again for nearly ten years. Frankly, I was sure he was dead – or, if not dead, merely awaiting his time to be ground up in the increasingly vast meat machine of Sri Lanka's ethnic politics. As a kind of memorial to him, then, I wrote a short paper – 'Learning Politics from Dharma' – and hawked it around among the leading anthropology journals in America. For I found that our 1984 conversation would not leave me, and I could still – as it were – taste the arrack of our discussion on my tongue. Still, even as I wrote it, I worried about how an account of Sivaram and his ideas would be perceived in academic America. After all, Sivaram was an unlikely figure even to his friends; and our last debate about the Foucauldian implications of intellectuality and militancy (I had not even realized till our all-night discussion that he had even *read* Foucault) had transpired in an air of theatrical unreality – a hint of Pinter in Sri Lanka. Would the stern puritanism of American anthropological prose even admit such a figure? And though American anthropology at the time was experiencing its 'reflexive moment,' would not an account of a failed Arts undergraduate under a midnight palm tree in Batticaloa quoting, by turns, Marx, Milton, Derrida, and Foucault appear simply too fantastic? After all, it was one thing to ask American academics to be (correctly) reflexive about their racial, geopolitical, and socio-economic position. It was quite another thing, alas, to ask them to be reflexive about the intellectual worth and political implications of their PhDs. So it proved to be. The paper was

universally rejected. Several reviewers suggested I had simply invented
Sivaram to advance my own arguments about anthropology. 'Get rid of the
stooge,' they seemed to be saying, 'and speak for yourself.' Egad.

Of course, I also had doubts of my own. First, I vigorously disagreed with
some parts of Sivaram's argument. I still did not know what one should
do when confronting, in one of Walter Benjamin's 'moments of danger,' a
plenum of almost equally destructive historical choices. (Frankly, I still do
not know the precise answer to this question, though Sivaram's arguments,
and subsequent events in America, have long since convinced me that mere
inactivity is not a viable option.) But I did think that, even if such uncertainty
posed no argument against risking oneself, it seemed to make for a good one
against putting anyone *else* at risk – such as those at the other end of one's
gun. Further, though aware of the extent to which Tamil nationalism had
been provoked into being by oppression, like most American academics I
remained generally skeptical of nationalist discourses of all sorts, and worried
about their destructive power. For one thing, even from a safe distance, I found
watching Sri Lanka's subsequent quick descent into the politics of the gun
terrifying. And this fear was only intensified, several years later, when I saw
my own country's gargantuan destructive capacity mobilized for the first Gulf
War by a home front whirlwind of nationalist rhetoric. Was it not, I worried
– unconsciously echoing arguments I did not yet know Ananthan had already
made to Sivaram – precisely the *responsibility* of an intellectual to remain
critically detached in such circumstances? Was not disengagement, at such
moments, a *good* thing? At the same time, however, whenever I remembered
Sivaram – head bowed, awaiting his death – or the blackened rubble of
Colombo after the riots, I knew that there was something raw and incalculable
at work in all this. I remember thinking, so often, while smelling the reek
of chaos: oh, so *this* is history. And perhaps only an American, pre-9/11,
middle-class, white, suburban child would not have known it beforehand for
the bitter, ambivalent, violent thing that it is. Confused, rebuffed, convinced
that Sivaram was dead or dying and that it did not really matter any more,
I put the paper away as a private memorial and concentrated on trying to
finish my dissertation and get a job.[1]

In this last regard, I will not bore you with my problems. Let me simply say
that there was, justly, very little market for a South Asianist with an archaic
(some might say 'Orientalist') interest in Hindu rituals and the application
of Anglo-American language philosophy to anthropology's epistemological
puzzles. After completing my PhD, therefore, I spent a hungry, semi-homeless
year working at minimum wage in several Princeton bookstores before friends
rescued me with a cheap room and a slightly better paying, temporary job at
the Carnegie Foundation for the Advancement of Teaching. Access to a bigger
paycheck allowed me to buy new clothes and to attend the American Anthropological Association meetings one year, where mutual friends introduced
me to Ann Kingsolver, a much more accomplished anthropologist and my
future wife, because we were both reading about *heteroglossia*. Access to

the Carnegie Foundation's computers allowed me to send out vitas and job applications, which resulted, thank goodness, in the first of three one-year substitute-teaching jobs. These led, in turn, to a modest but permanent job at the University of South Carolina, Aiken, where I remain to this day.

Meanwhile, the war in Sri Lanka roared on. After 1984, it became an ever more costly war, especially for civilians, and its bloodshed and kaleidoscopic fissioning seemed to me to mock equally my neutrality and Sivaram's activism. By 1992, the year before I finally returned to Sri Lanka, human rights organizations were estimating that there had been over 60,000 killed since 1982, many if not most non-combatants (Whitaker 1997: 204).[2] At the same time, the list of belligerents was growing longer by the day. For although Western newspapers, then, tended to characterize the fighting in simplistic terms as an 'ethnic conflict' between the governing majority of 11 million Sinhalese Buddhists, and the 3 million strong Tamil Hindu minority, Sri Lanka's strife was really much more complicated than that. For one thing, such a view missed the generational, class, caste, religious, and regional differences internally dividing both groups, and ignored the existence of a substantial Tamil-speaking Muslim population, not only in the east, where Muslims constitute almost 50 per cent of the population, but also in the north, where the Jaffna peninsula's smaller Muslim population was peremptorily expelled by the LTTE in October 1990 (Shanmugaratnam 2001: 9). In this war, as soon became evident, everyone was going to get a chance to fight or at least violate everyone else.

In any case, after 1983, the conflict in Sri Lanka developed in three phases. The first phase, 1983–7, called by Tamil people 'Eelam War One,' was a conflict between the Sinhalese-dominated Sri Lankan state and a bewildering number of independent Tamil separatist-nationalist militant groups (militants called them *yakkam* – 'movements')[3] in the north and east – for at one point 37 completely separate groups existed (Wilson 2000: 126). The two largest and best known of these groups, however, were the Liberation Tigers of Tamil Eelam, led by Velupillai Prabhakaran; and the People's Liberation Organization of Tamil Eelam (PLOTE), led by Uma Mahesvaran, formerly a member of the LTTE before he broke away to form his own organization in 1981 (Wilson 2000: 127). And PLOTE was, of course, Sivaram's future organization. Other important organizations were the Tamil Eelam Liberation Organization (TELO), the Eelam Revolutionary Organizatyion of Students (EROS), the Eelam People's Revolutionary Liberation Front (EPRLF), and the Tamil National Army (TNA). But Sivaram remembered that at one point after July 1983 there were so many separatist groups forming that 'one smart fellow came up with a chart. With words like: democratic, Eelam, national, revolutionary, and all these things. You would jumble it, and you would get a name for a new organization.' In any case, between 1983 and 1986, these groups together battled the Sri Lankan army to an initial standstill with guerrilla warfare, and the army responded by imposing ever harsher measures in the north and east. By 1986, however, competition between the groups exploded into a violent internecine power struggle, which, by December 1986, had left the LTTE alone in control of Jaffna and much of the east, and the other groups either shattered, subservient (EROS's fate), or, in Jaffna, completely disbanded. Sivaram's organization, according to reports reaching me then – just as I was trying to publish the 'Dharma' paper – was one of those decimated by the LTTE. One rumor had Sivaram caught and assassinated in Batticaloa, and even dying in his mother's arms. The reports were not far from the truth: Sivaram just missed being in the van in which one of his best friends, Ramalingam Vasutheva, the brother-in-law of his future wife, was killed in an LTTE ambush. Karuna, the LTTE commander at the time, was said to have kicked over the freshly killed bodies muttering, 'But where is SR?'

'SR' was Sivaram's PLOTE name.

By 1987, the overstretched LTTE was under grave pressure from the Sri Lankan army, and faced losing control of its core area, Jaffna, altogether. Further, the Sri Lankan air force began bombing parts of Jaffna fairly indiscriminately. Then India intervened. Of course, India's secret service, the Research and Analysis Wing (RAW) had been *covertly* intervening since July 1983. Gunaratna (1993, 1997: 16), for example, estimates that by 1987 as many as 20,000 Tamil militants had been provided with training in over 32 separate, Indian-funded training camps. In any case, the resulting Indo-Lankan accord of 1987, signed between Rajiv Gandhi's Congress Party government of India and the UNP government of J.R. Jeyawardene, brought the Indian Peace Keeping Force (IPKF) to the island, in theory to oversee a peaceful federalization of Sri Lanka. This set the stage for a second phase of the conflict. Although the LTTE was forced by its former ally initially to accept the accord, its leader, V. Pirabakaran, quickly rebelled against it, and between 1988 and 1990 his organization fought the Indian army as fiercely as they had earlier fought the Sri Lankan army – from whom it was, at this point, apparently, receiving arms (Balasingham 2003: 244). At the same time, in the Sinhala south, the miltant JVP, rallying against the accord from a Sinhalese nationalist/Marxist perspective, but inspired by the successful guerrilla tactics of the LTTE, was fighting the Sri Lankan United National Party (UNP) government of Jeyawardene's successor, R. Premadasa. All these conflicts told heavily on the civilian population, and Amnesty International documented Sri Lankan government, IPKF, JVP, and LTTE responsibility for thousands of 'disappearances,' assassinations, and cases of torture, during this period of time (ASA 1993: 21; see also Hoole et al. 1990).

By early 1990, after a notably 'dirty' war (Nordstrom 1992: 266), the JVP had been suppressed and its leader, Rohana Wejeweera, killed (in army custody) in the south while the IPKF had been forced by the LTTE to leave the north. After a brief, tense, peace, war broke out again in June between the LTTE and the Sri Lankan government, beginning with an LTTE massacre of nearly 600 captured Sinhalese policemen in the east. In Sri Lanka this phase of the conflict was called, by Tamils, Eelam War Two, and continued, despite fitful peace overtures by both sides, until well into 1994 – specifically, till October 1994, when the newly elected People's Alliance Party government of Chandrika Kumaratunge began its own brief period of peace talks with the LTTE. During this time the spectacular suicide bomber assassinations of Rajiv Ghandhi in 1991, and of President Ranasinghe Premadasa and the UNP presidential candidate Gamini Dissanayake in 1994 – attributed to the LTTE, though denied by them – gave the 'Tigers' a reputation for ruthless but efficient terrorism in the Western press. This phase of the war also saw an increase in bloodshed between Tamil-speaking Hindus and Muslims in the east, and an alliance between Sri Lankan government forces and some former militant groups such as PLOTE, TELO, EPRLF, and the EPDP (led by Douglas Devananda, as of 2004 a minister in the current UPFA government) against the LTTE. In the north, by the end of the year, this had translated into a war of attrition between the LTTE and the Sri Lankan army; in the east, into a continuous campaign of 'pacification,' conducted by Western-trained government special forces, such as the Special Task Force (STF), at great cost to the civilian population. It was at about this time, in the summer of 1993, that a small grant from my university allowed me to revisit Sri Lanka.

And Sivaram? In late 1989, during a lull in the fighting, a message reached me through friends in London that Sivaram was alive and (mostly) well in Colombo. His organization, it was true, had had the last of their fratricidal and, for them, ultimately fatal wars with the LTTE, and Uma Mahesvaram had been recently assassinated by unnamed dissidents within his own party. But by that time Sivaram, a weary veteran, and sick with chronic malaria, had already moved to Colombo, first to arrange his 'retirement' into the political wing of the party (of which he became General Secretary in 1988), and then to get married to Bavani, the sister of his dead friend's wife. When various differences with Mahesvaram forced him out of the party altogether in early 1989, he had to piece together some kind of life for himself, and did so: first, as a kind of fashionable oddity – the lone English-speaking militant – and then, in turn, and as a kind of evolution from the first, as the journalist 'Taraki.' It was only then that he sent word to me that, yes, he was alive – he had made it through. There followed several years of fitful attempts on my part to track him down which ended, finally, in July 1993, almost nine years from the day I last saw him, when he walked up onto the verandah of the house in Colombo where I was staying and said, with all his old blitheness, 'Well, *maccaang*, you have grown fat.'

And so I had.

What had happened to Sivaram in the intervening nine years? What I had not known that fateful night, though I had suspected as much, was that Sivaram had indeed joined one of the movements – indeed, had joined, in a sense, two of them. He was already a member of PLOTE through the Gandhian movement – in a 'remote' cell, as he put it, which just dealt with 'refugee issues' – but by July 1983 he had allowed his membership to become quiescent due to PLOTE's inactivity in Batticaloa. After the anti-Tamil riots, however, he was in a passion to do something, anything, definitively militant, and in no mood to await orders. So, not long after I left for the first time, in 1983, Sivaram joined with a group of like-minded young men – most, like him, already inactive members of other groups, and chafing for action – to form the Tamil Eelam Revolutionary Army (TERA), adding one more acronym to the separatist alphabet soup being generated at the time.[4] They decided that Batticaloa's many waterways offered them a unique tactical advantage, set up a safe-house on the Dutch Bar – the sandbar that separates the Batticaloa lagoon from the sea – and began to carry out 'operations' by boat. They had no weapons and so their initial forays were rather low key: some light sabotage and the stealing of an exploder from the Highway Department. But Sivaram's revelation that, from the shattered verandah of Stanley House, he could see across the lagoon to the door of the police armory in the old Dutch Fort, led them to try something more ambitious: they decided to steal the weapons. But to do so they would need a gun.

So Sivaram volunteered the old hunting rifle his father and brother had so often used to hunt deer and wild boar on the family's former estates. On the appointed night he wrapped the rifle in an old sheet, tucked it under his arm, and then went to find the bullets. He found, instead, Mahesvari – his mother – spitting mad. She had the bullets in her fist. Glaring at him, she turned, and walked away. 'It was the first time she realized, I think, that I was involved in the militant end of things,' said Sivaram, later. 'And she was really angry. So angry she wouldn't let me do anything.' First, she hid the bullets; then she moved to the steps of the verandah – now, of course, merely an empty concrete pad – and with a look (no doubt) of mingled fury and disdain – for no one, in my opinion, ever did fury and disdain as well as Mahesvari – sat down. She stayed there all night, silently erect, refusing to let him go, adamantly contemptuous of his pleas for her to give him the bullets, ignoring everything.

'Just go to bed!'

She waited till dawn. Then, stiff, but convinced that he had given up the venture, Mahesvari finally took herself off to bed. Sivaram crept out with the rifle under his arm, but without the bullets. That night, their plans revised, TERA raided the armory with the *unloaded* gun – loudly locking and unlocking its firing mechanism to convey the false message that they were ready to shoot. The security guards put their hands up and the boys ransacked the armory: they found 200 guns and about 12,000 rupees. The next day, however, one of the members – actually an LTTE plant – ran off with all the loot, leaving the group with just one World War I-vintage pistol. TERA instantly dissolved and its members scattered. Sivaram was disgusted by his own naïveté; never again would he be so trusting, or so ill prepared. He decided he would travel to Jaffna and revive his PLOTE membership – but keep his guard up.

In Jaffna, after reaffirming his membership, Sivaram met 'Glass' (*KaNNudi*) Chandran, the 'Land' commander of PLOTE who, seemingly impressed by him, appointed Sivaram, in turn, Land commander of what Chandran called the 'eastern border area.' Why 'Land' commander? Like most of the other *yakkam* or separatist groups at this time, PLOTE had a geographically inspired internal division of labor between its operational military wing, based in Sri Lanka or 'Land,' as they called it in English, and its political and command wing, located in Tamil Nadu, which they called the *pin thalam* or 'rear base' (Taraki 1991: 3) – a distinction that was latter to breed an inherent instability within the movement. In any case, Sivaram was told by Chandran to return to Batticaloa to find places in the jungles where camps could be set up and arms delivered; he was then to await further orders. But he was also told to keep his activities completely secret from PLOTE's overall area military and political commanders in the east, which Sivaram found odd. Nevertheless, keen to use his knowledge of Batticaloa's jungles – gleaned from years of tramping about them with his brother and his friends – he accepted the assignment.

It was while in Batticaloa scouting out jungle sites – and trying to stay out of the sights of the area military commander, as his orders specified – that Sivaram met a slim, intense, young man, just 21 at the time, whose PLOTE name was 'Paththan.' 'Paththan' was an old hand in the organization; indeed, he had trained as far back as 1981. But he presented, to Sivaram, a fascinating mixture of youthful rectitude and ruthless resolve. For since shortly after the 1983 riots Paththan had been operating as an assassin, using a .45 automatic to pick off, with cold efficiency, whomever – policemen, informers, *anyone* – Partthan, his local commander, at the behest of 'rear base,' ordered him to kill. At the same time, Paththan always acted with precise and almost fussy ethical delicacy, quickly paying back local Tamil people, for example, for food or bicycles appropriated in the heat of action, and being very careful about fighting or firing weapons in the presence of non-combatants lest they be caught in the crossfire. These were PLOTE rules, and he believed in and followed them religiously. The contrasts within Paththan's character fascinated Sivaram. Here was very poor young man of few words with a deeply inarticulate belief in Eelam. Yet he had a cool efficiency and a tactical brilliance in action that Sivaram admired; and he maintained a steadfast loyalty to his comrades and to the Tamil people that seemed – to Sivaram – almost the only 'pure' ethical principles still discernible in the increasingly vague fog of separatist politics. Paththan never doubted, never debated: Paththan just did and was. He would remain Sivaram's most trusted comrade for the rest of their war.

While Sivaram was in Batticaloa, however, he also gradually began to realize that he was a pawn in someone else's game. 'The plot was this,' said Sivaram to me, years later, in 2004: 'There was an extreme left wing in the organization which wanted to take over. And the leader of that wing, Santhathiyar, was very powerful – he was later killed. He appointed his own loyalist, Chandran, as Land commander of all the districts. Now India was going to give us the first batch of automatic weapons – all of which this faction of PLOTE wanted to keep to itself to bargain with the leadership, and to take over control. Anyway, that was why Chandran wanted everything kept secret. So I became suspicious and slowly probed the matter, and then the whole plot was unearthed.' In disgust, Sivaram took his findings to the overall area commander who immediately ordered him to take a letter detailing the conspiracy to Jaffna for Uma Mahesvaram, who was there at that time. He also told Sivaram that, henceforth, his PLOTE name would be 'SR.'

It was as Sivaram – now 'SR' – was preparing to go on this trip that Ananthan and Mahadeva came to see him. Times had been tough for them. Revolutionary storm clouds had driven the activities of the Readers' Circle underground; no longer could they risk having public meetings. Indeed, they were not to have another until 1989. Still, they continued to meet, continued to study, and were in fact growing – as they would continue to grow, a living fossil of an extinct civic society, for the next 20 years. But Ananthan and Mahadeva had been watching Sivaram's intensifying formal political involvement with great misgivings, and knew they would have to do something about it. His activities, they felt, were a danger: a danger to them but, even worse, a danger to him, and (they believed) a great waste. So they waited until July 1984, nearly a full year after the riots, and went to see him.

'Would you like some tea?' Mahadeva said to me, mildly concerned, thirteen years later. 'No? Ah, now you know that Sivaram had joined in this *other* activity. So we had to drop him from the organization. *After*, of course, quite a *lot* of discussion.'

'We had clearly said that there is no political activity in our organization,' said Mr Thevakuthan, helpfully.

'It was in our bylaws,' said Mr Mahadeva. 'There was to be no direct involvement by any person in our organization in political activity. This was one of the bylaws in our constitution. But Siva got involved. And we felt compelled to drop him.'

'You argued with him?' I said.

'Yes, myself and Ananthan. We took him to *Mamangam* temple and we had a long discussion. We said that he should not be involved in this political stuff; he should go back to Peradeniya, complete his higher studies, and become a university don or something like that – and in that way he would be able to do more than by being involved in the movement. That was our argument. But *he* argued that he had an intention of becoming a politician. He had this interest in politics. We said it was not your duty. There are lots of politicians in this country. But you should become an intellectual. And you should become a scholar.'

'This was 1984, very near the night that I talked to him too,' I said. 'I was making the same arguments. I said he was one of the smartest men I'd ever met and if he went and got himself shot it would be a tragedy. I said there would be no tragedy if there were one less politician, but there would be if there were one less smart man. He told me I was a domesticated intellectual.'

They all laughed.

'He called *us* "the armchair critics!"'

No, he would not listen. So Ananthan and Mahadeva told him that he would have to reach a final decision soon. He must choose either the Readers' Circle and a life of scholarship, or politics and the carnage that would come with it; that is, choose, as Ananthan later put it in a poem, between 'the *veena* (a classical Indian musical instrument, rather like a recumbent violin or a small sitar, and often used to accompany the recitation of poetry) and the sword' (*vaalai? ViiNaiyaa?*)[5] – and he must tell them his answer soon. Sivaram walked away. Several days later, as night was falling, Ananthan and Mahadeva caught him as he was returning to Stanley House on the back of my motorbike for *our* talk. Sivaram sent me on inside to where Mahesvari was waiting and told them his decision – a decision, of course, he had actually made long ago.

'I'm going to Jaffna.'

And so Sivaram left his Readers' Circle days behind him and set off for the war in earnest. Everything he would write and think about nationalism and military strategy in the ensuing years would be, in a sense, a product of this decision to push aside intellectual detachment and take an active role in the war. Ironically, heroically, it would be Ananthan who would die first in the conflict. Eleven years later, on 5 December 1995, according to Sivaram, Ananthan was one of 30 civilians pulled out of a bus on the Batticaloa–Kalmanai road and shot by the STF in retribution for the LTTE's over-running of a nearby STF camp.[6] His corpse was later found, riddled with bullets, futilely covering the body of a dead child (Ananthan 1997: 5). 'In 1996' said Mahadeva, sadly, 'we organized a memorial speech led by Sivaram.'

After delivering the letter to Uma – who swiftly relieved Chandran ('He's now working for a courier service in Toronto, last time I saw him,' said Sivaram, in 1996) – Sivaram stayed on in Jaffna till February 1985 or so, where his unorthodox philosophical views began to win him something of a following. He was, in fact, the lone English-speaking intellectual from Batticaloa in the party, which drew most of its Central Committee membership from Jaffna, and so was valued as such for 'representative' and liaison purposes by the political wing of the party.

Perhaps more important, though, was that Sivaram's knowledge of Marxism and his linguistic skills eventually led Uma Mahesvaran to start using him for PLOTE's central (but less public) project of establishing an alliance with the Sinhalese left. This ambition underlay the ideological difference between the PLOTE and the LTTE, and was the basic intellectual reason why Sivaram ultimately threw in his lot with the former group rather than the latter, despite some worries right from the beginning about PLOTE's organizational infelicities (Taraki 2004i). For Sivaram still believed, like Mahesvaran, in the Marxist thesis that the rights of the Tamil people could only be obtained within the context of an island-wide, 'proletarian' revolution. Hence, between 1984 and 1986, Sivaram was content to be sent south numerous times for this purpose. During this period Sivaram claimed he established friendly contact with leftists such as Dr Nalin De Silva of Colombo University's mathematics department (now, ironically, an important figure in the Sinhala nationalist *Jathika Chitanaya* movement), JVP intellectuals such as Dayan Jayatilake (who by this time had formed the armed, militant *Vikalpa Kandayama*, and whose speeches at the JVP's 'Stalinist Education Circle' had famously justified the Tamils' armed struggle), and eventually Vijaya Kumaratunge, an actor and husband of Sri Lanka's president-to-be, Chandrika Kumaratunge. Vijaya Kumaratunge had started his own leftist party, but would eventually be assassinated, probably by the JVP, because of his pro-Tamil pronouncements. In 1986, however, Kumaratunge helped Sivaram save Dayan Jayatilake's life. According to Sivaram (2004e):

Vikalpa Kandayama was banned in 1986 on the accusation that it conspired to topple the Sri Lankan government. Dayan Jayatilake went into hiding. When he was about to be captured, he contacted me. Even many of the good friends of Dayan Jayatilake refused to help me when he had to flee from his hiding place in Colombo. In the end we had to take him from his hiding place to another safe place outside Colombo. We did this after taking him to see the late Vijaya Kumaratunge ... at midnight. Vijaya helped me. (In this regard, without even asking his wife Chandrika or anybody else, he helped me immediately. He was a unique person.) (English translation, Tamil Canadian)

Sivaram maintained, later, that during this period he also grew to know and work with many people in the non-revolutionary Sinhalese left, including members of the SLFP. Among them was Thilak Karunaratne, who, Sivaram claims, used to allow cadres of the pre-1987 PLOTE to hide themselves in his residence, and who once was taken to court after the discovery of some PLOTE bullets in his car. Sivaram, of course, also had amiable political dealings with Chandrika Kumaratunge herself, who, with her husband Vijaya, 'allowed my friends and me to stay at their house in Colombo,' and who, 'during this time' once said to him: 'Do not speak to anyone who does not accept the rights of the Tamils for self-determination' (Sivaram 2004e). Years later, in 2004, a bitter Sivaram would lament the eventual betrayal of the possibility of such a Sinhalese–Tamil leftist alliance by all of these people and groups, with the singular exception of the martyred Vijaya Kumaratunge (Sivaram 2004e; Taraki 2004i).

At the time, however, and aside from his diplomatic skills, Sivaram was also interesting to the military wing of the party because of his practical knowledge of jungle routes in the east. This unique duality – for otherwise PLOTE's 'political' and 'military' people, according to Sivaram, kept very carefully to their own turf – eventually afforded him both opportunities and difficulties in the party. For the party's intellectuals could never bring themselves to entirely trust someone who was also involved in the military wing; and this, Sivaram believed, was merely a new version of the same controversy that he had just had with the Readers' Circle and with me. After being sent back briefly to the east to select more jungle sites, Sivaram had returned to Jaffna to work on documents related to party structure, when he was approached by Mendis – who had replaced Chandran as 'Land' military commander – and asked about taking a small party overland to Batticaloa.

The idea had originally been Sivaram's. Having witnessed, at a distance, the failure of an earlier attempt by Paththan to bring cadres and weapons to Batticaloa by sea – a failure that resulted in the death of most of the cadres involved and the loss of all the arms – Sivaram had suggested to Mendis that the only solution was to establish some overland routes to Batticaloa. So Mendis ordered Sivaram to take Paththan, only just returned from a brief exile in India, and two other cadres, Venkat and Raku, and try to find an overland route. Raku was supposed to be their guide for the first part of the journey to a town named Tiriyai, north of Trincomalee.

They took an AK-47, a revolver, a Sterling submachine gun, ammunition, six grenades, some biscuits and glucose tablets, but very little water, and set off from Kumulamurai, south of Mullaitivu on the Nayaru lagoon. They were clothed in what, at that time, was the traditional dress of the militant 'boys': plastic slippers, sarongs and shirts. For the next two days, having left the road to avoid army camps, they wandered, lost and thirsty, in the dry zone jungle. The thick, brambly woods of the north and east of Sri Lanka are called 'dry zone' jungle – or, more technically, Semi-Evergreen Monsoon Dry Forest (Popham 1993: 25) – for a reason: they receive on average less than 100 cm of rain per year during a brief north-east monsoon, or *Maha*, that generally runs from October to December; otherwise, the forest presents a consistent lesson in painful aridity with daytime temperatures averaging in the high 30s (or 90s, in Fahrenheit), and sandy soils that soak up and exude a raw, enveloping heat. So after their first day out of water, it is perhaps unsurprising that the boys became both desperate and rather lightheaded. Venkat, an urban boy, clutching the AK-47 to his chest, started muttering – then yelling – that he would kill *everyone* for bringing him to the jungle. Paththan, to distract him, climbed a *Palai* tree to pluck some of its tiny yellow berries, but they proved too few and too sweet to slake anyone's thirst for very long. At one point, exhausted, they sat down at a random tamarind tree and tied a string to Raku – so he would not get lost – and sent him out on a radial search for water. Eventually, he found some: filthy green water, odiferously congealing in an elephant's footprint near a dried out-water hole. They drank it anyway: 'It tasted,' said Sivaram, 'like the best beer.'

Finally, having found the coast, they followed it to the Yan Oya ferry – only about 25 km (or 17 miles) from where they set out, though they must have been wandering, lost, for many kilometers more. There they were surprised to find the ferry manned by a Sinhalese man; so they tied him up and stole his boat. Shedding Raku, who returned to Mullaitivu, they limped into Tiriyai where a Tamil family, fired with patriotic glee at the presence of 'boys' in their village, put them up for the night. The next day Sivaram decided to try to take the bus to Trincomalee – or Trinco town – in order to contact some PLOTE cadres there and get better walking directions. For Trincomalee, though a small town, has a huge port – most reckon it the finest natural harbor in South Asia, with enough deep water to anchor a fleet (a fact, as we shall see, of no small geostrategic importance) – and getting around it to the west was going to be a long slog, and tricky. So Sivaram decided to chance the bus. Since he alone among his comrades had his national identity card, he believed he should be able to travel unmolested. But along the way, he noticed that the army was doing a sweep of the area directly ahead of him, and in fact had the road blocked and were coming his way. So Sivaram told the driver he wanted to get down, jumped off the bus and, looking left and right, found himself staring straight into the workshop of a family of potters: an old woman and her two sons (or grandsons) shaping bowls over potter's wheels. 'I had no idea who they were,' Sivaram said to me later, 'I was absolutely clueless.' But he walked in and threw himself on their mercy.

'I'm a militant,' he said. 'The army is after me.'

The old woman did not even glance at him.

'Take your shirt off, hide your card, sit down, start work.' She threw a lump of wet clay at a free wheel as Sivaram scuttled behind it. Then, as Sivaram put it to me later, 'I was doing some bloody thing with clay; I didn't know what. And the army came there, and a major walked around, and he didn't even ask any questions. But I was sweating in my bloody balls.'

They decided they would forgo Trincomalee. After a short debate among the three of them, they decided to steal some bicycles. Paththan, always conscious of his ethics, insisted that they should steal only from families that already had more than one bike. 'Anything else,' he said to me later, 'would not have been fair.' So they set out, biking as far as Kinniyai, at least 20 km, where, at Paththan's insistence, they left the bicycles in a shop with instructions that they should be returned to their owners. Then they sought out a guide to get them to Tambalakamam through the thick jungle west of Trincomalee rather than by the main road. They found an apparently patriotic local farmer who swore he could get them to Tambalakamam through the jungle. By now it was the night of the sixth day of their journey.

As they traveled in the dark, however, it quickly became apparent to Sivaram and Paththan that their guide was increasingly nervous. After many kilometers of walking, he suddenly stopped and told them that his separatist ardor had led him to promise more than he could deliver: he had no idea how to get to Tambalakamam. What this meant, they realized, was that he wanted money, of which they had little. He then took off – knowing, apparently, well enough how to get home – leaving Sivaram, Paththan, and Venkat stranded in the darkness. They continued forward, nonetheless, until they came to a cluster of *cajan* (mud and straw) huts and, taking the chance that their inhabitants might be Tamil, they chose one at random and knocked. And that is how they met Rani.

Years later, in 1997, Sivaram and I traveled to Paththan's house by motorbike to discuss their old times in the movement together, and they spoke about this moment. It had not been an easy trip; every few miles we had been forced to dismount to pass through army checkpoints, relying on Sivaram's press pass and my white skin to see us through. Periodically, in the distance, we could hear firing and, once, the deep rumble of an electric road mine. But Paththan's modest green house, surrounded by palm trees and stands of banana, was peaceful, and Paththan was glad, as always, to see his old comrade again. Paththan, looking much older than his 34 years, and still thin, was graying at the temples and walked with a limp, a reminder of the many wounds he had received for his cause – twice from the Sri Lankan army, and once from the LTTE. His hands shook whenever he smoked a cigarette. But, over arrack, his memory of meeting Rani and her family in their wattle and daub hut became as clear as Sivaram's.

'This is quite a nostalgic part of the story for us,' said Sivaram.

'Nostalgia,' said Paththan, 'is taking us over.' He took a deep drag on his cigarette, stared thoughtfully at nothing for a moment, then picked up his weak leg and draped it over his good one.

'They were poverty-stricken people,' he continued, 'even so they made tea for us and looked after us. But they were very poor. The woman of the family was a pretty woman; her name was Rani. And she and they told us they were so desirous to see Tiger boys because it was by such people as us that the struggle was taken forward. And it was so important to them because they were so often raped and driven by the army. So we were *their* army. We gave them money to get our food, and we lectured to them about the movement, and we all became sentimental – particularly Rani.'

'Yes, and Rani told us a lot of stories,' Sivaram said. 'Once the army came checking and asked for Tigers, *Puli*. And Rani's sister, being an idiot, thought they meant *puLi* – Tamarind. And we thought that Rani might have been raped then, when the army came. They called their little town Pulankulam, but now they call it by a Sinhala name, a translation of Pulankulam.'

'We were really affected by Rani,' said Paththan, quietly. 'Rani was a great woman. Not any sort of sexual thing. She was a woman who had a feeling for liberation. How happy she was seeing us. We knew her only for a day.'

'We wanted to go back and give Rani some money,' said Sivaram. 'I told Uma that I wanted to do that. But when I went to the place it was burnt to the ground. Just one rose bush was left. The rest of the house was burnt out. And so every drink we have we talk about her. And yet she is a woman we knew only one day. We never forget to talk about her whenever we open a bottle. So anyway, that night she took us to Tampalakamam.'

'When we left,' said Paththan, 'we wanted to give them *something*, so we gave her a long torch that we had. But I can't even remember her face.'

'Was she very young?' I asked.

'Not so very young,' Sivaram said, 'But very pretty, and her sad history ...'

'Of those that saw us,' said Paththan, broke in, but quietly, 'she was the one most happy to see us.' Then, with sudden stridence, sitting up straight in his chair, imitating her memorial ghost, he shouted:

'Here are the liberators!'

Paththan subsided, was quiet for a moment, and then said: 'We gave her the torch light and that was the last we saw of her.'

The next night, their seventh of the trip, they slept behind a temple in Tambalakamam. Then, for the next two days, they made their way slowly toward Muttur, south of Trincomalee. Once they came to a bridge, and not knowing whether the army might have left a sentry there, Sivaram told the others to wait while he took a grenade and approached it. But there was no sentry.

'You would have been a dead duck,' Paththan said, complacently.

In Muttur they found PLOTE, but they also found a problem. The central party organizing member there, Selvan, had been caught having an affair with a young female cadre. As sex outside marriage was against PLOTE rules, local party members had complained, and Selvan had been followed to his trysting place. There he and his lover were discovered *in flagrante delicto*, but, more importantly, in his shirt pocket was found a letter detailing a conspiracy to take over PLOTE by the party's ultra-left wing. After marching Selvan, tied up, to a jungle base outside Muttur, it was decided in a quick meeting there that Sivaram should take a letter to Jaffna detailing what had happened. After Sivaram took off, Paththan was left with Venkat and a group of new, young, overly enthusiastic PLOTE members from Batticaloa – and with Selvan and his lover as prisoners. Fired up with loyalty to Uma, the Batticaloa cadre executed Selvan.

'I had tried to stop them,' said Sivaram. 'People will say I killed Selvan. But I tried to stop them. But they killed [him] and the responsibility was mine because they were under me. They killed [him] because they were so loyal to Uma.'[7]

The journey to Batticaloa was over.

After this Sivaram returned, for a time, to Jaffna and to work on the political side, although he continued to make periodic trips to Batticaloa as well. Later in 1985, Uma, from India, asked him to prepare a report on how PLOTE might be reorganized into a more 'revolutionary' party. Sivaram's report made what he regarded as a key point. 'This is not a revolutionary party,' he argued. 'That is a misnomer. It is a nationalist petit-bourgeois organization. In order to transform it into a party you would have to build trade unions, women's organizations, etc., and transfer political and decision-making power to them structurally. That is, you would have to bring more of these people into the central decision-making process, which should be replicated at every level. That way, it won't be just for Jaffna petit-bourgeois interests but for the interests of the less privileged groups like women and workers as well.' Uma, impressed with his arguments, asked Sivaram to proceed with this restructuring, and to set up classes to 'provide the ideological grounds for it.'

Both of these things Sivaram tried to do. Later he came to feel that while his restructuring of the party was a popular, long-lasting success, his classes were more ambiguously received. His sequence of seven classes tried to convey two things close to Sivaram's own core political beliefs. First, using a mix of his knowledge of both Marxism and post-structuralism, he tried to teach cadres how they, on their own, might analyze Sri Lanka's unique local conditions. 'They all,' Sivaram said, 'wanted to know what Marx had to say about nineteenth-century Berlin. But they knew nothing about society on the east coast, or even in Jaffna.' So, in this respect, Sivaram's 'indoctrination' program was really a short course in Foucault-influenced Marxist social analysis, with the names and fancy jargon left out. Second, Sivaram challenged the cadres' separatist assumptions, and sought to convince them of the necessity of eventually allying with Sinhala leftists in the south. He argued that Eelam's long border and economic interdependence with the south made this absolutely imperative. His classes, popular with many cadres, nonetheless aroused passionate distaste within the party among both doctrinaire separatists and doctrinaire Marxists.

Then, in late 1985, Santhathiyar, the leader of the party's ultra-left wing, was killed in Madras by assassins under orders from Uma, a murder that precipitated a party conference in February 1986, and a crisis which eventually split the party. For several months thereafter, having come out of the conference one of the losers – he was branded a 'neo-Marxist deviationist' – Sivaram was reduced to the role of cook at PLOTE's Inavil camp in Jaffna.

Why was Sivaram pushed aside?

'The main problem,' he told me in 1993, as we sat talking on the verandah in Colombo, 'was, first, that the political and military wing remained separate. Not that they were precluded from service with each other, but the political wing people thought that political intellectuals should remain pure. So the political people despised the military people; the division of labor was clearly inscribed in their minds. It was a combination of the Marxist "vanguard intelligentsia theory" (Lenin's idea) and the traditional Jaffna view of the intellectual as a professional, passive, quiet fellow who remains good and becomes a doctor or an engineer – derived from the *Varna* ideology no doubt. Yet the core of the party was the military people. *They* were the ones who came out of the womb of the TULF. *They* were the ones making the real decisions. So why all this nonsense? That is what *I* said.'

He put down his drink and looked at me blithely: 'You know, in our hatred of the West we fail to see a lot of rubbish that comes from our own tradition. That's why I think the subaltern studies people's writings have become *pathological*.'

'Anyway,' he said, continuing, 'the second problem is that they were willing to accept the pure SR, the intellectual. But they could not accept me as a fellow who could share the world of the military wing with all its unsavory aspects. But I didn't want to be just in the political wing. The ruffians in the military wing were honest fellows. And they wanted to make use of me. I was recognized among those fellows for two things: one, that I knew almost all the jungle routes in the north and east, which was a must for military operations; two, that I knew the north-western coast and the eastern coast to the extent of undertaking sea operations without a map or guide – that I could find a place to land, even without someone there to signal. Of course, these fellows vaguely knew I could speak English but they didn't care. These were the skills that got me their respect – and that was why the political people, not the military people, saw me as a problem.'

And then he looked exasperated.

'Also, what can you *do* by just being an intellectual? It was a complex question. My question to them was: how can you scream from the outside? You are dealing with the real world, and the rough and tumble of reality, and you just want to remain the pure intellectuals playing with all the sublime intellectual ideas, and you speak to all these fellows who wield the gun as through they don't have minds! Indeed, this was Uma's problem also – I always said: don't believe that these military wing people are mindless fellows. They are not fighting because they think you are Lono – you know, as that guy Sahlins argues in his book about Hawaii (1982). No, they have a certain "practical reason". They know what they are doing, and are doing what they do because they have their own reading of what is happening. And, in their own way, they are also doing a job, like the intellectual. So this whole thing about being a pure intellectual and the military guy being dispensable is rubbish. And if I had stuck with the purely political role, I would have had to go to London and would soon have been saying, like some other fashionable intellectuals, that it was all rubbish. It's an Empedoclean folly: being an apolitical intellectual is a bloody myth. But, of course, this was the same argument I had with Ananthan, and with you. But here it was more costly: it made me a cook!'[8]

But it did not leave Sivaram a cook for long. For when the organization split within a few months, with the leftists going on to form the ENDLF (Eelam National Democratic Liberation Front), Sivaram was instrumental in keeping the 'Land' military wing and, at least, a few of the 'Land' political cadres loyal to Uma. He was soon again very important within what was left of the Party.

But by September 1986 the LTTE, sensing weakness, began at first to suggest, and then to insist, to Sivaram and to PLOTE's Land military commander, Mendis, that PLOTE turn over to them the 500 or so trained (but largely unarmed) cadres that it had waiting in camps in Jaffna for deployment in the east. The LTTE that April, in the first of its various internecine attacks on other separatist groups, had already wiped out TELO with a quick series of murderously effective strikes; a move with which PLOTE had actually been in accord under the theory, as Sivaram put it, 'that TELO was being used by RAW[9] [India's foreign intelligence agency] to undermine the Tamil cause.' But now the hammer was poised to strike PLOTE. Sivaram stalled for time, hoping that Uma could come up with some solution. At one point, Sivaram went alone to the LTTE's office, convinced that he was going to be killed, and talked himself hoarse through the night. Understanding, when they finally let him go near dawn, that it was not going to be for long, he and Mendis immediately drafted a message for the newspapers announcing that 'to avoid a fratricidal war' in which 'many unarmed eastern cadres would be killed' PLOTE would be suspending military operations till further notice. Sivaram was convinced that 'playing the eastern card' had forestalled immediate attack, but he also knew the problem would not go away. In October he established radio contact with Uma – radio transmissions that he later learned were intercepted by the LTTE – and urged Uma to do something permanent about the problem. Instead, Uma told Sivaram to come to Madras.[10] So Sivaram crossed the Palk straits and traveled overland to Madras. But then: 'While I was there, in January or February, Mendis was arrested and killed by the LTTE. Then Pirabakaran came back to Jaffna for good. Mendis was probably killed because the LTTE did not want other military leaders of other groups in Jaffna when Pirabakaran was coming. And the intercepted messages gave them the impression that Mendis and I were in too close contact with Uma.'

In Madras Sivaram says he found the organization in a state of paralysis. PLOTE had thousands of trained cadres in camps in Tamil Nadu – at their peak, in 1985, more than 6000 – but had no money to arm or move them. There was no further money forthcoming from India either, for RAW was supporting the ENDLF, the ultra-left faction of PLOTE instead of PLOTE itself. Uma had tried to get round this problem by making a US $300,000 arms shipment deal with the PLO (Palestine Liberation Organization) – Sivaram also used to participate in these negotiations – but no one realized until it was too late that Saleem, the PLO dealer in London was also selling arms to RAW, which would never allow a shipment of weapons to go through to PLOTE. Eventually a message, passed through an EROS intermediary, confirmed this suspicion, and the money advanced was lost.

Sivaram and Sidhartan, who eventually became PLOTE's political leader in the late 1990s, argued to Uma that the organization 'was going to fall apart without an infusion of weapons – and since we had screwed up all avenues for doing this on our own,' they had better turn directly to India for help. Sivaram's point was that since their 'rear base' was in India, any alternative plan (such as dealing with Eastern Europe or the West) was not likely to succeed. So Sivaram urged that Uma turn to India directly, acquire the arms and trained cadres it would need to work independently in Sri Lanka, and then, as he put it, 'make other arrangements.' Either do this, he said, 'or we have to think of a future where we remain a small group talking Marxism and doing nothing.' Uma accepted the argument.

It was fortunate he did, at least for PLOTE, for this was precisely when India started arming and training the various separatist groups to bring pressure on Colombo (Gunaratna 1997: 17–19). By 1986, according to Sivaram, India was offering to arm all the organizations, including with SAM 7 missiles; so many of PLOTE's cadres were sent north to train. But not Sivaram: 'Uma took care,' said Sivaram to me, 'that I was not seen by RAW. That was routine practice – to not show people who worked in the Land to RAW, fearing that such exposure would lead to problems in the future.' Then, as trained cadres and weapons began to pile up at PLOTE bases in India, Uma, mindful of a certain political difficulty, took the advice of his military people and asked Sivaram to take charge of delivering the first shipment of them to Sri Lanka. The political difficulty was that RAW did not quite trust the PLOTE's ability to get the weapons landed, and wanted convincing that it could be done. Sivaram, Uma felt, was the man for the job.

So Sivaram was chosen. But by late 1986 Sivaram was going through a rough patch. He had caught chronic malaria on the 1985 jungle trek and was, periodically, deeply sick. Also, he was suffering remorse. A romance he had commenced in 1984 with a young woman in Batticaloa for, as he put it, largely sexual purposes, had caused her great sorrow and was now consuming Sivaram with guilt. He wanted to go home, atone for his 'sins' by marrying her, and settle down. And, beyond all this, as he said, simply: 'My body was tired.' So Uma's plan seemed to offer a way out. All Sivaram had to do, Uma suggested, was accomplish two little missions. First, establish a landing place and base in Mannar; second, do the same in the east; finally, finish each trip by training others how to navigate using Sivaram's trick (learned from experienced fisherman and smugglers) of setting course by counting the distant 'glow' of towns over the sea horizon. After doing these 'few' things, Uma said, Sivaram could remain in Batticaloa.

The first sea expedition to Mannar had to be aborted, however, when, one after another, the two outboard motors driving the boat conked out. After bouncing about in the swell of the Palk straits for a day – sitting ducks for aircraft or ships – they managed to get one engine running and return to India. So, in May 1987, they tried going to Batticaloa instead. Just before they departed, Sivaram noticed that the military commander of PLOTE called one of the two military group leaders Sivaram was supposed to be taking to Batticaloa and had a short, private discussion with him. Later, Sivaram discovered that he was told to bring Sivaram back to India at gunpoint.

'I had told them: this is my last journey. I am going to marry that girl. Uma obviously thought otherwise.'

The trip was harrowing. They survived a gale in the Bay of Bengal, a narrow scrape with a Sri Lankan navy gunboat, and were lost for a desperate while in the open sea – where even the experienced seamen were seeing palm trees, as Sivaram put it, '90 degrees east of where land should actually be.' Finally, however, by depending on an old British Admiralty chart, they sighted Trincomalee. The plan was for Sivaram and two other experienced cadres from the east to swim to shore from the ship and find a safe place to land – something that became necessary to do quickly, Sivaram realized, because all the other boys on board were violently seasick. So, in the dead of night,

Sivaram had them bring the boat in to within a half a mile of shore near a place he knew well, called Umiri, a small wedge of land between two coconut plantations. Then he and two other cadres swam ashore. But no sooner did Sivaram reach the sand than he heard a huge thud: the boat had grounded on the rocks. The waves quickly succeeded in turning the ungainly vessel on its side and spilling everyone and everything – cadres, guns, ammunition, and supplies – all about the churning shallows. What had happened? The boys in the boat, too seasick to bear staying at sea, had disobeyed Sivaram's instructions and had tried to land the boat themselves. And the cadres were so happy to be on land that they lay spread eagled on the beach, murmuring gratefully into the sand, completely ignoring the catastrophe.

Sivaram was terrified. For here they were but a mile or two from Tirukkovil, where there was a huge STF camp, centered on the Tirrukkovil hospital. Sivaram jerked people up by their collars and sent them off to collect what they could salvage of the supplies – they got all the weapons and ammunition, but lost the food – and then hustled them to an old, dilapidated fisherman's cabin to spend the night. There the surprised fisherman hurriedly boiled up the only food they had managed to save from the wreck: eggs. Sivaram was himself surprised that, given the commotion of their landing, the STF had not swooped down and wiped them out. He later learned that a nicely preventative rumor had reached the STF that a huge contingent of 'boys' had landed. The STF was too intimidated by this illusion to move. Even so, very early the next day, Sivaram shifted his cadres to a temporary camp he had them set up in a defensible mangrove swamp, and there carefully laid out – as was his standard practice – two secure lines of withdrawal. The next day, he called Madras.

Madras was angry at the grounding of the boat, and wanted it and Sivaram sent (at gunpoint) back to Madras to collect the next batch of cadres and arms, but the military cadre who had been ordered to do this shook his head and refused to do it. He confessed his orders to Sivaram and added, '*maccaang*, I don't want *anyone* to ever make this bloody journey again.'

So Sivaram stayed on in the jungles west of Tirrukovil until July 1987, when the Indo-Lankan Accord was signed.

Sivaram learned of the accord by radio, from Madras, and was ordered to make his way to Batticaloa to meet General Dhar, the IPKF Batticaloa commander, and arrange for the arrival there of PLOTE's military and political leaders – for PLOTE, as a signatory of the accord – was now a 'legal' political party. Among the leaders who arrived from India by helicopter soon thereafter was Ramalingam Vasutheva, PLOTE's deputy leader, a good friend whom Sivaram was very glad to see. Sivaram had often stayed with Vasutheva and his young wife, Rathi, and their children, whenever he was called to Madras. One of them, Sami, Vasutheva's daughter, still remembered, ten years later, how the playful 'SR-mama' (*mama* = uncle), as she called him, on especially hot nights, would sit up on their flat roof to catch the rare sea breezes off the

Indian ocean and beguile them with silly stories. In any case, when Vasutheva took over political control of Batticaloa, he relieved a grateful Sivaram of any immediate responsibilities, and set him free to pick up the pieces of his life for a time – if he could.

But he could not. Stanley House was in disrepair, the girl he had planned to marry had married someone else, and he found himself sick and penniless. Instead of the conquering hero, Sivaram arrived home barefoot, wracked by malaria, and dressed only in a torn shirt and a frayed sarong. Even his glasses were broken in half and tied together with a string (Ismail 1987). There was little for him to do but sit in the ruins of his dead father's house and wallow in his private distaste for the Indo-Lankan Accord. And so it was, I suppose, something of a relief when Vasutheva came again to Stanley House soon after to tell Sivaram that Uma once more had need of his English skills: for PLOTE required someone to go to Colombo to make contact with Vijaya Kumaratunge, husband of Chandrika Kumaratunge, Sri Lanka's future president. Kumaratunge's small political party, Uma thought, seemed positioned for Tamil allies. So Sivaram borrowed a pair of trousers and some slippers from GTR, one of his PLOTE comrades and fellow 'shipmates,' and 500 rupees from his aunt 'Baby,' and went to Colombo in late August 1987.

In Colombo Sivaram visited, briefly, with an old friend from Peradeniya University, Qadri Ismail – showing up at his doorstep one night, as Ismail says, looking a mess: 'shaggy hair, scraggy beard ....,' and looking for a good drink.[11] Only after that did he make contact with Vijaya Kumaratunge, who introduced him, in turn, to Dr A.T. Ariyaratne, the founder of the Sarvodaya ('self-help') Movement, Sri Lanka's most famous indigenous Sinhalese NGO. Ariyaratne, into whose care the weary Sivaram was placed, supplied him with shelter, money, clothes, and, briefly, even a car and driver. So, for the first time in three years, Sivaram was being well housed and well fed. Nevertheless, he was not happy. For his new fortune could not mask his uneasiness with the way his war had ended. In an article Ismail wrote about him for *The Island* newspaper that September, Sivaram (or 'Naresh,' as Ismail called him, to protect his identity) was presented as succumbing to the luxuries of the city even while wallowing in his sense of defeat. 'If his face smelled just that little of perfume,' Ismail wrote, 'his whole self stank of defeat.'

'The whole enterprise,' Ismail had Sivaram saying, disconsolately, over many drinks, 'was doomed from the very start. Our first mistake was theoretical. We called it a national liberation struggle and compared ourselves to Cuba and Vietnam. We should have thought of Biafra ... You know what Harold Wilson said about Biafra? He said he didn't care whether a million Ibos had to die, that Nigeria had to remain unified. The post-war international system does not permit the creation of new states.' And then: 'no one wants to think that a dream is not real. We had no mountains, no jungles, to retreat to and attack from. The Sri Lankan state was so developed that there was a police station within 15 miles of any place in the country. We had to use India as a rear-base. From that day onwards we were pawns in a larger chess game, though we thought we were going to liberate Thamil Eelam.' And further: 'Take the border ... It is more than 300 miles long – and there are Sinhalese at every end of it. Nobody ever thought of it. Nobody in any group came up with an intelligent idea of how it could be secured and then maintained ...' And then Sivaram went on, Ismail wrote, to tick off the presence of a large Muslim minority in the east, a peasantry uncommitted to the final goal of Eelam, and the opposition of India as additional factors leading, inevitably, to defeat. 'As guerrillas fighting for Tamil rights,' Ismail has Sivaram conclude, 'Our historical role is over' (Ismail 1987).

It is a bit difficult to know what to make of Sivaram's comments at this time. The general air of disillusionment seems right enough. Sivaram felt the Indo-Lankan Accord was merely a trap for the separatist movements; he was particularly opposed to the disarming of the jungle camps he had worked so hard to set up in the east, for he felt that any disarming on PLOTE's part would leave them sitting ducks. Confirmation of this suspicion came soon enough after Sivaram left for Colombo: on 13 September 1987, Ramalingam Vasutheva (Sivaram's old friend), the PLOTE military commander 'Kannan,' and five other third-level PLOTE leaders were returning from Pasikudah, a town north of Batticaloa, when they were ambushed and killed by the LTTE at Kiran. The LTTE commander leading the operation, Karuna, afterwards kicked over the bodies and stated his regret at not finding SR's among them. The LTTE went on that day to wipe out most of PLOTE's eastern cadres, including, almost, Paththan, who was left severely wounded, and had to be flown to India for emergency surgery. So Sivaram, mourning his dead friends, a member now of the rump of a shattered organization, had much to be bitter about.

Nonetheless, Sivaram remained a loyal member of PLOTE and was in Colombo, still, to advance PLOTE's aims. The dismal set of facts necessitating a separatist defeat that he had laid out for Ismail – the long indefensible border, the large Muslim minority, and an uncommitted peasantry – were no more than the very points he had made to fellow PLOTE members in the 'classes' he had set up at the behest of Uma in 1985. At this point, in fact, Sivaram, still a Marxist, continued to believe that Tamil aspirations could only be realized within a general, all-island proletarian revolution. And to that end his other, darker purpose for being in Colombo, unannounced to Ismail at this time, was to make contact with the JVP, which he also did.

As Sivaram said to me, at length, in 1995, after looking at Ismail's article: 'If I was disillusioned, how can I be negotiating with the JVP on behalf of PLOTE? My point was – and this was also Uma's position – that in the end, because of the above problems, the goal of a separate state was best achievable in a situation where the Sinhala would recognize the right of self-determination of the Tamils. Here my explanation hinged on the revelation of a "category mistake" at the heart of the Eelam movement. This was that everyone spoke of a "national liberation struggle", and when they did so they unconsciously imported a completely misleading referent into the definition of the Eelam question. This misleading referent was [the] "national liberation struggles" themselves, because, in the genre of literature that speaks about them, such struggles [took place] in countries shaking off the yoke of colonialism that were *already defined*, like Vietnam. So the assumption in the phrase was that there was a state *already*. That meant, in technical terms, [that winning equaled] the seizure of a nation's capital. But in the case of the Eelam question, the declaration of Eelam would mean the ability to secure and hold an undefined border over a period of time ... Therefore, [the phrase] "national liberation struggle" gave a set of wrong expectations and orientations that had little to do with reality. The reality was that there was a long bloody border, and the resources were on the other side ... And the task at hand was to redefine the concept of "national liberation" in this context. That *task* revealed the afore-mentioned problems. That was why [I said] Sri Lanka's problems were really more like Biafra's than Vietnam's or Cuba's – whose cases dominated the literature and ideology of national liberation in the Third World.'

Going on, Sivaram added, 'I used to call this the dialectical deconstruction of the national liberation concept of Tamil Eelam. And I the used the term "deconstruction" in the way it is misinterpreted in most of American academia – where they think of a deconstruction as a 'taking apart' rather than Derrida's notion of playing around with a concept to unbalance it within its own parameters.' In any case, Sivaram concluded, dismissively, 'Ismail fit all this into his thesis that everything was solved with the Indian intervention.'

Still, it seems as if contact with the JVP, finally, really did disillusion Sivaram. For the JVP cadres, when he met with them, were not interested in an alliance on equal terms between Sinhalese and Tamils. A more nationalist Sivaram, in 2004, would later claim this was because the JVP leaders' own innate Sinhala nationalism had overwhelmed or 'overdetermined' their entire political world view.[12] But perhaps, at the time, it was even more important that just as PLOTE was putting out feelers to the JVP, the JVP was making the decision to use nationalist rhetoric, and its opposition to the accord, as the spear-point of its new insurrection and of the terror that would follow. In any case, by the time Ismail was having his drunken conversation with Sivaram at the end of September, Sivaram was already beginning to digest the bitter fact that his long-held dream of an island-wide revolution was dissolving into nothingness.[13] Before his disillusionment would be complete, however, one more, intensely personal, disaster would befall him.

Casting about for something to do, Sivaram tried to take advantage of the general amnesty proclaimed by the accord by making a brief tour of the situation in Mannar, on the opposite coast. But this turned out to be a mistake. For Sivaram was arrested by the police under the Prevention of Terrorism Act, turned over to the Sri Lankan army, and tortured and beaten for about a week. On the fourth day, however, when allowed – briefly – to go to the squalid shared toilet, he discovered another boy there; a boy, more importantly, who was a regular prisoner and therefore allowed to have visitors. (Or, rather, had bribed a guard to be allowed to exercise this 'right.') Sivaram slipped him his address and begged him to ask his family to call Mahesvari. And so Sivaram was saved by his mother. For Mahesvari immediately stormed to Colombo and dragooned government officials until Sivaram was released to her under the Amnesty terms of the accord.

Speaking to me about his capture after 17 years, in February 2004, Sivaram said this torture had helped him later understand standard counter-insurgency tactics. He remembered talking about all this to a Sinhalese general, a co-attendee of a conference in Germany where Sivaram was scheduled to speak that year, who claimed that counter-insurgency strategy was basically torture collectivized. 'When you are tortured,' said Sivaram, becoming rather quiet, 'they beat and beat you until everything is pain. Until there is so much pain that you give up thinking it will stop. In fact you stop hoping it will stop. You start comparing pains instead and only hope that next time it will be kicking instead of burning or whatever. Then suddenly, one day, your cell opens and in comes a "nice" fellow who offers you a cigarette. For him you will do everything, anything. Well, this General told me that counter-insurgency is just like that except that instead of giving pain to a person you give pain to a whole community until it too stops hoping it will stop and starts only hoping for the lesser pain. Then you come in as the "nice fellow" and offer them a cigarette, or a constitution, and they will do anything for you.'[14]

In early October, Sivaram, nursing his bruises, dragged himself once more back to Colombo. There PLOTE had set up an apartment in Mt Lavinia to house both Sivaram and Paththan, then recovering slowly from his surgery in India. Sivaram and Paththan were also there to provide protection for the nearby apartment PLOTE had given to Radhi Vasutheva, widow of the dead Ramalingam Vasutheva. Also there, occasionally, starting in early October 1987, was Radhi's sister, Herly Yogaranjini Poopalapillai, a student of Ayervedic Medicine in Jaffna, with whom Sivaram began, gradually, to fall in love.

Herly Yogaranjini, called by her family 'Bavani' or 'little sister,' was a quiet, shy but highly intelligent young woman – fluent in all three of Sri Lanka's languages – from a large, well-regarded, though not particularly well-off family of Batticaloa teachers. In 1987, Bavani had five living brothers and two sisters and a widowed mother, Isabella Arulgnanam. Her father, Samuel Poopalapillai, a well-known school principal, had died of a massive heart attack twelve years before, in 1975. A relatively freethinking Methodist, Samuel's house had always been full of local intellectuals, pundits, and learned men. David, one of Isabella Arulgnanam and Samuel's sons, remembered there had always been lots of Tamil and English books lying about the house, as well as a continual procession of people borrowing and lending them. After Samuel's death, however, life became difficult for Bavani's family, both economically and politically. By 1985, the war had exiled one of her brothers, Daniel, to Canada, and landed David in prison under the Prevention of Terrorism

Act – though David's sole political participation in separatist politics had been distributing pamphlets for the TULF in the late 1970s. And, of course, by 1987 her sister's husband, Ramalingam Vasutheva, was dead. All these catastrophes had left Bavani with a deep distaste for politics. Despite this, Sivaram, wary and wounded though he was, caught her interest; and she caught Sivaram's as well.

By 1988 Sivaram had pursued several affairs with women – scholars, professors, even an international journalist – among the affluent Colombo intellectuals who, during the early, heady days of the accord, took up Sivaram, the ex-guerrilla fighter, as a curiosity. But Sivaram, though sexually engaged, felt emotionally alienated from the cosmopolitan women of Colombo's elite circles. A political radical, Sivaram was, in many ways, at least at this time, a deeply conventional Batticaloa man in his view of women and family life. Moreover, Bavani's intensely private nature seemed to offer him a refuge from the chaos of politics, particularly at a time when the politics of his own group, the PLOTE, were spiraling out of control. So Sivaram, as he once put it, in order 'not to have a revolution at home,' sought a marriage to Bavani arranged in the traditional manner. After the proper meddling of appropriate relatives, they were married on 9 September 1988 in a Christian ceremony conducted by the same Methodist minister who had presided over Sivaram's father's corpse in 1972, and who would eventually preside over Sivaram's own funeral in 2005.

By early 1989, however, Sivaram was beginning to drift away from politics and PLOTE. Of course, he had been appointed General Secretary of the Democratic People's Liberation Front (DPLF), PLOTE's political party, in 1988. But the failed attempts to form some sort of alliance with the JVP, the JVP's adoption of increasingly scattershot terrorist tactics, PLOTE's loss of cadres and camps in fighting with the LTTE in the north and east, and PLOTE's involvement in a ridiculous coup attempt in the Maldives in November 1988 – an attempt by Maldivian businessmen based in Sri Lanka to topple the government of President Gayoom using PLOTE cadres as mercenaries – all set Sivaram's teeth on edge. Further, by 1989, both the LTTE–IPKF war in the north and the JVP–government war in the south were at full intensity, and PLOTE was largely on the sidelines.

It was at this juncture, while still General Secretary of the DPLF, but losing interest in that role, that Sivaram often began meeting – or, rather, drinking with – Richard de Zoysa at the informal gatherings of intellectuals, actors, artists, and journalists that often occurred at the Arts Center Club, near the Lionel Wendt Theater in Colombo 7, a center for English-language theater in Sri Lanka since the 1940s, and an oasis of free speech in a Colombo becoming increasingly parched by JVP and Sri Lankan government terror. In 1989, a year prior to his murder, Richard de Zoysa was, to the general public, a famously handsome, much loved, Rupavahini (government) news anchor. From a prominent, bourgeois, Cinnamon Gardens, mixed-'race' family – his father was Sinhala, his mother was Tamil – Richard was also a talented journalist, playwright, actor, and poet. His depiction of Mark Anthony in Haig Karunaratne's production of *Julius Caesar* at the Lionel Wendt Theater is, apparently, still spoken of with awe by those who saw him (Siriwardena 2000: 157). But he had an intense sympathy for Sri Lanka's monolingual masses – those divided from wealth and power by the sword of English – and as big a desire to help. He once wrote a poem called 'Lepidoptera' in which he compared Sri Lanka's lost generation of the 1980s to broken specimens under an entomologist's glass.

> On broken butterfly wing, your crippled mind
> Fluttered into my schoolroom. Failed. And died.
> I couldn't do a thing to stir its organs
> Of poor maimed sense to life again ...
> The heavy-footed State, which made a mess
> Of your fragility, called this progress,
> Should pin you down on cardboard behind glass
> Specimen of the educated class.
> (Wijesinha 2000: 77)

'This fellow,' said Sivaram to me in 1993, 'was a brilliant product of the public school system, and all that. A "perfect Englishman".' And Sivaram laughed, but sadly. 'He knew Shakespeare by heart, and the whole works. But he was a great fellow to know, a great human being.'

'But how did Richard get you started writing your Taraki articles?' I asked him, two years later, in 1995. We were sitting in my apartment in Aiken, South Carolina, and Sivaram was slowly downing a glass of whisky and talking of old times.

'De Zoysa was working for a UN-funded feature service called the Inter Press Service [or IPS] which reported on development and Third World issues. But I knew Richard first while still General Secretary of the DPLF, PLOTE's political wing. Richard was a senior correspondent then, in 1987. [By 1989] I was drifting away from PLOTE due to its internal problems. After leaving PLOTE, I was trying to do international deals ...'

'That's when you were using the aliases "Ponambalam" and "Joseph"?'

'Right. Now Richard was drawn by my "holding forth" – that is, by our extensive discussions. And Richard said "Why don't you write for me – for IPS?" The pay was good. So I started to write things about development – some ... published under the name "Gnanasothy".'

He laughed.

'One of my articles was on buffalos! It was about how using buffalos was a better way to increase production and cut costs in wet zone paddy cultivation. But the pay was good. Anyway ... at that time Richard had gone to see the editor of *The Island*.'

This was the independent daily newspaper started by Upali Wijewardene, the Kandos chocalate magnate, in 1977, a time when all of Sri Lanka's other daily newspapers were controlled by the government.

'Why would he go to *The Island*?'

'At this time, IPS was trying to get the service into the local newspapers. Anyway, the conversation between Richard and the editor, Gamini Weerakon ... turned to Tamil politics. And the editor was lamenting the dearth of people who could write on Tamil affairs after the departure of the well-known *Island* Tamil journalist D.B.S. Jeyaraj. So Richard said he knew someone who could write for *The Island*. He didn't tell *my* name because he was afraid I would be gunned down. So Richard came to me and said, "*Maccaang*,[15] see whether you can write something for *The Island* on Tamil politics." They were keen to have someone because it was an interesting period with everyone getting worked up in the south about the Tamil National Army (TNA) being created by the IPKF in the north – so that was what the first article was about. Anyway, I agreed with Richard's proposal and gave an article on the TNA, which had a lot of inside information and "juicy stuff" that no one else had access to. I appended a Tamil name to it, "M. Jayaratnam". But the editor was of the view that you should not use this kind of name because there could really be a M. Jayaratnam who might object. So the normal thing was to invent a new name, something with no connection with a real person. So he gave the name "Tharaka", which means "star" in Sinhala and Sanskrit. But the notoriously careless English sub-editors of the Sri Lankan press screwed it up and made it "Taraki". The editor did not know who Taraki was for about three months until Richard introduced us. And I must say, in fairness to Gamini Weerakon, my editor, who liberals to this day criticize as an arch-Sinhala chauvinist, it was he nonetheless who pestered me into being the columnist that I am today.'[16]

'What happened to Richard?' I asked knowing de Zoysa was killed in 1990 – probably by one of the many anti-JVP death squads sponsored by Sri Lanka's state security forces (Wijesinha 2000: 12) – but I wanted to hear Sivaram's account.

Sivaram took a long drink. Then he gestured toward my computer, over which I was poised, as if to say: 'Start writing.'

'During this period, the later part of 1989, there was massive violence in the south. All kinds of people were being killed. It was safe to be a Tamil – I used to run around on my motorbike with my wife and just get passed through checkpoints when they discovered I was Tamil. One day, a boy who was a university undergraduate of one of the Western Province universities, and who used to work part time for the IPS as a translator, never got home. It became clear that he had been picked up and most probably killed. Meanwhile, apart from his IPS duties, Richard was engaged in some human rights work as well. He was sending material abroad about the massacres that were going on. One day, on my way to work, I bought a paper and saw the picture of Richard on the front page, which said he was missing. [The next evening]

I was at the IPS office in Bambalipitiya when word came that there was a body in the morgue at the Kalubowila hospital. They had found a body on the Moratuwa coast, washed up on the beach. I went and identified the body, because we were the ones in the office when the message arrived.'

Richard de Zoysa's body was found on the evening of 19 February 1990, the day after he was abducted. Five days later, on 25 February 1990, Sivaram wrote the following, uncharacteristically short, Taraki column.

Salute – To a Friend
I salute a friend and fellow journalist most gruesomely murdered by those who dare not show their faces nor advance or protect their interests as honourable and brave men do. In the land where the people were proud of the Sinhala lion, desperate jackals roam, seeking out their defenceless prey. What more justification, I may ask you, is there in continuing to call those who took up arms in the north-east terrorists, when more Sinhalese have become bloody victims of an insidious and cowardly terror in the south than the Sinhalese killed by the LTTE or EROS? Richard and many more have been brutally murdered; who or what is to be blamed? Remnants of the JVP which still have access to Pajeros with a nocturnal immunity? The collective psyche of the Sinhala people? Enough of this silent impotence. The terrorists have to be resisted. Extreme cowardice and a gnawing lack of self-esteem as usual seem to be at the source of this faceless terrorism. Therefore it should be collectively resisted before it knocks on every door looking for victims to torture and kill, thereby to reassure itself of its existence. (Taraki 1991: 32)

'I didn't want to work after that bugger died,' Sivaram said to me, in 1993. But he had to. Although IPS, out of fear, immediately dropped Sivaram (and everyone else close to Richard), Sivaram only stepped back from his *Island* column for two weeks. His need was simply too great to pass up the small salary of 3000 rupees a month (about US $120) *The Island* paid for his writing. Thus, newly married, with the first of his three children on the way, Sivaram's motivation for writing the Taraki column was, at first, not political but purely pragmatic: 'I did this to make a living and survive.' Or, as I remember him saying to me in February 2004, as we prepared for our ill-fated trip to Batticaloa, 'I had no political intentions at all at first. I was writing to eat.' But, gradually, Sivaram began to realize that his increasingly popular column might present other possibilities. For the Taraki column had become a decided success. Its incisive reviews of government, IPKF, and LTTE military and political strategies, often intentionally written in a tone (according to Sivaram) of 'cool and sometimes seemingly cruel sarcasm,' had become required reading for all sides in the conflict. So effective were his flashes of insight about possible next moves by the government, the IPKF, and the LTTE that some Taraki watchers began to suspect that all sides were occasionally using Taraki as a guide. By 1991, Taraki's writing had become so popular that his *Island* columns were collected by diasporic Tamils in France and published as a book, *The Eluding Peace (An Insider's Political Analysis of the Ethnic Conflict in Sri Lanka)*. He really had become, in a way, a kind of star – 'Tharaka' indeed.

Talking about all this, ruminatively, in 1995, Sivaram began to chuckle.

'The Indians were alarmed by the stuff I was writing. They felt I was revealing too much about the TNA. The EPRLF, which was in power at that time under the protection of the IPKF as the Northeastern Provincial Council government, were also very annoyed. And others were intrigued. I was in politics. Back in business, as it were.'

'And some people,' he said to me two weeks after our 1993 conversation, as we sat before the Batticaloa lagoon drinking arrack, 'some proper competent people find it a bit unpalatable, that past. They would rather find the "decent" past, where they can make sense. For it doesn't make sense, no? What sense does it make? What sense would it make to a bloody anthropologist ... or [urban] intellectual? The jumping, and the fighting, and all those things? [Those things] are absolutely alien because ... [they] ... don't make sense to the type of mind into which we are being molded. Ah, that is the thing.'[17]

I was confused. 'But isn't the whole point ...'

'The whole point was ... giving up being framed ... forgive me, that's the point I have made in our booze-laced conversations.'

We were sitting in silver darkness at Sivaram's brother-in-law's house, the moon-dappled lagoon spreading out before us in shimmering ripples. Across the waters, from the other shore where Batticaloa lay, we could hear distant music, Tamil show tunes, playing over loudspeakers on the town's gaudy, new clock tower – a gift from Sri Lanka's recently assassinated president, Ranasinghe Premadasa – the tinny music sounding fragile, happy, and evanescent in the night.[18]

'Romantic,' said Sivaram later, in 1995, glancing critically at my account, tapping the page.

'Whatever,' I said.

The music made Sivaram think of the days before the war, when he and his friends would take a boat and a bottle out onto the lagoon and drift through the warm night, drinking and arguing philosophy. But most of those boys were dead by 1993. So we, too, had bought a bottle of arrack, which we were mixing with slightly brackish water from the well.

I was, as we drank, feeling rather shell-shocked. The Batticaloa District to which I had just returned, after ten years, had been roasted by the war. Coming into it by bus had been like traversing overdone toast, with burnt houses, vehicles, and paddy fields lying along the road like cast-off crust. It was also a land under surveillance: there were 18 military checkpoints on the main trunk road between the border of the Eastern Province and Batticaloa town. And the trip from Batticaloa town to Mandur, which in 1982 had taken me about two hours, now took a full two days of inspection, suspicion, and delay. The same was true of all roads and all trips. Then, too, each security checkpoint was a place of carefully calculated intimidation: inspection aisles down which travelers had to run like cattle, flanked by desks to check papers, gun bunkers, armored cars, and lots of heavily armed, highly anxious security forces – all of the deadly bureaucracy of counter-insurgency. Occasionally there would also be informers, garbed in dark hoods to hide their faces, fingering the unlucky.

So we sat and talked in the moonlight. I told Sivaram about my trip back to Mandur, a town I had found still, somehow, surviving as a regional religious center, but nevertheless fearful, quiet, and empty of many of those I had known. And so, of course, we had to talk about Mandur's missing and dead. I felt an urge, suddenly, to ask Sivaram whether it had all been worth it – the killing and the dying. I remembered him telling me, at one point, about an abortive attack he had led on the bridge at Valaichennai – 'Where I learned,' he had said, 'how useful AK-47s are for retreating. You know, fire a burst, retreat; fire a burst, retreat ...' Jumping and fighting indeed; and my thoughts turned, again, to the dead. But it was a pleasant night, and we passed instead to a less painful topic. We talked about how Mandur's Sri Kantisvami temple elites, even now, continued to play out their competitions for power and prestige, despite the changed historical circumstances. We talked about how such competitions were always conducted as disputes about the temple's divine past – and argued about why elites would not admit, even in private, that they manipulated their temple's history to win such contests. Perhaps, I speculated, invoking Bourdieu's concept of *habitus*, they really did not know they were doing that; perhaps if they knew what they were doing, it would not work.

Sivaram agreed with this idea, but laughed at the notion that Mandur's temple officials were so unconscious. 'I think most of them know what history is. I can't speak with a US state department official and convince him to speak *his* mind!'

We both laughed at that. But then I persisted, pointing out that it was not just that temple elites refused to admit that they themselves manipulated history, they refused even to see their enemies as doing so.

'But [admitting] that is the same,' Sivaram argued, 'as saying "I have got the correct history." Because when you use something strategically, you shouldn't know that you are using it strategically. Once you know that, you know that it can be thrown aside, and ... you know you weren't seriously engaged in that strategy.'

Or, as he said to me ten years later, chuckling: 'You need to be *seriously unserious*!'

But in 1993 he paused, and then seemed to grow into himself.

'That seriousness with which a strategy has to apply is required more in political life. Any form of political life, even family or whatever ... It just doesn't work, you know, if you don't *buy* it, don't *believe* it, don't *engage* yourself in it. Because in every communicative act we are engaging ...'

'Maybe,' I said, 'that is what Derrida and Bourdieu are saying? That the fundamental difference between intellectuals and non-intellectuals is that intellectuals can never really engage in the same way people who are not intellectuals can engage?'

'Yeah,' he said, pointing his glass in my direction, 'that's why you'd never make a good politician – never make a good politician at all.'

He laughed, then blinked, and turned serious again.

'That's what I thought: that I couldn't be a good intellectual because – same thing – because it requires quite a lot of seriousness to believe, to participate in, the politics of intellectual games.' He laughed again. 'Like temple politics. The moment I realized that it was like that, I was thrown out of the intellectual [world]. Like how temple politics would end as soon as one has realized that, OK, this is how we are – as soon as one fellow [has] understood your thesis. In the same way, I was thrown out. I stopped being defined within that system called the intellectual world the moment I realized it; the moment I stopped being serious. Stopped being serious about being that kind of intellectual.'

And, suddenly, I could no longer resist.

'But didn't you find your life as a militant equally absurd?' I asked, thinking of all the burnt places, all the body bags bobbing in the lagoon.

'What do you mean? Why should it be absurd?' He sounded genuinely surprised, and eyed me speculatively.

'Didn't it make it difficult to do what you had to do if you weren't a believer? I mean, going without food, living in the jungle, fighting,' *killing*, I said to myself, 'and the whole business. I mean, doesn't it help to believe?'

He shook his head, 'That's where I come to this fecundity of being, right? As soon as you say "if you don't believe, you are without meaning", that is what I oppose.' And then he added, in 1995: 'My position is: take hold of all these things and exult in the proliferation of the possibilities. This is the idea you have never got. It is connected to my idea of social production. It is: when the myth of the individual producer is imposed on the reality of social production, creativity is blunted. What I mean by the proliferation of being is that it is the fact of the proliferate Being that is the very condition of being human. An example: my identities. Take an exercise: enumerate things you are, the modes of being you are in, in a single day. They are numerous, and lapse into one another. That is why I say they are fecund. That is the fecundity of being.'

Then, his voice sharpening, 'Why do you want it all upset? Why do you say this?'

'Well, I ...'

'When you asked me if I don't believe, and, therefore, how did I [fight] – right? – look at the other side! I left the intellectual world, refused it. Then how am I writing? How can I write? Here you are assuming that you have to believe in God to be happy, believe in something. So why?'

He stared as if expecting an answer. I squirmed a bit.

'Certainly not believe in God ...'

'You know what I mean. That you have to *believe* in what you are doing.'

He suddenly slapped at something. 'Ah, is that a mosquito?'

It certainly was. Moreover, accompanying it was a pestilential cloud of its sanguinary friends, a whining nimbus that formed above our heads like a cartoon depression. Soon we were both hopping about, slapping at them. Sivaram said we should burn a coil – one of those green spirals of evil-smelling insect repellent – and so we did. This seemed only to make the mosquitoes hungrier. We stood helplessly beside our chairs, grinning at each other in defeat, whatever tension there had been between us literally bleeding away. As we sat down again, he poured us both another drink, then, suddenly, laughed.

'Ayoo! You have been itching to ask this question. And you have been quite uncomfortable that I have been avoiding all this.'

'Yes, for about two weeks. So what is the question I am going to ask?'

'How come you risked your life and so forth.'

'Yes.'

He told me, first of all, that I did not really understand what death meant to people fighting in such circumstances. 'In a war,' he said, 'you come to terms with the positive side of death. That death doesn't mean a thing. You get to a point where you become a continuum; otherwise you can't fight the war. Death and life are in one continuum; when you are in a group you *see* death and life as a continuum. [Back then] I just [had to] come to terms with [the] *physical* aspect of death. My point was: look, if I die and am burnt then I'll be ashes. And if my ashes somehow get to be scattered on the road to Vadamunai – a jungle area, miles from anywhere – maybe when the next rain comes, I might still inhabit the world when the jungle is in glorious bloom – a thought which gave me a certain satisfaction. It doesn't mean you end there …'

It does though, I thought, years later.

Sivaram went on to argue that death got reconfigured in a war. 'Culturally, death assumes a different meaning altogether. It's a cultural thing, no? The concept "our death", the death of the self, is a cultural concept. The fact that it *is* a cultural concept makes it possible for another … culturally different concept of death [to replace it]. [Take] the LTTE, for example. Their new concept of death involves a combination of fairly conventional national renaissance ideology with a warrior ethic reclaimed from "ancient Tamil culture" as portrayed in the ancient war poetry of the Tamils. ("Here," wrote Sivaram in 1995, "I am talking about the LTTE. I am just making a comment about them; this has nothing to do with me.") The LTTE refers to dying as being "sown" (*vitaital*) and dead bodies as "seeds" (*vittukal*). So you can see this development particularly clearly [in the] culture of war that the LTTE has. That is the argument in my book.'

But, he asserted, all this was not unique to Sri Lanka. 'I think it must be common to all fighting. If you had gone and lived with that fellow – that bloody Christian pastor [David Koresh] who built up a fortress and blew up the whole thing – you could see … those people were just part of [his] committing suicide. So I think now all organizations at one point culturally also push that line: that your death is not *your* death.'

'I'm not sure I understand.'

'Neither have my friends,' he muttered, softly. Then he chuckled.

'Since I met you,' he said, suddenly loud again, 'I have become a bit nostalgic about my irresponsible philosophical past.'

'Why irresponsible?'

'Irresponsible in this sense: I was just pursuing all these interesting fellows – Russell, Frege, Wittgenstein, Foucault, Ryle, Rorty – all those fellows. But at that time when [we talked], I was trying to do something with all that I had acquired. Anyway, what you have not realized in your paper about me' – for I had shown Sivaram, a week before, the account I'd written of our 1984 conversation – 'is that the debate is not yet over.'

'It's not over?'

'No. My friends still blame me for doing what I did. And I still tell them, no, when I look back I am quite happy with what I did. [Still] ... they are complaining that I should have become a scholar; that I should contribute to the intellectual advancement of the eastern coast. Right? Even the other day I got drunk, and Ananthan, one of my closest buddies here in my intellectual adventures, scolded me, and I him, and we fought with each other – because we were drunk, and what to do? They still keep on blaming me for having abandoned the cause. And my point is that I would rather die Richard Burton than G.E. Moore.'[19]

I mulled this over in my mind a bit. The conceit about Richard Burton did not surprise me; that was vintage Sivaram. But I suddenly realized, with a bit of a jolt, the extent to which Sivaram had needed to steer a particularly idiosyncratic course, not only among his Readers' Circle friends, but also among local Batticaloa pundits and traditional scholars and university intellectuals as well. And I finally grasped that, in order for Sivaram to do so, and to feel justified in having done so, he had been required to invent for himself a whole new concept of 'local intellectual' or *paTicca aal*. This was startling because it brought home, all in a flash, the existential subtlety of Sivaram's yen for freedom. For, in a sense, Sivaram *was the only paTicca aal*, the only member of his new 'cultural' construction. To escape what he called being 'framed,' he had needed to cut a path between the home-grown captivity of even his Readers' Circle friends, and the epistemological and political hubris of Western-inspired (and funded) intellectuality. He had needed, that is, to escape both the moonlit boat and the Peradeniya University seminar. And that long night of talk, nine years before, had been really as much a matter of him carving out that cultural escape route as it had been an attack on my intellectual ethics. Of course, in doing so, he had also escaped me – and my sad attempts at anthropology. Staring now at the glass in my hands, and listening to the far-off music, I found myself rather glad.

But I also thought: how lonely.

'You know,' he said, interrupting my thoughts, 'this question you asked about [risking] death and all. It's like asking why the sky is blue or something like that. So many thousands of Tamil fellows, and so many fellows of your country, have [gone to war].'

'Oh yes, I know. My father went to war. But I guess the difference is ... You know, my father ...'

'What is the difference?'

'The difference is that my father went willingly off to war, believing in the cause. But before you went you spent the entire night talking to me about a thousand and one things, including how none of the organizations that you had to choose among were all that intellectually respectable.'

He laughed. 'No, but then the whole argument was ended. I can't just be saying that all these organizations are worthless. That's where you didn't get my point about the Empedoclean folly. That [if you go on thinking like that] the only thing left, [after] rising above and above and above [them] in these metanarratives, [is] ultimately [to] jump into Aetna – to prove you are a god.'

'So you jumped in?'

'You have got me completely wrong. What I am saying is that the *intellectual* says, do you not, "I have to be an intellectual, I have to *grasp* the world!" Right? "I have to come up with the perfect metanarrative. I have to come up with the ultimate vocabulary that will subsume all vocabularies. I will dream of full presence." And then *you* have to jump into it to prove all this. *That* is what I call the Empedoclean folly. And that is why *I* said the choice has to be made. Push the bloody thing! Push the thing! So you said that I had told you [that night] that all these organizations were not ideologically respectable. Right? I knew that. But that was not the point. The point is: OK, you push this thing. [You go in] further and further. And, like you, I might have been complaining that no one understands me. Right? It's possible to complain – to congratulate yourself and complain – "no one is understanding [me]!" [But] what is the problem with *me* if I am grumbling that no one understands me, or ... complaining that all these organizations are below [me]? Right?'

In 1995 Sivaram wanted to add: 'It is very important that it be understood that I am not saying I am above the organizations. The *rhetorical* import of the question must be emphasized.'

'My argument,' Sivaram continued, in 1993, 'is that the problem arises from the notion of intellectuality that I was at great pains to lambast during our last meeting in 1984 – if you remember the details. The logical extreme of this [notion of intellectuality] is that you will have to jump into Aetna, symbolically speaking, to prove that you are god. To prove that you have this ultimate metanarrative, to prove that, OK, we'll grasp this full presence. Jump into Aetna to make people believe that you have become *sub specie aeterni.*'

Chuckling over this on my dining room table in 1995, Sivaram wrote in my margin: 'My dear Mark! Does this make sense to you or should I expand? Anyway, please note that this is a Derridean phrase from the metaphysics of the presence discussion somewhere – perhaps in *Margins of Philosophy.*'

In 1993, however, Sivaram snorted his derision, and paused for a moment, staring off across the lagoon. The moon had now set; the night was completely dark. Behind us, in his brother-in-law's house, the shutters were drawn, though I could see that the door had been left unlatched for when we should want to come inside to sleep. Then Sivaram went on, more softly.

'What I was arguing was that this concept of intellectuality – the sociology, no, the political economy and epistemology of intellectuality – structures what makes sense; [but] that there could, culturally, be a different notion of intellectuality which [could] mean different things. So what I am trying to say is that this particular cultural [kind] of intellectuality that I was condemning results inevitably in the Empedoclean folly. However much you say that you understood Derrida or have unlocked the whole thing, you are caught up in the metanarrative. The moment that you say you understood Derrida, and you try to expound the thing to me, you have confounded yourself. That is why I like to tell the good story of this man Derrida. So push it up. Don't be caught by the comfort of the privileged vocabulary – as in that example from Rorty about the microbiologists. Push it up.'

'Push,' I muttered, rather sleepily.

'Push,' he said, this time to himself. 'Or end up in some tower guarding Aristotle's treatise on comedy. I mean, as in Eco's *The Name of the Rose*, and the philosophy that I understand is behind it: the idea that if laughter, pleasure, is found to be at the core of metaphysics, then the whole thing is gone. That is why the second book of the poetics, on comedy, had to be guarded with such deadly secrecy.'

And in 1995 Sivaram rooted around my untidy shelves until he found a copy of Eco's book. 'I do not propose here,' he said, leafing through my copy of the book, 'to expound on what Eco had in mind but I am using the relevant page as an instrument to illustrate my point.'

And then he read, aloud: 'But on the day when the Philosopher's word would justify the marginal jests of the debauched imagination, or when what has been marginal would leap to the center, every trace of the center would be lost' (Eco 1980: 475).

'That,' Sivaram wrote on my manuscript, 'is the blind monk Jorge explaining to William of Baskerville why he hid the second book of Aristotle on comedy from the gaze of mortals.'

Back in 1993, even more sleepily, I muttered, 'Is that where you think I should be? In that tower?'

He laughed, and downed the dregs in his glass. A sour look stole across his face.

'That last bit of arrack was ruined by the water.'

So then we did turn in. For there was no light left, and the arrack was gone, and Sivaram had a Taraki column due the next day. Sivaram took a sleeping mat. As a great honor, I was granted the bed. We slept soundly till the curfew ended the following morning. And then, through all the checkpoints, I went home again.

And Sivaram went back to work.

6 FROM TARAKI TO TAMILNET: SIVARAM AS JOURNALIST, MILITARY ANALYST, AND INTERNET PIONEER

For the LTTE the moral obligation is more important than political reality. It still feels that it should not betray those who like my friend laid down their lives for the cause while the dream was still in them. (Taraki 1991: 35)

The main aim of pacification in modern counter-insurgency techniques is the closure of the political space from which a rebellion derives it staying power and ability to spread its influence with ease. The military drive against a rebellion can consolidate its successes ultimately only if it can achieve a near total closure of the political space in which a rebellion is brought forth and thrives. (Taraki 1993b)

... [I said] I will enter the game on condition that no nationalist or propagandist shit gets on the website, and whatever of such shit that had been put on the resources pages earlier should be got rid of forthwith. Henceforth everything had to be neutral (in the ironic sense in which you and I have dealt with it). (Sivaram, email, 13 Aug. 2000)

My interest is to create a body of knowledge to help oppressed people all over the world help themselves get out from under oppression. (Sivaram in conversation, 2 March 2004)

SIVARAM COMES TO AMERICA

The first time Sivaram visited America was also the first time he told me that he thought his journalism was going to get him killed. It was the fall of 1995 and Sivaram had come to America that year on an exchange program sponsored by the US Information Agency (USIA). At that time, the USIA had such programs to spread 'democratic' and 'pluralistic' values to important journalists they had selected from the world's inter-ethnic hotspots, a purpose Sivaram found more amusing than helpful given that his visit coincided with America's burgeoning O.J. Simpson hysteria and the racial tensions revealed therein. In any case, this 'Building Democracy in Diverse Communities' program brought Sivaram to Washington DC on 14 September 1995, and from there, over the course of three weeks, to Los Angeles, California, Akron, Ohio, Miami, Florida, and eventually back to Washington DC. From Washington Sivaram was supposed to return immediately to Sri Lanka, on 12 October. Hence, the last page of his overly chatty USIA travel schedule chirped, encouragingly, 'Have a safe and pleasant journey!' But with a six-month, multiple-entry visa in hand he flew down to visit me instead.

He arrived in Aiken, South Carolina, wearing a natty gray sports coat, rolling a single small suitcase, and toting a large plastic carrying-bag full of pamphlets on democracy and grassroots political action which he gleefully deposited in my trash can since, as he put it, 'they appear to have all been written by insects.' But he told me, nonetheless, that he had been enjoying his first look at America and Americans. 'You are such a happy, naïve people. It's been really very pleasant, *maccaang*, like looking at children playing. Very cheering.' He was especially cheered by Aiken's local supermarkets, which, in those pre-Keels supermarket days (Keels being the Tesco or Publix of Sri Lanka), he found ridiculous in their fecundity. He liked being taken to Aiken's huge Wal-Mart Supercenter so he could stand in one of the food aisles and, simply, laugh. 'I could kill myself eating here, *maccaang*. I could easily murder myself.' After Ann, who was doing research in Mexico at the time, arrived for a visit, we took Sivaram to Charleston, South Carolina's tourist city, and the very place where the American Civil War started. It was partly for pleasure, of course, but partly for Sivaram's own research, for while Sivaram was thoroughly enjoying his first trip out of South Asia, his journalistic curiosity was fully engaged. He was forever striking up conversations, buttonholing, and generally chatting up strangers; and not the tame people USIA had paraded before him in their 'workshops.' Rather, in every city he visited, Sivaram had slipped out, and walked around, seeking the poor and the angry and the marginalized. By the time he got to me in Aiken he had spoken with Ethiopian political refugees in Washington DC, Mexican laborers in several states, a prominent Chinese-American dissident in LA, several annoyed black labor activists there too, a Marxist priest in Miami (with whom he had, one evening, sipped wine on Biscayne Bay while talking about the Haitian boat people disaster), and unorganized low wage workers everywhere – none of whom were on his official itinerary. He had an ear for those voices others like to ignore. So it was in Charleston, when, walking down Meeting Street with Ann and me, Sivaram noticed a picket line in front of a prominent hotel and shopping arcade. He immediately joined it, asking questions, striking up conversations, eventually finding out the whole story behind the strike. In about an hour he knew more about the sad labor politics of South Carolina than I had learned in several years. Buying a local paper, he pointed out that the event was simply not covered. 'And your USIA people, my friend, think they have a free press.'

And he laughed.

At various times, during that first long visit, I had to take him to dinner parties with other academics. These were invariably a disaster. We would go, and there would be nuts and cheese and attempts at witty talk over discreetly sipped goblets of expensive wine. If the academics were older or especially self-important they would then attempt to lecture Sivaram on what they thought he should know about the world, politics, philosophy, and literature.

Since Sivaram was generally better read than they were, and his experiences more concrete, these were intensely uncomfortable moments, made worse by Sivaram's penchant for subtly – and sometimes not so subtlty – baiting such people. I remember once a young, fancily-degreed academic attempting to explain Kojève's writing on Hegel to Sivaram, only to stand dumbfounded and stone-faced as Sivaram, after pointing out how profoundly mistaken this young man was in his interpretation of Kojève, proceeded to quote, from memory, the relevant passages. Sivaram was particularly, loudly, and rudely hard on academics who thought of themselves as 'politically active,' maintaining, with a dismissive wave of his wine glass, that the only true sign of political activism in an academic (or anyone else) was a death threat and imminent imprisonment. 'You have to *risk* something. Otherwise you are just *playing*,' he would say. He was also intemperately amused by the fashion for Buddhism in academic circles. At one party he flustered the guests by describing, in gruesome detail, the views and actions of some nationalist *bhikkus* (monks) in Sri Lanka. He ended the evening, as he often did such occasions, by laughing at the selection of tasteful 'eastern' music, the under-spiced food, the ersatz antique 'Third World' paraphernalia on the walls, and the politics. He also ostentatiously drank too much, and let it show, something which he rarely did unless he wanted to. After we left, I was furious.

'Couldn't you have been more polite? For God's sake!'

'*Maccaang, maccaang,* don't upset yourself. They will think nothing of it.'

'Come on! They're not completely naïve!'

'No, Mark, you are wrong. They are all *completely* naïve.'

On the way home from one of these affairs, I forget which one, Sivaram looked longingly at the moonlight silvering the oak trees flashing by and said that he hoped, when he died, that his molecules would mingle with the soil of the Batticaloa district so that, in this way, he would eventually become one with its jungles and flowers.

'Why are we talking about death?' I asked, still somewhat testy about the disastrous party.

'Because, young man, what I am doing now is eventually going to get me killed. It has to.'

We argued about this and he ended up telling me that when he died I would know it because a bottle of arrack would arrive in the mail. 'I've put it in my will,' he said. 'Unless you would prefer something else. Should it be a bottle of gin?'

'Arrack is fine. But you are not going to die.'

'Oh I *am* going to die, young man. Just remember the arrack.'

For the next seven years, however, Sivaram's fame as a journalist and military analyst grew, and, after 1996, as he did more traveling in connection with TamilNet, I saw him regularly. Of course, I was not the only academic Sivaram regularly visited in those years. Patricia Lawrence and Dennis McGilvray of the University of Colorado, Boulder, and Margaret Trawick of

Massey University, New Zealand, were all scholars Sivaram advised about their various projects; he often spent time in Boulder, for example, helping Dennis McGilvray prepare a new history of the Batticaloa District. Sivaram said he even briefly visited Stanley Tambiah at Harvard and Nicholas Dirks, now at Columbia University. But for Sivaram all this travel was foremost a golden opportunity to re-establish contact with his far-flung family. By the mid-1990s Sri Lanka's war had scattered perhaps 700,000 Sri Lankan Tamils over four continents (Fugelrud 1999: 1), and in this respect Sivaram's relatives and the old Stanley House 'gang' were no exception. His older brother Kuttan, and his cousins Lee Karu, Oppi, and later Surendaran, eventually followed their uncle Seervaratnam Velupillai to Britain, where they were more or less all established professionals by the mid-1990s. His younger brother, Sheshakumaran, after enduring Sri Lanka's war far longer than Kuttan and the 'gang,' had taken his degree and come to ground in New Zealand, and later Australia, as a doctor in the 1990s. Bavani's brothers, Daniel and David (the latter, after being sprung from prison by Amnesty International), her sister Radhi (widow of Sivaram's assassinated PLOTE friend, Vasutheva) and various cousins, nephews, and nieces had turned up in Toronto, a city, by that time, boasting the largest Sri Lankan Tamil population in the world.[1] Sivaram visited them all, spending especially long periods of time in London and Toronto, from where he would often call me, in the middle of the night, invariably from some noisy family reunion, to abuse me about what he claimed were my 'hard-working' ways. Even so, he continued to make time to visit me in my home too.

Indeed, until post 9/11 jitters limited his access to North America, Sivaram annually availed himself of our couch, our kitchen, our video (he loved Hollywood action pictures, the more unlikely the better), my school's library (where he ran down obscure books about nationalism and the novels of John Le Carré) and our spare bedroom (my study, actually), sometimes for weeks at a time. As a consequence he knew my son almost from the day he was born (had, in fact, for several years loudly and rudely lobbied for his birth, and arrived for a visit weeks before his birth), bought him his first toy truck, and was to my son, David, 'Uncle Sivaram' – no doubt about that – good for climbing about and sleeping on. One winter, in 2000, he brought his daughters with him. So we took them to Charleston also, to see the churning ocean from the Isle of Palms and the busy harbor from the Battery. Looking out over the slate-gray January waters toward Fort Sumter, vaguely huddling in the shifting light. Vaishnavi, Sivaram's eldest daughter, then 10 – who had been rather dubious about North America's winter landscapes – breathed deeply and pronounced it all beautiful.

'It looks like Batticaloa,' she said, contentedly. Looking closely, aided by her eyes, swapping an old Dutch fort for an old federal one, I suddenly realized that she was quite right. It did.

'But there are no bodies in the water now,' Sivaram said to me, conversationally, as we walked away, 'and no gunfire, *maccaang*.'

WHAT WAS IT ALL FOR?

How can I describe Sivaram's journalism? Subtle and prescient military analysis, a penchant for describing neglected details and ignored people, a pioneering way of using the internet to circumvent vast structural (and mortally violent) constraints on speech, an increasingly raw and tragic (some would say paradoxical and wrong-headed) nationalism? Do any of these moves and qualities sum it up? It is difficult, I suppose, to come to an understanding of the work of any journalist. Intellectually and physically peripatetic creatures, journalists necessarily wander unceasingly through a fractured landscape of crisis and spectacle, perpetually visiting and leaving behind the tragedies they record and comment upon. This was especially true in Sri Lanka, I think, not just because of the wild squalor of its politics but also because of the desperate economies of its journalists. The fee for an op-ed piece in the 1990s was a mere 100 rupees – about US $2.50 – and so, everyday, even the most respected columnists had to be always on the lookout for the next story, groping for anything just to survive. Still, great journalists, in Sri Lanka as elsewhere, are driven by grand themes, personal styles, even underlying ideologies or instincts for a certain kind of narrative; and these threads, or others like them, can weave numerous short works together into a sensible whole. This was certainly true of Sivaram's writings. But in Sivaram's case, I think, there was more at work than even this kind of aesthetic, attitudinal, or ideological unity. There was, or soon came to be, to his mind, a unifying intellectual and political project.

'Come on, Sivaram. What does it all add up to? What does it all mean? Why get yourself killed?'

I remember yelling this at him (or something like it) over the phone one day in May 2004. I was in Kandy and he was ... somewhere, he could not say. It was my birthday and I was angry with him. Sivaram had been living rough for months, running under a perpetual death threat, sleeping in a different bed every night, afraid to go home, worried that he might endanger his family. I kept telling him he should leave the country.

'You should leave the country!' I said.

'And do what? No, Mark, have a happy birthday. Get drunk. *Maccaang*, life is short.'

'What is the point!'

'The point? Just remember two things, *maccaang*. What I always say and always believe: first, never a dull day; second, only fools die!'

'That's the point?'

'Just remember those things.'

But nine weeks later, in a long conversation about his journalism and his theories of military strategy that lasted, eventually, for over nine hours, he also answered me, more soberly, this way: 'My interest is to create a body of knowledge to help oppressed people all over the world help themselves get out from under oppression. And to disseminate this body of knowledge.'

And this, really, *was* his project – or, at least, a central part of it. I could see anticipatory fragments of this as far back as our old, all-night conversations at Stanley House in 1984 about the social responsibilities of intellectuals. Of course, Sivaram had arrived at this rather grand goal through his more long-standing, and more local, desire to achieve what he called 'justice for the Tamil people.' For he never strayed far from his belief that a fundamental injustice was being perpetrated against his people, and that it was his duty to do something about it, or die trying. Nevertheless, even as early as 1984, Sivaram had begun to see Sri Lanka's conflict as one instance of a more general problem afflicting late modernity: the rise of what he later called 'counter-insurgency nation-states.' It came as no real surprise to me, therefore, that by the middle 1990s Sivaram had come to view Sri Lanka's conflict as a kind of military-political laboratory in which the various repressive forces of late modernity (local and international) were testing their clever, often cruel, counter-insurgency tactics, and in which others – the LTTE in particular – were, in response, coming up with equally savvy (and terrible) *counter* counter-insurgency antidotes. Since any counter-insurgency campaign is also a 'struggle for ... minds' (Kitson 1977: 282), as many military theorists say and as Sivaram also firmly believed, Sivaram began to regard his own recording and analysis of Sri Lanka's protracted struggle as a form of active subversion. Further, Sivaram believed that, by carefully selecting the military insights he gave in his columns, he could intervene in and, sometimes, influence outcomes. Thus, as he said, his writings had become again a way to be 'in the game.'

At the same time, Sivaram began to feel that if he could just leave behind in his writings a clear and meticulously accurate picture of exactly how a counter-insurgency campaign is conducted, won, and (most importantly) sometimes defeated, this in itself would constitute a telling blow against repression. I can see this most clearly in the pedagogical character of his writing: his careful definition of technical military terms (Taraki 1991: 34, 58, 69), his clear presentation of larger geopolitical contexts and players (1991: 89), his biographies of political actors (Taraki 1991: 30, 1994f), his comparative use of military history and theory (Taraki 1991: 58, 1993b, 1994a), his ethnographic and sometimes even socio-metric depictions of communities (Taraki 1994f, 1997a) and the way his articles, taken together, constitute an exceedingly graphic outline of counter-insurgency as a form of power. *Basically, Sivaram was trying to leave behind a set of instructions or a cookbook for defeating counter-insurgency* – a goal he believed not only right in itself, but also to which he felt the fortunes of the Sri Lankan Tamil people were completely hostage. So it was at this target that Sivaram aimed in his final years, from 1996 onwards. It was also, I think, to this ambition that Sivaram ultimately felt compelled to sacrifice (at least publicly) two of his most clearly stated, and firmly held, former views: his intense disdain for the LTTE's intolerance and totalitarian tendencies, and his hope that Tamils might one day unite with Sinhalese progressives for the good of all Sri Lankans. For he came to believe that discussing the first was playing into the hands of counter-insurgency strategists, and (betrayed, he felt, again and again) he simply lost faith in the ability of Sinhalese progressives to participate in the second. Ultimately, of course, to this idiosyncratic political effort he also sacrificed his comfort, his fortune, his safety, and his very life.

Now I think one can see the ripening of this project over time in Sivaram's writings alone, but only subtly and by reading each column with a weather eye toward Sivaram's own eventual course. But since Sivaram was working at the coalface of politics, his reportorial blows were often carefully aimed to carve out (and push his various readers toward) larger, unspecified designs of his own. Realizing this, I decided that it would be best if I could get him to spell out more explicitly his underlying ideas. So I arranged to have two long conversations with Sivaram at my rented house in Kandy: one in late March 2004, on his view of nationalism, and the second in the middle of July 2004, on his view of modern military strategy and the rise of 'counter-insurgency states.' Both conversations, as usual with us, involved a lot of drinking and eating, and a lot of arguing, but I had a tape-recorder, and Sivaram managed to free my computer from a few of its nastier viruses long enough for me to take dictation. In any case, because Sivaram carefully reviewed his journalistic writing in the second conversation, I have decided to defy chronology and present most of that second conversation here, first. The conversation on nationalism will be recounted in Chapter 7. Before turning to either conversation, however, I think a brief overview of Sivaram's journalistic wanderings, and an equally brusque précis of the progress of Sri Lanka's struggle between 1989 and 2004 are absolutely necessary as a backdrop.

AN OVERVIEW OF SIVARAM'S JOURNALISTIC CAREER

Sivaram's journalistic career lasted from late 1988 till April 2005, 17 years, during which, for various financial and political reasons, Sivaram wrote for a confusing number of venues under a bewildering variety of names. Hence, after losing his IPS job due to political fall-out following Richard de Zoysa's murder, Sivaram stayed with *The Island*, as Taraki, till 1996. But at the same time also wrote, under his own name, 'D. Sivaram,' for the human rights weekly *Sarinikar*. This paper, by the way, was run out of the Colombo office of a local human rights NGO, MERGE, and edited by the Marxist, Sivakumar, Sivaram's old friend and fellow ex-PLOTE member from his pre-war, Jaffna seminar days, who had been forced to leave Jaffna by the LTTE in 1990 for advocating democracy (as he reminded me, rather bitterly, at an interview in his ramshackle office in July 1997).

In any case, Sivaram was also writing for the left wing *Lanka Guardian*, as 'D.P. Sivaram,' turning out in 1992 a locally famous, 11-part, series 'On Tamil Militarism,' between May and November that year. This series was Sivaram's most scholarly work in English, and traced the South Asian historical origins of such characteristic LTTE ideals as its valorization of suicide in battle to the pre-colonial 'Maruvar' military caste mentality that, he believed, inspired the early developers of Dravidian nationalism in India to a degree hitherto neglected by historians. (The rather obscure sources needed for this carefully researched exercise were not to be found in Sri Lanka. So Sivaram had to repeatedly send his brother, Kuttan, to the British Library bearing Sivaram's epistolary requests for various moldering colonial books and documents.) Further, in 1995, Sivaram was approached by the editors of *Tamil Times*, a monthly news magazine run by London-based Sri Lankan Tamil professionals, who wanted him to contribute yet more articles. Bedeviled by government censorship at home, Sivaram found it possible to publish with the *Tamil Times* complete versions of articles that had been rendered senseless in *The Island* by the censor's increasingly freewheeling stamp. So for the next several years he wrote for the *Tamil Times*, sometimes as 'D. Sivaram' and sometimes as 'Our Defense Correspondent,' or even as 'Our Colombo Correspondent.'

By 1996 *The Island* had swerved its editorial view in a majoritarian direction and was less amenable to having Sivaram's column around, especially since Sivaram's criticisms of the People's Alliance (PA) government were becoming alarmingly and increasingly sarcastic, and his views of the LTTE more sympathetic. So in 1996 Sivaram shifted his Taraki franchise to the *Midweek Mirror* and the *Sunday Times* (the latter edited by Vijitha Yapa, the former *Island* editor, and current publisher of Vijitha Yapa books), both newspapers controlled by the 'liberal democratic'-leaning Ranjit Wijeyeardene (Jeyaraj: *TamilWeek*, 255/05). According to D.B.S. Jeyaraj (2005c) – the journalist whose famous 'Behind the Cajan Curtain' column preceded Sivaram's own at *The Island* – the *Sunday Times* in 1996 had not yet made its own move toward a 'Sinhala majoritarian outlook' and so was a good home for Sivaram's work. Sivaram, hence, continued writing for both newspapers until late in 1999 (Jeyaraj 2005c). But by the later half of the 1990s, Sivaram was finding his time increasingly taken up by two new activities: editing the internet news service, TamilNet.com, and advising various governments and foreign policy think-tanks.

Sivaram's work for TamilNet was a direct outgrowth of his fame as a journalist, mostly as Taraki, among the far-flung members of the Sri Lankan Tamil diaspora. Sivaram's Taraki writings had been in circulation among the diaspora in Europe, Australia, and North America for several years already before his 1995 trip because, during those early days of the internet, news-clipping services like TamilCanadian.com and chat-rooms such as the Tamil Circle Mailing List circulated his articles. But early in 1996, in North America, Sivaram was introduced to one of the organizers of a new but troubled internet site, TamilNet.com, a transparently nationalist and enthusiastically pro-LTTE site. TamilNet's organizers – none of whom were, at that time, members of the LTTE – had created the site out of disillusionment with the way the Western, English-language press was covering the war in Sri Lanka. Specifically, they were alarmed by how that coverage was being increasingly influenced by the Sri Lankan government's propaganda, and, even more, by the English-language reports of an organization called the University Teachers for Human Rights (Jaffna). The UTHR(J), as it was generally known, was originally started by four members of the science faculty at Jaffna University during the LTTE–IPKF war as an oversight group to monitor human rights abuses (Hoole et al. 1990). Over time, however, most of the contributing writers for UTHR(J) came to regard the LTTE (for various reasons, including its penchant for killing its critics) as an increasingly dangerous, fascist organization, and said so in their reports. When the LTTE responded by assassinating one of the group's central members in September 1989 – the victim was senior lecturer in anatomy, Dr Ranjani Thirananagama – the rest of the group dropped underground and, from there, continued to produce their reports, supported, many diasporic Tamils and the creators of TamilNet firmly believed, by the Sri Lankan government (Hoole 2001).[2] So TamilNet was originally created to provide an alternative English-language voice to counter the popularity of the UTHR(J)'s reports among the Western press.

But, at this, TamilNet was clearly failing: it was receiving very few hits, and there was no evidence that the Western press was paying any attention to it whatsoever. So, intrigued by Sivaram's work, and aware that TamilNet as then configured was having no impact, this man asked Sivaram if he would care to help them improve the site. Sivaram, for various reasons of his own (which we will turn to presently) was immediately fascinated by this prospect – especially by the possibilities the internet raised for what he termed the 'distribution' of his project – but very weary of its implications. Nonetheless, after further meetings in Europe, during which Sivaram argued that the very nature of the site would have to change – for one thing, if he was going to take it on, he would want it to abandon nationalist rhetoric and remain financially and editorially independent of the LTTE – it was agreed that he should re-establish TamilNet along lines he carefully described to them, that is, as an independent news agency publishing its own stories written by its own reporters. Henceforth, its news stories were to be double sourced and carefully fact-checked, so as to be accurate beyond challenge. Further, it was to be written and edited in a style reflecting, as Sivaram termed it, an 'ironic' but 'professional' use of the 'objective-neutral' language of international news agencies (Whitaker 2004) – the very language, Sivaram believed, that so often masked the biases (some accidental, some geographic, some strategic) that marred Western press reporting about Sri Lanka. Sivaram, for his part, would use the $1400 a month TamilNet's backers put at his disposal to set up the agency in Sri Lanka, retaining only $200 for his own salary. After training his reporters and issuing them with laptops and digital cameras, Sivaram would be linked to them by cell phone and email, and would edit the site as well as contribute periodic 'News Features,' all anonymously. The result would be, as it soon was, a cyber-web, with Sivaram (and the other TamilNet creators) the unnamed spiders at its center. By 1999, Sivaram, able to link his laptop to the net through his cell phone, was writing and editing almost continuously – even from, as he put it, some 'dingy bar somewhere while having a drink.' By 2004, Sivaram had a mobile phone with a flip-down front and a stylus that allowed him to word process and upload onto the net directly through his phone. I remember, for example, a dinner with him in Kandy one night in early February 2004 during which he wrote, rewrote, edited, and uploaded five stories, all the while furiously interviewing sources, collecting additional facts off the net, and composing parts of a news feature, even as the food was served and eaten. Watching him was exhausting.

'Don't you ever stop?' I asked, curiously.

'What to do, *maccaang?* Does *it* stop? How can I stop?'

The new venture began in 1997, and consumed him (I think, quite literally) from then to the end of his life. By 1999, Sivaram's attentions were so bound up with TamilNet.com that his other identity, Taraki began to wane. By 2000 he had ceased contributing articles to the *Midweek Mirror* and the *Sunday Times* altogether, and Taraki, temporarily, was gone. But not forever: Taraki revived again in January 2004 when Sivaram, concerned about school fees, agreed to contribute Taraki articles to the *Daily Mirror*, the newspaper into which the *Midweek Mirror* had eventually evolved. That same year, moreover, he also agreed to start sending in articles under his own name (D. Sivaram) to *Viirakeesari*,[3] Colombo's largest-circulation Tamil-language daily. These columns, too, were quickly circulated through the internet.

Still, even during Sivaram's period of greatest preoccupation with TamilNet (1998–2002), editing the site was not Sivaram's only activity. First, in 2002–3, Sivaram helped start another newspaper, the *Northeastern Herald*, a 'civil society' project originally sponsored by a grant from the Swedish government. Second, Sivaram's direct involvement in electoral politics was also increasing; Sivaram, for example, was one of the prime movers behind the Tamil National Alliance, as the loose, pro-LTTE coalition of several ex-militant Tamil parties and the TULF came to be called, which coalesced just in time to play a role in the 2001 elections that cost the PA control of Parliament.

Beyond this, as the 1990s ended, Sivaram's stock as a military analyst was going up, partly because he alone had predicted the spate of military setbacks the Sri Lankan government was then experiencing. Consequently, governments as diverse as the United States, Canada, the UK, Switzerland, Germany, India, and Japan arranged meetings, both in Sri Lanka and abroad, between Sivaram and their various security people and quasi-private advisers. (Meetings where, Sivaram always claimed, he learned far more than he ever revealed.) At the same time, NGOs learned of Sivaram's expertise and started inviting him to their conferences as well. Soon Sivaram was regularly appearing at conferences on ethnic conflict, press freedom, and security issues held at venues all over the world. These were the trips that allowed him to see his family in Britain every year until 2005, and his wife's family in Toronto (and mine, in South Carolina and New York) almost annually till 2001, when North America became too consumed by its post-9/11 fears to allow such travel.

This was Sivaram's journalistic career from 1989 to 2004. Of course, such an overview leaves a number of questions unanswered. For example, first, how and why did Sivaram's attitude toward the LTTE change between 1989 and 2004? For change it did, though perhaps more subtly, and for different reasons, than many of those who laud and condemn him might think. Second, how is it that Sivaram's advice became so important to all sides in the conflict? For it is well to remember that Sivaram's views were as actively sought by the Sri Lankan government and the various Western and regional governments backing it as by the LTTE – despite many in the first group believing that Sivaram was somehow linked to the LTTE and some in the LTTE insisting that Sivaram was an Indian (or a CIA or a Sri Lankan government) spy. And, finally, why did Sivaram persist, even after it became quite clear that continuing meant his death? For, as I said, Sivaram already knew by 1995 that his job was going to get him killed.

SIVARAM AND THE WAR

To a certain extent, answering any of these questions (particularly the last) presupposes having some grasp of the almost hallucinogenic mutability and obscure complexity of Sri Lanka's military-political history, particularly during the 1990s. For it was against that hazardous and confusing backdrop that Sivaram felt compelled to test, recast, and modify his work and beliefs again and again. So it matters, therefore, that within the ten-year (or so) span that concerns me here, the Sri Lankan conflict was going from bad to better to worse to good to bad again, in a roller-coaster of political hope and despair. A brief overview is required.

In late October 1989, when Sivaram wrote his first article as Taraki for *The Island*, the LTTE (subtly aided by the Sri Lankan government) was still at war with the already withdrawing IPKF, while the Sri Lankan government was yet in the midst of its own war with the JVP. By March 1990 the remaining IPKF forces had departed Sri Lanka, leaving the LTTE to quickly crush, and acquire the weapons of, the Tamil National Army (TNA), the stopgap replacement force the IPKF had spawned in its wake. A short period of negotiations between the LTTE and the Sri Lankan government then took place, even while Ranasinghe Premadasa's UNP government was continuing its reign of anti-JVP terror – or, rather, extending that terror to include other targets (such as anyone critical of the government), since the JVP had been effectively crushed as an insurgent force with the death of its leader, Rohana Wejeweera, in November 1989. These events fell within what Sivaram called his 'first phase' of writing as Taraki, when he had, as yet, no political agenda of his own, and was content simply to lay out the military, ideological, and strategic objectives of all players.[4] And so he did, while the talks dragged on.

By 10 June 1990, however, all such talks had broken down and there began what Tamils call 'Eelam War Two,' during which the LTTE quickly burned its political bridges with India by blowing up Rajiv Gandhi (by means of a female suicide bomber masquerading as a flower-garland wielding devotee at a campaign rally), withdrew the bulk of its guerrilla forces from the east, and concentrated instead on turning Jaffna into a proto-state, complete with its own police, tax collectors, judges, and colorful graveyards dedicated to its cult of Tiger martyrs – many lionized for suicide attacks and bombings. These were LTTE tactics that Taraki's columns both explained ('LTTE between positional and guerrilla warfare,' in 1991: 58) and, on occasion, condemned, as for example when he referred to the 'fascist fanaticism of the LTTE' (in Taraki 1991: 58).[5] At the same time, Sivaram's columns also noted that the LTTE was, gradually, transforming itself into a more 'conventional army' (1991: 82) – as shown by its attempts (unique in the history of insurgency) to establish a naval arm (Taraki 1993c), its increasingly sophisticated training methods (Taraki 1994a) and its efforts to create proper, battalion-sized units. These moves toward fielding a more conventional force were partly inspired, Sivaram believed, by the LTTE's impressively massive, very costly, and ultimately unsuccessful attack in 1991 on the huge Sri Lankan army base at Elephant Pass, the sandy choke-point causeway that links the Jaffna peninsula with the rest of Sri Lanka. Their failure there had shown them the need to reorganize, and this they quickly did.

The Sri Lankan government, for its part, seemed to have a two-pronged strategy. On the one hand, the Sri Lankan army, commanded by General Kobbekaduwa, began to mount attacks into the Wanni region just south of Jaffna, not with the aim, as Sivaram pointed out to me later, of taking back territory but of threatening the LTTE's various bases there in order to force the LTTE to expend its forces to defend them. ('A move straight out of Jomini,[6] though they would never have put it that way,' Sivaram said to me, in 2004.) On the other hand, the army also quickly mounted a massive, torturously repressive, and very bloody counter-insurgency campaign in the east, during which thousands upon thousands of people 'disappeared,' sometimes to turn up later as bloated corpses bobbing in the ocean off Kallady's Bar road – as I found, to my horror, when I interviewed survivors of that period in 1997.

Privately, Sivaram was highly distressed by the increasing levels of violence being directed at his beloved Batticaloa, though his columns by now rarely revealed any emotion other than a carefully cool, almost surgical, disdain. But, as a military analyst, he was curious: what explained these clearly calculated excesses, these efforts to smother a target population with terror? So Sivaram's columns, for the first time, began to systematically explore the role conventional Western counter-insurgency doctrine – what he called, then, 'pacification' – was playing in the conflict. Careful to supply definitions, as always, Sivaram/Taraki wrote:

The main aim of pacification in modern counter-insurgency techniques is the closure of the political space from which a rebellion derives its staying power and ability to spread its influence with ease. The military drive against a rebellion can consolidate its successes ultimately only if it can achieve a near total closure of the political space in which a rebellion is brought forth and thrives. (Taraki 1993b)

And it was with this strategic end in view, Sivaram argued, that most of the LTTE's tactics – its suicide bombings, its efforts to establish a conventional army, and its creation of a Jaffna proto-state – could best be understood. That is, as disparate parts of a well thought out, historically unique, if ruthless, 'counter-pacification strategy' primarily designed around the need to keep precisely such a rebellious political space open.

Meanwhile, in April and early May 1993, while combat between the Sri Lankan government and the LTTE took on an increasingly conventional and bloody character in the north, and the anti-insurgency campaign was proceeding toward a kind of apotheosis of terror in the east, the former National Security minister for Premadasa, Lalith Athulathmudali, who had recently turned into an opposition candidate, was assassinated – it is difficult to say by whom. This was followed a week later by the assassination of Premadasa himself, blown up by an LTTE suicide bomber who had been calmly penetrating the president's entourage for over a year (*Tamil Times* 2001). In addition to these disasters, the 'conventional' war in the north began to go badly for the government, especially after it lost its base at Pooneryn, on the Jaffna lagoon, to a spectacular LTTE attack (Taraki 1994d), turning the war into one of constant, wearing engagements, with the LTTE now generally taking the initiative (Taraki 1994g). In late 1994, even as desertions were rising in the army, Premedasa's replacement, UNP party stalwart D.B. Wijetunge, rejected the LTTE's call for unconditional talks – arguing that he would not negotiate with terrorists and claiming that there was no ethnic problem.

So the People's Alliance, led by the Sri Lankan Freedom Party (SLFP) and Chandrika Bandaranaike Kumaratunge rolled to victory in the 1994 parliamentary elections on a peace platform. Why? Many Sri Lankans, perhaps, felt that Chandrika Kumaratunge was somehow fated to lead Sri Lanka at that crucial time. In addition to being extensively and liberally educated, Kumaratunge was the daughter of two former prime ministers, S.W.R.D. Bandaranaike and Sirimavo Bandaranaike, and the widow of Sivaram's old acquaintance, Vijaya Kumaratunge, the former leader of the United Socialist Alliance, and a man who had reached out to Sri Lankan Tamils with such authentic sympathy that he was, apparently, assassinated for having done so by the JVP. Moreover, Chandrika Kumaratunge's platform promised unconditional talks, an end to the executive presidency, and vowed to find a solution to Sri Lanka's ethnic problem, all music to the ears of an increasingly war-weary population. And Gamini Dissanayake, who might have better challenged Kumaratunge from the anti-Tamil right, was blown up by the LTTE on 24 November 1994, leaving the maladroit Wijetunge her sole opposition. So soon thereafter Kumaratunge, still inspiring great hopes among Sinhalese progressives, former militant anti-LTTE Tamil parties, and

Tamil moderates alike, also won the ensuing presidential election and, in early 1995, signed a 'cessation of hostilities agreement' with the LTTE.

But Sivaram, for his part, was not sanguine about this agreement or the possibility for peace the ongoing talks ostensibly promised. He pointed out, as early as June 1994, that one fundamental impediment to Chandrika Kumaratunge's plans, which implied some real devolution of federal power, was that they required making changes to the Sri Lankan Constitution. But making such changes, in turn, depended upon controlling or contriving a two-thirds majority in Parliament, something Sivaram felt Kumaratunge (and all Sinhalese politicians) lacked the ability to accomplish (Sivaram 1994b). Moreover, he began to suspect that Chandrika Kumaratunge's peace plan was really (or also) an attempt to 'unhinge' and squeeze out the LTTE politically. But this, he claimed, revealed a serious misunderstanding of the extent to which the LTTE's victories on the battlefield, and steadfastness on the Eelam issue, had earned it the loyalty of many normal Tamil people outside Colombo, as well as the degree to which the LTTE was itself aware of this fact (Taraki 1995a). Moreover, Sivaram had long been concerned by the extent to which Chandrika Kumaratunge's efforts depended upon an alliance with the moderate TULF. Many Tamil people, as Sivaram had long pointed out, felt betrayed by the TULF (Taraki 1994b), casting the TULF's legitimacy as a party capable of acting for Sri Lankan Tamil people into question. At the same time, one weakly floated LTTE trial balloon – for a confederation, with a right-to-succeed clause added to the Constitution – seemed, to Sivaram, equally unrealistic and unlikely to fly (Taraki 1995b). When he visited me in 1995 he cautioned against my hopes that the peace would last.

And he was right. For after only a brief period of negotiations – four months – the LTTE called off the talks, and what Tamils call 'Eelam War Three' began with a bang. On 19 April 1995 LTTE 'sea Tigers' (as the LTTE called its naval arm) blew up two Sri Lankan navy ships in Trincomalee harbor. Enraged, Kumaratunge declared a 'war for peace,' and had her army launch a series of large-scale campaigns (operations named 'Leap Forward' and 'Riveresa') against the LTTE's peninsular Jaffna bastion in the north, an action that culminated in the fall of Jaffna town itself to government forces in early December 1995. The LTTE, apparently badly beaten, retreated (with much of the population of Jaffna, initially) to the Wanni, the vast and thickly forested area south of the Jaffna peninsula (*Tamil Times* 1995). Some military experts, in Sri Lanka and abroad, promptly agreed that this spelt the end of the Tigers as a conventional threat. But, after reviewing this action for the *Tamil Times*, Sivaram saw the offensive as only partly successful. He pointed out that while taking Jaffna appeared to have accomplished the government's main political aim – that is, delegitimizing the LTTE in the eyes of the international community by dismantling its Jaffna proto-state – its twin strategic goals of destroying the LTTE's tax base (which allowed it to field a conventional army) and, more importantly, of forcing the LTTE to waste its main strength defending the peninsula, were less successful. This latter goal, he wrote, stemmed 'from a long-standing belief among Western military strategists that an enemy would concentrate his critical military strength and resources in one place and thereby expose them to easy destruction ... if something considered strategically crucial ... is substantially and really threatened' (Sivaram 1995). Sivaram agreed that this was a good theory. But he noted that the LTTE's retreat from Jaffna had not been desperate but calculated, and that their resistance had stiffened only briefly, to provide extra time to withdraw key military assets to well-prepared positions in the Wanni jungles. So this, ultimately, was why the government had not, as it had hoped, dealt 'a decisive blow to the backbone of the Tiger military machine' (Sivaram 1995). Because, that is, the LTTE had decided that the decisive, Jomini style, showdown battles were going to take place elsewhere, in a territory they had carefully prepared: in the Wanni.

Few analysts agreed with Sivaram's assessment, however, and, in any case, Kumaratunge's PA government was feeling politically emboldened. So, while pounding away militarily, PA negotiators also continued trying to hammer out a constitutional, devolutionary solution to the conflict with the other, ex-militant, Tamil parties and the TULF. Chandrika Kumaratunge's hope, clearly, was to produce an agreement that would undercut the LTTE politically while satisfying, alike, non-LTTE Tamils, the eastern Muslims, and, most critically, her own Sinhala allies. And this aim of detaching the LTTE from its political support seemed, if anything, aided by the sanguinary attacks the LTTE started staging in Colombo. For Sivaram, these culminated most horribly on 31 January 1996, when a truck stuffed with explosives, driven by a suicide-Tiger, was rammed into Sri Lanka's Central Bank building, collapsing its front and killing over 100 people, including Sivaram's *maccaal* (cross-cousin), Vasumathy, who had stopped by simply to withdraw money for a friend.[7] 'So sad,' Sivaram said to me later, when I visited him in 1997. He was leafing pensively through her memorial funeral book, before passing it to me. 'So very sad – and *ridiculous*. Poor, poor woman.'

The government's political effort soon stalled, however, and eventually (in 1996) failed altogether. But the Sri Lankan government's military efforts seemed more successful – at least until 18 July 1996, when the LTTE overran Mullaitivu, a huge army camp on the north-east coast of Sri Lanka, costing the government between 1200 and 1400 soldiers and control of the north-east coast. Sivaram had warned that something like this was in the offing, especially in March and May 1996, when he reported that some disregarded army strategists feared the LTTE's strategic withdrawal from Jaffna bespoke an imminent counter-stroke (Sivaram 1996b, Taraki 1996a). After the battle, Sivaram quickly pointed out that by giving the LTTE control of the Mullaitivu coast, the Sri Lankan army's overall strategic aim of reducing the LTTE to an isolated, and thus containable, guerrilla group by cutting it off from its international suppliers had been effectively shattered by this one blow (Sivaram 1996b, Taraki 1996a).

As efforts to retake Mullaitivu eventually also fell apart, the government, in response to all the bad news, imposed censorship on the Colombo-based press, setting up rules and procedures for reporting 'military' news that became, over time, increasingly strict. Eventually, several newspapers were actually shut down for short periods of time, and, toward the end of the 1990s, several Tamil reporters were mysteriously killed and many other reporters, both Tamil and Sinhalese, were threatened. For his part, Sivaram, was twice officially threatened with arrest, and often (unofficially) promised much worse. From 1998 onwards, indeed, Sivaram was generally under a death threat of one sort or another, and rarely slept at home for more than two or three successive nights. That was also the year Sivaram and I began to build up a bank of phone numbers for me to call – politicians, other journalists, Amnesty International, the Committee to Protect Journalists, etc. – whenever he told me things were getting particularly bad. I began to dread Sivaram's emails and, worse, his late-night phone calls, his jarringly blithe, 'Well, Mr Whitaker, they are after me again. It's time to make your phone calls ...'

Nonetheless, the war continued. In May 1997, the army started a campaign called Operation *Jaya Sikurai* or 'Certain Victory' (Jeyaraj 1997: 12), to open up a land route to Jaffna by taking the A9 highway that runs north from the Wanni gateway town of Vivuniya through Kilinochchi to Elephant Pass and Jaffna, thus neatly bisecting the region held by the LTTE. The operation lasted over a year, quickly turning into a bloody battle of attrition that the Sri Lankan government, with its larger human and financial resources, and widespread international support, seemed destined to win. The government's prospects improved further, moreover, when the United States government designated the LTTE a 'terrorist organization' in October 1997 and quietly began to provide more tangible military aid and training. In December 1998, however, despite these advantages and support, an increasingly sanguinary and inert Operation *Jaya Sikurai* had to be called off. Moreover, against all expectations, the Sri Lankan government began to suffer a series of stinging military defeats. Beginning in September 1998, when the LTTE, in a campaign it called 'unceasing waves' (*Oyata alaikal*) retook Kilinochchi (Jeyaraj 1999: 15), the government's troubles culminated in late 1999 and early 2000, when the LTTE, in a series of quick and coordinated campaigns, regained not only all the territory acquired by *Jaya Sikurai*, but eventually moved on to capture Elephant Pass and most of the Jaffna peninsula as well. In the midst of this, President Kumaratunge was almost killed in a LTTE suicide attack (27 bystanders were, in fact, killed), and the leading TULF moderate Neelan Thiruchelvan was grenaded by an LTTE assassin. Although Chandrika Kumaratunge was re-elected president in 1999, her People's Alliance lost control of Parliament in December 2001 to a UNP-led United National Front alliance of parties and Ranil Wickremasinghe, head of the UNP, became prime minister. The UNF's victory was, perhaps, partly occasioned by war-weariness in the south, and the lingering effects of the LTTE's attack, on 24 July 2001, on Sri Lanka's only international airport. Two months later, in

February 2002, the Sri Lankan government (or, at least, the Parliament) and the LTTE signed a long-term ceasefire agreement and shortly thereafter began Norwegian-brokered peace negotiations. This is the backdrop against which Sivaram's ideas achieved their final form and must be understood.

SIVARAM'S 'TURN'

Now those last years, from 1996 to 2002, were also when many claim Sivaram fully turned toward the LTTE. Of course, this is not true in any formal sense. Sivaram joined no other political organization after he left the PLOTE; and in 1998 (as confirmed to me by one of the other editors), and again in 2000, he vigorously, and successfully, resisted efforts by the LTTE to take financial and editorial control of TamilNet. Still, even assuming that what is under discussion is a major *intellectual* shift toward the LTTE, I have always found this a complex claim to evaluate because by 1997 Sivaram was working in two distinctly different venues: as Taraki, for the newspapers; and on the internet, as an anonymous features writer and editor for Tamilnet. com. Moreover, when people say Sivaram 'turned' toward the LTTE, they tend to see this as a simple political change, distinct both from Sivaram's military analysis and his own idiosyncratic overarching political ambitions: that is, to achieve what he called 'justice for the Tamil people' (which he believed required at least a radically restructured state), and, more generally, to disseminate knowledge about how to defeat state repression. Having carefully read almost everything Sivaram wrote during this period, I am convinced, on the contrary, that all these things were very subtly intertwined, and that Sivaram never became, simply, an LTTE supporter. For Sivaram never became anything *simply*.

So about the supposed turn to the LTTE: it is there, it is clearly discernible, but, until 2002, it is a gradual rather than a dramatic shift. In Sivaram's early writings, particularly in 1990 and 1991, Sivaram clearly regarded the LTTE as, among other things, a fascist organization. By 1993 and 1994, however, while not completely ceasing to be derogatory about its totalitarian tendencies, Sivaram began more to admire the LTTE's military cleverness.[8] Moreover, the fall of Jaffna, in November 1995, did mark a kind of turning point for him, though of a complex kind. On the one hand, privately, Sivaram was haunted by the event, as I knew because I was with him when it fell, and saw his bitterness. And one could also discern this, somewhat, in his writing about Chandrika Kumaratunge's PA government: his articles in 1994 and 1995, for example, range from gently pessimistic to rather positive; his comments after 1995 become increasingly caustic, though rarely openly hostile.[9] Even so, Sivaram's view of the LTTE remained relatively neutral with respect to its ideological aims (as it did, in his public work, until *after* the ceasefire was signed in 2002) even as his writing grew more admiring of the LTTE's military strategy. In his Taraki writings right up to the end of 1999, I find little evidence of any *ideological* rapprochement with the LTTE.

(Indeed, given the death of his cousin, it is difficult to imagine such a thing.) More clear, however, is an increasing bitterness about the lack of accomplishments by the other Tamil parties, and a growing cynicism about the Sinhalese left and its claims to be seeking a just solution – this last putting the final nail in the coffin of his old Marxist hope of a class-based solution to the ethnic problem.[10] Hence, by 1997, as I knew from our many conversations, Sivaram had come to believe Tamil nationalism and the LTTE to be, for good or ill, the only real games in town. That is, the only Sri Lankan Tamil forces to which those Sinhalese elites in government (regardless of party) had ever shown themselves responsive, and to which they were likely ever to concede anything real, even something really small, in the future.

Moreover, there were geopolitical facts to be taken into account. For Sivaram, key among these were the geostrategic interests of the US, India, and China in South Asia – especially with regard to the sea-lanes around Sri Lanka (Sivaram 2001). Further, Sivaram felt that the end of the Cold War (as he told me in 1997) had caused a general unleashing of 'super' versus 'regional' power conflicts in South Asia; and that this was a competition in which Sri Lanka and his Tamil people were likely to end up mere pawns. Finally, as he also told me in 2004, his contacts with Western intelligence and counter-insurgency strategists both in the West and in India (in 1995 and 1996) had convinced him that Sri Lanka was becoming, for them, a kind of laboratory for their counter-insurgency experiments. This last development especially, he felt, should be stopped.

So for all these reasons Sivaram began to think that the LTTE, however objectionable one might think it in other ways, must be supported. This was why, after 1997, much of Sivaram's energy shifted over to his work for TamilNet.com. For Sivaram had come to believe that the UTHR(J)'s reports and the Sri Lankan government's propaganda efforts threatened Tamil interests by continually throwing the bad behavior of the LTTE (and Tamil nationalism in general) into broad relief, while largely ignoring the way the government's Western-style counter-insurgency efforts were hurting (numerically) far more Tamil people in Sri Lanka's rural hinterlands. This biased attention, he felt, was eroding any future ability either the LTTE or a more general Tamil nationalism might have to wrest fundamental concessions from the Sri Lankan government. His answer was TamilNet.com: a Sri Lankan Tamil news agency so accurate and professional in its reporting that it could effectively shift international coverage by skewing what was looked at rather than by attacking what was said. All this Sivaram considered part of his project: his own contribution, as it were, to *counter* counter-insurgency. Nonetheless, his bitterness about the UTHR(J) from the mid 1990s onwards always seemed quite remarkable to me, and sometimes even unreasonable.

But Sivaram's new interest in the LTTE as a political goad did not get in the way of his military analysis of its tricks. In his last three years of writing the Taraki column, in 1997, 1998 and 1999, Sivaram continued to argue that the LTTE's responses to Operation *Jaya Sikurai* were strategic rather than evidence of its gradual decline due to the Sri Lankan army's General Grant-like war of attrition. His reasoning was complicated, but basically he saw that the LTTE was playing rope-a-dope with a largely intelligence-blind Sri Lankan army, getting them to spread out thinly over a lot of useless territory, and fighting them fiercely only when they strayed from the trap lines laid out for them.[11] He was right. Had his advice been heeded, the Sri Lankan army might have saved itself from a remarkable defeat in November 1999, although the slow preparations (one could hardly call them a 'run-up') for this LTTE counter-campaign took so long that even Sivaram began to doubt whether he was right (Taraki 1997c). Still, Sivaram never stopped pointing out the likelihood of a massive counter-strike by the LTTE, even though one must assume it was no help to the LTTE to have its plans so publicly anticipated. Here Sivaram's own political ends, his project of 'disseminating' knowledge about how counter-insurgency and *counter* counter-insurgency work as forms of power, took precedence. Hence, almost a year before the LTTE unleashed 'Unceasing Waves III' – the counter-attack that in six days retook all the land that *Jaya Sikurai* had originally taken, and eventually also captured Elephant Pass, the gateway to Jaffna – Sivaram had laid out his prescient speculations.

Sivaram was largely silent, under both his own name and his *nom de plume*, in 2000 and 2001, for his efforts were devoted to TamilNet. He did, however, give some important talks during this time, largely, for 'strategic reasons' – that is, to influence strategic policy – in Western venues to specialists interested in his geopolitical picture of the region. It was during this period, however, that Sivaram really formalized his views about 'counter-insurgency' and nationalism. That is, he began to come up with a more systematic theory about how counter-insurgency works (and how it helps form and maintain modern nation-states), and a separate theory – or, rather, set of what he called, *à la* Foucault (1977), 'counter-knowledges' – about how this must be opposed. In this light, he began to see the LTTE as a *counter* counter-insurgency force, or as a kind of *counter*-state in skillful if painful evolution. In 2002, Sivaram devoted his energies, for a while, to the *Northeastern Herald*, but only really re-emerged as a journalist in a big way (apart from TamilNet) in 2003–4 when he reopened his Taraki column and, under his own name, began another series in the leading Tamil-language daily, *Viirakeesari*. Only then, especially in his *Viirakeesari* columns, did Sivaram really present himself both as an unapologetic nationalist (something he had never ceased to be) and as an unabashed fellow traveler – albeit still clearly for his own reasons – of the LTTE.

Nonetheless, I have never felt, nor, I believe, can it be shown from Sivaram's writings, that he was ever an *uncomplicated* fan of the LTTE. The Sri Lankan cause to which Sivaram was devoted, and for which he was prepared to die, was, as he always put it, 'justice for the Tamil people.' And by 'justice' he had long meant either Eelam or a Sri Lankan state so restructured that Tamil people could never again be dominated by a Sinhalese majority acting strictly on its own behalf. But any fragile hope for this 'justice,' he believed, rested upon maintaining a precarious military-political parity between a united Tamil public and the Sinhalese (as he perceived it) state – a parity he saw as constantly threatened by modern counter-insurgency techniques. Since this parity in turn depended upon the military prowess of the LTTE, the LTTE, for good or ill, was the best he felt he could hope for – at least for the present. For Sivaram, to defy what his military and political logic told him was practical for reasons of his own ideological preference would have been tantamount to committing the very kind of Empedoclean folly he had so railed against in our discussions back in 1984. No, he felt he had to carry on with what actually was, and while one could debate some of Sivaram's political principles here (as I had, since 1984), or even his analysis of the post-ceasefire situation (I would not dare), his consistency was clear. This was the substance of Sivaram's so-called 'turn.'

OUR DISCUSSIONS OF STRATEGY

But all of Sivaram's justifications, here, ultimately rested upon two foundations: first, his view that counter-insurgency (C-I) was a peculiarly dangerous form of modern power that, when locally employed, threatened any possible 'just' solution to the ethnic conflict in Sri Lanka; and, second, his belief that states, nations, and nationalism were not really as many trendy Western scholars liked to portray them (a discussion to which we shall turn in the next chapter) because such portrayals inevitably left out or underestimated the extent to which C-I practices had reformulated most nation-states after World War II. With regard to the first of these notions, I had a number of discussions with Sivaram in 2004. One of these took place at his extremely modest house in Mt Lavenia on the night of our ill-fated trip to Batticaloa. It was March 2004, and it was the first time I had ever got him to spell out, clearly, his 'project.'

'My job,' he said then, as he sat fiddling with an article he was uploading to TamilNet, 'is to challenge this business of taking the state for granted, and to provide counter-knowledge to resist oppression becoming normal.'

'Oh,' I said. But then I was puzzled, not so much about his project but about its aims. For if one used nationalism to resist nationalist state oppression, I wondered, would that not recreate the very thing being fought? And could one not argue that insurgency and counter-insurgency (and *counter* counter-insurgency) similarly generated each other? So I asked him.

'As usual, you are getting everything glibly confused,' said Sivaram equably. And we went on to decide that, before I left we would have to have two long discussions – one on nationalism and one on military strategy. But just then Sivaram got the phone call that informed him that Karuna, the LTTE commander of the east, had just declared himself in rebellion against the rest of the LTTE. So, to follow that story, we left for Batticaloa – immediately, in the middle of the night – and kept moving from lead to lead (and so Sivaram could try 'peace talks') through the next week until we washed up five days later, after a news conference at the spanking new 'Peace Secretariat,' at an LTTE bar in much fought over Kilinochchi, capital of the Tiger-controlled Wanni. It was an outdoor place, pastel painted, with fake concrete bridges and tiny *faux* buildings, and it looked suspiciously like a miniature golf course – except that the little hut that should have been renting golf balls and putters sold arrack, beer, and plates of fried meat – what serious Tamil drinkers call 'taste' – instead. The waiters looked sternly teetotal and suspiciously fit. In any case, we were still alone at the table, the rest of the reportorial horde having not yet arrived, and I suddenly realized that, with so much happening, we had not had a chance to talk about his views all week.

'Would this be a good time to talk about C-I strategy and, what do you call it, counter C-I strategy?'

Sivaram's face suddenly lit up with wolfish enthusiasm and mischief.

'*Maccaang*, you are sitting in an example of counter C-I.'

'What?'

And he explained that just as one primary goal of C-I strategy was to shrink the political space in which rebellions can grow, so one goal of the LTTE's counter C-I strategy was to preserve that space, not just physically but also financially. So the LTTE, among other things, had restaurants, bars, and other 'gadgets' (Sivaram's favorite word) to generate revenue – along with many tax collectors, and police in snappy blue uniforms, to back them up. Rebellions, he told me, had to be financed too.

Putting off the heart of the matter for the moment, I asked him how his views on military matters had influenced his journalism.

'When I got hired by *The Island*,' he said, 'they were enthusiastic about having me because I was writing about the Tamil National Army and the Indian involvement in it ... it was considered an insider's view. And it was the first time technical military analysis was seen in writings on war in Sri Lanka. Words like: deployment, strategic advantage, and so forth. Otherwise it was just basic reporting. So my writings were the first that contained real strategic analysis. Iqbal Athas [who writes the "Situation Report" column for the *Sunday Times*] is a good reporter, but he does not do this kind of analysis. In any case, initially, some thought it was all written by an Indian officer. Neelan thought so.'

'Neelan Thiruchelvam?'

Sivaram nodded, and carefully poured his first glass of arrack.

'He told someone he thought Richard [de Zoysa] was translating these pieces and giving them to me. He did not believe I had the English to write such work.'

'He didn't think that by the time I talked to him in 1997.'

'The first phase of my writing,' Sivaram continued, ignoring this, 'was just covering the decline and fall of the TNA and the involvement of the Indian army. So there it was: basic knowledge and analysis of each engagement between the LTTE and TNA ... using what my columns became known for – an intimate knowledge of terrain and how to exploit it for military advantage. The second phase of my writing was about the start and progress of Eelam War Two, from June 1990. However, as you can see in my book, I predicted that war when I used the word "brinkmanship." So I was basically covering the war. And in that there are two main aspects you should note. First, I analyzed the growth of the LTTE from a guerrilla organization to an embryonic conventional army. And I also analyzed their larger strategic perspective, and argued that they had such a perspective. One article was: "The LTTE is now a conventional army" (in Taraki 1991: 80).'

Sivaram shifted in his seat and swirled the arrack in his glass. Other reporters were just beginning to trickle in. Sivaram drew an imaginary line on the pastel blue, concrete tabletop.

'That was one track. The other track is that I started increasingly to look at the SLA's strategy in the east as a laboratory case of standard counter-insurgency as disseminated by the British and the Americans. So this was the second strand of my writings. And I think this twin approach has continued: looking at the larger strategic approach and then also at [specific examples.] To put it in a nutshell, I think I should also tell you that I was invited to the University of Palmerston North, in New Zealand, in 1999 [and] most of my thinking ... on counter-insurgency in the east and other parts of the world were presented in a lecture that I gave there.'

'And you have this lecture?'

'I remember the argument. Basically ...'

But just then several other journalists from Jaffna and Batticaloa showed up at our table, along with the professional Sri Lankan photographer Dominic Sansoni, who also owned *Barefoot*, the famous and stylish Colombo clothing store. He said he was in Kilinochchi to snap photos of 'happy-looking Tigers' for an Italian news magazine.

'Have you seen any?' he asked, looking about affably.

'Well,' said a journalist from Jaffna, 'if we drink enough arrack, I'm sure we will.'

After that, the evening turned vividly social. Enlivened by several bottles of arrack, and a number of general journalistic squabbles, Sivaram and Dominic traded nostalgic stories about the brilliantly hybrid intellectual scene that had once flourished in Colombo at the Arts Center Club, in the Paradise Gallery, and at the Lionel Wendt Theater just prior to the JVP-government terror that crushed it. We memorialized its sad destruction with frequent toasts, and, gradually fading out, I realized that there would be no further discussion of C-I strategy tonight.

So, in fact, it was long afterwards that Sivaram and I were able to pick up the thread of our discussion again. The Karuna rebellion kept him so occupied for the next month that I rarely saw him, and so for the most part I pursued my own research in Kandy. When he did come to Kandy for a long visit, at the very end of April 2004, he felt more like discussing nationalism than military strategy. And then he was off again, back into his journalism and his project, on the run, working, and hard to contact. So it was not until I was almost ready to leave Sri Lanka, in July 2004, that Sivaram, at my urging, came to my house again to 'finish off the business,' as he put it.

Ann and I had been renting a lovely house high atop a mountain near Kandy. Surrounded by stout concrete walls, our two-story house had large windows upstairs that looked out over cool green hills and the valley below toward a crenellated line of blue mountains, often misty with fog or distant rain. Ann said the sight reminded her, sometimes, of the Smokey Mountains she used to camp in as a child. Sivaram said it was the only place he felt safe in Sri Lanka any more, 'only because no one knows I'm here, *maccaang.*' And so we talked.

'Basically,' said Sivaram, settling into the chair by my desk, and simultaneously editing a TamilNet article on his mobile phone, 'this is the argument I made in that lecture.'

Sivaram said that there were four basic things he tended to look at when thinking about counter-insurgency. First, there was the history of counter-insurgency as a practice. Focusing on Britain, the former colonial power with the greatest influence over Sri Lanka, Sivaram saw the origin of counter-insurgency as lying in the colonial wars of the nineteenth century. Moreover, he believed C-I generally remained 'still basically colonial in character. The wars in Sri Lanka and Ireland are basically wars of internal and real colonialism.' But Sivaram felt that C-I in its modern form found its start in Britain's successful C-I war in Malaysia and in its other post-World War II colonial wars. (Many other European states, of course, used C-I too – for example, the French did in Algeria – but Sivaram liked to focus on Britain, India, and the US because their practices eventually so influenced Sri Lanka's war.) In any case, to really get a sense of this history, Sivaram urged me to look up the writings of Frank Kitson, a British army C-I commander who honed his skills in Kenya 1953–5, Malaya 1957, Cyprus 1962–4, and Northern Ireland 1970–2. Kitson's unself-conscious memoir, Sivaram claimed, provided the most reliable if upsetting history of what went on in C-I campaigns (Kitson 1977). Moreover, to Sivaram's mind, Kitson's earlier book, *Low Intensity Operations* (1971) provided the most succinct C-I cookbook for states interested in suppressing dissent of any kind at every level. For almost all the tactics were there: the use of penetration agents, the mounting of psychological operations (or 'psyops' – that is, propaganda, misinformation, PR), the making of fake political concessions to split the opposition, the wielding of army counter-terror, the cordoning off of communities, the deployment of informers in hoods, and, somewhat less forthrightly, the 'rough' interrogations and 'wetwork' (that is, the hooding, torture, 'turning,' disposal, or dispatching of captives) that underlie so many C-I campaigns.[12]

'I gave the fucking book to Karuna,' said Sivaram, shaking his head disgustedly. 'That bugger always liked to borrow books. He never gave it back.'

Second, Sivaram believed one had to look at C-I's modern manifestations, particularly at what he called the 'post-Cold War theories of terrorism and counter-insurgency.' He said: 'I see all this as an outgrowth of what was being done during the Cold War. But now what is being done has evolved into something else, into this discourse on terrorism and what some Pentagon theorists call "warriorism".' Sivaram felt that while this new discourse was still based on 'traditional counter-insurgency practice,' 'terrorism' had now become 'part of the conceptual baggage of counter-insurgency.'

'I presented a paper about all this in 1998 at the University of Oslo to a couple of people from the Norwegian foreign ministry in which I argued that it was all based on the concept of asymmetric warfare – basically guerrilla warfare in a new garb. In asymmetric warfare the US has to face an enemy quite different from the Marxist guerrillas of the Cold War. But, I must also say, you could see that their new enemy was being constructed, that they [were] fighting enemies they themselves created – [in] Afghanistan, Iraq; but Iraq might be different: we will see – whereas in counter-insurgency the enemy [started out] quite real. [In any case] in the post-Cold War world organizations like FARC [in Colombia], and the PKK [the Kurds], and the New People's Army, and a lot of these guerrilla organizations that were forces to be reckoned with, have seen some decline. This is all because counter-insurgency works.'

A third thing to look at, said Sivaram, was his specific studies of counter-insurgency in the Eastern Province. In this regard, Sivaram pointed me toward two articles he wrote in the early 1990s: 'Govt's counter-insurgency programme and LTTE's military response' (Sivaram 1994a), and 'Pacifying the East?' (Taraki 1993b). Taking them in reverse chronological order, Sivaram pointed out that his *Tamil Times* article was a meditation on the Sri Lankan army strategy being illustrated in two, then ongoing, operations: 'White Eagle,' south-west of Trincomalee (Sri Lanka's famous, eastern, deep-water port); and 'Jayamaga,' north-west of Vavuniya. Sivaram had started his written discussion of them by focusing on terrain:

The ability of a guerrilla group to operate successfully in the Eastern Province is derived from five vast hinterland zones comprising the dry zone jungle, shrub, marshes, slash and burn plots and paddy fields separated from the populated coastal areas of the province by lagoons and jungles. (Sivaram 1994a)

After discussing these zones in detail (he eventually concluded there were seven), Sivaram went on to argue that the British and American C-I model being used by the army here laid out three basic methods to 'limit and, if possible, ultimately destroy the LTTE's logistic and tactical mobility along with its popular support among the Tamils' (ibid). These methods were: (a) the complete evacuation or destruction of villages; (b) the destruction of crops and the prevention of cultivation – a 'scorched-earth policy'; (c) the control of supplies available to civilians living near rebel areas, for 'the army insures that in all seven zones there is direct control on, and supervision of, the amount of food and medicine each family buys and takes into their area of residence' (Sivaram 1994a). Moreover, he argued:

In addition to the standard C-I methods described above, the deployment of small and highly mobile special forces commandoes which are constantly roaming one part or the other of the hinterland zones has greatly reduced the tactical mobility of the LTTE in the field and resulted in the loss of a large number of important Tiger cadres. Probhakaran's answer to this problem has been to pull out his key commanders and political workers from the east. (Sivaram 1994a)

'So the army was winning?' I asked, curious, 'Their CI campaign was working?'

'That is what I thought then. I later realized I was partly mistaken, but that is what I *thought*. In this article I was criticizing the LTTE for not picking up on this strategy.'

Sivaram shook his head, laughing. He explained that while he had accurately observed the government's C-I techniques, he had missed the LTTE's *counter* counter-insurgency strategy.

'Anyway, I also wrote an [earlier] article after a dangerous trip I took in 1993 to Tirukkovil in which I talked about a counter-insurgency program.' That article, 'Pacifying the East?' written shortly after the fall of Pooneryn, began with a review of a similarly themed presidential speech. Sivaram wrote:

The widely held view in military, political and Western diplomatic circles that local government elections followed by economic development could expedite and consolidate the process of pacification in the east which in turn enable the government to hit hard at the LTTE in the north was thus expressed by the president [Premadasa] in his characteristic style at Ratnapura on October 28. (Taraki 1993b).

Sivaram pointed out that Premadasa's speech here betrayed the president's exposure to the language of C-I, where 'pacification' is a technical term with a long history, as well as one with a central place in the 'well-developed jargon' of C-I since World War II. In any case, Sivaram, always careful to define his terms, argued that there were in general three basic modes of 'pacification,' although which mode a government chooses should be determined by the root causes of its conflict. These modes were: (a) land reform plus some promise of political reform – where the rebellion derives its motivation from class inequality; (b) devolution and some regional autonomy – where ethnic grievances fueled the rebellion; or (c) disenfranchisement of local warrior groups, a no longer relevant technique once practiced by the British in colonial Tamil Nadu (as laid out in Sivaram's eleven-part series on the history of Tamil militarism in 1992). The key feature of all of these modes, of course, was the same: 'the closure of the political space from which a rebellion derives its staying power and ability to spread its influence with ease.'

But, again, Sivaram felt his analysis was incomplete because it fell short of a complete understanding of the full scope and pervasiveness of counter-insurgency doctrine. This remained so, he felt, until 1995, 'when I started traveling abroad and started buying books on these matters. Until then I had been reading piecemeal about counter-insurgency techniques. So it was after this that I started developing a more comprehensive perspective and understanding of counter-insurgency. Fortunately, the British defense attaché in Colombo, who became a good drinking buddy, was a specialist in the matter. He had first-hand experience in Ireland and Oman. And the most important thing: he was a protégé of Frank Kitson, the father of modern counter-insurgency techniques.'

'You're kidding.'

'No, young man, I am not kidding.'

The fourth thing Sivaram thought worth looking at were the political and global aspects of counter-insurgency doctrine and practice.

'Here,' said Sivaram, still working with his stylus at his phone, 'I will give a little bit of explanation.' He eyed me, flipped the front of his phone down, set it carefully on my desk, and put himself in lecture mode. That is, he swirled his glass and settled back even further in his chair.

'Counter-insurgency is not a military phenomenon. It has to be understood as a political-military phenomenon. So it has very strong political components, such as promoting Sistani, the Shia guy in Iraq who keeps telling Sadr to stop.[13] The political component itself – and how it is deployed by strategists to achieve the objective of a counter-insurgency campaign – is very important to understand. So here I have to say that when speaking of the political component we are also speaking of a certain amount of anthropological and sociological and religious-studies knowledge. These forms of knowledge are very important here ... because one of the main things about counter-insurgency is to divide the target population – to prevent them from coalescing into one body. So the political component is very important; and anthropological knowledge is very important. For example, in Vietnam consider the use the US made of the Montagnards and other small groups. And India is always doing this too. To fight the Nagas, they used a very small ethnic group called the Kukis [pronounced "cookies"].'

He stopped for a second, finished his glass, and pursed his lips.

'There is also a geostrategic component. In many counter-insurgency events multiple states get involved. Usually it is one state using insurgency to destabilize another. These are the four things we should look at.'

'So?'

'So we will go into each component tomorrow. I'm going to bed, *maccaang*.'

And he did. But as I mounted the stairs to go to bed, I noticed that Sivaram nervously checked the doors, twice. That night, in bed, Ann turned to me and said she had to tell me something about Sivaram. He had called her from Batticaloa several days before arriving to check where I was, and to make sure I was not headed his way.

'What? *Why?*'

'It was all about Karuna. He told me he was in danger. He was out there researching a story and got hemmed in, and he wasn't sure he was going to make it. But he made me promise not to tell you. He said you would try to come. He just wanted to make sure you wouldn't.'

'For God's sake Ann, you should have told me!'

'No, he asked me not to, and I thought he didn't need to worry about getting both of you out. But I'm telling you now.'

'Just how bad was it?'

'I don't know. Bad. But he made it. Someone smuggled him out of Batticaloa in the boot of a car. Let's all get some sleep. And hope nobody comes after him here.'

Before he left our house, Ann told me she had seen Sivaram standing alone in my office. He had been slowly pivoting, his eyes running carefully over all the documents that were scattered there. 'And,' she said, 'he had the saddest expression on his face. Infinitely sad. I thought he might be thinking of his father, of the futility of scholarship. But I think he also realized that this was it, the sum of his life in all those bits of paper. I think he knew you were his repository, and this might soon be his memorial.' Sivaram said that he could sleep in our house – as his snores proved. We never knew what visit might be his last.

CONTAINMENT

The next afternoon – for he had gone out during the morning to see journalists in Kandy – Sivaram did not feel like immediately picking up the intellectual threads of the night before.

'Before I go into conventional warfare strategies and so forth let me come to something that has been bothering me since 2001. The military strategy of containment – not in the Cold War sense, but in a military sense of the containment of insurgencies – and basically this is the paper I presented at the Center for Strategic and International Studies (CSIS) in Washington DC (Sivaram 2001). [I was invited by] Teresita Schaffer, the ex-ambassador from the US to Sri Lanka ([from] around 1994 or 1995); she is in charge of the South Asia section of CSIS.[14] [In the audience were people] from the Joint Chiefs of Staff's office, from the State Department, [one] from the Office of the Secretary of Defense, the CIA, the Sri Lankan embassy, and several other important guests.

'So there I did a comparative study of containment in which I argued that the Sri Lankan army in 2001, when things were not going well, had come to a point where it could only think of containing the LTTE because it had lost its offensive capability with the failure of Operation 'Rod of Fire' (*Agni Khiela*) [in April 2001][15] ... I argued that the Sri Lankan government's approach boiled down to a strategy of containing the LTTE by engaging it in talks. And I think I made the point that peace talks are a very important component of a containment strategy. I gave the example of FARC ... drawing a parallel to what happened in Colombia. The US Defense Intelligence Agency – there is a place in Alexandria, a sprawling massive operation – said in 1997 that the Colombian state was collapsing. They gave a lot of reasons, yet the bottom line was they said that Colombia was in a state of collapse: the military weak, the government tottering, and so forth. So I said: yet Colombia is still there. Why?'

'Well, why?' I said.

'It did not collapse,' Sivaram went on, 'because of several factors. Basically, the US was able to influence or direct the Colombian state to engage in various measures to contain the FARC. The main method was to ... concede 40 per cent of its territory to FARC and start talks. But during this period, while the FARC was contained by talks, the US pumped in the largest amount of military aid ... given to any country in Latin America – all under the excuse of fighting narcotics. There were also a few operations, which were designed to apply maximum pressure on FARC and to blunt its growing conventional capabilities. But the talks were the main thing.

'Now containment,' he continued, 'is what is applied in situations where counter-insurgency methods have failed to successfully deliver the desired results. Containment, as I see it, is the means by which one uses political means to stop a guerrilla organization that shows a clear capability to collapse a state. (I use "collapse" in the active voice. The best example is El Salvador.) Containment in the sense we are talking about here "locks" an insurgent movement into a political mood usually using the bait of political recognition through talks. Once locked into the negotiating mode, the insurgent movement will have to indefinitely postpone or, rather, put on hold, the timetable of its war strategy. (I am talking about war because we are discussing its war against the state.) This gives a wide range of opportunities for the state and its backers to strengthen the state's military, and get massive infusions of foreign defense aid and assistance – which are otherwise stymied during the war due to regular exposures of human rights violations.'

He stopped and looked fierce for a moment.

'Now I am saying all this about containment and negotiations as a key component of this military strategy regardless of those who will cry foul at me for taking a "cynical and militaristic" attitude to conflict resolution, peace processes, negotiations, etc. *But I say that the ultimate test of the real nature of talks that states engage in with insurgent movements – i.e., to see whether it is containment or a genuine desire to change – is whether any externally underwritten commitment has been made by the state in question to restructure itself at least in regard to those aspects which in the first place generated the insurgent movement.* [Emphasis his, judging by the way he was slapping the table at each word.]

'What are some test cases?' he asked, rhetorically.

'A classic example,' he answered himself, 'is provided by the talks between the FMLN in El Salvador. All the detail on that can be provided by your wife, Ann.' Calling out to her in her office, he said: 'Can you, Ann?'

'Can I what?'

'Can you tell us about the FMLN? Or the Zapatistas in Mexico?'

Ann provided us with a summary as she swept about the house picking up books, papers, and her briefcase. 'I'm headed out right now to give my seminar at the university. But we can talk more tonight, maybe, if you're here?'

'Fine. Fine.'

'Bye Ann!' I called out to her retreating form as she ran out to a waiting three-wheeler.

'Bye!'

Sivaram continued:

'The US got the FMLN to talk just as they were poised to overrun the country, but nothing happened in the talks. Example number two: the New People's Army (NPA) in the Philippines. It was the largest insurgent movement in the 1980s. Then they started talks with the Philippine government. Now they are split, weakened, their membership has dwindled, and they are fucked. And who is facilitating the talks? Norway. The coincidence is remarkable.'

'Why Norway?' I asked, fascinated but rather worried by the direction this was taking.

'The US during the Cold War developed them as a listening post. Norway is a US handmaiden. Anyway, so the NPA split, the leaders are in exile, the movement limps on. Still, there are talks; but the US has signed several defense treaties with the Philippines and there is nothing the NPA can do about it. You should look for an article called "Crumbs for Asia's Finest Puppet" by Sonny Africa (2004). And the FARC was also messed up by the same process. They talked, the army moved in, so the FARC got fucked. You see, modern states don't think of totally destroying insurgent movements. They aim to weaken and keep them within a tolerable level.'

'But isn't it possible,' I asked, 'that a state *might* be willing to restructure itself to end a conflict?'

'Such restructuring would have to include the monopoly of violence held by the state-controlling group. But this never happens for this monopoly is the last thing that a state-controlling group will give up. No,' he shook his head, and said, determinedly: '*the state never gives up its monopoly of violence.*

'So,' he continued, 'we talked about the FARC, Zapatistas, and a whole host of others who got fucked by this kind of containment. And, most important, is the example of the Nagas separatist movement – who have been locked in talks since 1997. What India could not achieve by fighting them for 50 years they achieved by locking them up in talks. I could go into this in detail. This is the kind of knowledge that no state wants to be disseminated.'

'You should write a book.'

'I did. But I don't have time to write another. That is why I'm talking to you. Only ...' he started laughing, 'for God's sake, don't make this sound like a book of fucking anthropology.'

Pausing only long enough to enjoy my chagrin, he went on:

'The second test of whether such talks are a component of a containment strategy is a state's hand in inducing or promoting splits in the insurgent movement – covertly, for the peace period offers the best opportunity for this. Karuna ...' Sivaram's voice momentarily roughened, 'is an example. He was not induced; but he is being promoted. But keep in mind throughout your book on me that this is all about the control that state-controlling groups have on some basic monopolies. These are not easily given up – this is what all my arguments are based on. So state-controlling groups won't – in fact, nobody will – part with money or power. This is just human nature. There is no arguing about that.

'The third test of such talks,' he said, gesturing at my computer screen for me to continue, 'is the degree to which the state and its international backers (here I largely mean the US – though the Russians, French, Indians, and Brits have been known to do this as well) show a greater interest in "pacifying" the target population with aid, psychological operations, so-called confidence-building measures, and NGOs than in restructuring fundamental aspects of the state that led to the insurgency. There is a RAND book on the Zapatistas that talks about all this. But I'll give an example. In Sri Lanka, talks have been going on for almost three years now. Fiscal devolution was important to the LTTE because the Parliament controlled all the wealth. So one of their key demands was devolution of fiscal policy. So what do we see? All sorts of aid that provides temporary band-aids while the key issue of fiscal devolution is not addressed. All this is aimed at preventing the population from backing another challenge by the insurgent movement to the state's monopoly of violence and wealth. This is a way to not break but erode the will of the people. Go to the CSIS website and type "Sivaram" and get what they said about what I said.'

'I will. But had you written about this anywhere else at the time?'

'When I came back from the US [in 2001] after giving my paper I wrote about containment in Tamil in the Batticaloa paper, *Thinakathir.* This is where my head got broke in the beating that occurred in December 2001. Anyway, I wrote this and then the LTTE's former leader of EROS – their house intellectual, Velupillai Balakumar – wrote an article saying that Taraki is saying all this, and that the LTTE is aware of these things and knows what to do. To some extent I think this was true.'

'Daddy! Uncle Sivaram!' My seven-year-old son, David, suddenly arrived, bearing tidings of dinner (from Ann, back from Peradeniya), and started crawling on Sivaram.

'Am I a chair! Am I a chair for you, young man?' said Sivaram, in mock anger. But he made no move to push him off.

'*David!*' I yelled, when he reached what seemed to be a particularly painful position, using Sivaram's hair as a handhold. I reached out to grab him; Sivaram waved me away.

'Leave him be, *maccaang.*'

SIVARAM DISCUSSES THE STRATEGIC ASPECTS OF THE WAR

After dinner, while I put David to bed, Ann and Sivaram spent time discussing various American interventions in Latin America. Then Ann had to retreat to her office to prepare a lecture for the next day, and we brought our computers (Sivaram had his laptop) and my tape-recorder out to the dining room table and worked there. Sivaram wanted to discuss his views of the strategic aspects of what he called 'the Eelam war.'

'When,' I asked, 'did you first start to write about the strategies being employed in the war?'

'My strategic view was first stated in the *Island* article, "The LTTE is now a conventional army" (in Taraki 1991: 80). Here I took a look at some of the larger strategic aspects of the war. Basically, that the LTTE was aspiring to emerge and function as a conventional army in the north. In essence, I was saying – and few people realized it at the time – that the Tigers had thought out a strategy, consciously or unconsciously, to overcome the aims of the counter-insurgency war that the Sri Lankan government was fighting against them. One of the objectives and intended or unintended effects of counter-insurgency is that it precludes the means of guerrilla warfare developing into a serious challenge to the state's monopoly on violence.'

'So counter-insurgency works?' I asked, again.

'Of course it works. Counter-insurgency has been successful in 80 out of 100 cases. But the point is that the LTTE's project of starting a conventional army was a direct challenge to the goal of counter-insurgency. Because, as we shall see when we discuss counter-insurgency, the aim of counter-insurgency is to prevent a guerrilla organization from acquiring enough material and political resources to pose a serious challenge to the state's monopoly on violence – something which guerrilla movements as such cannot do.'

At this point, Sivaram stood up, stretched, and walked into the kitchen to pour himself another shot of arrack. Then he wandered about the room, continuing his lecture.

'Of course, my observations were not properly understood at the time because the mindset of the Sri Lankan army then was entirely in a counter-insurgency mode. Mainly, they were being advised by British guys who just thought, "These are some slipper-wearing guys – what the hell do they know?" Their image of very poor Third World fellows in slippers had no connection with strategic thought.'

Sivaram paused, laughed, and then slipped back into lecturing.

'As the first phase of its project of becoming an army the LTTE concentrated its resources in the north by pulling out the majority of its fighters from the east as soon as the Indian army left. The LTTE had acquired a large stock of weapons from the TNA, which was being armed by the Indian army. These included the Swedish Bofors recoilless rifles (the Carl Gustavs). And once they had done this – concentrated in the north – they set about creating a liberated zone where they could raise adequate resources to establish and expand a conventional fighting force. Of course, on the government side, neither the army nor the political leaders had a strategic perspective on what was going on – and even their British and Indian advisers did not. One of the main effects of counter-insurgency is that it keeps the insurgent movement dispersed. The middle-class romantics who start out fighting such guerrilla wars often don't understand the nature of power. They think of Che in the jungles and get caught up in the romance of roughing it that way. But they do not understand the key issue involved in challenging a state. The key thing is whether you can really challenge the state's monopoly of violence. That is the only thing that can compromise the state. So I said they had no perspective on this matter.'

'Well, what happened then?'

'From 1990 to 1994 the Sri Lankan government under the UNP was focused largely on the east, and on winning the counter-insurgency operation there. They believed that if the east was completely pacified the LTTE could be contained in the north, and Eelam as a physical and political reality would be scuttled. At the same time, as the east was being pacified, the LTTE could be contained in the north – particularly in Jaffna – and dominated piecemeal by drawing out the LTTE in large numbers into battle and killing them and depleting their numbers with superior fire-power. This was embodied in General Kobbekaduwa's dictum: "I am not interested in real estate." By which he meant that his aim was not to take territory but to draw out the LTTE and kill as many of them as possible. He was commander in the early 1990s, and he is still considered one of the best commanders of the Sri Lankan army, and the one who first enunciated this dictum. So this was their approach.

'So there were several operations launched in the north to achieve this. The most well known was Operation Thunder. It was an attack on the LTTE's military heartland in southern Mullaitivu – which the LTTE moved into during the IPKF war and turned into their main base. The LTTE fought back, lost many fighters. But the fighting was so intense that the Sri Lankan army never got anywhere near the main base. And they did not really want to, although if they could have gotten the base that would have been fine. Their main idea was basically Jomini's; that is, when you threaten a place that is vital to the enemy, he will be compelled to pour a lot of his resources into defending it. So they were working on this idea in the north. They got a taste for it when the LTTE lost over 600 fighters in the battle for Elephant Pass in 1991, where most were killed in open spaces by Sri Lankan air force bombing and artillery fire. They thought they should keep doing this, and continued with this strategy of threatening a vital point, making them defend it, and killing them with superior fire-power. At the same time, they – the Sri Lankan army – adopted the strategy of isolating Jaffna by setting up a string of camps on the east–west access between the peninsula and the mainland.'

'Why was this necessary to the strategy?"

Sivaram sat down again at the table and swirled his drink.

'It was necessary to isolate the LTTE militarily inside Jaffna so they could be crushed there without any escape routes. The policy of strangling Jaffna involved blocking off any means the LTTE might have of withdrawing into the Wanni in the face of a Sri Lankan army assault – so the LTTE would be compelled to fight and lose a lot of fighters. But the LTTE attacked one of these key camps – Pooneryn – and overran it in November 1993. That was the first indication – which came as a bit of a shock to the Sri Lankan government – that the LTTE had developed conventional and amphibious capabilities. The LTTE called the operation 'frog' (*thavaLai*). So this showed that the LTTE's conventional fighting power had expanded despite the afore-mentioned strategy. Now the army re-established the camp when the LTTE withdrew, but it had made the point that the strategy had failed.'

'Did anything else happen to show this?' I was searching my memory, trying the review the many 'operations' he had written about.

'It was becoming increasingly clear. For there was another operation that demonstrated the expansion of the LTTE's conventional capabilities. This was called *Yarl Devi*, named after the train that used to run to Jaffna before the war. The operation was meant to interdict the only remaining route that the LTTE had between Jaffna and the mainland. The point of the operation was to go from Elephant Pass camp along the lagoon coast – and a dirt road there – to Kilali, from where the LTTE ran a ferry service to Nallur. So the LTTE counter-attacked and routed this operation. Bottom line, these showed that the LTTE's conventional capabilities had grown quite remarkable.'

I poured him another drink and asked what effect this growth in the LTTE's conventional power eventually had.

'By 1994, the big question was the LTTE's conventional military power. So that became the big problem. The UNP was planning a big operation to take Jaffna. It was all shelved due to the elections when Chandrika was elected to power. But the argument at this time among the Sri Lankan establishment and among the Tamil groups working with the army was that counter-insurgency was not yielding results. They were arguing that the only way to bring down the LTTE was to take out Jaffna. The argument was that Jaffna was the head, and if you knock off the head, the body will fall. And if Jaffna goes, then the expatriate Tamils [from whom much of the LTTE's funding comes] will lose faith in the LTTE and stop contributing money – because the majority of the expatriates are from Jaffna. However, from the military point of view, taking on Jaffna was aimed at destroying the means by which the LTTE could sustain its conventional fighting capabilities.'

'Sivaram,' I said, rather puzzled, 'I'm not sure I know what "sustaining its conventional fighting capabilities" means.'

'Well, here I have to make a small intervention: how do you precisely distinguish a conventional from a guerrilla war? Has it ever occurred to you?'

'Not really.'

'Conventional warfare is the kind of engagement in which battalion-sized (about 1000 soldiers – but it varies from country to country) or larger-sized formations fight each other, with supplies flowing from the rear. You can check my definitions against most books in the literature. But to support this you need to satisfy the following five conditions.'

He started ticking them off on his fingers, so I typed them out as a list.

1. You need a politically motivated population base from which you can raise several battalions.
2. You have to have an economy from which you can raise enough resources to clothe, arm, feed, and deploy these conventional forces.
3. You have to have a secure territory where you can train and barrack your forces.
4. You need an efficient logistics system, such as is described in Martin Van Creveld's *Supplying War: Logistics from Wallenstein to Patton* (1977).[16]

'Look,' he said, continuing, 'a guerrilla army has no logistics department. As a fish swimming in the sea, it gets its supplies from the population. But an army marches on its stomach. Now suppose a soldier on the move requires a kilo of supplies for a day. (You can get real estimates from books.) If you have a battalion, you must move 1000 kilos, and their ammunition, and the fuel for the whole battalion. And then there is one more condition:

5. Unless your soldier knows that he is going to be treated, he will not fight. So you have to have the facilities to treat at least a battalion of wounded fighters.

So the military thought that, *sans* Jaffna, all the requirements for sustaining and deploying a conventional force (except number three) would be denied to the LTTE. So the focus was on taking Jaffna and destroying the LTTE's conventional capability. This became the top priority.'

He paused and looked carefully at my screen and at what I had written there. Reaching over me, he corrected a spelling mistake, and then, nodding, pointed to where I had stopped. 'Here a small political note. The presence of another conventional force in the hands of somebody who is challenging the monopoly of violence of a state means that the state's monopoly of violence is gone. So a state will strive to its utmost to keep this from happening.'

'Are you saying that was what happened here?'

He nodded his assent, and continued:

'So when the talks failed, this was the strategic plan that was implemented and that people thought was best. Then Jaffna was taken in 1995 (that is, Jaffna town was taken in late 1995; the rest of the peninsula in early 1996) and the US, Britain, and everybody thought it was the beginning of the end for the LTTE. Now, they said, the LTTE is just a guerrilla organization confined to the Wanni. So I wrote an article, "Game plan for a grand slam" (Taraki 1996a). I said: Jaffna was being talked about as a victory. But you have to *define* victory in war. You win, I argued, when you have destroyed the enemy's will to fight you, and/or destroyed his military assets to a point where your enemy is no longer in a position to fight you. I argued that the LTTE had pulled out all its military assets – troops, ordnance, ordnance factories, everything. So, I said, it is not correct to talk about Jaffna as a "victory" that would permanently force the LTTE to become a guerrilla organization.'

Sivaram pointed out that the same principle was being invoked, however, when the government bombed Kilinochchi hospital in July 1996 to deny Tigers a place to take their wounded. But that was during the Tiger attack on Mullaitivu, the very battle that signaled the failure of the Sri Lankan army's strategy.

'It was the biggest attack that the SLA had ever seen,' said Sivaram. 'They lost 1400 men in just two days of fighting. And the LTTE made off with the armory and two 122 mm artillery guns. That was also the first time the LTTE could hold a place they overran – 'cause the army never went back. The army tried amphibious and paratroop operations with special forces to regain the place, but neither worked. The LTTE beat them back. This showed that my argument was right. And it also clearly showed that there was no strategic thinking among the army and its advisers – that the British and Americans and Indians had no strategic perspective on what was going on.'

'Were there American advisers around then?'

'They were around, but not in a big way yet. Anyway, now again the priority was to break the conventional fighting capability of the Tigers – which they found had, contrary to their expectations, actually *increased*. This showed that the LTTE was focused on its project of becoming a conventional army, the real challenge to a monopoly of power. [As early as] 1991, when the LTTE attacked Elephant Pass, I said "There are two armies in Sri Lanka now." I was also well-known for this; it was quoted everywhere.'

'So what happened then?' I asked.

'The LTTE stayed focused on its project. And the army wanted to prevent this. So how do you break the LTTE's conventional capability? There was a parallel concern: on the other hand, how do you keep [SLA-occupied] Jaffna supplied since it was cut off from the rest of Sri Lanka by the Wanni? Logically, the shortest overland route to Jaffna was from Mannar [a small peninsula, south of Jaffna on the north-west coast] to Pooneryn [on the Jaffna lagoon] – this was the shortest and safest route because on the one side is the sea so you only have to defend from the east. And that is what the army intelligence and planners were talking about. However, the Indians, who were also taking a great interest in seeing the LTTE reduced to a guerrilla organization, took another view. They pressed the government to apply Jomini's principle. They, of course, did not say precisely 'Jomini's principle'; but it was the same idea. Kill two birds with one stone: open up a supply route *and* destroy the conventional capability of the LTTE. They pushed the idea of attacking the A9 [the main highway from Vavuniya to Jaffna], saying it would pose the danger of cutting the Wanni, the LTTE heartland, in two. And that, understanding the dire consequences of having the Wanni divided into two, the LTTE would draw in all its resources, and then you [could] kill them. So the logical route was abandoned, this A9 route was taken, and the war starts.'

'Now,' said Sivaram, up and wandering about the dining room again, 'in 1997 I was in the US at a meeting with Pentagon guys – I was there for a long time – and a little later in England at a meeting with a senior British Military Intelligence officer. So on both sides of the Atlantic, though I first heard it in Washington, I got told the same argument. It was about *Jaya Sikurai* (which means 'victory assured'), which was what they called the A9 campaign, the largest operation the Sri Lankan army had ever launched against the LTTE. The argument went like this: a war of attrition along the A9 will eventually wear down the LTTE because, after all, the Sinhalese, being the majority, can throw more resources and people into the fray so that, at the end of the day, though the LTTE might win some victories, the preponderance of Sinhalese people and stuff will win it.'

I told Sivaram that, to me, this sounded suspiciously like a theory developed by a US Civil War buff enamored of Grant's strategy against Lee. Sivaram agreed; it did. But he called it, instead, the 'creeping advantage argument' (Taraki 1997c), and said that it seemed to him at first to have some truth to it. He was particularly interested in the possibility that attrition might wear away at the LTTE's raw recruitment numbers enough to ensure eventual defeat. So he decided to think about this in May 1997, in a long column entitled 'The cat, the bell, and a few strategists' (Taraki 1997a). Here he decided to test the 'creeping advantage argument' by applying the theories of the military sociologist, Stanislav Andreski, as outlined in his book, *Military Organization and Society* (1968), which has a curious introduction by Radcliffe-Brown. About Andreski's book, Sivaram wrote:

His is the only academic treatise ... on the connection between populations and the quantum of organized fighting men they can produce and sustain. He is best known among defense specialists for introducing the concept of Military Participation Ratio (MPR), by which, when other factors are taken into account, the degree to which a society is militarized may be measured. (Taraki 1997a)

According to Sivaram, the MPR of any population varies according to a lot of factors, not the least being whether recruitment is largely voluntary or enforced. During the American Civil War MPRs as high as 10 per cent were seen. But, in general, MPRs tend to be much lower in modern warfare and must be measured against a given army's ideal size or 'optimum force level.'

An optimum force level is the number of troops that can most effectively be used against a state's security forces which is compatible with a rebel military organization's financial resources, administrative efficiency, political cohesion, logistical capability, and the extent of safe terrain available for training and stationing troops in secrecy. (Taraki 1997a)

Sivaram's basic argument was that in order for any rebellion to continue, an insurgent population's MPR must be high enough to sustain its fighting force's optimum force level. In other words, MPR was *relative to* optimum force level. Now in Sri Lanka, attempts to deny the LTTE access to recruitment centers and to use terror to induce what counter-insurgency experts call 'war-weariness' in the Sri Lankan Tamil population to inhibit participation, had, according to Sivaram's calculations, temporarily reduced the Sri Lankan Tamil MPR from a high of 2.8 per cent to as low as .03 per cent in 1989 (under the Indians, who used a 'saturation strategy' to deny recruitment); but those low levels had recovered quickly to a sustained 1.1 per cent after 1991. MPR levels were highest (and well above 1.1 per cent) in the Batticaloa District, according to a statistical survey Sivaram carried out of recruitment in villages in the Tiger-occupied zone, suggesting that efforts there to suppress recruitment by creating 'war-weariness' had, if anything, produced the opposite result. At the same time, and perhaps more importantly, the LTTE had developed a special training regime that allowed it to keep a relatively low optimum force level compared, say, to the Sri Lankan army, which, given its completely different strategic necessities (i.e. of occupying, saturating, and defending hostile territory rather than staging opportunistic attacks) required a much higher optimum force level. Further, the LTTE had kept its optimum force levels small even while increasing its effectiveness as a fighting force – as measured, that is, by the damage it was able to inflict during this period. This, in turn, meant that an MPR of 1.1 per cent (about 2000 new recruits a year) was, in fact, more than enough to sustain the LTTE's 'optimum force level' indefinitely.[17] For Sivaram, in the end, this suggested that Operation *Jaya Sikurui*, the vaunted A9 highway campaign to wear down the LTTE, was not going to be the 'military textbook cake walk that many, including some Western defense specialists, think it has to be (Taraki 1997a).

'In November 1999,' Sivaram continued, 'the LTTE rolled back in six days everything the government achieved from May 1997. So I wrote an article for TamilNet.com on 16 December 1999 (a "News Feature" entitled "Tiger manoeuvres trouble gateway garrison", TamilNet 1999). I argued that it was becoming increasingly difficult to defend Elephant Pass. It was thought to be one of the most highly defended garrisons in South Asia. And the US army visited Elephant Pass and said it was impregnable. They thought that the LTTE were amateurs; they didn't think that the LTTE was capable of maneuver. But I foreshadowed that it could be taken.'

And it soon was.

THE AIMS AND METHODS OF C-I DOCTRINE

Sivaram paused for a moment, as if considering where to go next. He decided to pick up our discussion from where we had left off the day before. He reminded me of what we had already said about C-I doctrine and 'pacification.' He then asked me to reflect on the tactics Kitson and his ilk advocated, and that we both knew had been used with such devastating consequences (and some effectiveness) in the Batticaloa District.

'You must see that C-I,' he said, intently, 'is about forcing the target population to lose its collective will to achieve the objective which you are trying to destroy or head off. The problem is that quite often academics tend to miss the wood for the trees. The point that they miss is that the state is always focused on destroying the political will of the target population, and that the art and science of doing that is counter-insurgency – including its political components.'

'Well, how *do* you break the will of a population?' I asked.

'Not in any particular order,' he said, ticking them off on his fingers (so I listed them below):

1. Massacres and terror. Frank Kitson has a nice phrase for this. One of the proponents of this is Lunstead, in Mclintock's book. Of course, terror has been typically used since ancient times – Genghis Kahn used it: well displayed massacres; massacres done as spectacle so everyone knows about it.
2. Arrest, detention, torture, all indiscriminate, and interrogation to destroy the basis of civil society. All of this denies one's sense of rights. You want people to lose track of the idea that they have rights of any kind. You reduce them to a point where staying alive becomes their top priority.
3. Checkpoints, unreasonably positioned checkpoints, constant checks – Kitson has a nice phrase for this, something about 'reasonable discomfiture' – where normal life becomes tedium.
4. Promote vigilante groups that are not answerable to anyone. In the east, there were the Razi and Mahan groups. They were not answerable to anyone so there was no one you could complain to if they arrested you. That is what you want. Because these vigilante groups, further, create an atmosphere of terror and collapse the social fabric. Patricia Lawrence's thesis becomes important here [see Lawrence 2000]: people lose their psychological moorings and so become unable to make any kind of politically cohesive statement. So the vigilante groups become a regime of terror within a regime of terror.
5. Promotion of numerous political and interest groups from within the target population backed, covertly or overtly, by either the vigilante groups or by the state, to dilute and obfuscate the basic issue in question that in the first place gave rise to the insurgency.

Sivaram broke off from his list for a moment to comment: 'What are the real key issues? (a) Control of national wealth by the Sinhalese, as stipulated in the Constitution saying that the Parliament has complete control; (b) control of the monopoly of violence by the Sinhalese in a manner prejudicial to the Tamils – that is, the executive controls the army and the Parliament provides for it; but the executive is always Sinhala and so is the Parliament, and the army always remains Sinhala Buddhist; and (c) complete and inalienable control over the land. The Constitution specifies all these as inalienable – at least the first two. Now these are the fundamental issues. The state wants to obfuscate all this by promoting these other groups that focus on other issues.

'A good example is Ireland,' he said, sitting back in his chair. 'The problem in Northern Ireland is that the British army is occupying the place; and that in the island of Ireland the Irish are in the majority and that Ireland was colonized by the British armed forces. The Irish fought the British in a war of national liberation to get them to leave, and to give back Ireland to the Irish. That was the fundamental issue, and the IRA stated all this very clearly. But these fundamental facts were completely obfuscated by making a big issue out of the Protestants, and by introducing labor issues into the talks, and introducing a women's forum, and talking about the disarmament of the IRA. All this obfuscates the basic issue, and causes the population to forget what it originally set out to achieve. The emancipation of Irish women depends upon the emancipation of Ireland.'

I pointed out that for many feminists this argument must seem like an excuse to thrust aside the seriousness and basic sources of their oppression. Was there not a danger of ignoring very real injustices?

'As long as these discussions do not become a means in the hand of the state to obfuscate and dilute the original issues for which you are fighting, then it's fine. But it should also be understood that you should not turn up from nowhere and say, "Give us our rights!" My argument is that even women's inequality arises from the state's refusal to share resources, for economic stagnation also creates older forms of gender inequality. Take wife-beating. Wife-beating is higher in poor families. In conditions of inequality the patriarchy – like the conservative Jaffna patriarchal household – starts operating in devious and perverse ways. You have to trace the connection between the inequalities within a group of people and their oppression. It's like I told Radhika Coomaraswamy[18] at a conference once: being deracinated like her is too expensive for the poor. The poor can't go to Cambridge, the poor can't have their own house, and so forth. This is all fine to talk about in academic seminars. But criticizing talking in terms of racial categories is stupid: so and so is raped *because* she is a Tamil woman. One of the things that a regime of terror expects is the total submission of women to the regime of terror. Basically, the regime of terror expects women to be sex slaves.'

He often thought, Sivaram said, of what had happened to the wife of one of the members of the Readers' Circle to whom some member of the security forces had taken a fancy. She had had no choice but to grit her teeth and submit. And he reminded me of a similar rape case in Mannar. In general, Sivaram said, 'The police find women who are staying alone in lodges and take them in and rape them in brutal ways. So when you are fighting to dismantle this regime of terror and to keep your focus on the fundamental issue, women's issues should not be exploited by the state to support the regime of terror. Because the main thing the state does not want to talk about is the fundamental issue – like the US saying that blacks are lazy, or saying that red Indians are drunks.'

Then Sivaram went back to ticking off C-I tactics.

6. Criminalizing and delegitimizing the non-state party. Done largely through the media. The state's extortion is taxes; the non-state's extortion is extortion. You do dirty tricks to do things and put the blame on the non-state actors. To understand all this you have to go back to our conversation about nationalist discourse.[19]
7. The promotion and propagation of the conceptual/political dichotomy of the moderate and the militant/terrorist.

Sivaram paused, again, to expand on point seven: 'A good example is what the British did in India. The Indian National Congress was started by a British civil servant named Hume largely to get the opinion of leading members of Indian society who were not totally averse to British rule in India. Then there was the armed militant movement to totally free India from British rule. The British called this the "terrorist" movement – the discourse [on terrorism] starts there. While the others were promoted as moderates and liberals who were prepared to advocate the independence without jeopardizing British national security interests in India. The moderates were prepared to talk and negotiate with England; the "terrorists" were prepared to align with Germany and Japan to secure independence. So you promote moderates. So the Indians are very good at this, because they inherited it from the British. Moderates are people who will talk with the state, never press for radical restructuring. The SDLP in Ireland is a good example of this. And India always had this: Kashmir, the same.'

'Well, what about Gandhi?'

'Gandhi was a crook – expected Tamils to learn Hindi. This is just the *dharma* of the powerful; they will keep this up. By the way, the Tamil National Alliance (TNA) was a strategy to erase this divide – a strategy out of my own thinking.'

He shook his head and stopped talking for a moment. He looked, suddenly, very sober, despite the hour and the many glasses of arrack.

'My interest,' he said again, quietly, 'is to create a body of knowledge to help oppressed people all over the world help themselves get out from under oppression; to disseminate this body of knowledge.'

Then he went back to ticking off C-I practices:

8. A standard thing in all modern CI programs is to promote porn. Batticaloa had about four full-time blue film theaters during this period, from 1990 to 1994, and you could walk in any time – and these were backed by the army.
9. Laxity in the issuing of liquor licenses, as in Black and Indian places in the US. In Batticaloa there were the bars that were there for ages – but now you find them all over the place. So sex and booze are part of C-I – fuck, drink, and forget; don't talk about your rights.

He sighed and sat down again, settling into his chair for a story. 'Now all this was put to me in a nutshell one day in the late 1990s (I don't want to mention the year) at a beautiful lakeside town in Switzerland by a recently retired Sri Lankan army general who was an admirer of my writings. So we were having a long evening discussion about C-I and, after many glasses of Chivas Regal (I was telling him how the LTTE had fucked their counter-insurgency, 'cause with too much booze you tend to go over to top), he said that a population that is targeted by C-I is actually like the body of a prisoner who has been taken under the Prevention of Terrorism Act. He is beaten out of his wits in the first phase of his detention. He is tortured. He is deprived. He loses track of normalcy. The focus of his whole being after a few days of this kind of abuse would be to hope that when the door opens he won't be assaulted. His whole focus is on not getting beaten. His life's sole aim would be focused on that – he would lose track of everything else. Then, there walks in another officer who says, "Don't worry. These guys are sadists!", who brings him a cigarette. Now you have the prisoner's life pinned to those two things: one, is the hope that the nice man will come around; the other is the fear and constant terror that the torturers will turn up.

'Now, remember,' he said, gesturing at me with his glass, 'this general was talking about how the target population is like this prisoner under the Prevention of Terrorism Act. So you treat the target population as a prisoner: break its will, reduce its expectations to bare minimum, so Tamils who set out to demand a separate state would end up just arguing for not being tortured. So your aspirations are depressed from separatism to being allowed to travel without being shot. And then the nice guys – the NGOs, the paramilitaries, are the nice guys who come and talk to you and you start giving them intelligence and you become pliant. And you start learning the lesson of just being grateful for being alive.

'Another aim of counter-insurgency,' he continued, 'is to induce war-weariness in the target population. That is why State Department fellows are always talking about "war-weariness" – so that [the target population will] no longer support its original demands. Once that happens, support for the guerrilla movement also falls. A people's sense of sovereignty vanishes and they can be robbed at will – as has happened in Congo and Sierra Leone. Congo is one of the richest places, but the people of Congo cannot assert their sovereignty to get a cut of their national wealth because of the civil war, starting with the US intervention and killing of Patrice Lumumba. And if you read the book about oil in central Asia you will get another example, and you can see this a-plenty in Latin America.'

'Granting for the sake of argument that all this is so,' I said, 'how do you fight this? How do you counter C-I?'

'As I said before, in the 1994 article that I wrote about C-I, I did not understand the LTTE's strategy: because I saw C-I succeeding, while the LTTE seemed to be only thinking about dazzling victories in the north.' But by 1996–7, Sivaram claimed, he had shifted his view and come to the conclusion that there were six basic ways you could head off C-I. And, again, he ticked them off as a list.

1. If the target of the state is to break the will of the target population as a whole, counter it by concentrating your military resources to create a zone of control where the population would be committed to the cause.

'And thereby,' he explained, 'you undermine the state's project of breaking the whole population's will by keeping a part of the population from being subjected to these tactics. This is why the LTTE pulled out its troops from the east, let the C-I go on there, and concentrated in the north. You create a liberated zone by concentrating your resources rather than by scattering them. This way of countering C-I has to be parallel to the development of a conventional army as efficient, or more so, than the state's forces because you have to have the sophistication and power to counter the Jonomiesque 'I am not interested in real estate' move against your fixed base. And also an understanding that if the enemy wants you to do something, you don't rise to the bait. You never work according to the enemy's timetable.'

Then Sivaram ticked off another counter C-I tactic:

2.   Counter-media like Al Jazeera and TamilNet – these may be the only two examples in this whole wide world.

'Counter-media,' said Sivaram, explaining, 'breaks the obfuscation and helps the population stay focused on the injustices. And it also shakes the population out of the stupor induced by the normalization of injustice. For example, in Batticaloa, when we local journalists and some Eastern University lecturers – including Yuvi [i.e. Dr Yuvaraj Thangaraj, who is Meena's husband, Sivaram's brother in law, and a member of the Readers' Circle] – started a campaign to explain and campaign against the Prevention of Terrorism Act [PTA] and the emergency regulations, we found that there was a generation of young people in Batticaloa who had grown up thinking that this was normal law. We constantly came upon people who thought that it was normal, very normal, for the police or army to walk into your house, arrest you, or beat you up. They believed, this generation – just took it for granted – that if you are arrested, you are tortured. The surprising thing – and you can search TamilNet for these seminars – even old men from the era of normal law had forgotten a thing called a "search and arrest warrant." That is what I mean by the normalization of injustice. Hence, now the LTTE uses arrest warrants. It feels it has to dismantle the gains made by counter-insurgency and rebuild the will of the people. To rebuild a sense of their sovereignty. And you find them burning blue film cassettes in Jaffna. Then the *Pongu Thamil* [literally, 'Tamil uprising'; referring to a series of popular demonstrations in Tamil Sri Lanka and the diaspora] was another thing aimed at rebuilding the will of the people. Hence, our campaign against the PTA was successful to the extent that the Tigers, for the first time, took up the issue of the PTA being removed as part of restoring normal life in the north-east.'

Sivaram went on to say that I should include a discussion of TamilNet and the Sri Lankan security forces' use of Tirukkovil hospital in the east (see TamilNet 2002). 'The STF was just camped there for 15 years. People just took it for granted that the army could be in the Tirukkovil hospital ... that they could park themselves in a functioning hospital, so that patients had to go through an army checkpoint to go to the hospital. But in the TamilNet I have fought a big war against this normalization of injustice. They are still there, but at least it has become controversial now.

'And rape,' he said.[20] 'We started focusing on these things in English. If you read the ceasefire agreement (the CFA), you will find this whole thing about restoring normalcy. The key word is dismantling the gains of counter-insurgency. At least the people have realized that this is fucking wrong, and [in the case of the Tirukkovil hospital] the STF is negotiating this. But it's all about restoring to people their dignity and their sense of direction and rights.'

'And are there any other counter C-I practices?' I asked. According to Sivaram, there were three more:

3. Burn the porn. The LTTE says: if you are using it as an individual that is fine; but don't make it a distraction or destroy a student and people. If you are an adult, don't take school children, or whatever.
4. The LTTE campaign to stop drugs.
5. Fuck the moderates with the TNA [Tamil National Alliance].

'A couple of us did that,' said Sivaram proudly, sadly, somewhat drunkenly. But by this time it was very late, well past twelve, and the rest of the house was asleep. Rubbing my eyes, I suddenly realized, with a quiet internal 'ah,' that herein lay the reason why Sivaram had become so publicly enthusiastic about the LTTE after the ceasefire. That is, first and foremost, because he had become convinced that supporting the LTTE's centralizing power in the Tamil community was prerequisite to defeating the kind of divisive C-I practices that had for so long devastated Tamil Sri Lanka; tactics that were continuing, he clearly believed, albeit more subtly, in the stalling tactics, shadowy intelligence warfare, and support of Karuna of the current Sri Lankan government. I also realized, however, that Sivaram, in his old way, was still trying to influence the Tiger with whom he was dancing. His efforts to get the LTTE to take up the issue of the Prevention of Terrorism Act showed this clearly. He was not a *member*; he was a *mesmerizer*. He was not a new acolyte brightly aglow with the fresh blush of a new faith, but an old seducer, cool-eyed and calmly stalking, dazzling with experience, still intending, as always, to ease Tamil nationalism out of its old leanings and toward a fruitful tryst with the rationalism, justice, and egalitarianism he himself favored for the Tamil people, and that he feared most others had forgotten or betrayed. But this meant, in turn, that even his coldest calculations were still underlain by passions he rarely revealed, except when seriously in his cups. For ultimately it was his old romance with history; his staunch, almost existential belief in life's (always?) potential fecundity; as well as his anger that a history should be gainsaid or anyone's possibilities suppressed, that Sivaram was trying to whisper into the ear of Tamil society. And why did Sivaram feel nationalism, leaving aside the question of the LTTE, was the way to this mother-lode?

Well, by that time we had both had too much to drink. I was incapable of putting the question properly, and so began a desultory argument about whether it wasn't fair, after all, and nonetheless, to consider the LTTE a fascist organization. I cited the critics: Amnesty International, various UN agencies, and Hoole and the UTHR(J). But Sivaram was contemptuous, especially of Hoole – saying loudly, pounding the table, 'Let history judge!' He was not happy when I reminded him that Tony Blair had said exactly that to justify the invasion of Iraq. Sivaram responded by suggesting I had completely forgotten our discussion of several months before about nationalism and so, as we argued, I found myself trying to remember what we had actually talked about.

7 STATES, NATIONS, AND NATIONALISM

The problems of the nation are not, then, problems of 'Sinhalaness,' 'Tamilness,' or 'Moorness' *per se*. The problem rather is in the making of diverse peoples into 'Tamils,' 'Sinhalas,' or 'Moors'; and then in turn of making those people into Sri Lankans. (Jeganathan and Ismail 1995: 2)

We need these various bases of acting together, these language games. The individual is a myth; for we start from these various group identities. (Sivaram, in conversation, 23 April 2004)

We have not yet discussed what is beyond the nation-state. But I always presuppose that the nation-state (as opposed to nationalism and nations) is a historical phenomenon, and a modern one. It is, perhaps, only two centuries old; and not really even two centuries old. For if we are to understand the nation-state with its current capacity to mobilize violence, it is really a post-World War II phenomenon. If you carefully examine the matter, and look at the counter-insurgency handbooks that I mentioned the other day, then you are looking at developments in the technologies of violence that make the modern state possible. (Sivaram, in conversation, 23 April 2004)

In 1995 a group of young, mostly Western-trained, Sri Lankan academics put together an interesting anthology, edited by Pradeep Jaganathan and Qadri Ismail, called *Unmaking the Nation: The Politics of Identity and History in Modern Sri Lanka*. It was published in Colombo, where it was fairly widely circulated, and where it made a bit of a splash when it first came out due to its authors' incisive use of the very latest in Western theory in their efforts to take on and, as their title says, 'unmake' Sri Lanka's nationalisms. Gananath Obeyesekere, one of Sri Lanka's senior scholars, contributed a complimentary blurb to the book's back cover from his office at Princeton University, writing: 'Notions such as nation, nationalism, identity, and ethnicity are virtually axiomatic in the human sciences ... It is therefore refreshing to read these provocative essays, by a younger generation of scholars ... that "unmake" these terms and force us to think about Sri Lankan symbolic and social formations in an entirely novel fashion.' As for me, I was quite impressed by the anthology when it came out: most anthropology anthologies are, frankly, boring; this certainly was not. And its various clever attempts to discomfit the 'axioms' (as Obeyesekere puts it) of nationalism – or, as the book's editors assert in their introduction, to 'suspect the nation' (Jegnathan and Ismail 1995: 2) – struck a resonant chord in me. Not so my friend. Sivaram's response to the book, when first I asked him about it, was characteristically both unfair and *ad hominem.* 'I saw one of them at a May Day rally once. I was there with a friend of mine – drunk as a skunk – and there was one of those guys dressed in a Malcolm X t-shirt. That's all it is for them: fashion. *Everything* they do is just fashion.' What was Sivaram's problem? The fashion charge, of course, was one he made frequently about academics of all stripes and was only partly serious. And insofar as it was serious, we can take it up later. But Sivaram's fundamental problem here was not with this book but, as a nationalist, with its underlying premise: that the primordial claims of nationalism are completely false and that nations are, in fact, things that have been fairly recently 'imagined' by particular populations exposed to the conditions and technologies of modernity.

This way of thinking about nationalism has, indeed, been fairly *de rigueur* in anthropology and many of the other social sciences since the publication of Benedict Anderson's influential book, *Imagined Communities*, in 1983 – a book in many ways as radically important for scholars writing about nationalism as Thomas S. Kuhn's *The Structures of Scientific Revolutions* was for scholars writing about the history of science, and for much the same reason. That is, Anderson's book, like Kuhn's, eloquently posed a 'non-realist' and 'modernist' view of its particular subject in a way that solved many of the vexing problems realist or 'primordialist' views always face when trying to understand historically mutable entities that refuse to connect smoothly or linearly to their supposedly foundational (hence 'primordial') pasts. So, just as Kuhn got rid of 'scientific progress' when faced with the obvious disjuncture between, say, Ptolemy's and Galileo's astronomies, and replaced it with his notion of a paradigm-shifting 'scientific revolution,' so Anderson got rid of nationalism's 'primordial history' when faced by an equally obvious disjuncture between Sukarno's Indonesian nationalism and Java's precolonial theocratic states, and replaced it with his idea of an 'imagined community.' That is, his solution, again like Kuhn's, was to give priority to the role communities play in making certain forms of knowledge sociologically real under certain (modern) circumstances. It is crucial to understand that Anderson was not claiming that nations are the consequence of some kind of Nietzschean act of will. Nations are 'imagined communities' for Anderson not because of some collective, self-generating act of creativity, but because modern circumstances – borders, printing presses, newspapers, etc. – create historical contexts where groups (however originally thrown together) are bound to think of themselves as one. His 'non-realism' about nationality, thus, is surrounded by his 'realism' about the historical and socio-economic circumstances that he believes generate nationalism. Nevertheless, Anderson's thesis, in cutting the cord that supposedly binds nationalism to some 'really real' historical past, seemed to set historians and social scientists of nationalism free from the often thankless task of trying to sift 'real' history from its nationalist elaborations. Indeed, if his thesis were true, the whole concoction of nationalist rhetoric could be seen henceforth as a discursive whole, as a kind of semiotic text, to be read, decoded, and perhaps – and here is the aim of *Unmaking the Nation* – even deconstructed and eventually redirected onto a more benign path. Moreover, Anderson's general idea seemed confirmed when two other influential books came out the same year, Gellner's *Nations and Nationalism* (1983) and Hobsbawm and Ranger's influential anthology, *The Invention of Tradition* (1983), both of which also displayed 'modernist' (if not, in Gellner's case, as sociological determinist, completely 'non-realist') views of nationalism. In any case, Anderson's thesis provides a heady way of thinking about nationalism – particularly for horrified, sometimes justly frightened, desk-bound academics struggling to think about bloody 'street-nationalisms,' as they would term them, with high body counts and low tolerances for cultural or 'racial' difference such as those found in Sri Lanka. Indeed, in many ways, it is a theory that I continue to hold in some sympathy myself.

But for Sivaram, as a nationalist and, more importantly, as one who had experienced the violence of nationalism from both sides of the gun, this 'fashionable,' Andersonian, 'non-realist' and 'modernist' view of nationalism was arrant nonsense. Why? Sivaram's reaction to Anderson's thesis was not merely emotional, despite the above *ad hominem* bluster. Nor was Sivaram's distaste for Anderson's thesis (and others like his) the result of a street-level, pre-reflective, 'we deserve a state but you bums don't' nationalism of what political philosophers would call the 'invidious particularist' sort. Sivaram's views about nationalism were really more ecumenical, scholarly, and politically cynical than that. Sivaram, in fact, by the early 1990s, had evolved a detailed 'realist' response to Anderson's thesis – or, at least, a response to the abstract outline of Anderson's thesis that many Western or Western-trained scholars conventionally deploy in their writings on nationalism. It was a response, on the one hand, steeped in the specialist literature about nationalism that has grown up in the wake of Anderson's seminal book – particularly the works of the Subaltern school (see Chatterjee 1986), and of Charles Tilly (1975) and Anthony Smith (1986; 2001), that question, for various reasons, both the 'non-realist' and 'modernist' claims that underlie his thesis. Yet Sivaram's response was also flavored by a deep emotional attachment to Sri Lankan Tamil places and practices, a profoundly 'communitarian' sense of 'Tamilness' that he argued arises (in Sri Lanka as everywhere else) from the set of locally shared, empirically observable, 'language games' of daily life – how one eats, how one speaks, how one (as he put it) 'washes one's back' – that form our everyday, existential being. It was the existentially given feeling of group identity that arises from these shared language games that underlay, for Sivaram, both nationalist feelings as such and the seemingly inexplicable willingness people display to die or otherwise sacrifice their interests for 'their' group. For Sivaram's experiences in the war and with the JVP in the late 1980s had convinced him that such feelings of national identity were, in fact, fundamental rather than merely symptomatic of a nation-state. And so this was one sense in which Sivaram's view of nationalism was deeply 'realist.'

But the real heart of Sivaram's counter-view lay in his claim that violence plays the most important *constitutive* role in the formation of nation-states – an assertion he made based both on his experience as a Tamil victim of state-nationalist violence, and as a nationalist guerrilla fighter. It is this somewhat Weberian, or Maoist, view of the role of violence in nationalism that Sivaram had elaborated at great length both in his thinking and writing about nationalism, and in his many newspaper columns and addresses about the military strategies being used by established nation-states in 'low-intensity' conflicts such as Sri Lanka's civil war. What took me years to understand, however, is that Sivaram's critique of 'non-realist' and (to a certain extent) 'modernist' views of nationalism underlay, in a way, *everything* he had written and done since 1989.

So what, then, *were* Sivaram's views of nationalism? Sivaram's writings on nationalism were scattered and, although fairly numerous, did not quite cover his whole view of the matter. So one weekend in May 2004 I invited Sivaram up to my rented house in Bowellawatta, Kandy, high on Heerasigalla hill, to thrash them out. Sivaram, however, was in a peculiar mood that weekend. For in early March of that year the LTTE's eastern military commander, Vinayaamoorthy Muralitharan, or 'Colonel Karuna,' citing unfair treatment of eastern Tamils and cadres by the northern Wanni leadership of the LTTE, had withdrawn himself and his 6000–8000 trained cadres from their command. The subsequent 40-day Karuna rebellion had just come to a tentative and violent conclusion in early April, only weeks before, and Sivaram, who had played a key role in it, was exhausted. Exactly what that role was is a story for the next chapter, but here it is enough to note that, as one might expect, he was at the center of the thing right from the beginning. For, in addition to a controversial BBC interview, condemnatory of Karuna, that he gave soon after the crisis started, Sivaram wrote an 'Open Letter to Karuna' (*karuNaavukku oru kaTitam*) which appeared in *Viirakeesari* on 14 March 2004 (Sivaram 2004d), detailing an argument to the effect that Karuna's break from the LTTE was disastrous for the Tamil cause. The letter was much bandied about on the internet among the diaspora, and the LTTE photocopied thousands of copies and sent them as handbills around Batticaloa as part (Sivaram believed) of their 'psyops' pre-softening of Karuna's cadres in the lead-up to their Good Friday offensive to retake the district. Retake the district they did, it turned out, in short order. But with the rump of Karuna's faction still carrying out revenge killings in Colombo and Batticaloa, Sivaram felt that he could well be high on their hit list.

Moreover, beyond this fear, I think there was a lingering ambivalence in Sivaram about the whole Karuna affair. On the one hand Karuna, the killer (as Sivaram knew) of Vasutheva, his friend and Bavani's sister's husband, was gone from the scene. More importantly, gone also was the threat, as Sivaram saw it, to the military unity he believed was absolutely necessary to bring the Sri Lankan state to the bargaining table. For, as we shall see, given Sivaram's views both about the nature of nationalism and about the kinds of politico-military, C-I strategies nation-states employ to suppress rival nationalisms, he could have held no other view. But Karuna's charge that the LTTE leadership in the Wanni had been favoring the north rang powerfully true to many people in Batticaloa, including some of Sivaram's closest colleagues, relatives, and friends. And, given Sivaram's romantic attachment to his birthplace, and his own occasional distaste for the LTTE (which had, after all, once tried to kill him), this brief revolt must have touched something in him too. Backing the northern LTTE against the home-grown feelings of many Batticaloa Tamils – though he believed it absolutely necessary, and though he admitted to me absolutely no doubts – nonetheless cost him: friendships and family feelings, of course; but also, I suspect, a bit of himself. It was at moments like this, indeed, that I wondered at the personal cost of Sivaram's views.

To add to his woes, while Sivaram and I were still in Batticaloa, 30 or 40 policemen (accounts differ) raided his house, terrifying Bavani and the children, and turning everything upside down, looking, claimed the Inspector General of police later, 'for a cache of weapons.' Even the *Sunday Island*'s pro-government, and generally anti-TamilNet, op-ed writer 'Our Defense Correspondent' – a columnist who firmly believed Sivaram made some sort of deal with the LTTE back in 1996 and was therefore now directly linked to them – saw the Inspector General's rationale as absurd: 'This is clearly one of the most idiotic statements for an IGP to make ... So what was the real motive of the raid? It looks to all as though it was plain old-fashioned police intimidation of journalists. Given the fact that Sivaram had been writing critically against Karuna's factions, it appears clear that the raid was ordered by someone in government who supports Karuna' (Our Defense Correspondent 2004). So it seemed.

Sivaram's visit to Bowellawatta came the week after this disaster. And he was, perhaps understandably, full of nervous energy. Much of what follows about nationalism was worked out consequently while we were walking down Heerasigalla Road – a precipitous track that makes three-wheeler drivers dive for their reserve tanks every time they creep painfully toward its top – and while tramping ceaselessly about the extraordinary grounds of the Peradeniya Gardens where, we quickly discovered, sitting down to talk was almost impossible because of the ubiquitous presence on every bench and tree stump of courting lovers.

'It's biology, Mr Whitaker. Biology is everywhere. And infidelity.'

'Infidelity? How do you reckon that?'

Sivaram's laugh boomed out, causing several nearby couples to swerve their eyes worriedly in our direction. 'Mark, your innocence always makes me laugh.'

'Well, I'm always happy to oblige. Ah, look over there.'

Close to the rickety Mahaweli Suspension bridge was a wooden gazebo that held only two silent lovers, momentarily unentangled. It was buzzing with mosquitoes but otherwise quiet. So we took our chance, sat down on one of the structure's rough benches, and began our talk about nationalism

– loudly, for my attempts to conduct our conversation in hushed tones were to no avail. Sivaram boomed out. The lovers contented themselves with quietly holding hands and casting frustrated glances our way. Eventually, an hour or so later, at Sivaram's insistence, we shambled off to find a three-wheeler and continue our discussion back up at my house. 'We must not be completely insensitive,' said Sivaram. 'They must be allowed to get down to business too.' I could hear them sighing with real relief as we left, two old fat men talking about irrelevant things. In any case, for the next two days, we thrashed out, very carefully, Sivaram's view of nationalism. So here it is:

SIVARAM'S VIEW OF NATIONALISM

Sivaram began by arguing that an ethnically based nationalism cannot be understood separately from the state. It can not be understood separately, he asserted, because nationalism is actually a way of organizing states that achieves, for the elites that run them, maximal efficiency and the greatest degree of comprehensibility – and thus, for them, the greatest return. So, given a state, elites these days will try to run it using ethno-nationalism. This notion sounds, I pointed out, a bit like the primitive thesis that 'nationalism is just elites manipulating things for their own benefit' that newspaper editorialists in the US like to trot out to accompany their ethno-nationalism bashing. It also sounds, I thought, like the kind of nationalism that liberal nationalist 'communitarian' academics, anxious to distinguish their nobler cause from other, baser, kinds of nationalism, often describe as 'street-nationalism.' But Sivaram claimed that both of these reactions to nationalism are based on a false distinction that arises either from disingenuousness or from a complete misunderstanding of the nature of nationalism. That is, on the one hand, American editorialists provide an example of disingenuousness about nationalism when they claim that they don't believe that they themselves *have* a form of ethno-nationalism (only the other guys do), because their kind of American exceptionalism is only possible when the role Christianity and 'whiteness' play in harmonizing American 'patriotism' (as they would call their nationalism) is *disingenuously* placed beyond the pale of polite public debate.[1] In fact, Sivaram claimed, *all nationalisms are really ethno-nationalisms* – a point he said we would have to get back to. On the other hand, the attempt by both liberal and 'communitarian' scholars to distinguish between 'legitimate' nationalism and 'illegitimate,' elite-manipulated, 'street nationalism' was, Sivaram claimed, merely a philosophical nicety that ignored basic political realities about how states actually work – particularly the way states are *constituted* by violence. Moreover, argued Sivaram, suspicious as always, there was a kind of hidden neocolonial agenda behind these 'descriptions' of nationalism. 'There is a *politics* to all these popular and academic theories about nationalism, Mark. They are not innocent. Which one is fashionable; which one is ignored? *It's all politics – neocolonial politics.*'

Still, it soon became clear for a variety of reasons that Sivaram's theoretical description of nationalism was not really like the descriptions of 'bad' nationalism that American journalists and academics tend to trot out. But those reasons were only apparent in Sivaram's preliminary thesis about the state, and so, while the doleful lovers continued to give us suspicious looks, for we were still in their garden, we turned to the vexing question of the nature of the state.

SIVARAM'S THESIS ABOUT THE STATE:

Sivaram started with the claim that human beings are inherently social and live in groups, or social organizations, of varying size and inclusiveness. It is within these groups, he claimed, that we participate in the 'language games' and 'forms of life' that give us not just collective but individual identity. For human individuality outside such groups – as envisioned, say, in the social contract fables of the English empiricists – is, he asserted, impossible. Or, as he said, 'We need these various bases of acting together, these language games. The individual is a myth; for we start from these various group identities.' Now these social groups are of all sizes. They can range, as Sivaram pointed out by means of a chart he later drew for me back up at my house, all the way from a family to a football club to a caste to a clan (although I was not sure what he meant by this last step since, even abstractly, clans tend to be less inclusive than castes) to a clan of people traditionally resident in Batticaloa and, finally, to a class of people who consider themselves Sri Lankan Tamils. At all levels, he argued, one finds socially organized groups. Also, these groups display different amounts of permanency: families being more permanent than football clubs but, perhaps, less permanent than castes and so on. But some forms of identity are relatively permanent. As Sivaram put it, waving an equivocal hand in my vague direction:

'Some of these identities can be acquired and dropped depending on the groups to which we belong. Some identities, like Mark being a white man, are more durable than others. It is, of course, possible to think of "whiteness" being in some future utopia not important. But this is certainly not a historical likelihood. So certain language games have a contextual staying power. Those contexts don't go away.'

Now all of these groups, Sivaram argued, constitute forms of social organization. For a social organization, as Sivaram defined it, is any group that is organized according to rules. These rules can be *memorized* rules, such as those found in a football club's charter or, I supposed, a state's written Constitution (although these are more often consulted than memorized); or they can be *internalized* rules (what Bourdieu would call *habitus* and Durkheim would call *norms* – though Sivaram did not use either of these terms) such as one would find displayed in family behavior. The key thing here, for Sivaram, was that all social organizations, at whatever level, involve such rules, and that one obvious consequence of this fact is that control of such rules constitutes control of the group – though, he was quick to add, such control would have to follow from the more fundamental, violent, kind of control that we would be discussing shortly.

Sivaram then observed, rather magisterially, that at some point very early in human history very large social organizations formed which are conventionally called *states*. Or, as he put it: 'In this group of social organizations we find that a larger group identity that tends to include all these smaller social organizations and that is largely defined by language, region, common history – the usual culprits which national scholars have identified – organizes around a thing called a state.' But while this kind of comprehensive group identity is, in this rather weak sense, antecedent to any further development, what makes this potential social organization a state, according to his thesis, is the establishment, to a greater or lesser degree, of three *monopolies*: (1) a monopoly of surplus extraction, (2) a monopoly of violence, and (3) a monopoly of adjudication. Of these three monopolies, (1), the monopoly of surplus extraction (as he terms it, after Smith 1986), is *prior*, for, according to Sivaram's theory, elites are motivated to form states in order to control the surplus of their group – 'surplus' being that part of a group's production that is not needed for physical and cultural reproduction. Or, as he put it, 'the state as a form of social organization arises in societies where organized surplus extraction takes place.' And it is an interesting part of Sivaram's theory that for him states are not formed willingly, as in social contract theory, neoclassical rational choice theory, and in most kinds of 'communitarian' theory, nor even 'organically,' as in classical nationalism (*à la* Herder), but *coercively* by self-interested elites – rather as Robert Carnieros suggested in his 'circumscription theories' about the formation of early states. But while surplus extraction, in the form of taxes, tithes, tribute, etc., is, for Sivaram, the formative motivator of state formation, it is (2), the monopoly of violence, that actually *constitutes* a state. For, as he put it, bluntly, 'Let's say the others resist this extraction. You need force to break that resistance. Therefore force and violence are inextricably bound up with surplus extraction. That is why tithes, taxes, tribute – whatever you may call it – is extraction rather than redistribution.'

Hence violence, Sivaram claimed, is what in fact always lies behind the existence of any state. It may be meditated through ideology, symbolic forms, and the kind of internalized 'symbolic violence' (those 'internalized rules'), which, in this kind of circumstance, Bourdieu would call 'symbolic violence' or 'misrecognition.' But whenever any kind of real challenge to a state's monopoly of violence presents itself, all of these mediations, according to Sivaram, fall by the wayside and sheer, naked, violence is wielded by the state to restore its monopoly. Or as he put it to me, wielding a chicken bone for emphasis – for by this time we had settled back up at the house and were having dinner – 'Whether the violence is symbolic or internal or whatever – that entire facade goes off the moment there is a real challenge. Then they set out to kill people and establish their authority.' But then, rather carefully replacing the chicken bone, he pointed out that constant violence would be self-negating, since a society always confronted by the violence of its elites would quickly destroy itself. 'The surplus cannot be extracted though violence all the time because the society will be destroyed. It is self-negating. Instead a certain equilibrium has to be maintained.' So, once a ruling elite's monopoly of violence is established beyond a doubt, its actual deployment, he claimed, is held as a last resort, and it is then that the various forms of mediated violence come into play.

After dinner he pointed out that perhaps the primary form of mediated violence is the final monopoly, (3), the monopoly of adjudication. As I understand this one – for Sivaram did not expand upon it at any length, but only strongly asserted, over his small glass of postprandial wine, that it is necessary – a state requires this monopoly in order to be able to supply its populace with a constant reminder of the existence of its unitary power (and hence of its monopoly of violence). That is, states every day demonstrate their primary existence (and their people's secondary dependence upon the state) by demanding that people turn to the state, and only the state, for settlement of their differences and, also, to a greater or lesser extent (depending, I assume, on how 'totalitarian' the state is), for judgments of their public behavior.

Here it is probably appropriate to note that there is something idiosyncratically wide about Sivaram's thesis about the state. That is, until relatively recently, conventional definitions of the state – such as those found, for example, in introductory anthropology textbooks (Miller 2002: 225) – tended to include both relatively large size and a fairly high degree of political centrality as important criteria for determining whether some social group is or is not a state. Other anthropologists debate this, of course, arguing that such internal criteria are arbitrary and turning instead to criteria generated by interstate practice. For example, Kingsolver (2001) points out, correctly I think (in a rather Barthian way), that what actually tends to determine in practice whether the term 'state' is used about a particular political entity is how it is 'acknowledged' by surrounding 'states.' That is, if an entity is 'acknowledged' with negotiations and treaties then it tends to be seen as a 'state'; if it is 'acknowledged,' on the other hand, with violence then it tends to be seen as something other than a state (a 'terrorist' group perhaps). She observes, for example, that at one point in the early 1990s the would-be state of Québec, itself in a stand-off over its own 'stateness' with Canada in the Meech Lake meetings, was at one and the same time engaged in transnational *negotiations* with Mexico and the US over trade issues (hence, being state-like) while *violently repressing* its own Mohawk Nation's assertions of sovereignty (and hence seeking to demonstrate the Mohawk Nation's non-stateness) (2001: 52–3). For Kingsolver as for Sivaram, then, though for different reasons, neither size nor political centrality are central to 'stateness.' Still, by most *conventional* reckoning, the Yanomami, for example, would not be considered a people who 'have' a state – indeed, they tend to be called in contemporary literature 'stateless' people – and the reasoning here is that the

Yanomami are both too small in population and too decentralized politically to be seen as constituting a 'state.'

Yet Sivaram, who knew about the Yanomami (he read about them in a newspaper article), disagreed with this. By his reckoning such a group does have a 'state' (he called it a 'patriarchal' state in this instance) because a certain group – Yanomami men – have a monopoly of violence that allows them to control the surplus and adjudicate conduct. Moreover they have a territory – Sivaram called it a 'habitat' – within which the various language games involved in 'being Yanomami' are most likely and easily accomplished, and which they mobilize to defend when threatened. 'Even the Australian Aborigines, as decentralized as they were, mobilized to protect their habitat, Mark.' So rather than the application of criteria such as size or political form, what determines whether something is a state, according to Sivaram, is the mere existence (in some degree) of the three monopolies within a social organization that occupies a 'habitat.' 'Even a football club *could* be a state. *Briefly.*'

In any case, in modern times, Sivaram continued, states tend to be controlled by ruling elites that are drawn from a particular group. Ruling elites, in other words, are not multicultural. This was not necessarily true in the past, and Sivaram pointed out that he had tried to demonstrate this in several of his published historical articles; nor is it true, he claimed, in the present in 'collapsed' states like Sudan or Afghanistan. But it is true of most modern nation-states, including Sri Lanka and, of course, the United States. *In general, therefore, all modern states, according to Sivaram's argument, are 'ethno-national' states, despite local ideologies (like liberal US 'patriotism') that may assert the contrary.*

'But wait a moment,' I said. 'Surely there are some counter-examples to this. What about India and Canada? Aren't they rather famous examples of multicultural democracies?'

'Ha! Young man, India survives by constantly, ceaselessly, violently suppressing regional rebellions. How many has it been now? Let's see: the Sikhs, Assam, the Tamils earlier, Kashmir. It's a long list, and there is no sign of the violence ending. And Canada, like the United States, was created by destroying the native-Canadians, and continues today as an uneasy alliance of ethnicities that can barely stand each other. Look at the failure of the Meech Lake accords. Indian and Canada are not counter-examples; in fact, they are good examples of just what I am saying.'

'Well, I'm not so sure what you say is true. After all, on this issue it can't be how sloppy, or even occasionally violent, their arrangements are that counts – indeed, maybe sloppy but mostly peaceful is all that can be hoped for. Surely, what counts is whether they can maintain some sort of nation-state without forswearing or suppressing cultural diversity. I mean, in that sense, it seems to me, both Canada and India remain good examples of multicultural nation-states that have handled their diversity problems in a way that, most of the time, avoids both violence and the suppression of diversity. Take India, for example. Tamil Nadu and the Dravidian movement seem quite happy to exist within a unitary, federal state; and the Indian federal state seems quite happy – as your friend Jude Fernando points out – to allow Tamil Nadu to pass language laws and such that actually limit Delhi's influence. No, I just don't buy it that there are no examples of successful multicultural states.'

'No, no, no! The Indian state used all sorts of force to suppress the Dravidian movement in India. The accommodation with the Congress Party and with Delhi all came later. But, young man, I'm getting to all that. Don't be hasty and jump ahead or we will never get this chapter finished. Have a drink and calm your fevered brow instead. And let me explain.'

'I'll have a drink. But I still don't buy this part.'

'Wait. Wait.'

The single most important characteristic of such ethno-national states, he continued, ignoring my continued grumbling, is that their ruling elites are the main producers and reproducers of 'high culture': of, that is, that part of the state's national 'culture' that is used to constitute its various mediated forms of authority, or what a lot of social scientists these days, after Gramsci, would call the nation-state's 'hegemony.' Elites have this role, of course, because only they, given their control of the state's surplus, have the time for it. But their cultural activities are also absolutely central not only to the running of an ethno-national state but, more importantly, to why this kind of state has come to dominate the world. According to Sivaram, these cultural activities are central because their ethnic-nationalist, homogenizing character is the key component of the increased effectiveness of modern nation-states.

Why? According to Sivaram, modern ethno-national states have come to dominate the world because they provide the best way for elites to completely and comprehensively organize the three monopolies that constitute a state. Pre-modern states, like feudal Europe or precolonial India, according to him, often parceled out their various monopolies of surplus extraction, power, and adjudication among a number of subordinate, semi-independent, often culturally distinct sub-elites – thanes, knights, the Church, Vanniyars, Podiyars, regional temples, and so forth. This type of 'devolved' system of authority allowed large, albeit unwieldy, pre-modern states to control huge territories that often contained several populations with whom the state's ruling elites had little in common linguistically or culturally. Ruling elites at the center could do this because they relied on a tiered hierarchy of local elites – themselves members of the various regional cultures – to implement local rule. (In this regard Sivaram's description of pre-modern states seemed to me to be in accord with the work of people like Stein, [1980] whose work he nevertheless claimed to detest, and with Tambiah [1976] and Geertz's work on 'cosmic states,' which he seemed grudgingly to admire.) But this kind of state control, Sivaram maintained, was inefficient. For setting up a state in this pre-modern way ensures that none of the state-constitutive monopolies will be complete, and, most importantly, that a goodly portion of the state's surplus will be sacrificed up and down the line to pay for the hierarchy of sub-elites involved in keeping the pre-modern 'multicultural' entity together. So modern and modernizing elites, realizing that this kind of organization was both inefficient and expensive, turned instead, to ethno-nationalism.

With ethno-nationalism, Sivaram argued, the key feature is that the culture and language of the ruling elites, whatever they are, are used as templates for homogenizing the cultures and languages of the state's various populaces. This move, Sivaram went on, eliminates the need for an intermediary tiered system of sub-elites capable of communicating with local populations. For communication with the populace can be done now by the elites themselves. Hence, given ethno-nationalism, the whole, unwieldy, and expensive system of intermediary centers of power and surplus extraction can be replaced with a centralized, streamlined, state authority. Ethno-nationalism also, of course, ensures that the advantage in this interaction will remain with the ruling elites since it is *their* culture and language that will form the homogenizing national template. That is, the culture and language of the state will be henceforth that with which *they* are most comfortable.

At this point it was after eleven o'clock and we all went to sleep.

A HISTORICAL EXAMPLE

The next day, after breakfast, Sivaram gave the following historical example – derived from an article he wrote for the *Lanka Guardian* (1992) – to illustrate the difference he sees between pre-modern and modern states. In the early eighteenth century much of Tamil Nadu, he argued, was controlled by the Nawab of Arcot, a Muslim, Urdu-speaking ruler. The Nawab maintained his authority over Tamil Nadu, Sivaram argued, by controlling an army that could extract tribute from the region's local rulers, the *Paalayakarar*, who were the Tamil-speaking, Hindu (generally Maruwar, Kallar, and perhaps Vanniyar caste) warriors who dominated the local countryside from their camps or *paalayam*. This system was, as Sivaram pointed out, the very form of local rule, based on the *uurkaval* or 'village guard' system, that is so well described in Nick Dirk's *The Hollow Crown* (1993), which Sivaram admitted he greatly admired. But Sivaram's point, here, is that the Nawab's rule nicely illustrates how a tiered system of violence worked in a pre-modern state. As he later wrote out long-hand in my notebook, 'in such an ancient regime, as in a collapsed modern state, the work of justifying the monopoly of violence on the lower rungs or levels of the system is left to the local warlord, feudal chief, or *Paalaya*.'

All this the British dismantled when they took over the region. As Sivaram put it: 'The first thing that the British did when they took over the Tamil country from the Nawab of Arcot was to issue a proclamation, by one Major Bannerman, prohibiting the inhabitants from carrying or owning weapons. The *Paalayams* were systematically dismantled. The *kaaval* system was banished. Bishop Caldwell, the writer of the *Comparative Grammar of the Dravidian Languages*, and Edgar Thurston, author of *Caste and Tribes of South India*, then wrote about the "evils" of the *kaaval* system. With the introduction of the Criminal Tribes Act, the Tamil martial castes, which enjoyed these local monopolies on violence, were completely disfranchised. Residual local monopolies of violence that could not be stamped out were classified as criminal – hence the word "criminal" in the title of the Criminal Tribes Act. And early descriptions by East India company officials and British travelers refer to the Kallar and Manavar as "martial" and "warlike," and as "warriors."'

Further: 'The British state then proceeded to complete its monopoly at the local and state levels, by replacing the Nawab of Arcot and the *Paalayam* with one single monopoly of force. The British colonial state then erased the tiered monopolies of violence that existed in the ancient regime. For the British did not recognize, as the ancient regime did, other centers of violence – except in a ceremonial sense in the case of the Princely States. Hence, once these were abolished by law and in practice, the British state also endeavored to delegitimize the *kaaval* system and the *Paalayam* altogether by erasing the symbols that reminded people of these former systems. Some *Paalayam* forts that rose in rebellion were razed to the ground and removed from official maps. It took the Dravidian movement being in power in Tamil Nadu to put these things back on the map, in every sense of the term. In short, in creating the modern Indian nation-state the British strove to completely and comprehensively monopolize the raising and deployment of organized armed violence.'

How does this example relate to Sivaram's argument about nationalism? Sivaram's point here was that pre-modern states, such as those run by rulers like the Nawab of Arcot, do not need cultural commonality, because the tiered system of local monopolies of violence upon which they rely is controlled by various local elites who share the culture and language of the various people they rule. In a sense, then, by Sivaram's definition, these ancient empires or states were not really states at all in the modern sense but rather conglomerations of states – the actual 'states' within them being defined by the local regional identities and monopolies of violence, as found in the *Paalayam*, that these larger entities pulled together (at first) through sheer military power. Sivaram argued that in such circumstances an ideology may eventually be constructed to link elites at various levels – as feudal Catholicism linked European kingdoms or as Asokan 'cosmic' ideology linked South Asian ones – but that such ideologies are largely for elites, and are secondary to the 'first among equals' military power that establishes such entities.

But when elites in charge of an ancient state such as this centralize their ability to deploy violence, as the British in India did by criminalizing the martial castes, then, Sivaram argued, conditions are created which inevitably set in train two contradictory processes: cultural-linguistic homogenization on the one hand and rebellion on the other. That is, linguistic and cultural homogenization are set in train because elites, once they have established their monopoly of violence, need to justify it, and this is most easily done by gesturing toward some of the 'culprits' of ethnic identity, such as a common culture and heritage, and then invoking the need to use the monopoly of violence to preserve the habitat which gave rise to these things. Rebellion is equally set in train, however, because a newly established monopoly of violence will always draw attention to an as yet unbridged (and perhaps unbridgeable) gap of cultural and linguistic differences between central rulers and those they rule; and when elites try to close this distance through cultural homogenization, the cast-off sub-elites of the old centers of violence will tend to resist. Hence, in Sivaram's view, it was not possible for the British to continue to rule India once they had established their comprehensive monopoly of violence, for doing so merely emphasized their foreignness. They *might* have continued to rule, of course, as the Moguls did, through local monopolies of violence, for had they done so their foreignness would not have mattered at the local level. But this they could not do, Sivaram argued, because the inefficiencies (particularly the financial inefficiencies) that are part and parcel of this kind of pre-modern devolved rule made it simply too expensive to do so. So the Raj eventually fell, a victim of this paradox.

Sivaram argued, further, that America's neo-imperialists (as he called them) face a similar choice in the 'collapsed state' of Afghanistan. That is, as he saw it, they can either seek to rule indirectly through various warlords (with the current President Hamid Karzai as little more than a first-among-equals warlord); or they can seek to establish a modern nation-state by establishing a monopoly of violence at the center. If they do the first – which Sivaram believed was what was happening – they *will* be able to rule, but only in a way that will leak resources (parts of the 'surplus') all up and down the hierarchy of warlords. This kind of indirect rule, he believes, they will find very expensive, as the British also found it to be earlier. But if the US seeks to establish a monopoly of violence (perhaps for the current president), then the ensuing need for cultural and linguistic homogenization will surely inspire rebellion in all the old centers of violence – which is, in fact, exactly what happened before when the Soviet puppet government in Kabul tried to turn Afghanistan into a modern nation-state over 20 years ago.

SUMMING UP NATIONALISM

Before leaving to return to Colombo, Sivaram thought it might be a good idea to back up and summarize his argument up to this point. He did so with the following nine points.

1.   States are sets of language games that are comprehensive of the language games of smaller social organizations such as clans, castes, families, clubs, etc.
2.   This is true of all kinds of states, at all levels, including small pre-modern entities such as the *paalayam* (military camps).
3.   Such states can be said to exist as states when they have achieved in some degree the three monopolies of violence, surplus extraction, and adjudication.

4. States, however (or the elites that rule them), must soon justify their possession of these monopolies in terms of a common language, culture and so forth.
5. Justification of this sort is necessary because violence alone, though it establishes the monopolies, is self-negating.
6. So it is necessary to make people feel that the monopolies are held for their benefit.
7. And this is best done in terms of a code composed out of a shared language, history, and so forth.
8. So ruling elites deploy and reproduce 'high' culture, and this common 'code,' to reduce the possibility of challenges to their monopolies.
9. It is this reproducing and deploying of 'high' culture and a common hegemonic code that is the basis of nationalism.

The implications of these nine points, Sivaram argued, are pretty clear. When *modern* nation-states – that is, ones *comprehensively organized* – take on the role of reproducing and deploying a common code in this way, then we have modern nationalism. And when groups that are for some reason excluded from the common code – and some will always inevitably be excluded by language or religion or history – then their *resistance* to the nation-state's homogenizing project is modern nationalism too. Their reaction, their nationalism, Sivaram argued, must first take the form of seeking to limit the monopolies enjoyed by the nation-state. But even as they seek to do this, Sivaram claimed, they will nonetheless share with the ethno-national elites they are opposing (though they might not admit this) a sense that it is the sovereign right of a group to hold those monopolies. (I told Sivaram that I doubted this – 'invidious nationalism' being the inevitable result of a successful nationalism, but he said he would get to that point, or prognosis, later.) So the nationalist challenge always amounts to establishing or maintaining this sovereignty. Hence, a successful nationalist struggle will always entail establishing either an entirely separate state, or at the very least a separate semi-state such as that currently held by the Kurds in northern Iraq, which wields the key monopolies at least in some degree. In the end, since nationalisms are always seeking to establish the three monopolies and thus a state – for survival, otherwise, is impossible – nationalism and the state are inextricably bound together.

From all this the argument justifying Tamil nationalism, he said, follows pretty directly. Tamil people, he declared, did not cede their sovereignty when the British left in 1948. Nor did the Tamil people cede their sovereignty when the republican Constitution of Sri Lanka was crafted in 1972. Instead, in the 1976 Vaddokoddai meetings, the Tamil people agreed to establish their own state. Now, he continued, a republican Constitution rests upon the idea that sovereignty resides in the people and is inalienable. But, to exercise this sovereignty, a 'people' require representatives who can wield exclusive executive, legislative, and judicial power – which are, by another name, simply the three monopolies of violence, surplus extraction, and adjudication spoken of earlier. So the establishment of Tamil sovereignty required, in turn, he concluded, the establishment of these three monopolies. But in order to try to do this, Tamil elites had first to convince Sri Lankan Tamils as a whole to participate and support their project; and this meant that they, in turn, needed to create a homogenizing national project to mobilize the Tamil people. (I almost but did not quite ask, at this point, in what sense the 'Tamil people' as a collectivity did all these things if, later, elites had to create a national project to convince the same Tamil people to support it. He would likely have pointed out that his conception presupposes elite leadership.)

Now, in an already established nation-state, Sivaram argued, the comprehensive deployment of a homogenizing national project requires resources on a huge scale: TV stations, radio stations, newspapers, a system of formal education, and so forth. So the capitalist class that controls such states will tend to lead in deploying the homogenizing national project, for, of course, *their* interest is to create, expand, and maintain workforces and markets, and all this a common national code or 'narration' (Sivaram 1993, after Bhabha 1990;) also allows them to do. Sivaram then paused for a moment, looked somewhat uncomfortable, and admitted that in contemporary circumstances global capitalism in some ways tends to undercut, challenge, and destabilize this kind of nationalism. But, again, he said that he would have to deal with this difficulty later. And so he did, in fact, by invoking Smith's 'international-ization of nationalism' argument that globalization's transnational legal forms – treaties, trade agreements, etc. – actually tend to confirm or 'normalize' nation-states even as they undercut their sovereignty in other ways (2001: 138). The national state, for Sivaram (as for Smith), is clearly itself a form of globalization. In any case, leaving globalization momentarily to one side, homogenizing nationalisms are clearly dependent on state resources.

But counter-nationalisms that are resisting such homogenizing nationalisms, like Tamil separatism, do not, at first, have access to state or state-like resources. So instead, he asserted, they must fall back on a mix of *pre-existent* 'high' culture (or 'narration' – for here he differs from Bhabha) and on their common *existential* bonds – on, that is, in the Sri Lankan case, what Sivaram called their 'Tamilness' – to forge their modern national code. This, then, was the substance of Sivaram's 'realist' response to 'non-realist' notions of nationalism: that when (violent) push comes to (violent) shove, pre-existent (though not eternal or immutable) ethno-discursive 'narrations' *and* experiences of 'Tamilness' are simply so inextricably bound up with the *making* of states *per se* – let alone, in modern circumstances, with the making and resisting of nation states – that to claim national identities are merely the epiphenomenal byproducts of modern nation-states (as Gellner, Anderson, and Hobsbawm variously do) is to put the cart very much before the horse. At this point Sivaram, tired of talking and walking, went back to Colombo and left me to ponder his view of nationalism.

THE MATTER OF HUMAN RIGHTS AND GROUP RIGHTS

He returned a week later to visit an old friend, Jude Fernando, a batchmate of his from Peradeniya University days who is now an assistant professor of geography at Clark University. We all had dinner together at Jude's house – at that time, a partially constructed three-story shell hinting of nicer things to come – which is high atop a hill overlooking Kandy. A host of similarly incomplete houses surrounded it, globalization having excited a hectic building boom in the cool Hintanna hills. We ate our hoppers, rotis, and mutton curry at Jude's red plastic kitchen table and then took our chairs, glasses, and bottles (red wine for Jude and me, and, for Sivaram, Johnny Walker black label – Jude's duty-free) up to Jude's incomplete third story.

'Don't drink too much,' said Jude, leading the way up.

'Why not, *maccaang?*' Sivaram huffed, making rather heavy going of the stairs. 'The night is young.'

'You'll see.'

The 'third story,' when we came out of the stairway hut, was simply a concrete pad open to the stars. On three sides a deeper darkness beyond the dim gray of the pad proclaimed the 30-foot drop that would pre-emptorily conclude any incautious wandering.

'A man could easily die,' said Sivaram reflectively. He paced, rather ostentatiously, but cautiously, to the very center of the pad and placed his chair down facing the busy lights of Kandy. I walked, with equal caution, to one of the precipices.

'Jesus!'

'Don't walk about, *maccaang*. Don't look. Sit down and drink. If we don't move we won't die.'

'Well,' said Jude, thoughtfully, 'at least not immediately.'

In any case, at some point that night, I raised some objections to Sivaram – for I had spent the intervening week thinking about how conventional Western liberalism would react to these views. Take the issue of human rights. Surely, I said to Sivaram, Western liberals would argue that your description of states and nation-states leaves individual human rights, and hence individuals, in a precarious position. That is, your definition of a 'nation' posits the utter dependence of human identity and status on the group identity that underlies the nation. But Western liberals would surely argue that this assumption that an individual human's status is so utterly dependent on their membership in some 'national' group leaves individuals too vulnerable. For, by this definition, liberals might say, people who cannot participate in a national project (perhaps because they are too culturally distinct) are not only *going* to be mistreated, but (it could be argued) even *deserve* to be mistreated because of the threat they pose to the essential, nationalizing project. That is, since the excluded, by your thesis, will necessarily resist, they also, by merely existing, threaten the national project upon which all individuals depend for their identity and rights, and so can be justly attacked or forcibly removed. (Of course, communitarians and Burkian conservatives run into this same issue.) Now to most Western-style liberals – indeed, to me as well – this all sounds rather frighteningly like the very logic used by the Sri Lankan state to attack

Tamils in 1983 and by the LTTE to exclude Muslims from Jaffna in 1990. Nor could any *individual*, under your definition, question such attacks on the grounds that they violate the individual human rights of the members of the excluded group since such rights, according to your thesis, derive from the nation-state itself, and therefore can only be applied *after* its establishment. But given this, liberals could argue, the only recourse for individuals seeking to protect themselves or others from such abuses is to turn to a competing ethnic group. And the only recourse for such an ethnic group, in turn, would be collective, violent, and equally repressive – for in the Hobbesian war of all ethnic groups against all other ethnic groups that you describe, there will only be room for the strong and the gone. But surely, liberals might well conclude, this is all morally questionable; for there must be *something* wrong with a definition of nationalism that not only explains but would also seem to justify attacks on minority groups.

Beyond this, I said, could not a Western liberal argue that when nationalism is defined, as it is by you, as emerging from the context of a Hobbesian inter-group war, then this amounts to justifying and even valorizing 'invidious particularism' – that is, the kind of nationalism that not only asserts a group's sovereign identity, but also denies both the identity and sovereignty of all immediately proximate but weaker groups? They might admit, I said, that you are not advancing 'invidious particularism' as a *positive* ethical claim about nationalism – that nationalism *should* be this way – and grant that you are making an empirical claim about the way nations, in fact, are, based on the cultural constraints you claim are basic to their formation. But even with this proviso, they might still assert, correctly, that it remains a logical implication of your thesis that all nationalisms must (at least at some point) necessarily take on an 'invidious particularist' form.[2] But if this were so, then it would likely raise two questions for Western liberals. First, empirically, they would likely ask if it is it really the case that nationalisms always take this 'invidious particularist' form? Are there not, in history, they might say, examples of nationalisms that explicitly supported other, proximate nationalisms? For instance, was not such support shown in South America during the Creole wars of independence from Spain? And, for that matter, did not the Sri Lankan Tamil nationalist struggle receive support from nearby Tamil Nadu?

Second, more fundamentally, liberals might ask whether your definition of nationalism, looked at from within the context of the Hobbesian inter-group war you presuppose, implies not only something essentially immoral about nationalism but also, perhaps more importantly, something *impractical* about any nation-state so conceived. For there seems to be, they might argue, a kind of practical paradox involved in a nation-state so invidiously described. And they could argue this as follows: all national states, by your logic, are justified in suppressing all other national identities; for to allow alternative identities to exist would be to impede the national project and threaten the nation-state's continued existence. (This, they might note, is why you point out that even ostensibly 'multicultural' nation-states like the United States in fact continue to violently repress their ethnic and 'racial' minorities.) But in suppressing other national identities, surely the nation-state thereby not only rejects the very rationale that underlies its own legitimacy (that is, that a 'nation' deserves and requires sovereignty), but provokes the very resistance its invidiousness is predicated upon and is deployed to suppress? Indeed, they might claim that you described an occurrence of this very paradox in your example of British practices in South India. Ultimately, therefore, would not nationalism so described be a matter of continually cutting off one's (minority) nose to spite one's (majority) face? And could they not argue that it was this very practical paradox, arising from just this kind of 'invidious nationalism,' that underlay the failure of nationalism in Sri Lanka? For did not Sinhala 'chauvinism,' they might say, end up breeding its own worst nightmares (that is, the LTTE and the JVP) precisely because it 'invidiously' insisted upon the effective elision of all other national identities? Finally, might they not conclude, given that 90 per cent of the world's existing states are in fact multi-ethnic (Connor 1995: 39), and that most such states are largely peaceful, that it is most unlikely that this invidious form *is* the only form nationalism can take? For ultimately, they might say, if this is the only form nationalism can take, then the implication – a war everywhere, all the time – would seem to involve the very sort of continuous violence that you earlier said was 'self-negating.'

Surely, therefore, out of group and state self-interest if nothing else, liberals could argue that a national state or nationalism *must admit to some individual rights that are prior to national rights*, and thus are not dependent upon a person being lucky enough to be part of a majority group or a group big enough to struggle for an independent state. That is, at the very least, they might say, *the right to belong to a group identity must be admitted*. But if this is so, then liberals could argue that there are and should be, for both moral and practical reasons, human rights that are in some sense prior to the state, and that can block the full implementation of national projects, particularly when national states are striving for the degree of modern 'comprehensibility' – to use your term – that appears to require the mistreatment of minorities. The alternative, they might point out, would appear to be 'self-negating.' But if their argument were true, then, by your own argument, a fully 'comprehensive state – with all three monopolies in place – would be actually not only immoral but impractical.

Sivaram looked pained at all this and said that, in his opinion, while there might be some merit in these liberal theories, this kind of privileging of individual human rights only tends to be done in practice by people – usually rich Westerners 'like you, *maccaang*' – who came from already established nation-states where they happen to be a members of the majority. In actual practice, he claimed, this kind of gesturing toward universal human rights tends to occur only when established powers are interested in limiting the resistance of opposing national projects. 'Look at the US in Iraq, Mark! They invade, they claim, to protect the Iraqi people's human rights, which they say were being violated by Saddam Hussein because he killed and tortured people from groups that opposed him; then they turned right around and used his very prison to torture Iraqi people from groups that, guess what, oppose the US. And they argued, at least at first, that they had to do this to combat "terrorism"!'

'Yes, but look at the ruckus that kicked up. They screwed up their whole deal by doing it. Surely, then, Iraq is actually an example of the moral-practical paradox that liberals can point to?'

'No, it's an example of how human rights discourse is completely implicated in nationalist politics. In this case, American nationalist politics.'

And so he referred me, first, to the arguments put forward by M. Sornarajah, a Jaffna law professor, on this very issue. Sornarajah, in an address to the International Tamil Foundation in London on 25 June 2000, argued that the right to secede from a state depends upon world recognition of group rights. Such rights, he believed, have been sadly undervalued by the Western liberal focus on individual rights. But the pre-eminence of this Western view, he claimed, was an artifact of colonialism held in place, after World War II, by the polarizing international relations born of the struggle between the US and the Soviet Union for world dominance. In a post-Cold War, globalizing world, he claimed, this undervaluing of group rights was altering in the direction of the recognition of group rights:

The Western liberal tradition emphasizing individual human rights is on the wane, as it comes increasingly to be recognized, even in the West, that there is a case for the protection of the rights of linguistic and religious groups within societies. Thus, the 1991 Proposal for the European Convention on the Protection of Minorities clearly acknowledges the collective dimension of the rights of ethnic groups. As Western societies become multi-ethnic, the emphasis on individual rights continues to remain but there is also an increasing awareness that ethnic rights have to be protected. The Western tradition that has remained impervious to group rights may now be shifting. This may portend a greater acceptability of the right of secession by states accustomed to the liberal tradition and make them more aware of the need for the assertion of group rights. (Sornarajah 2000: 3)

Sornarajah then pointed out that one basic problem of international law has long been how to preserve the nation-state system while at the same time protecting the collective rights of ethnic groups. Thus the UN Resolution 'On friendly relations between states' (UN 1970), he claimed, is an attempt to reconcile both these principles when it asserts the global legal integrity of nation-states, but with the proviso that secession from them is justified if (and only if) it can be shown that a particular group within a state has persistently received unequal treatment. This, according to the professor, is precisely what could be shown in Sri Lanka. There, he claimed, adequate legal protection of Tamils' rights has obviously been withheld since independence – despite attempts by the Sri Lankan state to cover this discrimination up – and so the right of Tamils to secede from the state follows legally and justly from this persistent recorded inequality. Moreover, since peaceful methods of pursuing secession were violently suppressed by the Sri Lankan government, Tamils obviously have the right to use violence to establish a separate state.

'But even granting what Sornarajah says is true – and I think his historical account of how group rights were pushed to the background by the Western imperialism is true – does that really deal with the point liberals make about nationalism being, at least as you describe it, essentially repressive?'

'But my point is that such charges involve an essential misunderstanding of the nature of nationalism and national states because they treat nationalism like some kind of ideology. In fact, when they try to compare nationalism to other ideologies or to Western human rights discourse they involve a category mistake.'

Sivaram, pouring himself another drink, explained that he had once come across an article in *Foreign Affairs* by a post-Soviet Georgian reacting to various Western liberal arguments to the effect that nationalism *per se* – or, for liberal and communitarian nationalists, *some* 'invidious' forms of nationalism – was inferior ideologically to democratic, rights-based, liberalism. The man's counter-argument, as Sivaram remembered it, was twofold. First, he argued that, historically, democratic liberalism and rights discourse both show up only after the establishment of modern-style nation-states. More importantly, when they do show up, such ideologies always presuppose a national state, for it is only within the arena of action – Sivaram called it the 'space' or the 'playing field' – provided by the national state that ideologies can take place. In the same way, he argued, it is only *citizens* who have rights.

'I think this guy is right. Comparing nationalism to ideologies is like comparing a house to a ... a *rafter*; it makes no sense. It's a complete category mistake. But everybody,' said Sivaram, 'falls into this trap of trying to think of nationalism as a kind of ideology that can be contrasted with democracy, communism, fascism, or what have you. Look at how Anthony Smith – who otherwise gets nationalism right, I think – starts talking about nationalism in his conclusion.'

Sivaram picked up Smith's book, which he had wanted present for our conversation, and leafed through its conclusion. He started jabbing his finger at various passages – at random, apparently, because it was still completely dark.

'Here. First he says something right: that nationalism is a "politicized form of culture" [Smith 2001: 142]. That is exactly what I am saying. But he also persists in thinking of nationalism as a kind of "ideology" with "sacred foundations". As, in fact, a kind of religion. Now here, it seems to me, he makes two errors – errors that a lot of others make too. First, he tends to speak of nationalism as some kind of reified thing. No. Nationalism is a *dynamic* thing. It comes when the requirement arises – when a habitat is threatened – and it goes when it is not needed. But this is true of all language games. Some language games, the football club, have less hold than others

– say, that of Mandur's temple. So language games have different degrees of permanence.'

'And this brings me to this "sacred foundations" stuff. Here he is falling into the trap of contrasting liberal values with the values of nationalism. And I am saying this is a category mistake. Because these values that he is talking about themselves exist within the playing field defined by nationalism, and stand on the "sacred foundations" of the state as they would be seen by, say,' he laughed, 'George Bush!'

He shook his head.

'This Smith is a British fellow, right? How does he explain that mad ass, Tony Blair? Isn't he going after the same "sacred" nationalism as George Bush? I am saying that this business of contrasting "transcendental" liberal values with nationalism is something that cannot be done. That it is a false contrast based on a category mistake.'

I wanted to nail this down so, putting down my glass, I said:

'So what you are saying is that nationalism is not an ideology. And that to compare it to other ideologies is a mistake. Rather than an ideology you are saying it is a phenomenon of social organization at a certain level?'

'Yes. And that is why I say so many times that it cannot be compared to other ideologies. It is nations and nationalism that define the playing fields. And all these things – economics, rights, culture, ideologies – all this stuff occurs within the framework defined by a nation-state.'

'But then what do you do with the anti-globalization movements which are transnational and so forth?'

'We have not yet discussed what is beyond the nation-state. But I always presuppose that the nation-state (as opposed to nationalism and nations) is a historical phenomenon, and a modern one. It is, perhaps, only two centuries old; and not really even two centuries old. For if we are to understand the nation-state with its current capacity to mobilize violence, it is really a post-World War II phenomenon. If you carefully examine the matter, and look at the counter-insurgency handbooks that I mentioned the other day, then you are looking at developments in the technologies of violence that make the modern state possible.'

'Surely, Sivaram, Hitler had the modern technologies of repression all worked out.'

'No, and this is why my discussion of counter-insurgency is also integral to our discussion here – for the counter-insurgency handbooks were developed – although they have their origin in the small wars of the British Empire ...'

But at this point it began to rain. We looked about, somewhat dazed, and noted that Jude had already beat a judicious retreat – taking the flashlight with him.

'OK. Now we are going to die,' I said.

'Maybe the stairs are this way,' said Sivaram, setting off resolutely in the wrong direction, and almost consigning himself to the depths. I grabbed his arm, pulled him around, and pointed toward the dim outline of the stair shack. The rain quickened. And suddenly we heard the anemic horn of the three-wheeler we had earlier ordered to come and pick us up.

On our way up the mountain to my house in the three-wheeler, Sivaram started feeling his whisky. The climb was steep, and our battered green three-wheeler was both ancient and underpowered, with sprung wheels that caused it to list worryingly whenever we went around corners. The driver was shaking slightly; I hoped, with cold. At one point we hung out over a curve that displayed lights so small that they could have been stars but were actually cars on the road below, twinkling minutely. Sivaram laughed.

'Ah, *maccaang*! This is the life. Late at night, a three-wheeler, drunk, the wind blowing through everything. I have lived a full life, my good son. A full life. And do you know why I continue to be friends with you for all these years?'

Caught somewhat off guard, I said. 'Why? Surely not my matchless wits.'

'It is nothing intellectual. It is because you are a warrior. A warrior. Had you not fought for me that night 20 years ago at the checkpoint I would have been a dead duck, *maccaang*. And all of my life since would have been nothing. Nothing.'

A warrior? Me? Hardly that – hardly me being anything of the kind, except terrified. The thought filled me with a vague alarm that mingled with the wine and the lurching of the three-wheeler into a kind of nauseous vertigo. For I still, occasionally, thought of the frightened soldier and the infinite hole his rifle barrel had been. Sometimes, during a lecture in class, I would turn the corner of an argument and see his finger tightening on the trigger, and Sivaram standing in the background, over his shoulder, hands folded politely in front of him, head bowed slightly, like one already dead. And then it would be gone, and there would be students again, looking slightly puzzled. '*Dr Whitaker? Dr Whitaker? You were saying?*' But as we bounced along, the wind whipping my face, I suddenly wondered something that I did not say. For if Sivaram was right, and the nation-state defined the arena for all public morality, then why were we not both *dead*?

8 RETURN TO BATTICALOA

> Myself when young did eagerly frequent
> Doctor and Saint, and heard great Argument
> About it and about: but evermore
> Came out by the same Door as in I went.
> (*The Rubáiyat of Omar Khayyám*, Fitzgerald 1942: 28)

> This column tries deliberately to be the 'other voice' in this scene, out of tune with
> the litany that saturates the political atmosphere on the southern side of this island's
> ethnic divide, so that people can see a need to hedge their bets on the ethnic question.
> (Taraki 2005d)

> People cannot live by ethnic politics alone. (Taraki 2005g)

On 19 October 2000 the 38-year-old Tamil reporter Mylvaganam Nimalarajan was sitting at his desk at home in Jaffna typing up a story when assassins shot him through his open window. They then rolled a grenade into the family living room, which fortunately killed no one else when it exploded, and quickly fled into the night (TamilNet 19 October 2000). Nimalarajan wrote for *Viirakeesari*, and both the Sinhala and Tamil sections of the BBC, but also, more secretly, for TamilNet, for whom he was the premier Jaffna correspondent. Many knowing analysts suspected that members of the EPDP, an armed Tamil paramilitary group allied to the government, were guilty of the killing, since it was the EPDP's more shadowy activities in the north that Nimalarajan had been reporting on lately. Others, particularly reporters for the Tamil and Sinhala sections of the BBC whom I talked to eight months later, saw the murder more as a government 'message' to the effect that reporting embarrassing government doings in the north and east was not going to be tolerated. Sivaram, though he believed both theories likely, thought the death was also aimed at TamilNet. Soon after, as if to confirm this suspicion, anti-Sivaram editorials began to appear with regularity in the Sinhala press. The most vitriolic of these, however, was not in one of the various, government-controlled, Lake House newspapers,[1] but in *Divaina*, *The Island*'s Sinhala-language sister paper, and in the columns of Keerthi Warnakulasuriya. There, as time wore on, Warnarkulasuriya repeatedly called for the army to act against Sivaram, whom he called a 'tiger propagandist' living 'freely and without problems' in Colombo.[2] As this kind of tension mounted, I tried convincing Sivaram by email that he should leave Sri Lanka for a while to let things cool down; but he was not responsive. Then I had another idea, and started to write a grant proposal.

So, in July 2001, Sivaram and I took a trip together to see his family in Toronto and London. The notion had been brewing between the two of us for some time, and he could hardly say no. For Sivaram had long argued to me that I could not understand him or what his career had become without meeting the Tamil diaspora and more of his widely scattered family. Hence, upon receipt of the grant that would (barely) cover our expenses, we began our trip from where we had arranged to meet over email: Poughkeepsie, New York, my old home town, and the somewhat care-worn Mid-Hudson Valley city of 50,000, about 70 miles north of New York City, where my parents still live. When I finally got to town, however (I had to drive up from South Carolina), and had swung by to pick up Sivaram at the address he had provided me, I found myself disoriented by its being the long-time residence of a friendly Sri Lankan Tamil medical doctor, Rajan Sriskandarajah. What surprised me was that this amiable man, who asked to be called Dr Rajan, had lived in Poughkeepsie completely unbeknownst to me for many years – having arrived in my home town not long after I first departed it to conduct fieldwork in *his* country. Indeed, I was bemused to discover that Dr Rajan knew my cousin Karen, a nurse who, like him, also worked at Poughkeepsie's Vassar Hospital. The Tamil diaspora, clearly, and once again, had made an utter mockery of the various cultural and geographic distances that my profession once so naïvely presupposed. And so it was with a weird sense of seemingly alien worlds converging – or of worlds never, in actuality, far apart suddenly revealed as one – that I drove off with Sivaram from the good doctor's house.

That evening we went out to dinner with my family at Gentleman Jim's, a modest American-style restaurant, where I watched with amazement Sivaram deploying a courteous and gentle charm with my parents and brother that he rarely displayed to me. He complimented my parents on their home, their appearance, their health, and (flashing a quick, wry glance my way) their younger son with courtly aplomb. He decorously devoured his dinner and sipped his one glass of wine. He charmed our high-school-age waitress, who kept glancing at him from the safety of her waitress station, while gossiping about him with her friends. He praised my older brother's colorful descriptions of local watering holes, and promised to try them out with him should he have the chance. He let my son to climb all over his feet under the table. My parents said they had rarely met anyone so gracious. I was agog. And Sivaram laughed at my reaction as we loaded the car, 'Don't looked so shocked, young man. I don't *have* to be cantankerous.' Then we set out for Newark airport and our flight to Toronto.

So this was how Sivaram first introduced me to the Tamil diaspora: through his in-laws. For in Toronto, we visited Bavani's family: her brothers, Daniel and David, and their families; her parents; her sister Rathi, widow of the LTTE-assassinated Vasutheva; and various other cousins and their families. Most of these people, I found, had been drawn together by each other's example, and were living in fairly modest apartments and houses in Mississaugu, not far from the lakeshore. A partial exception was Daniel, whose more substantial (though hardly ostentatious) two-story house was a testimony to his earlier arrival, his passionate industry, and his having founded a successful paper recycling business in alliance with two white Canadian partners. Like many other Tamils in Toronto, the migratory journeys of Sivaram's in-laws (starting in the mid-1980s and running through the late 1990s) correlated neatly with Sri Lanka's datable spasms of violence. Interviewing them was like reviewing the war.

Beyond the family, we toured Jamestown, according to Sivaram the oldest public housing project in the world, and now occupied almost exclusively by Tamils – most rather poor, and sometimes beset by the Tamil gangs (named after Jaffna peninsula villages) that clash there. We walked down Gerrard Street, called 'little India' by white Canadians, but dominated by Sri Lankan Tamil shops selling South Asian groceries, Tamil movies (videos or DVDs), Tamil music CDs, Hindu religious paraphernalia, multicolored sarongs and saris, and often advertising '24 carat gold jewelry' (for, Sivaram said, 'Tamils want nothing less'); in short, a street selling just what you might once have found in any good-sized Tamil town in Sri Lanka. We visited Scarborough, along Eglinton Avenue, and the offices there of several threadbare Tamil human rights organizations; after which we had a quick lunch in a rather seedy Chinese restaurant with a group of their frustrated lawyers, all nostalgic for their profession, all seeming somewhat shocked at finding their skills neglected in a land where they could hold few briefs. Later that day, we went to a party in a newly built brick house in an expensive suburb outside Toronto, a place with a huge cathedral ceiling in the front, four bedrooms, a formal dining room, and a vast white kitchen, the whole carpeted in furry white like the top of an old man's head.

And all the time I felt, emotionally, dizzy; because everywhere there were Tamils, so many (over 150,000) that I felt like I was in Sri Lanka; so many that the Toronto Tamils had developed their own (quite thick) phone book, and myriad temples, support groups, refugee organizations, 'old boy' school societies, newspapers, and radio stations (many though not all pro-LTTE), and, of course, businesses. Walking down a street in Mississaugu or Scarborough I kept meeting Tamils from Jaffna, Tamils from Batticaloa, even Tamils from Mandur. At a party, I met by chance an old friend, an NGO worker I had known well years before in Batticaloa who had just arrived, that very night, from two years of refugee limbo in Manila. Though always resolutely non-political (he was one of the Readers' Circle stalwarts), he had been nonetheless remanded under the Prevention of Terrorism Act in 1998, tortured at Boosa military camp, and then, when international pressure forced his release, forced to flee the country to the Philippines and further, much more benign, internment as a stateless refugee. He looked drawn and grayly frail, like a set of frayed work clothes; and the traces of torture were still on him and flitted through his eyes. But he was incredulous and very glad to meet me, and kept shaking and shaking my hand. He was, he said, dazed to be in Canada. A philosopher by training and inclination – that was his affiliation with Sivaram and with me – he knew that he must be resigned to years of hardship in Canada. 'It's hard here. I know. Everyone says so. But I am alive and life ... life ...' He shook his head, bemusedly.

'Is life,' said Sivaram, turning toward the buffet table.

I talked to a number of people in Toronto besides members of Bavani's immediate family, but only 20 altogether, enough for impressions rather than conclusions. Politically, these people ranged from emphatically nationalist anti-LTTE through various shades of increasing enthusiasm for the Tigers to deeply nationalist pro-LTTE, though there were definitely far more in the latter category than in the first. There were also a few who seemed determinedly disillusioned with politics altogether. One man, in his 30s, who also had been tortured by the security forces in Sri Lanka in the late 1990s, was emphatic: when the LTTE came round asking for contributions, he told them to get out. He did not want to have anything to do with politics any more. 'No more. Me. *Finished.*' He hated the cold of Toronto, but 'What to do? I am here, no?' Others seemed to feel burnt clean of their identity by the horrors they experienced, echoing what Bavani's brother, Daniel later told me. 'I can't describe,' said the young businessman, 'how I felt when I flew out of Amsterdam airport. I knew that if I could just get through there that Canada would not turn me back. They didn't then. So as I flew out I just had this intense feeling that I was going to make it; I was going to survive. And after I got here I didn't think about culture or language or anything. I just worked and learned to survive. I was very lonely. But I had to survive.' Most, however, also felt an intense guilt at having left 'the struggle' behind – as David did, Bavani's younger brother, who had been active politically in Sri Lanka in the early 1980s, and who had also been twice imprisoned and tortured. 'Now,' he said, 'we live blood lives.' He meant, he told me, lives made good through the suffering and blood of those left behind – not just in Sri Lanka, but in the rest of the 'poor world.'

Most told me stories of some burst of terror or destruction that launched them on their course to Toronto. Still, many also told me that life in Toronto was harder than in Sri Lanka; that they felt they were working all the time, driving all the time ('Life, here, is through a windshield!'), with barely a moment to do or know anything else. I was pleased to be able to talk more freely with women in Toronto, something difficult for a male to do in Sri Lanka, and a new freedom and a growing sense of empowerment that women I spoke to were both aware of and for which they seemed genuinely grateful. Yet they too generally said life was hard; that the new freedom was paid for with great labor. 'Here we women have to work hard. Not like Sri Lanka. But I'm used to it now,' said one 45-year-old woman in Missisaugua about her workdays of twelve hours or more. But no one I talked to believed they would ever return permanently to Sri Lanka; there was no 'myth of return' so far as I could see, and many said they could feel their children drifting away, losing (or never receiving) their Tamil, perhaps finding more in common with Rap than Karnatic dance or Madras movie music. In one case a 50-year-old woman anxiously reported that her son, with his hair in prominent dreads, had announced disdainfully: 'I'm rasta now, *Amma*. Not Tamil. *Rasta!*' Her eldest son, however, still smiled down from a photo in a gold frame with the wings he had just won glittering on his new commercial pilot's uniform. His face, she told me, conspiratorially, was so happy because he was full of the plans he now had for the wife he intended to marry from Sri Lanka – as soon as that could be safely arranged.

I should mention that everywhere we moved in Toronto Sivaram was received with a respect that bordered on reverence. Sivaram, many people told me, was their only window on what was really happening in Sri Lanka – not just the facts, which they could now get off the internet, but of what the facts meant. And his voice was all the more valued because, unlike most Sri Lankan Tamil intellectuals who had been politically active in the 1980s, Sivaram had stayed in Sri Lanka. It was this precise fact, however, that most concerned his brothers-in-law, who argued that Sivaram had risked himself long enough. He should come to Canada with Bavani and the children, they said, anxiously. It was just too dangerous, and he had done enough. Sivaram, affectionately, shrugged them off: 'If I am not in Sri Lanka, what am I? What would I do in Toronto? What would I be? No.'

We moved on to England. There we found a reprieve from the war, albeit by stepping back into the alternative universe still emanating from distant Stanley House. For then we spent time with all 'the gang.' We stopped several days with Sivaram's brother, Kuttan, at his suburban home in Dorridge. There, one night, we ate partridge, drank good wine, and Kuttan talked, in his rather quiet way, far into the night about family history. 'We lived in our own world, Mark,' he said to me, refilling my wine glass while Sibelius' *Finlandia*, which he had just put on, swelled in the background. 'We had our own nicknames, our own language; we were a clan apart. You have no idea. It was all very strange.' We spent a few days with Oppi – like Kuttan married to another medical doctor – at his home in London. Oppi immediately drew us into discussing his new intellectual enthusiasms: mathematics and Tamil linguistics, and spent a vivid hour describing the story of the family elephant. Oppi also put on a CD of Jules Massenet's *Thais: Meditation*, which Sivaram said was his father's favorite piece. Brought back as a 78 from his disastrous year at Cambridge, Sivaram's father, Keerthi, had often put the record on in the bedroom of the plantation bungalow in Tirukkovil, at their old Dharmarajah estate. There, Sivaram said, his father would listen while watching the dawn through his bedroom window. Oppi, nodding, said that in his mind he still sometimes saw the sea through the open French doors of that old house. Later that week, sticking with our theme, we met Lee Karu, the barrister, barely out of his robes and still bristling with self-confidence and verbal cheer after a long but successful day in court. Like all the gang,

Lee Karu still called Sivaram 'Kunchie,' and greeted him with warm pride. He stood us to an elaborate Italian dinner at a fashionable restaurant – ordering a succession of wines I'd never heard of and could never afford – and then took us back to his three-story house in an expensive, clearly upper-middle class, London neighborhood, where he regaled me with elegantly told stories about family history till 4:30 in the morning, while Sivaram roared like an old bus engine on the sofa nearby, asleep. The next day, Oppi, Sivaram and I (the latter two of us, however, rather tired) also spent a pleasant afternoon chatting with Sivaram's Uncle Veluppillai, the old accountant, who served us tea in good china with little muffins he must have made himself – his wife, Elizabeth, having already died.

Then we visited Surendaran, the son of the stubborn Mylvaganam, Sivaram's mother's brother – the same who rejected marriage with Sivaram's father's sister, Ranjani, out of love for his wife to be, and thus started off the family feud that eventually helped destroy the wealth of Stanley House. Consequently Surendaran's path in England had been, economically, more thorny than the gang's. The unease between his family and Stanley House had meant that he was ten years in Britain before he contacted any of his cousins. The antipathy of the Stanley House women – the 'old stones' as Oppi said everyone had called them – toward Surendaran's mother, whom they called, dismissively, a 'country woman' (she was actually a teacher, like Mylvaganam), had entailed not only a fall in the family's fortunes and class position in Batticaloa but the persistence of this misfortune in England, and the continued familial tension it encouraged. In any case, Surendaran lived in a modest house in Leicester, with his wife and three children. And Leicester itself was a revelation. For it was a largely South Asian city by then; so much so that as Surendaran drove us down the Melton Road, it seemed like being transported to Madras or Delhi – or perhaps, more accurately, Gujarat. The street was completely full of South Asians, mostly (according to Surendaran) Gujaratis, but there were also Tamils and Sinhalese, and Sikhs and Pakistanis, and very few whites – a mingling weave of vibrant diasporas that seemed imprinted nonetheless with a subtle background batik of the washed-out, nineteenth-century industrial city that Leicester once was.

Then, on 24 July 2001, a small group of Black Tigers, apparently swaddled in explosives, and carrying machine guns, rocket-propelled grenades, anti-tank weapons, and 40 mm grenade launchers, attacked Katunayake airport, the main international airport in Sri Lanka, about 20 miles north of Colombo, and destroyed much of Sri Lanka's military and civilian air fleet (*Tamil Times* 15 July 2005). As soon as we heard this, our trip collapsed like a punctured balloon, and I, for one, felt a great but familiar weight pull me down. For it seemed once again that whenever I was with Sivaram a crisis would follow; as, in fact, crises always did – one after another – right to the end. So Sivaram and I broke off our peregrinations and returned to central London where Sivaram, with his military analyst hat firmly back on, rushed about giving interviews, including one at BBC headquarters for BBC TV to which I tagged along, admitted only because I was his biographer.

It took place deep in the bowels of the old BBC headquarters in a tiny, completely dark room that smelled vaguely of cabbages, photocopy machines, and old cigarette smoke. The room was empty of everyone and everything but a TV camera and a chair (both painted black), and an abstract backdrop. Biographers not being provided for, I had to squat in the corner, holding out my tape-recorder like a fishing lure. Suddenly bright lights exploded, and a female voice boomed hollowly from a wall speaker.

'Hello? Hello?'

'Hello?' said Sivaram back, experimentally.

'I'm Rita Pain,' said the voice. 'We will just be talking to you about the tactics and the timing. OK?'

'OK,' said Sivaram, unfazed, knowing the drill. I kept craning my neck, looking for the speakers.

After a long pause, there was a male voice. Dusky, deep, smoothly authoritative: the voice of the BBC at work.

'Hello.'

'Hello,' said Sivaram.

'Mr Sivaram? Can you hear me? What is your reaction to this attack?'

Before Sivaram could answer, the voice roared out again, suddenly bossy and Sergeant Majorish: '*Look at the camera, if you will!* Straight in. *Right down the barrel.*'

Sivaram's eyes merely flickered at this unfortunate metaphor.

'Straight into the camera,' he said.

'What is your reaction to this attack?'

'My reaction,' said Sivaram, in his slowest, deepest voice, as if he were laying carpet rather than speaking: 'like everyone else: that the LTTE has been able to get into the base and attack the vital installations – how they did it is what I have been thinking about.'

'So your first reaction,' said the voice, sounding now slightly dismissive and theatrically incredulous, 'is not to be horrified at the number of deaths but to wonder at how they did it?'

'Yes,' said Sivaram, phlegmatically, 'because anyone who lives in Colombo and who has been to that airport knows how secure that place is, and how absolutely difficult it appeared to get in there. For anyone. Particularly for Tamils.'

'So you think,' said the voice, somewhat less dismissively, 'that they must have had inside help?'

'I don't think. If you look at the other big attacks they have carried out in the north and east, the LTTE attacks usually begin *inside* the camp.'

'How significant would you say,' said the voice, professionally smooth again, 'is the timing of this attack, which Tamil Tigers say is as much on the economy as anything else?'

'I think the significance of the attack is that once again the Tigers have shown the Sri Lankan government that they can strike anywhere at will, and within Sinhala areas, within the capital. And, particularly now with this attack, they have shown that they can strike even in areas where there aren't any Tamils.'

Later, over drinks in the pub in the basement of BBC headquarters, I interviewed a BBC Sinhala section senior producer, Chandana Keerthi Bandara, a man who once reported for the leftist, Sinhala-language *Haraya* newspaper in Colombo, until coming to London in 1984. I was interested in what he thought of TamilNet, in whether he thought its reporting was balanced or (as many by then were saying) blatantly pro-Tiger, and how he accounted for the influence the news site had among those on all sides of the conflict who concerned themselves with Sri Lankan Tamil affairs. I was also interested in what he thought of Sivaram as a journalist, and whether he felt Sivaram was risking his reputation and, for that matter, his life by editing the site.

As I put these questions, Bandara, an urbane man with affable (but careful) eyes, his hair neatly drawn back behind his head in a tight ponytail, his hands slowly toying with his glass, was cautious before my spinning tape-recorder – not reticent, I think, but professional, taking care to say only what he wanted said. He told me that TamilNet 'was a unique thing' because it was 'getting the news out from the war-torn areas' when no other agency could – particularly after the death of Nimalarajan. He felt that politicians in the south labeled TamilNet pro-Tiger because they were labeling anything that gave accurate information about the war 'pro-Tiger.' He argued that although its web-based character made it something new in one sense, the attention it paid to what he called the 'death, destruction, rape, mayhem' of the war-torn areas – which he felt to be its real 'bias' – was in keeping with a long history of other papers in Sri Lanka that spoke up for the rights of neglected groups. For 'there have been papers for a long time crying for human rights, crying for environmentalist rights, crying for workers' rights – fascist rights also. So why not a paper for the oppressed when the Tamils are the most oppressed in the country?' Bandara regarded TamilNet as mainly accurate, though he pointed to one story that he could not verify, and which he felt had hurt the site's credibility, about the army once having put up posters in the east begging forgiveness for past atrocities. For the most part, however, he counted on and used the site's stuff. Its real fault, Bandara felt, was that TamilNet paid too little attention to the efforts of the anti-war left in the south, which elision fed the myth that the war was 'OK for the Sinhala masses'; though he admitted that Sinhala leftists (the JVP, for example) might feel being highlighted by TamilNet more 'shameful' than good. Nevertheless, he saw Sivaram as 'treading a very fine line in doing this show.'

'Really?' I said. 'Between what and what?'

'Between not being a journalist in the broader, unbiased arena – not falling into that – and also not falling into the pro-Tiger, war-mongering camp. And also at the same time he has to keep his journalistic integrity. Because he has built up his whole life among the Sinhala masses – or, I would say, the English-reading southern masses – as a journalist.'

I told him I was worried about Sivaram's safety and he agreed that what Sivaram was doing was not safe. Yet he felt, all the same, that Sivaram's work protected him. First, he said, 'Sivaram is a world-renowned journalist. He is not just an island phenomenon, or a peninsular phenomenon for that.' Moreover, because many people, Tamil and Sinhala, pro and anti-Tiger, depended upon TamilNet's information: 'People are always checking on whether he lives, what are his movements, is he all right. You see, he is a news provider. I mean, I am a newsmonger, and he provides it *free* to me. And if my provider dies ... I mean, this is a market world; he is a free provider; and if he is not there, how are we to sell the best news about Sri Lanka, which is the war?'

But I told Bandara that I remained worried. And so, when Sivaram found his way to the pub, I tried again to talk him into staying in Britian until things cooled down. There had been more threats on his life, as Bandara also pointed out, and talk of him being a 'traitor' in the government-controlled press. There had even been talk of his arrest; but Sivaram, as always, was contemptuous of the latter possibility: 'Let them arrest me. What would be the charge?' Later, while Sivaram was off finding the loo, I seem to remember Bandara turning to me, sympathetically, and just shaking his head.

The next day was to be my last in England; Sivaram was to return to Colombo a week later. I took the train to London from where I was staying with friends in suburban Redhill and met Sivaram at Victoria station. He had had a bad night. He had stayed with a friend who worked for the International Broadcasting Corporation-Tamil (IBCT), a satellite radio station that was one of a number of similar stations in Europe and Canada in which the LTTE had a controlling interest. Years later, Sivaram told me that IBCT had a standing offer to employ him in London but that he was reluctant to take them up on it because he felt that he would then no longer be a free agent. In any case, he had suffered all night (he suspected) from the oily lamb curry his friend had served him for dinner, and was very sleepy. We went to a large Waterstone's bookstore (which used to be Dillon's) to meet one of his TamilNet subeditors, a cosmopolitan young man who had lived in Britain since he was five, and then went on to an Italian restaurant near Piccadilly for a late lunch. Sivaram was delighted with his calamari and his glass of Tuscan red. Then the three of us wandered about Leicester Square, Soho, and China Town, all the time continuing, in a desultory way, the argument we had been having for days about his returning to Sri Lanka.

Gradually, as the three of us drifted back toward Victoria station for my departure, Sivaram grew rather depressed and depressing. He noted that his new electric watch had stopped and said, 'So shall my life stop. If soon after this I should die, that is what would dominate your thoughts about me. That I noted that my watch stopped and so will my life.' He said that the people reading my book would welcome this. 'Out of fear,' he intoned, lightly sneering, 'the "native" turns aside from Western philosophical sophistication and back to the snake charms and omens of his savagery.' I said I would say no such thing; it would contradict my thesis. He sniffed at this. I then said:

'So do you think we are all prisoners of our last interpretation?'

He genuinely laughed at that. Eventually, we ended up at a small pub in Victoria station. I bought Sivaram and the subeditor pints, and got a half for myself – knowing that I was going to be leaving shortly on the train to Gatwick. We were very thirsty by this time and drank with genuine pleasure. Sivaram then sat back, momentarily content, and started surveying the scene around us – the vast space, the rushing people, the huge digital train board, the row of shops, the hustle and the bustle, the colors and the roar – and slowly, carefully, he drew the moment into himself. I could see it filling his eyes, flooding his brain, washing over him until it culminated in his letting out a big breath, as if he had just successfully surfaced from a dangerously deep dive, or perhaps, the opposite, had finally given in to his drowning. 'Ah, *maccaang*,' he said to me, laughing, slapping his chest with sudden glee, 'I could die right now. That lunch was perfect, this beer is cool and good, and I have seen everything, done everything, and gone everywhere. It would not be such a shame to die now. Not now.' He shook his head slowly, turning his head deliberately again, like a surveillance camera, drawing it in.

'You know,' he said, fixing my eye for a moment, 'you are going to call the book "Learning Politics" but maybe it also should be "Learning Life". It's not just politics you know. It's all life. It's about really doing *all* life, not just the politics. That is just one part of it.'

'Well if it's about life,' I said, suddenly angry, 'then, dammit, why don't you stay in Britian and *live*? Why go back and be killed?'

'*Inshallah*, we shall meet again.'

'He says that,' said the subeditor, 'but like a bad penny he always shows up again. And I have his picture ready for the obituary and everything!'

We laughed at that, though a bit grimly. And then I was gone.

LAST WORK

After July 2001 I did not see Sivaram again for more than two years. The September 11 attack on the Twin Towers made subsequent travel to North America difficult for him and, beyond that, Sri Lanka in 2001, tottering toward an uneasy ceasefire, was going through its own upheavals. As for me, well, the vicissitudes of teaching closed in. Still, I could tell Sivaram was in the thick of things again when he emailed on 12 August, briefly, to say he was safely back. 'The place is going down the drain,' he wrote, 'everything is a mess.' And, several weeks later, on 30 August: 'Fellows are still after my blood. But life goes on ...' For the most part, however, there was silence, though Sivaram always remembered to call on my birthdays. Sivaram did email me once more in 2001, on 13 September, worried about how close the attacks on New York had been to Poughkeepsie; but, after being assured of my family's safety —'say hello to your family for me' – he soon slipped away again into the maelstrom of Sri Lanka's politics and his own projects. He was simply too busy to chat, as usual.

One of his tasks during those years, surprisingly, was formally political; for Sri Lanka was facing a new parliamentary election. With the failure of the PA government's last military campaigns in 2001, and with international pressure on both sides mounting for some kind of negotiated peace (though, as Sivaram always pointed out, the LTTE had been making serious offers of a ceasefire since December 2000), it seemed likely that a big change was coming. At this point, the UNP, under Ranil Wickramasinghe, had forged a new alliance, a United National Front (UNF), and was entering the electoral lists against a weakened People's Alliance with good prospects of winning. For his part, Sivaram was convinced that a ceasefire was indeed coming and would entail an altered political landscape in which political unity among Sri Lankan Tamils would be at a premium.

So Sivaram, after ten years of carefully steering clear of formal political entanglement with any of the Tamil parties, suddenly took an active part in creating a nationalist political alliance. This alliance was to be between many of the most important Tamil groups, including both ex-militant groups such as the PLOTE, EPRLF (Saresh) and TELO, and straightforward political parties such as the TULF and the All Ceylon Tamil Congress (ACTC), a small party Kumar Ponnambalam (son of a former government minister) had led before he was assassinated on 5 January 2000. Sivaram began his new activism by joining a group of Batticaloa District journalists and university lecturers, called the Tamil Renaissance Organization (*Tamilar marumalarci kaLakam*), and helping them draft a statement advocating unity among the various Tamil groups. By 'unity' they meant that the LTTE alone should be henceforth regarded by all parties as the sole representatives of the Sri Lankan Tamil people in any future peace talks. This idea was an anathema to many Tamil anti-LTTE groups, who in general regarded it as a tragic, LTTE-led cooption of what little remained of an independent Sri Lankan Tamil, civil society. But Sivaram claimed to me, later, that this kind of political unity was something the independent Sri Lankan Tamil press rather than the LTTE first advocated, and that Sivaram himself was pushing it (as always) for his own reasons. As for the LTTE, Sivaram said they at first seemed rather cool about the idea.

In any case, in November Sivaram helped smooth over difficulties within the potential alliance that arose when some Batticaloa TULF members, particularly Joseph Pararajasingham, objected to working with TELO because it had once been actively allied with the Sri Lankan army (and, earlier, the IPKF) against the LTTE. Pararajasingham argued that the LTTE would object to the whole alliance if it included TELO. At a tense meeting with TULF and TELO members at the Lakeview Inn, a small Batticaloa hotel, Sivaram suggested that they should simply go talk to the LTTE to see if they had any objections. So Sivaram and Indrakumar Prasanna, the General Secretary of TELO, slipped over the border into Tiger-controlled territory for an odd meeting with LTTE political officers. According to Sivaram, the Tigers at this meeting radiated an air of bemused indifference toward the whole alliance idea – but said, at last, no, they had no objections to TELO taking part. In any case, at a meeting in Colombo a few days before the election, Sivaram (among others) also helped convince the reluctant leaders of the ACTC to join the alliance by claiming that staying out would destroy their party's influence. As he told me, later, chuckling at his own hubris: 'I said if you are not going to do something for Tamil unity, we will go back to Batti and your effigy will be burned!' Sivaram also claimed that it was he, eventually, who gave the alliance its 'TNA' name by insisting on calling it the 'Tamil National Alliance' in TamilNet's articles rather than the lugubrious name the politicians had preferred: 'The Alliance of Tamil Parties.'

On 5 December 2001, as the UNF was winning control of Parliament, the TNA took 14 seats and 3.89 per cent of the popular vote, thereby denying most Tamil areas to the PA-allied EPDP. For his efforts, on 27 December, Sivaram was attacked and severely beaten when thugs armed with 'clubs, batons and swords' (TamilNet 30 Dec. 2001) came to destroy the offices of Batticaloa's *Thinakathir* newspaper while he was there typing up a TamilNet article.[3] Sivaram survived the attack with six stitches on his head and a bloody shirt. Two months later, on 22 February 2002, the UPF-dominated Sri Lankan government signed a ceasefire with the LTTE.

Why did Sivaram throw his efforts into this alliance after ten solid years of steering clear of any direct involvement in electoral politics? And why did he do so in expectation of a ceasefire? Speaking to me about these events in retrospect, on 3 March 2003, just a few hours before we first heard that Karuna was in rebellion against the LTTE in Batticaloa, Sivaram argued as follows. During periods of active fighting, he claimed, standard counter-insurgency doctrine holds that governments should pursue two objectives at the same time. On the one hand, governments should try to destroy the military ability of their insurgents. On the other hand, they should also work to erode what Sivaram called the 'will of the (insurgent) people to fight.' For 18 years, the Sri Lankan government, with its large army and draconian Prevention of Terrorism Act, had pursued both of these objectives assiduously. But the Sri Lankan government's efforts to defeat the LTTE *militarily* had failed, and the manner of that failure had actually worked against the other objective of eroding the Sri Lankan Tamil people's will to fight. Moreover, by late 2001 the US was seeking a simplified geopolitical landscape for its 'war on terror,' and the LTTE, stung by the successful efforts of the Sri Lankan government to deny it world political legitimacy (for example, the UK was convinced to ban the LTTE on 28 February 2001), was anxious to win back some international sympathy. The pressure on both sides to negotiate a ceasefire was, therefore, irresistible. Given that a protracted government–LTTE ceasefire was inevitable, Sivaram felt that, for Tamil people in general, the moment presented both an opportunity and a danger.

That is, given a ceasefire, Sivaram argued that the Sri Lankan government would face two choices: it could either negotiate an actual settlement of the conflict by agreeing to radically restructure the Sri Lankan state to address Tamil concerns, or it could use a ceasefire to engage in alternative counter-insurgency tactics (such as 'containment') under the cover of peace. Sivaram was dubious about the former possibility, given both constitutional impediments and what he called 'history' (he meant the long history of Sinhalese politicians being pulled back from the brink of political settlement by the anti-Tamil flanking moves of whomever constituted their opposition), but in 2001 he was still willing to hope. In his opinion, so long as the Sri Lankan government and the LTTE maintained what he called a 'strategic parity of military status' with one another (that is, each capable of posing a credible threat to the other), there would continue to be a small hope for a negotiated final settlement (Taraki 2004a). Still, he thought it more likely that the Sri Lankan government would be tempted to view the ceasefire primarily as an opportunity to erode political support for the LTTE and, more generally, for Tamil nationalism. He thought they would use a combination of soft 'confidence-building measures' (such as building up 'civil society' – that is, political pluralism – in the north) and harder 'shadow war' tactics to 'contain' the LTTE by, first, decreasing the stomach of its supporters for any continued insurgency and then either gradually melding the LTTE to the state in ways that mitigated its war-making powers (such as, for example, removing its tax base) or by splitting the LTTE from within through psyops tactics and internal subversion (Sivaram 2003a).

It occurred to me later how ironic it was that we were discussing these strategies on the very night that Karuna announced his rebellion – although Sivaram always believed that active Sri Lankan government involvement in Karuna's activities only came after the initial break. In any case, Sivaram suspected that this kind of 'progressive' dismantling of the LTTE's military and political power was what Ranil Wickremasinghe and his international supporters really had in mind. Nevertheless, formal Tamil political unity, Sivaram argued, might head this strategy off and keep alive the possibility of real negotiations (that is, 'real' in Sivaram's sense, involving consequential change in the structure of the state). It could do this by offering the Sri Lankan government fewer opportunities for pursuing its 'peaceful' C-I strategy and thus maintaining the military threat potential of the LTTE – this latter being the only thing, in Sivaram's opinion, bringing the Sri Lankan government to the table. This was why Sivaram got involved in the formation of the TNA.

That night, before we got the call saying that Karuna had rebelled, I pressed him on the goal of all this. You do this, I said, so that you can oppose and escape the hegemonic power of the Sinhalese-dominated Sri Lankan nation-state. More to the point, you do this to show that it is possible to oppose the hegemonic power of any nation-state. But suppose your *counter* counter-insurgency strategy really works and the LTTE-led negotiations result in some kind of LTTE-dominated *de facto* federal Eelam? Given the LTTE's propensity for one-party rule, has anything been improved? Would you really be willing to live in such a state? Would there be any room in it, for example, for obstreperous journalists? But Sivaram would not be drawn that night into directly answering my question. He remarked, instead, that he was less interested in any potential, final state-to-be than in the almost Derridean, public educational possibilities of the current political moment. During Sri Lanka's peculiar peace, he claimed, people everywhere could be shown the normally hidden ligaments of the modern national security state; for here they were being nakedly suspended between the mutually opposed military poles of the Sri Lankan state and the LTTE in a way that brightly displayed both entities. In fact, their public illumination was really a kind of dynamic artifact of the tension between them. This, he insisted, was what he wanted to teach people. And I realized that for Sivaram, as always, it was all about showing how things worked, and thus how they could be fought.

During this period Sivaram was also working on his scholarly history of the Batticaloa District. Even when I knew him as a young man, Sivaram had always had an ambition to rewrite the Batticaloa District's history in light of the Tamil, Dutch, and Portuguese documents he knew of (in Colombo archives) that previous scholars had either failed to consult or could not read. He was particularly scathing about historical claims made by anthropologists, like me, who based their work largely on oral histories leavened with relatively recent colonial documents. Thus, from the mid-1990s onwards, Sivaram had worked on a book-length response. This work had been several hundred pages long, as he told me sadly, when (perhaps in 1999 or 2000) it was lost when his laptop was stolen in Zurich railway station. Sivaram had set the laptop down by his side to check his ticket, and when he had looked up seconds later it was gone (Emmanuel 2005).[4]

With this grave setback, Sivaram had given up (temporarily, he thought) his efforts to write a book about Batticaloa history. Soon thereafter, though, he began working with Dennis McGilvray on several Dutch documents he had unearthed in the archives in Colombo. He also continued collaborating with E. Kamalanathan, his old teacher at St Michael's, with whom he had been diligently hunting down and translating the District's disorganized collections (generally found in dusty temple storage rooms) of old palm-leaf manuscripts (*eeTu*) since 1998. By August 2000, he was busy preparing a seminar on ancient Batticaloa history for Eastern University based on those sources. Sivaram had many contacts at Eastern University by this time, but none closer than the American-trained anthropologist Dr Yavaraj Thangaraj, a friend and former member of the Batticaloa Readers' Circle, who had by this time also become Sivaram's brother-in-law. 'Yuvi,' as Sivaram called him, had married Dr Meena Dharmeratnam, one of Sivaram's favorite sisters, also a professor at Eastern University.

In any case, I asked Sivaram about this seminar, and was piqued to find it was largely (as he viewed it) a refutation my own earlier work on the history and politics of Batticaloa's largest temples. As he replied, by email, on 2 August 2000:

You asked about my work. I basically argue in the Batticaloa university paper that all forms of temple-centered social organization in Batticaloa have evolved from a well-defined, text-centered/generated Chola system – one based on a clearly formulated Sanskritic social order and Tamil colonization schema in which the king constitutes a community by building a temple, clearing land for cultivation and, for the sustenance of it, settles cultivating castes and temple service castes, settles Brahmins and a warrior caste for maintaining the social order so established. The regeneration of such social order is through the sharing of temple honors in the following order: 1. Wannia chieftan (Kshatriya) 2. Brahim 3. Chetties (Vaisya) 4. Vellala [*VeLLaaLar*] (Sudras) and others. I analyze how the Mukkuwas [*Mukkuvar*] and Sirpathar [*Ciirpaatar*] have insinuated themselves through such a social order and finally established their respective positions and histories by meddling with texts on which the temple-based social order was 'predicated.' I show that the meddling, particularly in the case of [the] Sirpadar, has left traces of the story that they intended to gloss over – for the stakes included not just honor but paddy fields.

The moral of my story for you would be that the fieldwork, field-note prejudice of anthropology, which essentially assumes the oral native (whatever fine arguments to the contrary you may come up with) is a hopeless method of understanding this text-centered – 'Name of the Rose'-level society.

It was no surprise to me, therefore, that when Sivaram returned to Sri Lanka in 2001 he again took up this intellectual campaign to 'textualize' Batticaloa history. Along with Mr and Mrs Kamalanathan, Sivaram began to look into the *MaTTakkaLappu Maanmiyam*, the District's putative chronicle, really a hodge-podge collection of caste-tales and temple myths that apparently described Batticaloa's founding and precolonial history. The pundit F.X.C. Nadarajah had translated and published the *Maanmiyam* as a book in 1962, but Sivaram and the two Kamalanathans had become convinced that Nadarajah's version was actually based on an even earlier work, found in several *eeDu* versions, called the *MaTTakkalappu purva carittiram*, which they reconciled and translated into contemporary Tamil for publication as a book, with a brief 'Introductory Note' by Sivaram, in April 2005.

It was also during this period that Sivaram began to re-dedicate himself to journalism. By the time of our trip, it should be remembered, Sivaram had pretty well withdrawn from journalism. For a short period in 2000, Sivaram had even let his work for TamilNet slide. He never offered me any reason for this lapse in activity, except the general one that he was tired. I suspect, however, that his turning away from journalism might have had something to do with a delayed reaction to, and perhaps some guilt over, the death of his mother, Mahesvari, from cancer in 1996. 'Poor, poor woman,' he said to me, several times, 'She never stopped working.' I believe he never quite forgave himself for his inability to convince her to give up her endless legal struggles over the old family lands, or to restore her to the comfort and security she had known when young. Beyond this familial grief, however, there were also political concerns. Sivaram, for a time, lost faith in his ability to influence political opinion in the south through his Taraki columns, and saw the power TamilNet.com had to more subtly shape international coverage of Sri Lankan Tamil affairs as, simply, more important. Its importance was confirmed, for Sivaram, by the increasing risk editing it entailed – as demonstrated, for example, when Sivaram and three other journalists were singled out, in an ITV broadcast on 3 June 2000 (ITV is government-controlled), and accused of having direct links to the LTTE.[5] The three other journalists, sensibly, fled the country; Sivaram stayed.

But all this had a cost. By 2000, even TamilNet was beginning to tire Sivaram, for, in addition to the risks involved, editing the site was exhausting. Speed, of course, was central to TamilNet's ability to shape international coverage. It was because the site generally posted its stories ahead of the news cycles of the international news agencies (in addition to having better access to news in Tamil areas) that Reuters, Associated Press and the BBC grew increasingly dependent on TamilNet in their coverage of the war after 1997. But for Sivaram this meant constant, unceasing, labor. And although Sivaram did not like to admit to me that he worked hard, he would occasionally let slip that constantly being on call 24 hours a day – with his mobile phone often ringing in his sleep, or in his bath – was indeed wearing him down. Sivaram bore the pace patiently, partly by drinking more; but for this, too, there were consequences. He began to have liver and heart problems, and although in his final years he increasingly turned to Kuttan for temporary, medical palliatives, what he clearly needed most (as Kuttan often reminded him) was rest. At the same time, equally wearing for him perhaps, were the struggles over TamilNet.com itself. Twice, in 1998 and again in 2000, Sivaram had fended off offers by the LTTE to take over editorial and financial control of the site. With the help of two of the original founders of the site, Sivaram was able to keep TamilNet independent, but the effort involved was exhausting psychologically and, of course, in other more concrete ways, dangerous.

The ceasefire agreement between the Sri Lankan government and the LTTE, however, as well as the need to pay tutor and school fees for his children, galvanized Sivaram back into print journalism. In late 2001, after the elections, Sivaram joined with two friends, the journalist J.S. Tissainayagam and the anthropologist and geographer Jude Fernando, to start the *Northeastern Herald* (now *Northeastern Monthly*) with money from the Swedish Embassy. He wrote assiduously for the *Northeastern Herald* (as D. Sivaram) for the next year. By June 2003, however, he was also writing a column in Tamil for the leading Tamil newspaper, *Viirakeesari*. Moreover, in January 2004, 'Taraki' returned when Sivaram began writing weekly Taraki articles for the *Daily Mirror*.

Sivaram's new Taraki columns ran pretty much true to their earlier form, still both teasing and pedagogic, though with perhaps a slightly harder, more bitter edge to them than before. But his *Viirakeesari* writings marked a real departure.[6] Written at speed – even, frequently, dictated off the top of his head to a fellow reporter sent round by the *Viirakeesari* editor when worried by a pressing deadline – the results nonetheless were always carefully constructed. As many Sri Lankan Tamils with whom I discussed them pointed out, the *Viirakeesari* pieces were written in virtuoso local or *sen*-Tamil; and, since written for an exclusively Tamil audience, they were also more partisan, inclusive, and intimate than Sivaram's English work, with Sivaram often using the inclusive Tamil 'we' (*naam*) form, as if speaking, collectively, for (or as) all Tamil people, men and women (David Buck, personal communication). Moreover, in these Tamil columns Sivaram freely, almost exuberantly, displayed his nationalism, frequently referring to 'our freedom fight,' 'our homeland,' or 'our struggle,' as if finally leaving the reticence and coded circumspection of his English writing behind. It is important to understand, however, that these seemingly open effusions were, for Sivaram, still strategic. For Sivaram had particular political and pedagogic aims in mind in speaking so warmly to his Tamil readers. Politically, Sivaram was trying to prepare the Tamil public for a possible disappointment: the ultimate failure of the ceasefire and peace negotiations. Hence, in one piece (Sivaram 2003b) – an interview with a Sinhalese political scientist, Colombo University's Jayadeva Uyangoda – Sivaram asks Uyangoda to review the ways in which various clumsy interventions by the US and Japan in the peace talks had altered the 'strategic equilibrium' between the two sides in the Sri Lankan government's favor, and forced the LTTE to cancel negotiations. The resulting 'globalization' of the conflict, Uyangoda and Sivaram agreed, left less hope that a permanent peace could be arrived at. Pedagogically, Sivaram was trying to teach his Tamil readers to focus more broadly, first by laying out and explaining the strategic geopolitical factors he saw influencing Sri Lankan affairs, and then by arguing that Sri Lankan Tamils must realize that their 'freedom fight' had become hostage to the geopolitical competition between India, China, and the United States over the sea routes between the Bay of Bengal and the Indian Ocean region. He also claimed as important here American ambitions to head off the rise of any potential regional 'hegemons' (like India and China), and to gain access to usable runways and port facilities in South Asia. Thus any attempt to settle Sri Lanka's ethnic woes without reference to this global background, he seemed to suggest, was doomed to failure (Sivaram 2003c, 2003d, 2004a, 2004b). In any case, by the time I arrived in Sri Lanka again, both Sivaram and Taraki were back as a major 'voices' in southern politics.

RETURN TO BATTICALOA

As for me, I came to Sri Lanka with my family on 26 December 2003 and we stayed there until 23 July 2004. I had long had a dream of 'bringing' Ann and David to see Sri Lanka, but had been afraid to do so due to the war and, anyway, had little prospect of being able to fund such an expedition. But Sivaram had begun urging me to bring my family to Sri Lanka as soon as the ceasefire was signed, claiming there would be peace, of a sort, for at least two years. In the end, however, our coming had little enough to do with me. It was my wife's sabbatical, and a Fulbright grant she obtained to teach at Peradeniya University while conducting research on the tea industry in the up-country, that actually provided the occasion. So we came to Sri Lanka, rented our house on a hill outside Kandy, and I prepared to finish this book off by returning to Batticaloa with Sivaram one last time.

On 3 March 2004, I traveled down to Colombo to meet Sivaram at his tiny house in Mt Lavenia, a mostly Sinhalese suburb of Colombo. When I bounced up to his house in my three-wheeler taxi, I saw his green sheet-metal front gate was as banged up as I remembered it. But a small verandah, a new toilet, and an incomplete second story had been added since I first visited it in 1997. With Sivaram busy writing, I wandered about the house chatting with the children while thinking, in the back of my mind, that this trip would make a good ending for our book. Of course, I knew the purpose of the trip for Sivaram was professional. He wanted to cover preparations for the upcoming parliamentary elections. For on 4 November 2003, President Chandrika Kumaratunge had pushed Ranil Wickramasinghe's fragile UNF government into crisis by relieving its ministers of Defense, Interior, and Media of their portfolios – claiming that their ineffectiveness in the face of the LTTE rearming was endangering the nation – and thus forcing elections. As these were scheduled for 2 April 2004, barely a month away, Sivaram wanted to make the rounds as campaigning was winding down. But for me the trip appeared a great chance for a summing up – a last chance for a long conversation with Sivaram by the rippling waters of the Batticaloa lagoon. I imagined it would provide a fine way to end the book on an appropriately ambiguous note: a conversation with Sivaram in a Sri Lanka at peace, but hardly settled. This way I would be able to write an ending with Sivaram scarred but undaunted, and still very much alive – like his cause. But all that was not to be. For that night, 3 March 2004, Vinayagamoorthy Muralitharan (a.k.a. 'Colonel' Karuna), eastern military commander for the LTTE, began his rebellion. And so instead Sivaram and I set off pell-mell through the night in a hurtling *Daily Mirror* van to chase yet another story – a story, to his mind, of a disaster. It would turn out to be the first of many.

Days later, tired and bedraggled, Sivaram had the van drop us off at an outdoor bar near Kalmanai, a largely Muslim city roughly 30 km south down the coast road from Batticalao. For the two previous days Sivaram had spent his mornings out of sight (of me, anyway) engaged in what he tersely called 'peace talks.' I had passed the time mostly chatting with Sheshadri, Sivaram's 29-year-old nephew. Like his uncle, Sheshadri was a school 'drop-out' and unconventionally brilliant. Deeply interested in electronics, computers, postmodernism, and Derrida, and profoundly uninterested in politics, he was a bit of a recluse. After a brief and frightening run-in with the war, Sheshadri had withdrawn into crumbling Stanley House – now, with Mahesvari dead, the home of his mother and Sivaram's sister Suriyakumari – and read his way systematically through all the musty books Sivaram and Sivaram's father had left behind. One morning, after picking my brain about post-structuralism for several hours, he took me to Stanley House to see the functioning satellite TV dish he had made by hand out of cast-off local junk – mostly reworked aluminum cans. He had hooked it up once to a borrowed TV to see that it worked, and then disconnected it permanently, finding TV, on the whole, acutely underwhelming.

The 'peace talks,' whatever they were, failed both days. So, in the afternoons, Sivaram and I had made the rounds of TNA politicians campaigning in Batticaloa. Sivaram had stayed talking the longest with S. Jeyananthamoorthy, a former TamilNet correspondent for Batticaloa, who was running for Parliament on the TNA ticket, and with Joseph Pararajasingham, also a former journalist, and the senior TNA MP for Batticaloa.[7] Jeyananthamoorthy and Sivaram were, of course, great friends. In April, shortly after Jeyananthamoorthy's election to Parliament, Sivaram would save his life from a Karuna group kidnap squad by bodily pulling him from their van – vans and SUVs being the vehicles of choice for assassination by all sides (Taraki 2004d). Pararajasingham, however, 20 months later, would be shot and killed while attending Christmas services at St Mary's church in Batticaloa town (TamilNet 2005g). In any case, both Jeyananthamoorthy and Pararajasingham proclaimed themselves unmoved by Karuna's gambit. Pararajasingham said – mostly, I believe, for my benefit – 'I don't believe the LTTE – a formidable group – will permit a split.' And Jeyananthamoorthy also claimed to be unfazed. But I could tell they were both deeply worried. At one point, in Pararajasingham's office, they anxiously discussed a rather effective handbill printed by Karuna that was currently circulating through town. Sivaram later told me that the pamphlet had pushed all the right buttons for the Batticaloa district. It had pointed to long-standing tensions between largely urban Jaffna and largely rural Batticaloa over such matters as the condescending *hauteur* with which Jaffna Tamils occasionally treated even educated Batticaloa Tamils; the scarcity of Batticaloa Tamils in the inner circles of the LTTE; the heavier burden of recruiting – especially of children – and thus the larger number of casualties borne by the east; the on-going clashes with the district's Muslim population, particularly over land tenure disrupted by the war; and, finally, to the rumor that money earmarked for rebuilding war-torn communities was mostly flowing north to fund the opulent lives of northern LTTE commanders. All these grievances, Sivaram said, Karuna, as a 'son of the soil,' claimed to understand better than the Jaffna-oriented LTTE. 'I will do my duty to the people of south Eelam,' Karuna apparently said.[8] And Sivaram could see Karuna's stance was finding some real support in Batticaloa, particularly among the educated middle class in Batticaloa town. In the end, looking at the handbill, Sivaram just shook his head and grew silent.

Later, on the road, we stopped two Tiger women riding bicycles and interviewed them. We asked them what they thought about the split. They said, unemotionally, that there was no split and they would fight for Eelam.

They were both dressed and coifed identically. Short and Spartan hair, baseball caps, green shirts buttoned to the neck, wide black belts, black pants, thick shoes. They looked tough. They neither smiled nor waved, and seemed as if they had been through it. Their arms were whipcord strong, their faces chiseled and hard, and their eyes were like marbles – suspicious marbles. I could make nothing of the encounter but Sivaram seemed to glean something troubling.[9]

So when the two news reporters wanted to tour the rest of the district to pick up clues, Sivaram grew thoughtful and asked the van to drop the two of us off in Kalmanai at the outdoor bar.

'*Maccaang,*' he said to me, 'this is going to be a long, busy time for us from now on. So let's sit in this bar and drink a bit before the storm comes.'[10]

The bar's little tables were scattered under palm trees and covered by green and red sheet-metal umbrellas. Out front, a small tin hut with a grilled window sold arrack and tepid bottles of beer. Distributed about the tables were a number of lounging men – and only men – mostly goldsmiths from Paddiruppu, talking quietly and drinking. As soon as we sat down – me with a beer, Sivaram with a half bottle of Old Reserve arrack – Sivaram's phone rang, and he was in the thick of the crisis. 'The thing to remember,' I wrote in my field notebook then, 'is how Sivaram works.' And so it was. Sivaram's phone was linked to the internet, and, with its front flipped down, he worked a tiny keyboard with a toothpick stylus writing and uploaded TamilNet stories in between making and receiving hundreds of calls in three languages to people all over Sri Lanka and the world. Calls to and from, for example, TamilNet reporters in Jaffna, Kandy, and Trincomalee; reporters from other agencies in London, Paris, Delhi, Madras, and New York; Karuna's spokesman and personal secretary, Varathan, hiding somewhere in the Batticaloa jungles with his own hand phone and internet link; Sri Lankan government, intelligence, and army spokesmen; and finally TamilNet.com software people in Norway and his co-editors in North America and Europe. At one point the BBC Tamil service called to interview *him* and Sivaram told them, on air, loudly and (I felt) intemperately that Karuna was an 'idiot' for splitting the LTTE. Soon afterwards, someone called to announce that Karuna had just threatened Sivaram's life. I glanced at the surrounding tables, where I noticed men staring at us, and, rather anxiously, asked Sivaram if, maybe, we should move somewhere else. 'No, *maccaang*, this is just fine.' Eventually so many calls were coming in from so many places, and so many stories were being written and uploaded, that he started using my phone for backup. Like a spider in his web he neatly wove between the two phones, his stylus, and his glass of arrack without dropping a stitch. And he loved it. Eventually, he looked up at me with a kind of ecstasy on his face.

'I am full. And I don't mean with food or arrack. I love this. I don't want routine to kill me.'

'You'd rather something else did,' I said, trying for light sarcasm.

He paused, though, taking the question seriously.

'Yeah.'[11]

From this point on, for the next year, Sivaram's life was a whirlwind of work and danger. Sivaram firmly believed that Karuna's rebellion was a disaster for the Tamil people because he felt it would eventually play into the hands of the Sri Lankan government's counter-insurgency strategy and leave Tamils, again, defenseless. So, shortly after returning from Batticaloa, he launched a two-pronged journalistic attack on Karuna. On 14 March, Sivaram wrote a scathingly polite 'open letter to Karuna' (*karuNaavukku oru kaTitam*) for his *Viirakeesari* column, publicly questioning Karuna's military reasoning (Sivaram 2004d). And on 17 March, as Taraki, Sivaram wrote an article for the *Daily Mirror* arguing that the real motivation behind Karuna's rebellion was 50 million rupees in missing funds (Taraki 2004b). As the crisis deepened, and the LTTE and the Karuna group began violently jockeying (by means of assassination and intimidation) to control the TNA candidates for the upcoming election, Sivaram continued to hammer away, arguing in subsequent articles that the real motivation for Karuna's rebellion was shame (Taraki 2004c, 2004e). That is, dismissing rumors that Sri Lankan military intelligence or even the Americans had cultivated Karuna's revolt – and setting aside the very real regional tensions that were garnering Karuna eastern support – Sivaram argued that Karuna's financial scandal had simply left him too ashamed to face Prabhakaran, a man he revered 'like a god' and called '*Annai*,' or elder brother. This kind of analysis infuriated Karuna's supporters, particularly after the LTTE regained control of the east in a brief, fierce campaign that began on 9 April 2004 and was over by 12 April, when Karuna, with a few of his trusted lieutenants, fled to sanctuary with the Sri Lankan army in Colombo.

In any case, soon thereafter began a sudden intensification of the 'shadow war' that had long gone on at a lower level between the intelligence wings of the Sri Lankan army and the LTTE. With both sides now able to cite the activities of the 'Karuna group,' as the papers soon called it, as an excuse for their efforts, tit-for-tat killings became the rule, and violence began to reach out beyond intelligence agents to politicians, academics, and journalists perceived as supporters of one side or another. This became particularly true after the 2 April 2004 parliamentary elections, which were barely won by a new United People's Freedom Alliance (UPFA) between the JVP and the SLFP. This fragile alliance only seemed to add to the growing instability and air of danger settling over Sri Lanka once again. And after the LTTE regained nominal control of the east, both the Sri Lankan government and the LTTE began to turn more attention to squelching dissent.

In this spirit, on 3 May 2004 – ironically 'Press Freedom Day' in Sri Lanka – Sivaram's house in Mount Lavenia was raided by the police. They were looking, they claimed, for weapons – a justification even Sivaram's Sinhalese colleagues (and critics) found ridiculous.[12] Sivaram was not there, but Bavani and the children were terrified and called us on the phone in Kandy. The police had apparently milled aimlessly about their house, not quite knowing what to do with Sivaram's copies of the *Times Literary Supplement* and his books of history and political theory. They eventually retreated in some confusion. Thereafter Sivaram began spending most of his time away, coming home only infrequently and unpredictably, keeping his schedule as random as possible to throw off potential assassins. But it was not just the government exerting pressure on Sivaram and other reporters. According to *Reporters sans frontières*, just before the elections Tiger officials, worried about TamilNet's coverage, twice summoned Sivaram for interrogations (Reporters sans frontières 2004). And, in Batticaloa, academics and reporters who had supported Karuna were threatened, and some were killed. Also, after the elections on 31 May, Aiyadurai Nadesan, a well-respected Batticaloa correspondent for *Viirakeesari* was shot down in the street, probably by the Karuna group (Selvanayagam 2004), and then officially mourned by the LTTE. By June, 16 people had been killed in the east by one side or the other and I began to suggest to Sivaram that this might be a good time for him to leave the country.

To my surprise, for the first time, he seemed seriously to consider doing so. There was a long-standing offer from the Tiger-controlled IBCT radio station in London for him to join their staff as an analyst, at least for a year. Although Sivaram had always been extremely unwilling to be tied to the LTTE's media empire before, now he was tempted, if only to get his family out of Sri Lanka. We talked about it one day in June as we walked down the steep hill in Kandy that led from my house to the main road. The road banked and twirled as it circled down the mountain, and Sivaram walked slightly ahead of me, jumpy, worried, and full of strange energy. We passed shops, a Buddhist temple, more shops, fields full of tall mountain grass and huge tamarind trees; high above, by craning my neck, I could see the upper slopes where tea was still grown and Tamil laborers lived. Down below, blue with distance, I could see the road and the river. Sivaram had shown up, as usual, out of that blue, wanting to have our final conversation about his military and strategic views and be done with it. But he had been unable to settle down inside our house. Our walking was really his pacing.

'Did you ever get beat up?' he asked me as we walked.

'When I was little, in school I suppose. Not since. Why?'

'Everyone should get beat up once. It's an education.' He stopped and eyed me dangerously for a moment, deadpan, like a predator just beginning to crouch. 'Or beat somebody up. Do you ever feel like you could just beat somebody up? Just beat them. Feel that energy, that fire?'

'No. I never wanted to beat somebody up.'

Then we both had to leap aside as a three-wheeler taxi hurtled around the corner, bleating with its high-pitched horn.

'You are *too* good, Mr Whitaker.'

'So,' I said, wanting to ignore this particular conversational gambit, 'will you go to Britain? Take that job?'

'I might.'

But he would not. He explained to me later, over arrack, that taking the job would be the end of his freedom. He would no longer be his own man with his own project. Ultimately, he would just be a hired hand and that idea was impossible. Beyond and behind that impossibility, I feel, lay his continued ambivalence about the LTTE. On the one hand, he could not, at this point, conceive of a solution to the ethnic struggle that did not involve Sri Lankan Tamils unifying behind the LTTE. On the other hand, I knew he could never forget the killing of his best friend, Vasutheva (and Bavani's brother-in-law), or the many attempts to kill him, or the death of his cousin in the Central Bank bombing. And he remained, as he said many times, still an old PLOTE man deep down, nostalgic for PLOTE's abandoned vision of a north–south, Tamil–Sinhalese, left-based alliance, even though he now felt that the Sinhalese left was, simply, too unreliable for this ever to be. Still, he mourned that lost vision, though quietly, until the very end.[13] So he said again what he had said many times before: 'Where should I die but here?'

At the end of July, Ann, David, and I were to return to the United States. Our last night was to be spent in Colombo at the Mount Lavenia Hotel, a huge colonial eminence located on a spectacular seaside bluff overlooking Colombo. This was a special treat so that David and Sivaram's son, Seralaathan, who had become close friends, could spend the day swimming in the hotel pool together. But as I watched them playing I remembered, suddenly, stopping there 22 years ago just after the riots to have a nervous cup of tea – it being the only place open and tea all I could afford – and watching the peculiar haze of a still burning city drift low over the 10 km curve of picturesque beach between me and central Colombo. In any case, that night Sivaram was supposed to go to Kilinochchi – whether to gather news or because he had been 'summoned' I never found out. Beforehand we dined at a private Colombo club with a wealthy older couple from the diaspora. Originally from Jaffna, they were in Sri Lanka briefly for nostalgic reasons, and wished to pay homage to Taraki. Sivaram was very gentle with them as we sipped our mulligatawny soup, listening attentively to opinions I knew he believed ill-informed, and then sending them on their way feeling as if they now had the inside scoop. Afterwards, as we stood outside in the lane waiting for the three-wheelers that would take him to the Vavuniya night bus and me to my hotel, I again implored him to think about getting out of the country. In the intervening month, the police had again searched Sivaram's house, and there had been more death threats from the Karuna group. But he was unmoved, and so we got into our three-wheelers and rode away. It was the last time I ever saw him.

But it was not my last time talking to him. About five minutes later, as I was barreling down the Galle road toward Mount Lavenia, I got a call from Ann telling me that Bavani had just rung her completely terrified by a new death threat from a high-level policeman who had just appeared on the TV news. So, in a subsequent four-way conversation between Ann, Sivaram (already heading to Vavuniya), Bavani, and myself – all while bouncing down the road

– it was decided that I should spend the night at Sivaram's house to head off the threat of another police home invasion with my innocuous Americanness. Joining me there would be the well-known Sinhalese journalist, Rajpal Abeynayake, a man largely opposed to Sivaram politically but completely loyal to him personally. Bavani brought a table out to the verandah so we could sit and watch the gate, and we got our papers and cell phones in order, ready to flash passports, press passes, and call for reinforcements if someone came. Then we sat and drank a bottle of arrack that Sivaram had instructed us, by mobile phone, was hidden behind his door 'for special occasions, *maccaang*, like getting shot.' But no one came – that night. And in the morning Ann, David, and I flew home.

For the next four months I kept track of Sivaram from afar. This was easier in the new millennium than it had been in the past. In addition to email and TamilNet, the *Daily Mirror* was now online, so I could follow Sivaram's Taraki writings; and, of course, we also talked on the phone. What he was writing about both sides in the conflict was interesting but bound to get him in trouble. It was also more and more pessimistic. In August, as Taraki, Sivaram wrote that the LTTE had fashioned its 'Interim Self-Governing Authority' (or ISGA) proposal – its offer of a transitional agreement with the Sri Lankan government, put forward the year before, on 31 October 2003 – after Sudan's Machakos Protocol of July 2002 (Taraki 2004f). Arrived at with heavy international involvement, that protocol (like the ISGA) had involved a power-sharing agreement and provision for a referendum at the end of an interim period in which the south could decide whether to stay part of Sudan. Sivaram suggested that international forces, knowing this provenience, would find simple, outright rejection of the ISGA politically uncomfortable, and make it so too for the new UPFA government. Yet, argued Sivaram, because the UPFA knew that the Sinhala people of the south did, in fact, reject the ISGA, they were left anxiously, perhaps disastrously, poised between the rock of their displeased political base and the hard place of international displeasure.

Similarly, on 18 August 2004, again as Taraki, Sivaram asked why the Tigers had been so successful in Sri Lanka (Taraki 2004g). The answer, he claimed, rested upon two further questions: why other militant Tamil groups had failed and why the Sri Lanka government's C-I tacticians had never succeeded in creating either a viable political alternative to the LTTE or a viable military threat (in the form of Latin American style militias 'like the right-wing AUC that controls large areas in Columbia and terrorizes peasants who support FARC, the main Marxist guerrilla organization fighting the state in that country'). His answer to both of these questions was that there was a lack of what he called 'political space.' Under the Sri Lanka Constitution, he claimed, Tamil *democratic* political parties constantly faced legitimacy problems because the Constitution prevented them from addressing issues of state structure, including the Eelam or separate state demand that lay at the heart of the conflict, on pain of being expelled from Parliament. In the same way potential militias – such as the rump of the old militant parties

– that might have been useful to C-I tacticians, also could not grow or long survive without having a position on the Eelam question, something any alliance with the government would have forbidden. Either way, the result was the same: political paralysis, with the LTTE, in its utter rejection of the Sri Lankan state, the only entity left able to move. Or so Sivaram claimed, leaving out the Karuna group, by that time rumored to be running its operations in the east with at least covert Sri Lankan army support.

By September and October, Sivaram's dark pronouncements were increasing. He saw the US as having tilted the playing field toward a 'Sinhala Buddhist state victory' by having made its Millennium Challenge Account funds available to the government of Sri Lanka. This, he argued, undercut the EU's earlier attempts to tie aid to movement toward a federal solution (Taraki 2004h).[14] More direly, in a *Viirakeesari* article in October, apparently entitled 'On the psyche of the Sinhala nation,' Sivaram answered a critic who argued that more effort should be made to explain Tamil views to, at least, sympathetic Sinhalese people. 'There should,' Sivaram wrote, 'be no second thought about taking our reasonable views to the Sinhalese people on a regular basis. However, my genuine concern is that we should not fall into the illusion that such acts from us will result in receiving our rights from the Sri Lankan rulers' (Sivaram 2004e). History, he believed, proved the best guide here, pointing out that S.W.R.D. Bandaranaike, founder of the Sri Lankan Freedom Party (SLFP), had once supported a federal state with a 'Tamil homeland'; that the Trotskyist LSSP (*Lanka Sama Samaja* Party), and the Communist Party of Sri Lanka had both once supported Tamil rights and later reversed themselves. He reviewed, bitterly, his own personal relationships with a long line of left-wing, once sympathetic, Sinhalese politicians and militants who later became, to his mind, determined enemies of the Tamil people. Among them, he cited Thilak Karunaratne, once of the SLFP, who later became a co-founder of the nationalist *Sinhala Urumaya* Party; Dayan Jayatilleke, once a member of the 'Stalinist Education Circle,' a JVP splinter group that supported Tamil self-determination – and whom Sivaram helped save from the Sri Lankan government when he was forced underground in 1986 – who later became an ardent anti-LTTE crusader; and Chandrika Kumaratunge, then still the president, who Sivaram claimed once said to him: 'Do not speak to anyone who does not accept the rights of the Tamils for self-determination' (Sivaram 2004e). Why, then, Sivaram asked rhetorically, 'did she unleash the horror of the "War for Peace" on Tamils?' (2004e).

On 26 November, Vellupillai Pirabakaran's birthday – as if to answer the other, unasked part of the above question: 'Why, then, did Pirabakaran start Eelam War Three?' – Sivaram, writing as Taraki, undertook to defend the LTTE leader from the charge that he was simply a self-aggrandizing militarist (Taraki 2004j). It was a canard, Sivaram wrote, that Pirabakaran established the LTTE's 'Great Heroes Day' – its annual celebration of Tiger martyrs – on his own birthday. Pirabakaran's birthday was actually one day earlier, and he spent it fasting to commemorate the birthday of Shanker, the first

LTTE cadre to die in the war. Pirabakaran's politics, according to Sivaram, found their true source not in macho grandstanding but in the history of the old Tamil Federal Party. In the 1950s, Sivaram related, there were two schools of thought in the Federal Party: one, led by S.J.V. Chelvanayagam, emphasized negotiating with the Sri Lankan state; the other, led by Federal Party co-founder, V. Navaratanam, remained suspicious of the idea that the Sinhalese would ever cede anything and believed that Tamils should try to develop sovereignty independently – yet non-violently – on their own. This split, Sivaram argued, eventually led to Navaratanam being sacked from the Federal Party in 1968. But Navaratanam went on to found the 'Self-rule Party' (Sayadchi Kazhagam),[15] whose eventual representative for Valvettithurai and Port Pedro was Venugopal Master, Pirabakaran's home town school teacher. 'Pirabaharan,' Sivaram continued:

...has come a long way politically since he was one of Venugopal Master's nocturnal students. At fifty, his biggest political achievement is the confluence of the Chelvanayagam and Navaratanam schools of the Tamil movement. The Tamil National Alliance is the manifestation of this political confluence which he has brought about. The remarkable failure of his opponents to plead even an iota [of] political concessions for the Tamils from the Sinhala polity for the last 17 years (1987–2004) has contributed in no small measure to strengthen Pirabaharan's political strategies in taking forward his current 'peace offensive.' (Taraki 2004j)

In early December Sivaram called me from London. He was on another trip, and would be swinging through the United States – with his cousin Oppi, for part of the time – partly in the hope of spending the last week or two at our house in South Carolina. Thereafter, periodically, every two or three days, Sivaram called me from various way stations. He gave talks to appreciative Tamil audiences in Washington DC and New Brunswick, New Jersey – where he teased one acolyte, who wanted to take a picture, by suggesting that she just wanted a good photograph to use at his memorial. Eventually, he went on to Colorado to visit Dennis McGilvray and Patricia Lawrence at the University of Colorado. But one night somewhere in between, during my final exam week, he called me up, very drunk, from I know not where, demanding to know why I hadn't called him. 'Should I just die alone? How can you leave me here like this, you bugger?' I told him he should come to South Carolina immediately. Then, judging the real issue, I said he simply needed to leave Sri Lanka, at least, for now. 'No, Mark, my friend, there will be no leaving. Not for me.' Later, calmer, he said that I was his true friend.

'You're drunk.'

'Nevertheless.'

Then on 26 December 2004, the Asian tsunami hit Sri Lanka. It came in three waves and killed tens of thousands of people – perhaps 35,000 in Sri Lanka alone[16] – its effects stretching almost completely around the eastern side of the island from Colombo to Jaffna. But the east coast was particularly hard hit. In Batticaloa, the Kallars, Kalmanai, Akkaraipattu, all the haunts of

Sivaram's youth, there was great destruction and loss of life. Thousands were drowned when their clothes were caught on suddenly submarine barbwire fences, or when smashed by debris, or when carried out to sea with the retreating waves (Gaasbeek 2005). But 'Bavani and the children are safe,' Sivaram told me, when he called from Colorado with the news. For me, ten hours behind Batticaloa time, it was still, surreally, Christmas night, and as Sivaram talked, describing catastrophe in Sri Lanka, it started to snow picturesquely, the flakes outside my sister's Massachusetts kitchen window spinning festively, delicately, against the colored lights. Hoarsely, in my ear, Sivaram told me that Bavani and the children had been visiting Bavani's old home in Batticaloa for the holidays when the waves struck. The house, on high ground for Batticaloa, had been completely flooded with 5 feet of water, but everyone there had survived. Everyone, that is, but Shashadri, Sivaram's nephew. He had gone to visit a Hindu temple that morning on the Dutch Bar in Kallidy – a thin hump of sand that separates the lagoon from the sea. When the water hit, the bar was scraped clean by its waves. Afterwards, Bavani went out looking for him, walking through the slurry streets, horrified – as she later told us on the phone – by the many dead. She could not find him. 'He was probably just washed out to sea,' said Sivaram as the snow continued falling outside my sister's window. 'Poor boy, I don't think they will ever find him.'

Sivaram was desperate to return to Sri Lanka. He spent the next week struggling to change his ticket so he could return immediately. Meanwhile, Ann, David, and I drove back to South Carolina, the new semester looming. At first it seemed as if Sivaram would have to stick to his original ticket; and, selfishly, I almost hoped for this, as it would mean we could still fly him south to see us before he departed. But the mounting death toll throughout South-East Asia and the Bay of Bengal caused airlines to loosen their rules, and Sivaram was able to convert his ticket. Since he had to fly out of New York, he arranged a ride to Poughkeepsie to see my parents before he left. His old friend in Poughkeepsie, Dr Rajan Sriskandarajah, drove him over to my old house.

My parents served them tea and Christmas cookies, which my Mom could tell Sivaram drank and ate out of politeness, to honor them. They sat in my parents' tiny living room in gold velour easy chairs by the fieldstone fireplace, with my mother's antique bust of George Washington on the floor between them, and accepted my parent's condolences. My father noticed that Sivaram was 'nicely' dressed in dark slacks, loafers, a good shirt and a blue blazer – a jacket, Oppi later told me, Sivaram bought for £10 at an Oxfam shop on one of his first trips to England. He would later be buried in it. My Dad also saw that Sivaram was very quiet and tense. 'He told us about his nephew being missing,' my father said. 'And they never found him, did they?' My Mom could see that 'this was something he wanted to do – but it was difficult for him. His mind was miles away, on his nephew, on his wife and his country.' They all made small talk. He asked after my brother, who was at work; they talked about the tsunami; and about his children. My Mom, worried about Sivaram, wanted to give him a hug before he left but felt, somehow, that it would not have been appropriate, not Tamil. My Dad realized that Sivaram had brought no overcoat. 'And it was cold out there,' my father said, 'colder than a witch's elbow.' After about an hour he was gone.

In despair over the death of his nephew, horrified by the destruction he saw in the east, Sivaram threw himself into his work when he returned to Sri Lanka. He barely spent any time in Colombo – where, anyway, it was not safe for him to be. Instead, he ceaselessly roamed the east coast talking to survivors, poking into the recovery efforts, watching with a jaundiced eye the maneuvering – already beginning – between the various groups vying for influence there. One wealthy American Tamil couple, heavily involved in Tamil Rehabilitation Organization (TRO) work, who were in Batticaloa for a brief visit to survey its efforts, remembered running into Sivaram on the street. They were acquainted with him from his trips to North America as an amiable if crusty raconteur. They were surprised, therefore, when an angry-seeming Sivaram, without preamble or preliminary politeness, practically snarled at them that in Amparai, south of Batticaloa, the JVP was actually providing more aid, and garnering more good will, than the TRO. If the TRO wanted influence down there, he told them, harshly, it had better get moving more quickly.[17] Then Sivaram was off again like a gust of wind.

I was following Sivaram through his writing, leavened with an occasional phone call. It was clear from his columns that he was rapidly losing whatever faith he once had that the ceasefire was working, or that further war could be avoided. And while others saw the brief, but quite real, burst of inter-ethnic cooperation that occurred after the tsunami as an amiable portent, Sivaram believed the old forces were already gearing up for more battle.[18] Hence, in one article, Taraki argued against the notion, then being bandied about, that the humanitarian needs created by the tsunami had opened a 'window of opportunity' for restarting the peace talks. On the contrary, Sivaram argued, 'no window of opportunity is wide enough when the fundamentals remain wrong' (Taraki 2005b). In fact, to Sivaram's mind, the tsunami actually damaged the 'peace process' by revealing even more garishly the same structural flaws in the Sri Lankan state that had scuttled the peace talks in the first place. Namely, that the kind of resource- and local authority-sharing needed for both tsunami recovery and a final, federal peace settlement were, simply, illegal under the Sri Lankan Constitution in its current form, and politically unlikely given the general reticence of Sinhalese elites to share power with anyone. Hence: 'Any hope that a common ground could be found to coax the two sides to the negotiating table has been dashed to smithereens by the tsunami' (Taraki 2005b). This was Sivaram's old 'lack of political space' argument and, sadly, shortly after his death, he would be proven right on this point, at least with respect to the tsunami. On 15 July 2005 Sri Lanka's Supreme Count, acting on a complaint filed by the JVP, would strike down the resource- and authority-sharing parts of the Post-Tsunami Operation

Management Structure (or P-Toms) agreement between the Sri Lankan government and the LTTE – the agreement, arrived at only two weeks earlier, under which international aid funds for post-tsunami recovery were finally to be distributed to the north and east by an impartial third party. In the end, the P-Toms agreement itself was never implemented, even in its truncated form, and was later entirely revoked by Sri Lanka's new president, Mahinda Rajapakse – thereby indeed confirming the tsunami as more an occasion for conflict than any inspiration to resolve it.

From February onward, Sivaram devoted much of his remaining writing to accessing the strategic, political, and military condition of the LTTE. Moreover, in tone, his Taraki articles began to move closer to the more unrestrained voice found in his *Viirakeesari* writings – though always retaining that little bit of pedagogic diffidence, restrained sarcasm, and almost pedantic devotion to the startling fact always characteristic of Sivaram's writing for his English-speaking, Sinhalese audience. Thus, in one article (Taraki 2005c), Sivaram discussed the LTTE's troubled position in the Batticaloa and Amparai districts, pointing out that the LTTE's strategic emphasis on maintaining a 'base area' in the north and winning victories there had sacrificed the multi-ethnic east by leaving its people (especially its Muslims) open to mistreatment not only by the Sri Lankan state but also by the LTTE itself (particularly as once commanded by Karuna). After reviewing LTTE efforts to reverse some of this damage by implementing reforms and introducing the same kinds of governmental features it was experimenting with in the north – police, law courts, less taxation, ending the appropriation of paddy lands, rapprochement with Muslims, some 'social justice' – Sivaram concluded that, for the east, such efforts might be too little too late. 'In the final analysis,' he concluded, 'the key to winning people's undivided political allegiance is good governance. Unless every LTTE cadre in the east fully grasps this truth the Tigers will find it difficult to accomplish what they have set to achieve in this long troubled land' (Taraki 2005c).

At the same time, Sivaram tried to both widen and trouble his audience's focus by placing all these concerns in a more strategic and geopolitical context. He argued, for example, that there was good evidence not only that the Sri Lankan army but also India were getting increasingly involved in the growing 'shadow war' in the north and east, though each for their own strategic purposes (Taraki 2005h). Elsewhere he tried to gage the relative strength of the LTTE versus the Sri Lankan army after four years of the ceasefire by enumerating, in precise detail, the overseas weapons purchases of each. He concluded, surprisingly, that while the LTTE had actually *lost* ground to the Sri Lankan army in terms of fire-power, its 'martial self-confidence' remained nevertheless, mysteriously, undiminished (Tarkai 2005e). Why? Perhaps part of the answer, for Sivaram, lay in Taraki's earlier claim that 'Southern pundits' seemed too distracted by the Karuna group's deadly activities in the east to see the LTTE's real strategic aims. Sivaram went on in that article (Taraki 2005d) to chide those who underestimated Pirabakaran's military and political skill, warning that with him little was as it seemed. When Pirabakaran, five years earlier, had stopped his troops at the gates of Jaffna he did so, Sivaram claimed, for political rather than military reasons, for he was then already well aware that Sri Lanka's conflict was being played out within the context of a global competition for power. What people should be asking therefore, Sivaram claimed, is: 'What is the larger picture that Pirapakaran has in mind while the south is entertained by Karuna?' (Taraki 2005d). At the same time, Taraki was not above teasing Sri Lankan army intelligence by pointing out that the LTTE had used the Karuna affair 'to send the largest number of moles' – that is, 'sleeping LTTE intelligence agents who bide their time and await the signal to strike' – 'into the country and the intelligence establishment' (Taraki 2005h). He also winked, knowingly, at the Tigers' recently established National Television of Thamileelam (NTT), saying it appeared to be an attempt by the LTTE to upend the so-called 'CNN effect' – that is, the strategic problems caused by too much media coverage – and use TV images instead as a 'force multiplier,' like the US did in the beginning of its second Iraq war by allowing CNN to film overwhelming forces taking off from its carriers, hoping in this way to undermine Iraqi morale (Taraki 2005f).

In all of these Taraki articles Sivaram was clearly attempting to poke holes in elite Sinhalese over-confidence. That is, he was trying to be, as he put it:

... the 'other voice' on this scene, out of tune with the litany that saturates the political atmosphere on the southern side of this island's ethnic divide, so that people see a need to hedge their bets on the ethnic question. It is easy to jump on the bandwagon by saying 'Pirapakaran [Pirabakaran] is losing' or 'down with the Tigers,' if one wants to be feted and quoted. This is immoral – particularly when we see an increasingly collective compulsion in the Sinhala polity to hear only what people want to hear about the ethnic conflict. (Taraki 2005d)

Meanwhile, I was at home writing, fitfully trying to finish the book, and growing more and more worried. I could tell by following the news, and the increasing 'shadow war' body count, that Sivaram was in great danger. Specifically, in addition to Karuna's periodic threats, I knew that on 6 April Wimal Weerawansa, propaganda secretary of the JVP, had done his best to whip up hatred against Sivaram (among others), by identifying him as 'the one who runs [the] Tiger terrorists' TamilNet web site' (TamilNet 2005a; Jeyaraj 2005c). Weerawansa's ire was perhaps fueled by a series of articles Sivaram had written in *Viirakeesari* in 2004 about the JVP – articles which, among other things, revealed the JVP's turbulent history in unflattering detail, particularly its inconsistent views of 'the Tamil question' (Sivaram 2004c).[19] Typically, Sivaram responded to Weerawansa by writing even more articles about the JVP, pointing out in one of them that the current, rather odd, ideological justification for the party's current antipathy to the Tamil cause lay in a speech its dead leader, Rohana Wijeweera, made to his inner circle in 1986 declaring Tamil nationalism a United States-supported, imperialist plot (Taraki 2005g). I also knew (because Sivaram told me) that the 22 April abduction in Colombo – most likely by the LTTE – of T. Jayaratnam, a senior investigator of the Terrorism Investigation Division of the Sri Lankan police, had also aroused 'great resentment' within the police (as the journalist D.B.S. Jeyaraj [2005c] put it) and that some of this ill-feeling was likely turning toward Sivaram.

So I was nervous. And on those occasions when we talked to Bavani by phone – for Sivaram was rarely at home – we could tell she was nervous too. Nonetheless, my work continued, and I periodically sent off things by email for Sivaram to check. Then, on 24 April, Sivaram surprised us with a call from his house. Ann, earlier, had sent birthday gifts to Mt Lavenia, for both of Sivaram's daughters had birthdays that week. Sivaram was calling so the children could thank us. We talked to the children, then Bavani, and, finally, I chatted briefly with Sivaram. He seemed to me in a gentle mood, calmer then I remember him being in years. I told him I wanted to send more chapters for him to check. He said, 'No young man, wait.' He was flying to Japan in a week; I should hold off sending things until after he was back. I told him to have fun in Japan; he told me, genially, to do the same in South Carolina. 'Have some fun, *maccaang*. But finish the book.' Then he was gone.

Four days later he was dead.

I heard the news by phone. Because classes had just ended, I was sitting at my home computer working on the book, just thinking about calling Sivaram with some questions – calculating that he would not yet have left for Japan – when Ann called me with the news that Sivaram had been kidnapped. Unable to reach me, Daniel had phoned her immediately after Bavani had got to him, crying, to report that Sivaram was missing. I then called Kuttan and Oppi – interrupting the latter at a concert – whereupon we all waited for news. According to the journalist D.B.S. Jeyaraj (2005c), what had happened was this: Sivaram had been drinking at the Bambalapitiya restaurant on the Gall Road, near the Majestic Mall and the Bambalapitiya police station. He was there with three Sinhalese acquaintances: Kusal Perera, a freelance journalist; Ravi Kumudesh, a trade unionist for the health sector; and Prasanna Ratnayake, an NGO coordinator. At 10:20 p.m. they left the bar and Perera and Sivaram headed for a bus stop while the other two men crossed the street. Sivaram then received a phone call, and stepped aside to answer it. At that moment, a silver-gray Toyota Pajeiro pulled up with four men inside (TamilNet 2005d). Two of them leaped out and pulled Sivaram, fighting all the way, into the SUV. Perera, appalled, fled home and started calling people, including Bavani, to alert them to Sivaram's abduction. Soon thereafter, Bavani went with her brother to file a complaint at the Bambalipitiya police station. That was around 11:30 p.m. Sivaram's body was later found by police – aided by an anonymous tip-off – at 1:00 a.m., bound, gagged, and dumped behind the Parliament building in a high security zone (*Daily Mirror* 2005). An autopsy later revealed Sivaram had first been knocked out – probably to stop him from fighting – and then shot twice while unconscious on the ground. Later that morning, Bavani and Sivaram's eldest daughter Vaishnavi were brought by police to identify the body.

Things moved very quickly after that. Bavani and the children, shattered, retreated to Mt Lavenia in shock. Soon Sivaram's body was taken there too, and a parade of mourning friends and suddenly self-conscious politicians descended upon them to pay their respects. Within days people started flying in for the funeral, in particular Oppi and Kuttan from the UK, and David and Daniel from Toronto. And, inevitably, political complications arose. The LTTE declared Sivaram a 'great man,' a *maamanitar*, and asked Bavani if they could have his body transported to Kilinochchi so Tamils there – including the leader, V. Prabarkaran – might pay their respects. But Bavani, vehement about keeping the funeral a non-political family affair, and knowing Sivaram had never joined the LTTE, declined. (Besides, Sivaram had remarked to her, shortly before he died, that carting bodies around in the heat was, as he put it, 'smelly'.) For its part, the Sri Lankan government, perhaps embarrassed by rumors of its own involvement in his death, quickly responded to Bavani's worries about her family's safety by ordering the police and, eventually, the army to escort Sivaram's body all the way to Batticaloa. This amazed Oppi. He described to me riding along in the family procession, accompanied by armored cars, puzzled by the show of force the Sri Lanka government was devoting to conducting its greatest gadfly to his grave. In any case, in Batticaloa the complexities of postcolonial religion had to be satisfied. There was a Christian prayer service at Bavani's house, then a Hindu ritual at Stanley House – where 10-year-old Seralaathan, trembling with shock, but properly dressed in a white *versti*, bravely inserted the rice into his dead father's mouth – whereupon it was back to Bavani's house for a Christian funeral. Then it was time for politics again. The LTTE insisted that they should be allowed to take the body to a memorial service on their side of the ceasefire line, so Bavani and her other brother, David, accompanied it to patriotic memorials in the hinterland. Sivaram's burial ultimately took place on 2 May 2005, in Alaiyadicholai cemetery, Batticaloa, in an army high security zone where special permission had to be sought to allow the ceremony. Alaiyadicholai cemetery had been chosen by Sivaram long before because so many of his old PLOTE comrades had been buried or cremated there (Abeynayake 2005b). Ironically, an ex-PLOTE member, Arumugam Sriskandarajah, would later be arrested for involvement in Sivaram's murder, though, as of this writing, it still remains unclear to me who exactly participated in or ordered it (TamilNet 2005e, 2005f). Perhaps, in a way, many did. In any case, that was that. I could not believe it; but it was so – as Daniel called and, gently, told me. Sivaram was dead and gone, his return to Batticaloa complete.

POST MORTEM

I could not go to Sivaram's funeral. So for several weeks, rather numb with shock, I sleepwalked through school duties: turning in grades, chatting with students, walking in graduation. I kept thinking, unreasonably, that some night Sivaram would phone and say, as he often did, 'Ah, Mr Whitaker, what have you been up to *maccaang?*' Of course, I knew this would not happen. Oppi had called and told me that when he had touched Sivaram's surprisingly cold face in the casket, he knew Sivaram was really gone. Still, the ridiculous impression that he would call lingered on. And as I talked on the phone to other people appalled by his death – family members, but also journalists and academics – I began to realize that this elliptical fog was an almost universal condition among those who knew him well. Sivaram had always been a man in perpetual motion; how could he stop now? He *would* call, he *would* show up, it *was* a hoax, the bad penny *would* return again, time for one more glass. '*Maccaang*, the night is young!'

Dully, I began to dig through the avalanche of things suddenly being written about my dead friend. Sivaram was a complicated man, impossible to sum up even in death, so perhaps it is little wonder that summing him up is just what so many tried to do after he died. Within weeks of his death tributes, examinations, summaries, condemnations, and declarations for and against poured in from all around the world. The newspapers and, in particular, the web were alive with articles and blogs about his death and the significance of his life.[20] Some vilified him, particularly in the Sinhala-nationalist press and blogosphere. But many of Sivaram's old leftist friends and enemies (often the same people) wrote emotional eulogies, including Dayan Jayatilleka, Qadri Ismail, Jayadeva Uyangoda, J.S. Tissainayagam, and D.B.S. Jeyaraj. I thought some of their pieces were complicated, however, by their ambivalence about the exact nature of Sivaram's nationalist politics and his apparent support (or, for one of them, the inadequacy of his support) for the LTTE. With the exception of Uyangoda's brief declaration of sadness, moreover, I saw they also betrayed some puzzlement about what Sivaram's 'real' views on this and other topics actually had been (Ismail 2005; Jeyaraj 2005b; Jayatilleka 2005; Tissainayagam 2005; Uyangoda 2005). But I noted that Professor Karthigesu Sivathamby, the same who once stood on the stairs at Jaffna University marveling at Sivaram's first letter to him, wrote a warmer, more straight-forward tribute. He described a Sivaram I could recognize, sitting back in an easy chair at Sivathamby's house, momentarily at ease, forming clever insults to goad him back into scholarly work – criticism often being, as Sivathamby pointed out, Sivaram's biggest compliment (Sivathamby 2005). I also noticed the effect that Sivaram seemed to have had on a younger generation of reporters, regardless of ethnicity. For example, one young South Indian Tamil reporter from the BBC called soon after his death to tell me, almost tearfully, how Sivaram had become a model for young reporters like him, despite reservations about his politics. And the young Sinhalese journalist Rohitha B. Abeywardane, prevented by work from meeting up with Sivaram on the night he was killed, wrote of working with him on a Sinhala–Tamil arts festival that his employer, the leftist, *Hiru* newspaper, had organized in 2003 – a festival broken up by anti-Tamil thugs. Abeywardane then sounded themes repeated by many others, citing Sivaram's companionship, the excitement of conversing and arguing with him, his capacity for extraordinary charm, and his rigorous but generous professionalism. Importantly, Abeywardane also wrote about Sivaram's continued sympathetic interest in the non-JVP Sinhalese left, and detailed Sivaram's efforts to use his journalism to aid southern labor unions (Abeywardane 2005). Reporting from further afield, I noticed that C.K. Bandara, Sivaram's old friend from the BBC Sinhala service, wrote about being unable to break the news of the death of 'Siva Mama' (Uncle Sivaram) to his 11-year-old son (Bandara 2005). And I saw that V.S. Sambandan, Sri Lanka correspondent for *The Hindu*, in an article entitled 'The end of a dissenter' (2005), had suggested that Sivaram's death recalled the murder of Richard de Zoysa, Sivaram's old mentor, and boded ill for Sri Lanka's future tolerance of dissent. I also saw that Teresita Schaffer – the former US ambassador to Sri Lanka (1992–5) – had sent a surprisingly passionate message to TamilNet. 'I am,' she wrote, 'so distressed by this. I knew Sivaram as one of the best political analysts in Sri Lanka, and someone who valued and defended his independence of thought and action. His loss is a true tragedy, and whoever killed him has done great harm to the country and the community' (TamilNet 2005b). And I remembered that representatives from a number of foreign embassies, including the US, had attended the memorial held for Sivaram on 29 May in St Andrew's Scots Kirk Church in Colpetty, Colombo. I also saw that many of Sivaram's Sinhalese colleagues, including anti-LTTE or nationalist ones, genuinely and publicly mourned Sivaram's passing; and some, later, were subjected to death threats because of this. Among the most eloquent and angry was Sivaram's old friend, Rajpal Abeynayake, a columnist and deputy editor for the *Sunday Times*, the same man who had waited with me at Sivaram's house for the coming of the police. Abeynayake spoke movingly at Sivaram's memorial of their 'close friendship' that had 'transcended racial politics,' and later wrote contemptuously of those confused by his loyalty to a man whose politics he argued against: 'We have no such obfuscations or confusions – a friend is a friend is a friend' (Abeynayake 2005a; TamilNet 2005c).

Then, in late May, a member of the American Sri Lankan Tamil community contacted me about speaking at two memorials that were to take place in Washington DC and New Brunswick, New Jersey on 5 and 6 June. I knew Oppi was flying in from London for the events, and David and Daniel were driving down from Toronto, so I wanted to go. But I began to wonder what I could possibly conclude about Sivaram's life and work? To this day I still do not fully know.

Of course, for my speech I knew I could simply outline the basic importance of Sivaram's work. I knew, for example, that Sivaram could not be reduced to what anthropologists might call – intending no disrespect, but with unavoidable condescension – an 'artisan of nationalism,' a merely local mediator between 'communitarian sentiment' and 'technical knowledge,' however nuanced and reflexive such a characterization might try to be (Boyer and Lomnitz 2005: 113). For one thing, by the time of his death Sivaram was hardly local any more, either in audience or in importance. Rather, Sivaram had become an internationally influential journalist, analyst, and politician who spoke to many communities, even if always ultimately on behalf of one of them. Beyond this, as an unconventional but rigorous nationalist thinker, Sivaram had developed a carefully worked out account of the nation and what he called the 'modern counter-insurgency state' that combined insights drawn from a variety of sources – Marxism, postmodernism, Wittgenstein, Indian philosophy, the history of warfare, and more – into a unique vision. Ultimately, Sivaram's ruthlessly unorthodox view challenged people both inside and outside Sri Lanka, including academics like me, to rethink, or at least feel compelled to defend, more conventional views of the state, nationalism, democracy, violence, and the proper place of intellectuals amidst these things. Moreover, I knew that his many military and political analyses – scattered now in cyberspace through a thousand articles – constituted a sustained, if staccato and strategic, ethnography of nationalism and violence. An ethnography, that is, not only of Sri Lanka's ethnic conflict, but also of the globally distributed political and military discourses most elites now use to manage 'small-scale' conflicts like Sri Lanka's, and to play out their larger geostrategic games. If nothing else, I could say Sivaram's work demonstrated that an adequate account of nationalist or 'inter-ethnic' conflict requires a thorough discussion of the geostrategic, C-I, and tactical forms of life that now, inevitably, surround such struggles. And I could note, in this regard, the way Sivaram's subtle understanding of the role violence plays in the running of modern nation states – even supposedly peaceful and democratic ones – underlay his oft-repeated claim that the current Sri Lankan state was, in fact, and precisely because of its majoritarian democratic politics, *structurally dependent upon* the oppression of Tamil people; and that, hence, any real settlement of its conflict would require (as in Sudan) not only a radical restructuring of the state but also an equally fundamental reordering of the means of violence currently at its disposal. Beyond this, I knew I could speak of Sivaram's innovative transformation of TamilNet into a subversively effective online news agency; or of his prescient analyses in the early 1990s of Sri Lanka's complex place in a post-Cold War world; or of his ability to retain, despite a forthrightly expressed devotion to the Tamil nationalist cause, friendly contacts with Sri Lankans of all stripes and political persuasions. And I could point out that Sivaram's ability to talk openly to all contestants and, occasionally, build a span of insight between them, was not just a shallow conviviality over drinks but the deep undergirding of both his journalism and his political practice. Finally, I knew I could point to Sivaram's belief in giving voice, with both accuracy and sympathy, to the people he called 'the voiceless': the poorest and most rural Tamils, the east coast's beleaguered Muslims, and even, sometimes, up-country Tamils or the south's Sinhalese masses. All this was easy enough to say; and, at the two memorials, that is roughly what I did say.[21]

But about Sivaram, I also know, there will always be controversy, ambiguity, and questions. A year after his death, Jude Fernando, Sivaram's old batchmate at Peradeniya University, and an astute observer of his friend, wrote about how difficult it was 'to ideologically place him within one camp or another.' After noting that attempts to do so by various commentators often revealed more about their own ideological positions than about Sivaram, Fernando went on to say, accurately, why pinning Sivaram down is so difficult. 'Siva,' as Fernando called him:

... was a complex and highly sophisticated individual whose thinking and political loyalties shifted periodically. These shifts cannot be entirely attributed to his personal interests and conveniences, but are rather an integral part of his politically engaged intellectual development over many years. From Siva's perspective such changes were a historic and strategic necessity rather than clear statements about his moral and utopian ideals. This also placed him in [a] highly controversial and life-threatening position within Sri Lankan society. (Fernando 2005: 23)

Of course, it was precisely Sivaram's efforts to remain a 'politically engaged intellectual,' and to commit himself to political action despite the inherent ambiguity and what he called 'dirt' of history, that started all our conversations off in the first place in 1984, 21 years before. It was the background to all the arrack, the talking, the midnight calls, the friendship between our families, and his death. It was the substance, too, of his dispute with the Batticaloa Readers' Circle and with most of his critics today. It was that politics, for Sivaram, was ultimately an existential act, a necessary leap into the darkness of history inextricably linked to living life in general. To linger on the brink, to stand back with judicious distain from the filthy actions of those struggling in the mire, and to imagine this distance as morally superior (or possible) was, for him, the ultimate illusion, an 'Empedoclean' folly of betrayal and spiritual suicide. This, he always said, was why he was my friend: not because of what I thought about intellectual things but because of what I once did for him. Specifically, what I did that night, long ago, on a Colombo street, when a soldier aimed his rifle at me. Knowing that he felt this way always made me deeply uncomfortable, but I also knew it was true. That act was all that mattered to him; it was the foundation of our friendship and the only reason why our conversations ever happened or continued.

Thinking about this now I am reminded of our last arguments about violence and the state, and about the uncomfortable moral paradoxes of political engagement. Of course, we never finished that argument or forged a common agreement. But his arguments and his being moved me. He made me realize that my comfortable, scholarly, middle-class dissections of Tamil separatist politics, and of its violence, were often premised on the privilege of distance – in space, in race, in class, and from danger. Nationalism, I now realize, is largely a proximity issue. Far away, it seems obviously 'constructed,' 'imagined,' discussable, and de-constructable: a kind of collective fantasy that is perhaps best kept at arm's length, and thus something about which it is easy to make clear-cut moral choices and invent palatable alternatives. But close up, particularly when a state is after you – or when, because you are too poor, or too different, or too powerless, you become its target and cannot get out of its way – nationalism, both 'your' nationalism and 'theirs,' becomes undeniably palpable, like the sound of distant shelling coming closer, bracketing you, getting your range. And for me, now, the complexities of nationalism are all and forever twisted up with my memories of Sivaram and my grief, and are thus all too grimly real.

So perhaps I should give Sivaram the final word. I remember us sitting in my office in Bowellawatta at two o'clock in the morning tired and angry. I had just rehearsed the strong arguments put forward by Rajan Hoole of the UTHR(J) against having anything to do with the LTTE because of its 'fascism' and dismal human rights record. I was particularly bothered, as I continue to be, by acts like the LTTE's assassination of Ranjani Thiranagama, the Jaffna University professor who co-founded the UTHR(J)'s human rights watch project. Could supporting the LTTE really be justified given that kind of killing?

'Let history judge!' said Sivaram, slamming his fist on my table. 'To Hoole and all these people I ask, do you sell off your mother because your brother has cut off your arm? Because your brother is a scoundrel? So are we just going to say that the LTTE is a static thing, that it is fascist, and that it killed a lot of people? Yes, it killed a lot of people; other lives, not just special people like Ranjani Thiranagama. You can't just say she was special and all the others were nothing. There have been others who have been killed by the LTTE, like my cousin. But we are fighting the LTTE; we are fighting the Sri Lankan state. And in the end of the day ... you can tell them to go fly a fucking kite. Because people were telling me this in 1984. "Siva, how can you deal with people that have blood-stained hands? Don't go!" You are an intellectual, be an intellectual, teach in the university. I don't want to be like that. I don't care a fuck about being called an LTTE apologist. Because I am fighting another war – *my* war. The original cause for which I set out is not just my selfish motive to make a hero of myself, to say hundreds of my colleagues were shot dead, to work with Chandrika to betray the cause – no I won't.'

'But can the LTTE be reformed?'

'You are posing this as a question. This is a typical intellectual thing to do. You don't ask "if", you just do it. That is what I have been arguing since 1984. When a farmer looks at his farm, he does not ask "Does this soil help when I plant the seed?" You don't sit on the shore and ask: "Can the fish swim in this sea?" To acquire that knowledge some farmer thousands of years ago had to do it.'

'Well, what do you think are likely ways the LTTE *can* be reformed?'

'But this is just like your typical Sri Lankan intellectual. Because this problem has nothing to do with the LTTE. It started long before there was an LTTE, in the 1950s, when Pirapakaran was a fucking kid. So don't obfuscate the real problem – the Sri Lankan Tamil problem. I know a lot of people who say this: focus on the LTTE, destroy the LTTE, it is fascist, it is a killer. But if the LTTE were not here, we would all be fucked. We need them to defend us. At the end of the day, that is why the Tamils do not want the LTTE gone. Because we know what the Sri Lankan state has done. The LTTE has shot hundreds of guys; the Sri Lankan state has killed thousands. So you have to make practical choices – that this is your own man, was a brother once, so you try to reform him. And it is not just him who is the problem.'

And then he turned to me, bleary-eyed and very tired.

'But what I am saying is: *make my arguments*. Because the answers to their concerns will already be contained in the body of the book ... Anyway, my argument remains the same, from 1984 to now. There will be a consistency in your book because of your first chapter on what I am. I don't care a fuck about keeping my hands clean – no. I have done a lot for people – for example, in Tirukkovil, about the hospital. I don't care about some intellectual asshole. I care about people like them. And this is why I have a certain respect, even with my enemies. And I have good Sinhalese friends. They know I will do what I think is right.'

NOTES

THREE PROLOGUES

1 'Peon' is the local English word for a uniformed physical laborer.

1 INTRODUCTION: WHY AN INTELLECTUAL BIOGRAPHY OF SIVARAM DHARMERATNAM?

1 The *Daily Mirror* columnist, Sathya, for example, calls TamilNet the ' "unofficial" organ of the LTTE (if there is such a term)' (*Daily Mirror*, 23 Feb. 2004).

2 Sri Lanka's civil conflict has been conducted with great ruthlessness by all sides. The Sri Lankan government and all its various challengers, Tamil and Sinhalese, have amassed a sad record that includes years of attacks on noncombatants, large scale massacres, torture, disappearances, bombings, the forced recruitment of children, the killing of journalists and 'ethnic cleansing.' These human rights violations have been most consistently documented by Amnesty International, and are still continuing despite the current 'cease-fire' between the Sri Lankan government and the LTTE, as can be seen by a visit to Amnesty International's online archive ([http://web.amnesty.org/library/eng-lka/index] accessed 22 July 2006). As for the casualty figures given above, Chandraprema (1991) estimates that about 40,000 people lost their lives in the 1987–9 war between the Sri Lankan government and the JVP (*Janatha Vimukthi Peramuna* or People's Liberation Front), a Sinhala nationalist, quasi-Maoist revolutionary group. Most sources estimate, meanwhile, that the various Eelam wars have cost over 60,000 lives (see the fly-leaf on Swamy 2003, for example), although, since this is a figure that has been cited since at least 1996, four years before the conflict ended, it is pretty clear that many more than this actually died. The combined total is obviously more than 100,000.

3 *Jathika Chinthanaya* is difficult to translate into English. Chandraprema, for example, does not even try. 'National Spirit' or 'National Aspiration,' apparently, somewhat capture the idea.

4 Peiris is a switch-hitter, having been, for a time, Minister of Justice and Constitutional Affairs and Deputy Minister of Finance and Planning for the SLFP (Sri Lankan Freedom Party) led the People's Alliance (PA) before becoming disillusioned and joining the UNP's United Parties Freedom Alliance (UPFA) government for the 2002 parliamentary elections. He was once the Vice-Chancellor of the University of Colombo.

5 TamilNet.com ran on $1400 a month at first. This was later raised to $2000 a month.

6 I am well aware, of course, that this is a middle-class salary in Sri Lanka.

7 Das argues that 'allowing the pain' of a past victim of communal violence to 'happen to' her was what showed her how to 'redeem life from the violations to which she had been submitted' (2003: 297). This is something like what I am saying here, in that it points to the importance of having a kind of gritty, concrete, existential understanding of tragic historical events like these that goes beyond mere reportage or rhetorical

218

outrage. Of course, Sri Lanka's terrors did not happen to me (or, at least, not much), and that important phenomenological distance must be borne in mind.

8   This view is found, of course, in most contemporary versions of Aquinas's 'just war' doctrine. But in an interesting editorial in the journal *Philosophy* (Editors 2003: 317–18), the editors call attention to how problematic applying this idea has become these days, given both modern weaponry and the increasing uncertainty about what legitimately constitutes a state, 'universal' human rights, a 'humanitarian' war, and so forth.

9   I do not mean to be obscure here. Bourdieu's term (2004: 272–4) 'misrecognition' refers to his observation that victims of violence are sometimes complicit in the violence that assails them when such violence occurs in forms of life that victims and perpetrators both share or 'embody.' Bourdieu's observations about this kind of 'symbolic violence' were offered within the context of his discussion of gender violence among the Kabyle. Here Bourdieu argued that Kabyle women internalized or 'embodied' a language game of acting in the world (a 'habitus') that rendered their violation, culturally speaking, 'natural.' Although I have doubts about the justice of using the term 'complicit' here when referring to such embodied cultural practices – for does not 'complicity' suggest a degree of active if momentarily forsworn consciousness inconsistent with something so preconscious as an embodied cultural practice? – I nevertheless suspect that both nationalism and modern military culture ('low-intensity conflict,' 'containment,' etc.) also produce this kind of self-inflicted, 'symbolic' violence. Think, in this regard, of the 'gun culture' that has grown up in Sri Lanka; of the intra-communal conflicts the war occasioned; of the various (sometimes violent) reductions of difference under the necessity of nationalist unity; and so forth (see also Spencer 2000: 120–40).

10   What virtues? First, despite almost 30 years of passionate, aggressive, and, in many ways, well-deserved self-criticism, anthropological ethnography remains, I think, unique among scholarly endeavors in its commitment to actually *listening* to people: that is, ethnography. Whether one speaks here of Ann Kingsolver's notion of 'engaged listening' (2001) or Scheper-Hughes's 'witnessing' (2003), the implication is the same: that it is the practice, perhaps even the duty, of anthropologists to sit down and try to hear what people, any people, have to say; and to do so in a way that is relatively unmediated (at least at first) by theory or scientistic pretenses about 'representativeness' in the form of research 'instruments,' protocols, questionnaires, and survey forms. As a consequence, one notable characteristic of this kind of engaged listening is that it entails maintaining an extraordinary sensitivity to (and willingness to describe and explain) context; and by 'context' here I mean the messy multitude of things historical, linguistic, social, economic, and 'cultural' that surround a person and, in Wittgenstein's sense, conjoin their actions to various discernible forms of life (for example, doing philosophy, Hinduism, Buddhism, neoconservativism, born-again Christianity, marketing, warfare, *Jathika Chinthanaya*, Tamil separatism, partying, playing chess, and so forth). The relevance of this kind of commitment to context-sensitive listening or ethnography to the writing of an intellectual biography should be fairly self-evident.

A second notable virtue of ethnographic listening involves an almost perverse willingness to be continually, and publicly, *mistaken* – mistakes being inevitable since ethnographic listening takes place in the midst of actual conversations (among other kinds of active interactions) where everyone (including the generally clueless anthropologist) is expected to competently take part. As I have argued extensively elsewhere, from a Wittgensteinian point of view, while the experimental utterances and actions (or 'tries') that anthropologists (and others) fumblingly put forward in such conversations often fail, observing *how and why they fail* is precisely what gives them some overall sense of the various forms of life (local and otherwise) they failed within. It is, indeed, the record of such observed failures, though these are painful to record and often (if honestly recounted) comical to read, that constitutes the core of ethnographic knowledge. And since, in this conception of 'culture,' what is being learned is a set of acted practices and embodied knowledges that only exist, and are always changed, in their moments of acted emergence, recording even these evanescent glimpses of them is always also to be recording history, albeit on a minute scale. Again, the value of this kind of engaged listening to the writing of an *intellectual* history is relatively easy to see.

Finally, anthropologists at their best tend to be rather dogged about their listening. One thinks, here, about the many years Karen McCarthy Brown (1991) listened to Mama Lola; of Margaret Trawick (1992) listening for years to her adopted Tamil family; of Veena Das (2003) and Patricia Lawrence (2000) recording testimony after terrifying testimony in North India or Sri Lanka; or of Paul Farmer (1992) returning, summer after summer, to listen to (and treat medically) mortally sick Haitian farmers, and so forth. One could go on and on here, for there are many examples. Indeed, until recently (and I think this a dire trend for the field) anthropologists were simply expected to take a long time, even a lifetime, listening – and listening, sometimes, to just a few 'unrepresentative' people. But, again, the relevance of this to an intellectual history of Sivaram Dharmeratnam should be fairly evident. Of course, lots of people know they should be interested in listening to Sivaram *now*; that is why his column became so popular, his views so sought after, his opinions so celebrated and vilified, especially after he died. I listened before all this, and continued to listen for over 20 years.

2   LEARNING POLITICS FROM SIVARAM

1   At the time, I hardly understood just how complex this distribution of ideologies was, especially among the Tamil separatist groups. Just to give some idea of the contrast there, the Eelam People's Revolutionary Liberation Front (EPRLF) espouses a form of revolutionary Marxism in which separatism *per se* is officially secondary to socialist liberation; on the other hand, the LTTE, though sometimes utilizing Marxist rhetoric, especially in their English-language publications, more often envision and justify separatism in terms of a heroic, classical past. Indeed, their very name alludes to the royal emblem of the ninth- to thirteenth-century Chola kings. It is, perhaps, no accident that this group has had the most enduring popular support among the Tamil population of the north and east. See Dagmar-Hellmann Rajanayagam (1994: 54–84, 169–207), and my subsequent discussion of Sivaram's views on this issue.

2   For a more detailed picture of what was happening in Sri Lanka in 1983–4, the period of this account, see Tambiah (1986), Kapferer (1988: 29–120), and Obeyesekere (1984).

3   'Muttusvami' is a pseudonym. This is a hybrid book about a hybrid man and so follows a hybrid practice with regard to naming people. Generally, in contexts in this book that are 'ethnographic,' where people might be endangered by having their names known, or where they have not given me permission to use their names, I have followed anthropological practice and used pseudonyms or avoided using names altogether. On the other hand, this is a biography of a (now important) historical figure, so I have used the names of people in Sivaram's family and wide circle of friends, past and present, where they have given me their permission to do so or if they, too, are already public figures. For members of the various Tamil separatist political parties, however, I have used 'party names' but not real names, except in cases where they, too, have became public figures.

4   This scene between Muttusvami, Sivaram, and myself is recreated from memory and fieldnotes rather than from a verbatim record. Our conversation was initially in Tamil, although I took notes in English when I wrote down this part of the encounter later. Sivaram and I switched to English, in which Sivaram was fluent, as soon as Muttusvami left. I had no tape-recorder with me at the time and was not initially regarding this

as an 'ethnographic' encounter. Sivaram went over this section of the paper several times after I wrote it, and claimed that I did a good job capturing the gist of both how he spoke and what he said.

5   Sivaram disputed my interpretation here. His note on this statement was simple: 'Cut this out!' I cannot quite bring myself to do so. In one way, of course, Sivaram was right. Sivaram was using discourses – of which, as we shall see, he (more than I) was fully aware – that either disregarded caste (Dravidian nationalism), saw it as an object of study (social science), or actively objected to it as a structure of oppression (neo-Marxist, Foucauldian discourses). Moreover, Sivaram was using even these discourses as discourses, with all the ironic, postmodern distance that implies. But Mr M was not. Although fully aware of older, Tamil Nadu style DMK (Dravidian Progressive Front) nationalism and its disregard not only for caste but for religion as well, Mr M, as the maternal nephew of one of Mandur's Sri Kantisvami key temple board members, was very much involved in the caste- and honor-based politics that swirled about that temple. Sivaram, who just happened to be from the same caste as one of the three that, as caste groups, vied for power in the temple, was naturally viewed with suspicion by Mr M. This was not, as I have explained at length elsewhere, a sign of Mr M's 'traditionalism.' Temple politics are contemporary politics that simply happen to be based on principles that appear opaque to those using other, more self-consciously modern discourses to appraise them (see Whitaker 1999). In any case, I have altered the account here to make it clear that it was Mr M who viewed the situation in this way – as I know he did from having asked him why he so objected to Sivaram's visits.

6   From this point on in the 1984 conversation, all of Sivaram's comments were recorded either verbatim or as amended by him that night or later, in 1993, when he reviewed this section. My own comments were only put down by me in sketchy notes the next day, or in even briefer notes written in the time available between Sivaram's comments, and it is this inadequate record I have used to recreate my side of the dialogue. I am sure I have inadvertently rendered myself far more clever than I actually was.

7   Colombo, on the south-west shore of the island, is the capital of Sri Lanka. Peradeniya, a small town just outside of Kandy in the central highlands, is the site of the University of Peradeniya. Both the south-west and the center of Sri Lanka are areas dominated by ethnic Sinhalese, although there is also a large population of 'stateless' Tamil workers employed on tea estates in the central highlands, whose status has troubled both Sinhalese and Tamil nationalists (De Silva 1981: 274, 552, 560). Jaffna, at the extreme north of the island, is a Tamil enclave and the historical point of origin for much of the separatist sentiment of Sri Lankan, Tamil-speaking people (Russell 1982). Trincomalee, a deep-water port on the north-east coast, was, until the late 1960s, a predominantly Tamil town. Now, however, due to years of government-sponsored Sinhalese colonization, it is very much a mixed Tamil and Sinhalese community, and has been the scene of much inter-ethnic violence.

8   Sivaram later pointed out that I here transformed his phrase, 'ethical discourse,' into the more neutral 'technical discourse' – a bit of rhetorical sleight of hand by which I obviously hoped to avoid the critical claim he was making about my professional intellectual practices.

9   Sivaram is referring here to the section on 'Intellectuals' in Gramsci's *Prison Notebooks* (1971: 1–23). Sivaram had access to many such texts through bookstores in Colombo, and through the library of the university of which he was a nominal student. Most of his copies of these texts were photocopies. The importance of the photocopy machine in the spread of information among intellectuals in Sri Lanka should be noted.

10 For a summary description of the complex and unusual caste system found in the eastern province of Sri Lanka see McGilvray's article 'Mukkuvar vannimai: Tamil caste and matriclan ideology in Batticaloa, Sri Lanka' (1982: 34–97). Sivaram's view of caste is not representative. As a *paTicca aal*, of course, Sivaram's view would not be. I

have described elsewhere the complex range of east-coast views of caste and related concepts of history, merit, and status (Whitaker 1986: 147–240, 1990).

11   Velalar are an agricultural caste, often associated on the east coast with the executive end of temple control. As McGilvray notes, in east-coast traditional history, the Velalar are often seen as vying for 'social preeminence' with another caste, the Mukkuvar, the latter being celebrated in the province's historical chronicle, the *maTTakaLappu maanmiyam* (1982: 58–67). The relationship between these castes is complex, but both would be considered 'high' caste in the opinion of most east-coast people.

12   Sivaram is referring here to Noam Chomsky and Edward S. Herman's *The Washington Connection and Third Word Fascism* (1979), a book we had discussed numerous times in the past.

13   Sivaram's great-grandfather was his father's mother's father. East-coast Tamils are matrilineal.

14   This ritual is similar to the *dakum* or 'respects' ceremony that took place between landlords and tenants in Sinhalese villages during the Kandyan period. In that ritual, tenants presented their 'lord' (*gamladda*) with betel leaves and worshiped him. In Kandyan ideology, this asymmetrical prestation tied such tenants, as the lord's retinue (*pirivara*), into a larger system of royal service (*rajakariya*) from which both tenants and lords ultimately derived their limited rights in land and each other. Such rights were granted to landlords by superior landlords and, finally, the king, who, in theory, alone owned all the land and all rights in people under a warrant bestowed by the Buddha. As Obeyesekere (1967: 213–23) points out, this is a Kandyan working out of the *chakravarti* or 'world ruler' ideal. The temple-centered landlord–tenant ideologies of the east coast apparently drew upon both this Kandyan ideology and the *chakravarti* ideal in general in forging their own systems.

15   Sivaram said that, at that time, this was a fairly large amount of money. A teacher then was paid about 700 rupees a month.

16   Sivaram also said that at that time he was more of an existentialist than anything else, as diary entries from that time reveal. Beyond this, it is important to note that this was not the end of Sivaram's formal schooling. He studied successfully at home for his O- and A-levels, exams necessary for university entrance, and began to attend university as an Arts student, majoring in English. He was only there part of one semester, however, before anti-Tamil rioting and his own growing involvement in nationalist politics forced him to leave. The schools were shut down shortly thereafter. Sivaram was not a success as a student. His mother told me – and Sivaram himself confirmed this – that his wide reading and *paTicca aal* contempt for narrow gauge academia made it difficult for him to accept instruction, especially in the rigidly hierarchical setting of a Sri Lankan university.

17   Sivaram had a photocopy of the whole of Vincent Descombes' *Modern French Philosophy* (1980), from which he drew a lot of his thinking about French philosophy.

18   That is, 'Mother.'

19   This example, from Wittgenstein, was brought to Sivaram's attention by me. But Sivaram had already read *Philosophical Investigations* (1958) during his year as an undergraduate. His father's library had a copy of the *Tractatus Logico-Philosophicus* (1974 [1921]). He did read my copy of *On Certainty* (1969) while I was there.

20   Sivaram had been reading Thomas McCarthy's *The Critical Theory of Jurgen Habermas* (1981). He also had read Habermas's *Legitimation Crisis* (1975). His comments about Derrida derive chiefly, I believe, from Descombes (1980).

21   Since the town in question was Akkaraipattu, Sivaram must have been reading from some work of that town's very able ethnographer, Dennis McGilvray (1973, 1974). I must honestly report that I did not note down the precise text from which he was reading. It does not matter. Sivaram's criticism here is generic, and he had made similar comments in the past about Yalman's work on Panama, a town south of Akkaraipattu (1967: 310–24), and about my own work, all of which he had read.

22 *Paticca akkal ninka ellam cumma irukka, aru kekkira?*
23 Sivaram later told me that he was also thinking here of Lyotard's notion of esthetic 'masochism' – that is, what happens when imagination, facing the unimaginable, tortures itself so that at least its pain will signal the ineffable it cannot otherwise present. For a good explanation see Lyotard (1994: 55).
24 Interestingly, Sivaram misquoted Milton here. In his recitation from *Paradise Lost,* lines 250 to 259, he dropped line 256, 'And what matter where, if I be still the same' (Milton 1957: 217–18).
25 Sivaram's view of Milton was influenced by E.M.W. Tillyard (1966), whose book he read in Colombo before entering university.
26 Sivaram is referring here to my copy of Feyerabend (1975), which he had borrowed and read.

3   THE FAMILY ELEPHANT

1   His city firm was Ford, Rhodes and Thornton.
2   And see Canagaratnam (1921: 6) for further details about how Batticaloa's fish might be singing through their gills.
3   Or, in Tamil, *veLLaaLar, timilar, ciirpaatar,* and *karaiyaar.* These caste names are conventionally written in English as above.
4   See Jayawardena (2000) for a good description of the development of the bourgeoisie in colonial Sri Lanka.
5   Testamentary Jurisdiction No. 15284, in the District Court of Colombo, 16 May 1954.
6   *Maccaan,* in Batticaloa Tamil, refers to a mother's brother's son. In anthropological parlance such kin are called 'cross-cousins' since the sexes of the linking parental kin are different or 'crossed.' More generally, though, as in Sinhalese, Batticaloa Tamil people might refer to any other male 'cross-cousin' who is about one's own age and a friend as *maccaan.* The implication is that a *maccaan* is a convivial peer, a buddy. The cousins all call Lee Karu *maccaan* in this sense. As I will discuss below, cross-cousin marriages represent an ideal in Batticaloa Tamil society, and hence an alternative translation of *maccaan* might be 'brother-in-law' or 'potential husband.'
7   Dharmavasan, Sivaram's fraternal cousin, claims that the elephant was actually part of a matched set of baby elephants given to Keerthi's father by the Bandaranaike family. Sivaram's grandfather Dharmeratnam had attended the wedding of the future presidents S.W.R.D. and Srimavo Bandaranaike.
8   From Keerthi's diary: '15th December. Saturday ... I realize that my choice of Mahes has been as far as I am concerned better than any in all England, better than any in all the Ceylon ... better than any other in all Batticaloa. No other girl will suit me better I am convinced. To bed at 12:30.'
9   'To Father: I am sending this to you so that you may get some idea of how I am getting along here. You may find quite a number of things which may be shocking or which may qualify me for a bit of madness or silliness. I too do not look favourably on some things I have done. But that is what I *did* ... I must be honest and not merely show the better side of myself. Please let sister also read this diary. Certain things, which may mean much to me, may not suggest anything to you. Don't misunderstand. From son, 17 Jan. 46.'
10 But all these rifts eventually healed. Nagesvari, who later regretted her relationship with Keerthi, which she felt she was pressured into, was always well liked and respected by Sivaram. Somasundaram and Ranjani's children, Dharmavasan and Vasumathy, eventually became quite close to Sivaram and Kuttan. Indeed, it was Dharmavasan, now a successful computer entrepreneur, who took the lead in making the funeral arrangements when Sivaram died. And, as we shall see, Sivaram was shattered when the Central Bank bombing eventually claimed the life of Vasumathy. Somasundaram,

Ranjani's husband, a kindly man now quite elderly, became very close to Sivaram and frequently helped his wife and children.

11   As Wilson (2000: 99) notes, a good example of this kind of rhetoric is provided by the 1956 release of a report of the Unofficial Buddhist Commission of Inquiry entitled *The Betrayal of Buddhism*.

12   It should be mentioned that this move was actually supported by many Sri Lankan (i.e. non-plantation Jaffna and Batticaloa) Tamils, who do not see up-country Tamils as part of their community.

13   That is, the Illankai Thamil Arasu Kadchi or 'the party for a Ceylon Tamil government' (see Wilson 2000: 4).

14   That is, Gandhian style civil disobedience.

15   This is a rather important point. As Nesiah argues, mainstream Tamil politicians were still seeking a solution within a united state at this time.

16   As Wilson points out, the Tamil New Tigers themselves emerged out of the founding, in 1970, of the Tamil Students' Federation (2000: 124–5).

17   Such schools were excluded from the education nationalization reforms because they did not grant degrees. They were 'tutories' designed to get students past their exams.

4   ANANTHAN AND THE READERS' CIRCLE

1   Rohan Gunaratna (1997: 125) gives a slightly different account of the LTTE's origins, emphasizing its early relationships with the TULF, and claiming that Appapillai Amirthalingam, who succeeded Chelvanayagam as the TULF's leader, 'clandestinely' supported the LTTE right from the beginning for tactical political reasons. Both Wilson (2000) and Gunaratna, however, note the overlapping membership between the early LTTE and the TULF youth wing (TYF), pointing out that Uma Maheswaran – who later split with Prabharkaran and formed the PLOTE, which Sivaram joined – was, as Wilson says, 'at first both chairman of the LTTE and Colombo secretary of the TYF' (2000:). The early history of the LTTE, however, is very difficult and dangerous to ascertain: difficult, because those involved in its early history are either dead or are not talking other than in the official, propaganda-laden publications of the LTTE; dangerous, because Tamil scholars (especially 'insiders') who have attempted to write too frankly about the early history of the movement have sometimes been killed.

2   Shanmugathasan (1920–93), who was a Tamil, died in his sleep in exile in Birmingham, UK. Shanmugathasan's Maoist Communist Party of Ceylon split from the Communist Party in the 1960s as a result of arguments at the time in the communist world between the Maoist 'revolutionary' and Soviet 'parliamentary' approaches to capturing political power (Shanmugaratnam 1993: 22). It is ironic that Shanmugathasan, a dynamic teacher and a 'guru' of Marxism-Leninism for a generation of young Sri Lankan intellectuals in the 1960s and 1970s, inspired both the founders of the JVP and many of the young Marxists who went on to found Tamil separatist groups in the 1970s and 1980s, although not – notably – the LTTE. Sivaram, in an article on the history of the JVP, suggested that Shanmugathasan's Maoism, tainted at the time by China's geopolitical suspicions about India, inspired the anxieties about India given voice to in the last of the JVP's famous 'five classes'; and that this, in turn, eventually increased the likelihood of violence against 'up-country Tamils' (Sivaram 2004c). If so, this is an irony indeed since it was Shanmugathasan who attempted to mobilize plantation workers with the Red Flag Movement from 1966 to 1970. Shanmugathasan also tried to mobilize a mass movement against untouchability, rather a challenge to the orthodox Saiva Velalar who controlled Jaffna.

3   Of course, as Chandraprema notes, Wijeweera's brief period as a member of Shanmu-gathasan's Ceylon Communist Party was marked by 'distress' over the leadership of the party being in the hands of a Tamil. Further, 'There were times when Wijeweera openly

accused Shanmugathasan of communal mindedness and favouritism toward Tamils' (1991: 23) The point, however, is that both Wijeweera and Sivaram's mentor were exposed to Shanmugathasan's arguments in favor of an all-island, Sinhala–Tamil, peasant revolution.

4   It is interesting to compare this debate among Tamil nationalists about Marxism with a debate, in some ways similar, that was going on in the 1980s among Sri Lankan leftists. Chandraprema discusses this in his comparison of the ideologies of the JVP and the *Jathika Chinthanaya* nationalist intellectual movement (1991: 110–17), having noted first how the Tamil national issue had already troubled the JVP. In a 'Young Socialist' pamphlet Nanayakkara, for his part, sees *Jathika Chinthanaya*'s amalgam of Marxism and distinctly chauvinist Sinhala nationalism as a form of petit-bourgeois false consciousness emerging 'in reaction to the profound economic, social and cultural changes they were undergoing in the post 1977 period' (2002: 17), echoing Newton Gunasinghe's well-known argument detailing how the neoliberal 'Open Economy' of what was, in 1977, the newly elected UNP government quickly increased ethnic tensions (1994; see also Jayawardena [1986] for a helpful, longer, historical account of the development of ethnic chauvinism as the distinctive 'false consciousness' of the Sinhala petit bourgeoisie). In this Nanayakkara stands in basic agreement with Tambiah (1986), whose analysis of Sri Lanka's 'ethnic fratricide' makes a similar argument in non-Marxist terms. Be that as it may, what is also interesting to note is that in all three cases – Tamil secessionists, JVP self-avowed Marxists, and *Jathika Chinthanaya* – debates about nationalism had to be approached, albeit sometimes rather oddly, as debates about Marxism. Sivathamby (1995: 186) also points out the extent to which the Tamil secessionist movements of the 1980s, however instinctive their nationalism, all 'spoke in Marxist terminologies.'

5   Examples of literary journals cited by the *puluvar*, and published in Tamil Nadu at the time, are *Steps (paTikal)*, *Lotus (taamrai)*, *Dimensions (parimaanam)* and *Letters (eLuttu)*. These journals all boasted an eclectic mix of poetry, prose, and literary criticism.

6   I want to thank some of the other members of the Batticaloa Readers' Circle who were there that day: Mr Ravintaran; Mr Nullatompi, the treasurer; Mr Rajaratnam; and Mr Daiyananthan, the former secretary. They also contributed to the conversation that day.

7   This is the way Sivaram told the story to me. D.B.S. Jeyaraj, the journalist Sivaram eventually replaced at *The Island* in 1989, tells a different one. According to him, Sivaram tried to join the LTTE, speaking first to Mhathaya and then with Kittu (Krishnakumar) but was rejected by both – rejected, Jeyaraj suggests, because he was too enthusiastic and too intellectual. According to Jeyaraj, Kittu 'declined asking Sivaram to concentrate on his studies and help them in writing tracts and pamphlets. A deeply disappointed Sivaram now tried his chances with PLOTE.' (www.tamilweek. com/Sivaram_Gun_to_Pen_009html, accessed 3 June 2005). This all may be true. But I believe it is also true that Sivaram was more attracted to PLOTE than the LTTE because PLOTE's Marxist orientation more deeply fit with his own beliefs, and because PLOTE, at that time, had (to Sivaram's mind) a better view of the east and south. This would also seem to square with Ismail's account (2005) of an early discussion he had with Sivaram apparently in either 1985 or 1986 (see also Ismail 1987).

8   Kailasapathy, as the writer of the definitive study *Tamil Heroic Poetry* (1968), was perhaps more famous than Sivathamby as a scholar in the West. But Sivathamby is well known too, both as a scholar of Tamil language and literature and for having started in the 1950s, along with K. Kailasapathy, the Progressive Writers' Association (PWA). That was a failed attempt, as Wilson explains, to benefit from what Tamil Marxists hoped were the underlying progressive aspects of the Sinhala people's 1956 social revolution. As Wilson puts it: 'This did not happen and they were to be sadly disillusioned, although they persisted in their thinking and writings till the full tide of Sinhala Buddhist chauvinism overtook the "progressivism" they had hoped to achieve'

(2000: 37). Thereafter, according the Sivathamby, Kailaspathy became interested in the Chinese wing of the Communist Party and, in articles written under a pen name, endorsed violence as a legitimate weapon of revolution. Of himself, Sivathamby told me in an interview that he then worked for many years for various civil society reform schemes, including the Jaffna citizens' council, until he was convinced by Sivaram in 1993, in a curious reversal of roles, that such political efforts were wasting his scholarly potential, whereupon he returned to full-time academic writing.

9   Sivathamby's analysis here, of course, is derived from his knowledge of Jaffna Tamil society. Things work a bit differently in matrilineal Batticalao. However, Sivathamby's point about how a formerly imaginable and predictable future was no longer possible, and the role this played in the sense of urgency with which young men and women embraced the separatist cause in the early 1980s, is I think pertinent in both the north and east.

10 All of these scholars were associated with the Social Scientists' Association, with which Sivathamby was also periodically associated, with the exception of Newton Gunasinghe, who was in the department of sociology at the University of Colombo.

11 Sivakumar's career trajectory mirrors that of so many of the brilliant young middle-class people who originally supported the Eelam cause in the early 1980s in tracing a path from passionate involvement to disillusion. Sivakumar was involved in the PLOTE student movement, but he left PLOTE in 1986. Sivakumar's abiding interest, aside from a desire for Eelam, was human rights, and so he was driven out of Jaffna in 1990 by the LTTE for calling for democracy. By 1997, when I spoke with him, he was a journalist publishing a literary magazine, *ciringikar*, out of the office of the local human rights NGO, MERGE. Sivaram frequently wrote for him.

12 *Oru aRiviyaR pakaiTTulathtin palaviinngkal.*

13 One can see this in the following diary entry (10 Sept. 1983): 'One knows the jungle for quite some time. But one suddenly finds when talking to somebody who lives there that certain kinds of trees "existed" in that jungle whose "existence" was not known to him or that he was not "aware" of their existence. I learn the names of those trees. I enter into a certain relation. I learn a certain rule from them – a rule that is necessary for this domain characterized by this rule for production. At first I learn only *a* rule – that of using a particular symbol. Then when I went with them into the jungle to "produce" timber, I find that this rule is part of a language game of production: rules of using the axe, rules of what to do with which kind of timber, etc. This shows that all this philosophical chatter about a world "there" is nonsense. People may object that we see or experience things or referents even in the absence of words. The objection is baseless once we are aware that "seeing" and "experiencing" things is a social relation.' But lest one think that Sivaram here was arguing for an anti-materialist position, one should be aware that he wrote earlier: 'Here we place the Derridean maxim "there is nothing outside the text" in a materialist framework' (12 Aug. 1983).

14 Hoole says there was also violence on the campus on 10–11 May 1983 (2001: 64) But Laxman Kumara Keerthi, currently a journalism lecturer but at that time a student, told me that the left-wing student groups told the UNP groups to lay off the Tamil students. The historian K.M. De Silva points out that during the 1983 riots the Vice-Chancellor of the university opened the residence halls to Tamil refugees from the surrounding area – and was sorry he did so because, De Silva claims, inter-caste tensions then occurred within the dorms (personal communication).

5   FROM SR TO TARAKI – A 'SERIOUS UNSERIOUS' JOURNEY

1   This paper was published years later in Sri Lanka, after Taraki (if not Sivaram) had become well known, as 'Learning politics from Taraki: a biographical fragment (see Whitaker 1998).

2   But, note, recent estimates of the number of deaths by 2001 are not much higher. The National Peace Council (2003), for example, estimates that 65,000 people have died in the war, half civilians. But if 60,000 had already died by 1992, before the worst of the attritional warfare that followed, then these figures are suspect.

3   Sivaram pointed out that this was an over-literal translation of the English word 'movement' since an *yakkam* indicates merely a physical movement. A more proper word, in his opinion, would have been *kaLakam* or *cangkam*.

4   About the phenomenal proliferation of new separatist groups Wilson (2000: 130) argues: 'the only explanation for their multiplicity is the tendency towards individuality, competitiveness, and private enterprise among the Jaffna Tamils. This may be a general stereotyping but there is much to be said for it.' Obviously, TERA does not fit this theory. Another explanation, it seems to me, is that TULF rhetoric had so primed the pump of youthful expectations that, when an obvious 'trigger-event' such as the July riots occurred, the desire for action outweighed the organizational abilities of any of the existing groups. A former military commander for Batticaloa once pointed out to me, for example, that at one point in 1984, PLOTE was receiving applications to join from 300–400 young men per week – far more than the 10–15 they were set up to handle. Even the LTTE seems to have been swamped (Balasingham 2003: 75–86).

5   This is a line from Ananthan's poem 'Your poet is born' (*unkal kavirnam piRantullaan*). The key verse reads: 'The poet from the lineage/that sold its sword/to buy the Veena/ may sell the Veena/to buy a sword./Sword or veena?/Which will make history?/ Knowing the answer/chooses the right one' (*vaalai viRRu/viilai vaankiya/vamsam tannil/vantha kalinan./vaalum vaankuvaan/vaalaa? viinaiyaa?/varalaaRRai aakum/enpatai aRintu/eRRatait terivaan*) (Ananthan 1997: 19).

6   Mahadeva tells the same tale a bit differently. 'It was December 5, 1995. He was coming from Samantarai post office to Batticaloa. Because his family was in Batticaloa. And on the way there was a fight between the LTTE and the STF taking place. And he got caught in the crossfire.'

7   Jeyaraj (2005b) reports, differently, that Sivaram 'ordered the execution' of Selvan and Ahilan, and that 'This led to a disciplinary inquiry in which SR was exonerated. His detractors however continue to rake up this matter to denigrate him. This is happening even after death.'

8   Sivaram also points out that most of the organizations, including the LTTE, merely made use of intellectuals. Anton Balasingham, for example, according to Sivaram, is an *adviser* to the LTTE rather than a core decision-maker. 'But I,' said Sivaram, 'had crossed the line; I had become the nastiest of them all. It is just a matter of learning skills. One skill: when you see opposition building to a certain project, you should know who to single out in the opposition and talk him out of it while keeping him in the opposition; and thereby destabilizing the opposition by cultivating an unbeliever. Or you simply know more about guns. And these are skills that can be developed just as you can develop a skill in philosophy.'

9   That is, Research and Analysis Wing.

10   Although most of this story, and most of the quotes, come from several long taped interviews I conducted with Sivaram in 1993, Sivaram also supplied a long supplementary account of what happened (dictated to my computer) when he read an earlier draft of this chapter in 1996, and further details in 2004.

11   Quadri Ismail was a columnist for the *Sunday Times* between 1984 and 1989. Eventually, like so many intellectuals of Sivaram's generation, Ismail found it necessary to leave Sri Lanka to seek graduate education elsewhere. After studying with Edward Said at Columbia University, he went on to become an Associate Professor of English, specializing in postcolonial studies, at the University of Minnesota.

12   Sivaram wrote about this in 2004, saying: 'In the end, all the immense investments Uma Maheswaran made in forging a common Sinhala–Tamil cause came to naught. The last nail on the coffin of his project was hammered in by the JVP when it demanded that

the PLOTE should completely give up its identity and be subsumed in a revolutionary front where Tamil aspirations obviously had no place' (Taraki 2004i).

13   Sivaram's views on how or whether he was disillusioned by the Eelam cause by end of 1987 shifted over time. In 1995 when asked about all this Sivaram rejected Ismail's assessment. 'All this has to be cut. If I was disillusioned, how can I be negotiating with the JVP on behalf of PLOTE?' Ismail, by the way, for his part, remains convinced that Sivaram was deeply disillusioned by the Eelam cause by 1987, as can be seen in his 2005 *Tamilweek* article, 'Mourning Sivaram.'

14   In 2004, Sivaram spoke to me twice about his detention and torture in 1987 and about his strange conversation with the Sinhalese general. Both times he said roughly the same thing. Unfortunately, on this first occasion I did not have my tape-recorder running when he made this comment and so had to reconstruct it by comparing my rough notes about what he said then to our, later, recorded conversation on this topic.

15   Sivaram sometimes pronounced *maccaan* '*maccaang*.'

16   Gamini Weerakon, who remains an editor for *The Island*, though ideologically opposed to Sivaram, was still a fan of his work and personality when I spoke with him in 1997. He also came to Sivaram's memorial in Colombo on 29 May 2005.

17   The following conversation was recorded in July 1993. However, Sivaram read my earlier account of that conversation in 1995 and added comments. I have incorporated these into the conversation here. The gaps signaled by ellipses and words in brackets indicate places where I have trimmed the discussion or added words for the sake of economy.

18   A suicide bomber assassinated President Premadasa on 1 May 1993, while addressing a UNP campaign rally. It has generally been assumed that this was the work of the LTTE, although it should be mentioned that Premadasa's death occurred within eight days of the assassination of Lalith Athulathmudali, his main Sinhalese political rival. A UNP political nonentity, Dingiri Banda Wijetunge, filled the remaining two years of Premadasa's term.

19   Sivaram is referring to Sir Richard Francis Burton (1821–90), the colonial explorer and, sometimes, spy.

6   FROM TARAKI TO TAMILNET: SIVARAM AS JOURNALIST, MILITARY ANALYST, AND INTERNET PIONEER

1   To be specific, there were substantial refugee populations in Australia, Norway, Switzerland, France, Spain, Italy, the UK, the US, and Canada, all countries Sivaram visited in the 1990s. A 2005 Canadian Broadcasting Corporation radio feature, for example estimated the city of Toronto to contain over 150,000 Sri Lankan Tamils (http://www.cbc.ca/toronto/features/whose_truth/, accessed 17 July 2006).

2   I have seen no evidence that the Sri Lankan government has in fact supported the UTHR(J). What is true is that many Tamils in the diaspora believe they have.

3   *Viirakeesari*'s full name is *Viirakeesari vaaraveLiyiiTu*, or, according to its masthead the 'Virakesari Illustrated Weekly.' But people generally simply call it *Viirakeesari*.

4   And the titles of his articles bespeak this: consider, 'Strategies for the TNA' (in Taraki 1991: 1), 'Tigers still for Eelam' (1991: 7), 'The struggle for the Wanni' (1991: 22), and 'LTTE – the Tamil–Muslim equation' (1991: 27). His writing was also quite neutral in tone – as it was to remain, for the most part, till the end of his life. His writing expressed vivid emotion only once: when Richard was killed.

5   For example, Taraki wrote 'the lethal intolerance of Pirabhakaran is not the result of a brutality perpetrated for the sake of safeguarding democracy, it is a necessary condition of what he believes in: the one-party state' (Taraki 1991: 45).

6   Baron Antoine-Henri Jomini (1779–1869) was a Swiss-born general in Napoleon's army, most famous for his writings on the 'art' of war. Sivaram was a fan of Jomini's *The Art of War* (1971 [1862]).

7   Vasumathy was Sivaram's father's sister's daughter. Cross-cousins are generally very close in the matrilineal Batticaloa District, and intermarriage between male and female cross-cousins is often considered ideal. Vasumathy, born in 1959, was also close to Sivaram's age, and they were playmates as children. Tragically, Vasumathy was due to emigrate to Australia two days after her death. For a description of this event see 'News review: the bomb that rocked Colombo' (*Tamil Times* 1996). Yet Sivaram allowed no hint of his anger to show in his subsequent dispassionate article about the political consequences of the bombing 'Devolution, the bank bomb and the dilemma of Tamil parties' (Sivaram 1996).

8   Sivaram's continued hostility to the LTTE's intolerance is very clear, for example, in his response to the assassination in Paris of his old friend Sabalingam. See 'The exclusive right to Eelam history' (Taraki 1994c). For an example of Sivaram's growing admiration for the LTTE's military strategies and tactics see 'Govt's counter-insurgency programme and LTTE's military response' (Sivaram 1994a).

9   An example of Sivaram's positive view of Chandrika Kumaratunge's take on the ethnic conflict see 'LTTE's response to peace overtures' (Taraki 1994e); Sivaram's more caustic view can be seen in 'Tamils' suffering on the rise under PA' (Taraki 1998a).

10 Examples of Sivaram's increasing disdain for what he called the 'ex-militant' Tamil groups is found in such articles as 'In political wilderness, ex-militants go berserk' (Taraki 1998b) and 'Those who wear the Tiger mask' (Taraki 1999). But all this clearly stems from his feeling that all the non-LTTE Tamil parties were getting very little out of their association with the PA and the Sinhala left. See 'Is there a future for the moderates?' (Taraki 1997g).

11 For an article on the army's intelligence failures see 'Blinded in the Wanni' (Taraki 1997e) and 'Surprise in Prabha's strategy' (Taraki 197b). For examples of Sivaram's suspicion that the whole Wanni offensive was actually a trap, see 'Sojourn to Vanni tells all' (Taraki 1997f) and 'Creeping advantage: can the government hold on to it?' (Taraki 1997c); see also 'Troops in Tiger trap: electronic intelligence gathering can be useless if not matched and confirmed by ground intelligence' (Taraki 1997d).

12 Not that Kitson himself actually advocated 'wetwork.' In his 1977 book *Bunch of Five* Kitson said, about prisoners, 'There must certainly be no brutality ...' (290). Kitson's concern here was more practical than moral; he believed brutality was counter-productive.

13 Sivaram is referring here to Iraq's Ayatollah Ali Sistani, the senior Shia cleric and prime *marja*, or spiritual reference point; and to Moqtada Sadr, the anti-US Shia cleric whose followers fought US troops in April 2004 (see BBC News 2004).

14 Teresita C. Schaffer, a thirty-year US Foreign Service professional, was ambassador to Sri Lanka from 1992 to 1995. She is now Director of the CSIS South Asia Program. CSIS is the Center for Strategic and International Studies, a non-partisan Washington strategic think-tank.

15 See 'News Feature: Sustaining Strategic Parity and Beyond,' TamilNet 30 April 2003, for a description of the *Agni Khiela* (Rod of Fire) offensive. Sivaram told me that he wrote this particular news feature. The *Agni Khiela* offensive occurred after the four-month ceasefire unilaterally declared by the LTTE, and was launched by the Sri Lankan army to regain territory it lost near Jaffna after the fall of Elephant Pass in 2000. The offensive, according to Sivaram, was prepared under US guidance in accordance with the swift, blitz-like, combined air–armor maneuver warfare tactics later used in Iraq. Here those tactics failed. Sivaram argued, in this feature, that the government would never have signed the 2002 ceasefire had *Agni Khiela* succeeded. He also argued that the ceasefire was not entered into due to a parity of forces between the Sri Lankan

government and the LTTE, but because, given this defeat, the Sri Lankan government actually felt that the strategic balance had tilted against them.

16   Or, as Sivaram put it in the written version of his CSIS talk: an 'anti-state' movement required five things to 'develop and sustain conventional fighting capability: 1) A revenue base large enough to support a standing army comprising at least four brigade groups, to run a civil administration and to maintain law and order. 2) A population large enough to draw volunteer recruits from. 3) An absolute area of control to safely station and train large fighting formations. 4.) Medical facilities capable of absorbing more than a battalion of war-wounded from high-intensity engagements. 5) A logistics system compatible with the standing force and capable of backing a total engagement by it' (Sivaram 2001).

17   Sivaram in this article briefly addresses the issue of the recruitment of women and child soldiers. Many human rights organizations have taken the LTTE to task for doing both, and especially the latter. Moreover, such recruitment was seen in the late 1990s as evidence of LTTE decline due to recruitment problems. Sivaram responded by claiming that, statistically, the recruitment of women 'is the effect of a trend' and therefore 'cannot be taken as a manifestation of "manpower" shortages.' Sivaram rather dismissed the evidence of child recruitment as 'prejudiced in most cases by extreme political hatred or cultural disdain.' We disagreed about this latter point; I strongly felt that the evidence relating to child recruitment could not be dismissed.

18   Dr Radhika Coomaraswamy, at this time, was the United Nations Special Rapporteur on Violence, and Director of the International Centre for Ethnic Studies (ICES), Colombo.

19   See next chapter.

20   TamilNet's search engine reveals 253 articles about politically motivated rape between 17 June 1997 and 22 March 2005.

7   STATES, NATIONS, AND NATIONALISM

1   Here Sivaram disagreed with Smith (2001: 42), for example, who claimed that the formative role that WASP ethnicity played in American nationalism had been eroded by immigration and the abandonment, in the 1960s, of a 'melting pot' ideology. Sivaram thought, on the contrary, that WASPS (with, at best, some admission of Catholics and Jews) still controlled the American state as an ethno-national state.

2   Lest Sivaram's view here be thought unique, it should be remembered that Howard (in Hutchinson and Smith 1994: 256) also makes an argument, similar to Sivaram's, that war against competing nations and nationalisms has been the 'principal determinant in the shaping of nation-states.' And that Giddens (1994: 33–5), in his description of the nation as a 'power-container', posited a constitutive role for violence that was, basically, the same as Sivaram's. I would argue that these views equally imply that 'invidious nationalism' is nationalism *per se*.

8   RETURN TO BATTICALOA

1   In 1972, the Sri Lankan government nationalized the Lake House and Times publishing groups, which by that time owned most of the nation's high-circulation Sinhala and English newspapers, as well as one of its most important Tamil dailies, thus ensuring itself a dominant voice in the Sinhala public sphere (Peiris 1997: 45).

2   I am in debt for this information to Chandana Keerthi Bandara, senior producer for the Sinhala section of the BBC, whom I interviewed on 24 July 2001.

3   All this is according to TamilNet (http://www.tamilnet.com/art.html?catid=13&artid =6588, accessed 10 Jan. 2005) and the Sri Lanka Tamil Media Alliance (http://www. sltma.com/gn.html, accessed 10 Jan. 2005). Of course, Sivaram, knowing I would

read about it on TamilNet the next day, called me from the hospital on 26 December and told me he had been attacked.

4 Emmanuel, who witnessed the event, does not say what year this occurred. But I believe Sivaram mentioned it to me as happening either in late 1999 or early 2000.

5 ITV was reporting a charge made by the Deshabakthi media movement. This movement accused Sivaram, P. Seevagan (BBC Tamil service), Saman Wagaarachchi (editor of the *Irida Peramuna*), and Roy Denish (defense correspondent of the *Sunday Leader*) of having direct ties to the LTTE. All fled Sri Lanka shortly after this broadcast except Sivaram.

6 Although my largely conversational Tamil was not up to allowing me to read Sivaram's Tamil work properly alone, I worked through twelve of his articles carefully with the help of N.B. Jeyaraman, my Tamil instructor in 2004, and later discussed their style with the translator and Tamil scholar David Buck, my old Tamil instructor from the 1980s. N.B. Jeyaraman works for the University of Parediniya. David Buck's most recent translation is *Melagaram Tirikutarasekppa Kavirayar's A Kuravanji in Kutralam: A Tamil Tale of Love and Fortunes Told* (Buck 2005).

7 According to TamilNet.com, Joseph Pararajasingham once wrote for the Tamil daily, *Thinapathi* under the name 'Sugunam Joseph'. He was elected to Parliament in 1990 and re-elected in 1994, 2000, 2002, and 2004 (TamilNet.com 24/12/05, http://www. tamilnet.com/art.html?catid=13&artid=16629, accessed on 1 Sept. 2006).

8 *ten tamiLLeemakkaLukkaaka kaTamai ceyvatai virumpukiReen.*

9 For a fascinating discussion of the LTTE's female cadres in Batticaloa see Trawick (1999).

10 The following scene and paragraph is drawn, with a few modifications, from a book chapter I wrote entitled 'Internet *Counter* Counter-Insurgency: TamilNet.com and Ethnic Conflict in Sri Lanka,' for the book *Native on the Net: Indigenous and Diasporic Peoples in the Virtual Age* (Landzelius, forthcoming).

11 Although I have drawn upon an earlier, soon to be published, account of this conversation to write this one (see note 12), my notebook and memories of that day have Sivaram saying a number of times, in a number of different ways, that he loved a moment of crisis. On this occasion he also said 'this is what it means to be alive. To be really alive,' and, when I again pressed him about taking so many chances: 'My philosophy is: life is too short for worry.'

12 For example, as reported in a column by 'Our Defense Correspondent' in the *Sunday Island* (9 May 2004): 'The IGP has gone on record as saying that the police had information that Sivaram was hiding a cache of weapons in his home. This is clearly one of the most idiotic statements for the IGP to make.'

13 For an excellent discussion of Sivaram's ambivalent attitude toward the LTTE see Fernando (2005).

14 Sivaram was referring to a United States aid program called the Millennium Challenge Account, called for in a speech by President Bush on 14 March 2002. Meant to be the carrot component of his new 'war on terrorism,' the new fund, according to President Bush, would be 'devoted to projects in nations that govern justly, invest in their people, and encourage economic freedom' (see: http://www.whitehouse.gov/infocus/devel-opingnations/millennium.html, accessed 29 Dec. 2005).

15 This is how the phrase was transliterated in the original article.

16 In the twelve countries hit by the waves there were perhaps as many as 225,000 killed. But there are, of course, various causality estimates. These figures come from a *New York Times* article by Kaplan, a kind of *post mortem* written a year after the event. (*New York Times* 24 Dec. 2005; http://www.nytimes.com/cfr/international-ist/slot3_122405.html, accessed 26 Dec. 2005).

17 Taraki would soon write an article making much the same argument (see 'The writing is on the wall, and it is in red,' 2005g).

18   Sivaram, of course, was not the only one who could see this. Timmo Gaasbeek, a Dutch
      relief worker with a Sri Lankan wife, who was working in Batticaloa when the tsunami
      hit, has pointed out that the LTTE (through the TRO) quickly used the disaster as a
      means to recover lost ground in the east, perhaps aided, as Sivaram's columns attest,
      by the populace's memories of past government failures to deliver aid (Gaasbeek 2005
      and personal communication). As evidence of this, in one article Taraki noted that a
      number of tsunami victims had been displaced once before – from hinterland homes
      in 1990–1 by the STF (Strategic Task Force), the government's elite 'counter-terrorist'
      police unit, and as part of a counter-insurgency policy rather than by natural calamity.
      These survivors, Sivaram averred, saw little reason to place trust in the government's
      recovery promises because they had been promised resettlement and homes by the
      government before, after their first displacement, but were instead left for ten years
      in crumbling refugee camps by the sea so the tsunami could make them refugees (or
      worse) again (Taraki 2005b). At the same time, more generally, Sivaram began to
      suspect that Sinhalese elites were greatly overestimating the effects of both the Karuna
      affair and the tsunami on the LTTE, and were on the edge of talking themselves into
      abandoning the ceasefire altogether for war. His articles, therefore, began to work
      around the edges of this idea, first assessing the likely effect of the tsunami, then
      reviewing the LTTE's strengths and weaknesses, and finally boring in on the strategic
      picture overall.

19   This article, '*jee. vi. pi. neeRRu, inRu, naalai*' ('JVP yesterday, today, and tomorrow,'
      Sivaram 2004c), was supposed to be part one of a two-part essay on the history of
      the JVP. Unfortunately, I was unable to obtain part two. In part one, Sivaram traced
      the early history of the party, its founding by Rohana Wijeweera as a revolutionary
      party in 1964, its initial indifference to and later sympathy for the Tamil national
      struggle. Sivaram ended the article promising to show how the JVP fell into 'the power
      of communalism' (*inavartic caktikkuL*) the following week. I never found that article,
      but his 13 April 2005 *Daily Mirror* article, 'The writing is on the wall, and it is in red'
      (Taraki 2005g) covered much the same ground.

20   Sivaram's presence online became so pervasive after he died that that Harinda Ranura
      Vidanage, an anthropologist writing for Tamil Canadian, suggested that a 'virtual Siva'
      was defying his assassins online by being 'alive and well in cyberspace' (http://www/
      tamilcanadian.com/pageview/phd?ID=3265&SID=512, accessed 4 May).

21   A copy of the memorial volume handed out at those memorials is available at www.
      tamilnation.org/hundredtamils/sivaram.edf

BIBLIOGRAPHY

PRIMARY SOURCES

Diary of Puvirajakirthi Dharmeratnam, 2 October–31 December 1945.
Diaries of Sivaram Dharmeratnam for the years 1979, 1982, 1983.
In the District Court of Colombo, Testamentary Jurisdiction No. 1584/T.
Proposal of the Liberation Tigers of Tamil Eelam on behalf of the Tamil people for an agreement to establish an interim self-governing authority for the north-east of the island of Sri Lanka, 31 October 2003 (ISGA proposal). URL: http://www.tamilnation. org/conflictresolution/tamilleelam/norway/031101isga.htm, accessed 8/6/2005.

Daily Mirror
New York Times
Sunday Times
Tamil Times
The Island
Viirakeesari Illustrated Weekly.

WEBSITES

www.Newswire.ik
www.Tamilnation.org
www.TamilNet.com

SECONDARY SOURCES

Abeynayake, R. (2005a) 'One more leader for the assassination nation,' 28 Aug. URL: http://www.sundaytimes.Ik/050828/index.html, accessed 28 Aug. 2005.
—— (2005b) 'A funeral – an unusual end to an unusual life,' 8 May. URL: http://www. sundaytimes.Ik/050508/index.html, accessed 8 May 2005.
Abeywardane, R.B. (2005) 'Awaiting the winds, shrouded in sorrow,' *Daily Mirror* 11 May. URL: http://www.dailymirror.IK/2005/05/11/opinion/3.asp, accessed 11 May.
Africa, J.E. (2004) *Crumbs for Asia's Finest Puppet*, CAIS (Center for Anti-Imperialist Studies) Monograph, No. 2 (April–May). Quezon City, Philippines: CAIS.
Ananthan, V. (1997) *Ananthan Kavithaikal*. Batticaloa: Batticaloa Readers' Circle.
Anderson, B. (1991) *Imagined Communities*. London: Verso.
Andreski, S. (1954) *Military Organization and Society*, with a Foreword by A.R. Radcliffe-Brown. London: Routledge and Kegan Paul.
ASA (1993) *Sri Lanka: Assessment of the Human Rights Situation* (February, AI Index: ASA 37/1/93).
Balasingham, A. (2003) *The Will to Freedom: An Inside View of Tamil Resistance*, 2nd edn. Mitcham, UK: Fairmax Publishing Ltd.

Bandara, C.K. (2005) 'Siva is no more!' BBC Sinhala.com, 29 April. URL: http://www.bbc.co.uk/sinhala/news/story/2005/04/050429_sivaram_no_more.shtml, accessed 2 May 2005.

BBC News (2004) 'Who's who in Iraq: Ayatollah Sistani,' 26 Aug. URL: http://news.bbc.us/2/hi/middle_east/3033306.stm, accessed 17 July 2005.

Behar, R. (1993) *Translated Woman: Crossing the Border with Esperanza's Story*. Boston, MA: Beacon Press.

Bhabha, H.K. (ed.) (1990) *Nation and Narration*. London: Routledge.

Bhagavad Gita (1962) trans. Juan Mascaro. New York: Penguin Books.

Blakeney, E.H. (ed.) (1910) *A Smaller Classical Dictionary*. London: E.P. Dutton.

Bourdieu, P. (2004) 'Gender and symbolic violence.' In N. Scheper-Hughes and P. Bourgois (eds) *Violence in War and Peace: An Anthology*, pp. 339–442. Oxford: Blackwell.

Boyer, D. and C. Lomnitz (2005) 'Intellectuals and nationalism: anthropological engagements,' *Annual Review of Anthropology* 34: 105–20.

Brown, K.M. (1991) *Mama Lola: A Vodou Priestess in Brooklyn*. Berkeley: University of California Press.

Buck, D. (trans.) (2005) *Melagaram Tirikutarasekppa Kavirayar's A Kuravanji in Kutralam: A Tamil Tale of Love and Fortunes Told*. Chemmancheery, Chennai: Institute of Asian Studies.

Canagaratnam, S.O. (1921) *Monograph of the Batticaloa District of the Eastern Province, Ceylon*. Colombo: H.R. Cottle, Government Printer, Ceylon.

CBC (2005) 'Whose truth?' URL: http://www.cbc.ca/Toronto/features/whose_truth/, accessed 15 July 2005.

Chandraprema, C.A. (1991) *Sri Lanka: The Years of Terror – The JVP Insurrection 1987–1989*. Colombo: Lake House Bookshop.

Chatterjee, P. (1986) *Nationalist Thought and the Colonial World: A Derivative Discourse*. Minneapolis: University of Minnesota Press.

Chomsky, N. (2004) 'The new war against terror: responding to 9/11.' In N. Scheper-Hughes and P. Bourgois (eds) *Violence in War and Peace: An Anthology*, pp. 217–23. Oxford: Blackwell.

Chomsky, N. and E.S. Herman (1979) *The Washington Connection and Third World Fascism*. Boston, MA: South End Press.

Connor, W. (1994) 'A nation is a nation, is a state, is an ethnic group, is a ...,' in J. Hutchinson and A.D. Smith (eds) *Nationalism*, pp. 36–46. Oxford: Oxford University Press.

Creveld, M. Van (1977) *Supplying War: Logistics from Wallenstein to Patton*. New York: Cambridge University Press.

Daily Mirror (2005) 'Apprehend killers forthwith: magistrate directs CCD,' 21 June. URL: http://www.dailymirror.ik/2005/06/21/front/9.asp, accessed 21 June 2005.

Das, V. (2003) 'Trauma and testimony: implications for political communality,' *Anthropological Theory* 3(3): 293–307.

Derrida, J. (1982) *Margins of Philosophy*, trans., with Additional Notes by A. Bass. Chicago: University of Chicago Press.

Descombes, V. (1980) *Modern French Philosophy*. Cambridge: Cambridge University Press.

De Silva, K.M. (1981) *A History of Sri Lanka*. Delhi: Oxford University Press.

Dirks, N.B. (1993) *The Hollow Crown: Ethnohistory of an Indian Kingdom*, 2nd edn. Ann Arbor: University of Michigan Press.

Eco, U. (1983) *The Name of the Rose*, trans. W. Weaver. San Diego, CA: Harcourt Brace Jovanovich.

Editors of *Philosophy* (2003) 'Editorial: just war,' *Philosophy: The Journal of the Royal Institute of Philosophy* 78: 317–18.

Emmanuel, Rev. Fr. Dr. S.J. (2005) 'I weep for Sivaram,' in *Memorial Tribute to Mamanithar Dharmaratnam Sivaram (Taraki)*, pp. 16–17. (Memorial booklet handed out at the Memorial gathering at New Brunswick, NJ, USA, 6 June 2005.)

Farmer, P. (1992) *Aids and Accusation: Haiti and the Geography of Blame*. Berkeley: University of California Press.

Feldman, A. (1991) *Formations of Violence: The Narrative of the Body and Political Terror in Northern Ireland*. Chicago: University of Chicago Press.

Ferguson, B.R. (ed.) (2003) *The State, Identity and Violence: Political Disintegration in the Post-Cold War World*. London: Routledge.

Fernando, J.L. (2005) 'Sivaram on state, politics and class,' *Northeastern Monthly*, June, pp. 22–4.

Feyerabend, P. (1975) *Against Method: Outline of an Anarchic Theory of Knowledge*. London: Verso.

Fitzgerald, E. (1942) *The Rubáiyat of Omar Khayyám*. New York: Walter J. Black.

Foucault, M. (1977) *Language, Counter-Memory, Practice: Selected Essays and Interviews by Michel Foucault*. Ithaca, NY: Cornell University Press.

—— (1979) *Discipline and Punish*. New York: Vintage Books.

Fox, R.G. (1989) *Gandhian Utopia: Experiments with Culture*. Boston, MA: Beacon Press.

Freeman, J.M. (1979) *Untouchable: An Indian Life History*. Stanford, CA: Stanford University Press.

Fugelrud, O. (1999) *Life on the Outside: The Tamil Diaspora and Long-distance Nationalism*. London: Pluto Press.

Gaasbeek, T. (2005) 'Factors influencing post-tsunami recovery in East Sri Lanka,' MS of a paper presented to the tsunami research team, University of Colorado, Boulder.

Geertz, C. (1980) *Negara: The Theatre State in Nineteenth-century Bali*. Princeton, NJ: Princeton University Press.

Gellner, E. (1983) *Nations and Nationalism*. London: Blackwell.

Giddens, A. (1994) 'The nation as power-container,' in J. Hutchinson and A.D. Smith (eds) *Nationalism*, pp. 34–6. Oxford: Oxford University Press.

Gramsci, A. (1971) *Selection from the Prison Notebooks of Antonio Gramsci*. New York: International Publishers.

Gunasinghe, N. (1984) 'The open economy and its impact on ethnic relations,' *Lanka Guardian* 15 Jan.

Gunaratna, R. (1993) *Indian Intervention in Sri Lanka: The Role of India's Intelligence Agencies*. Colombo: South Asian Network on Conflict Research.

—— (1997) International and Regional Security Implications of the Sri Lankan Tamil Insurgency. Colombo: Unie Arts (Pvt) Ltd.

Habermas, J. (1975) *Legitimation Crisis*. Boston, MA: Beacon Press.

Harding, S.F. (2001) *The Book of Jerry Falwell: Fundamentalist Language and Politics*. Princeton, NJ: Princeton University Press.

Hobsbawm, E. and T. Ranger (eds) (1983) *The Invention of Tradition*. Cambridge: Cambridge University Press.

Hoole, R. (2001) *Sri Lanka: The Arrogance of Power: Myths, Decadence and Murder*. Colombo: University Teachers for Human Rights (Jaffna).

Hoole, R., D. Somasundaram, K. Sritharan, R. Thiranagama (1990) *The Broken Palmyra: The Tamil Crisis in Sri Lanka – An Inside Account*. Claremont, CA: Sri Lanka Studies Institute: Harvey Mudd College Press.

Hutchinson, J. and A.D. Smith (eds) (1994) *Nationalism*. Oxford: Oxford University Press.

Ismail, Q. (1987) 'Militants' historical role is over,' *The Island* 29 Sept.

—— (2005) 'Mourning Sivaram,' *TamilWeek* 12 June. URL: www.tamilweek.com/Mourning_Sivaram_0023.html, accessed 17 June 2005.

Jaimon, M. (2004) 'Lankan Websites in All Three Languages,' *Daily Mirror* 18 Feb.

Jayatilleka, D. (2005) 'The brutal slaying of Sivaram,' *Daily Mirror* 30 March. URL: http://www/dailymirror.Ik/2005/04/30/opinion/2.asp, accessed 29 April 2005.

Jayawardena, K. (1986) *Ethnic and Class Conflicts in Sri Lanka: Some Aspects of Sinhala Buddhist Consciousness over the Past 100 Years*. Colombo, Dehiwala: Centre for Social Analysis.

—— (2000) *Nobodies to Somebodies: The Rise of the Colonial Bourgoisie in Sri Lanka*. Colombo, Sri Lanka: Sanjiva Books.

Jeganathan, P. and Q. Ismail (1995) *Unmaking the Nation: The Politics of Identity and History in Modern Sri Lanka*. Colombo: Social Scientists' Association.

Jeyaraj, D.B.S. (1999) 'Camp after camp falls in Tiger blitzkrieg,' *Tamil Times* 18(11): 5–7.

Jeyaraj, D.B.S (2005a) 'Tigers strike back in "do or die" battle," *Tamil Times* 16(6): 12–16.

—— (2005b) 'From gun to pen: the story of Sivaram, Parts 1–4.' URL: (part 1) www.tamilweek.com/Sivaram_Gun_to_Pen_0009.html, (part 2) www.tamilweek.com/Sivaram_Gun_to_Pen_0010.html, (part 3) www.tamilweek.com/Sivaram_Gun_to_Pen_0011.html, (part 4) www.tamilweek.com/Sivaram_Gun_to_Pen_0012.html, accessed 6 June 2005.

—— (2005c) 'The abduction and assassination of "Taraki" Sivaram,' *Tamil Week* 1 May. URL: http://tamilweek.com/Assasination_Sivaram_0011.html, accessed 1 May.

Jomini, Baron de (1971 [1862]) *The Art of War: A New Edition, with Appendices and Maps*, trans. Capt. G.H. Mendell, Lieut. W.P. Graighill. Westport, CT: Greenwood.

Kailasapathy, K. (1968) *Tamil Heroic Poetry*. Oxford: Oxford University Press.

Kapferer, B. (1988) *Legends of People, Myths of State: Violence, Intolerance, and Political Culture in Sri Lanka and Australia*. Washington, DC: Smithsonian Institution Press.

Kaplan, E. (2005) 'Q&A: TSUNAMI: Tsunami rebuilding efforts, one year later,' *New York Times* 24 Dec. URL: http://www.nytimes.com/cfr/international/slot3_122405.html, accessed 26 Dec. 2005.

Keegan, J. (1993) *A History of Warfare*. New York: Vintage Books.

Kingsolver, A.E. (2001) *NAFTA Stories: Fears and Hopes in Mexico and the United States*. Boulder, CO: Lynne Rienner.

Kitson, F. (1971) *Low Intensity Operations: Subversion, Insurgency, Peacekeeping*. Harrisburg, PA: Stackpole Books.

—— (1977) *Bunch of Five*. London: Faber and Faber.

Kroeber, T. (1961) *Ishi in Two Worlds: A Biography of the Last Wild Indian in North America*. Berkeley: University of California Press.

Kuhn, T. (1962) *The Structure of Scientific Revolutions*. Chicago: University of Chicago Press.

Landzelius, K. (ed.) (forthcoming) *Native on the Net: Indigenous and Diasporic Peoples in the Virtual Age*. London: Routledge.

Laqueur, W. (1999) *The New Terrorism: Fanaticism and the Arms of Mass Destruction*. Oxford: Oxford University Press.

Lavie, S. (1990) *The Poetics of Military Occupation: Mzeina Allegories of Bedouin Identity Under Israeli and Egyptian Rule*. Los Angeles: University of California Press.

Lawrence, P. (2000) 'Violence, suffering, Amman: the work of oracles in Sri Lanka's eastern war zone.' In V. Das, A. Kleinman, M. Ramphele, and P. Reynolds (eds) *Violence and Subjectivity*, pp. 171–204. Berkeley: University of California Press.

Lyotard, J.-F. (1984) *The Postmodern Condition: A Report on Knowledge*. Minneapolis: University of Minnesota Press.

Lyotard, J.F. (1994) *Lessons on the Analytic of the Sublime: Kant's Critique of Judgment*, sections 23–9, trans. E. Rottenberg. Stanford, CA: Stanford University Press.

The Mahavamsa (1934) trans. W. Geiger. London: Oxford University Press for the Pali Text Society.

Marx, K. (1963) *The Eighteenth Brumaire of Louis Bonaparte*. New York: International Publishers.

McAlpin, D. (1976) *A Core Vocabulary for Tamil*. Philadelphia: South Asia Regional Studies, University of Pennsylvania.

McCarthy, T. (1981) *The Critical Theory of Jurgen Habermas*. Cambridge: MIT Press.

McGilvray, D.B. (1973) 'Caste and matriclan structure in Sri Lanka: a preliminary report on fieldwork in Akkaraipattu,' *Modern Ceylon Studies* 4: 5–20.

—— (1974) 'Tamils and Moors: caste and matriclan structure in eastern Sri Lanka.' Unpublished PhD thesis, University of Chicago.

—— (1982) ' "Mukkuvar vannimai": Tamil caste and matriclan ideology Batticaloa, Sri Lanka.' In D.B. McGilvray (ed.) *Caste Ideology and Interaction*, pp. 35–97. Cambridge: Cambridge University Press.

Miller, B.D. (2002) *Cultural Anthropology*. Boston: Allyn and Bacon.

Miller, B.H. (1974) 'St Michael's College: the private years.' In *Centenary Volume of St Michael's College, Batticaloa*. Batticaloa: St Michael's College.

Milton, J. (1957) *John Milton: Complete Poems and Major Prose*, edited by M.Y. Hughes. Indianapolis, IN: Bobbs-Merrill Educational Publishing.

Nadarajah, F.X.C., (ed.) (1962) *MaTTakkaLappu Maanmiyam* (The Glory of Batticaloa). Colombo: Kalanilayam.

Nanayakkara, S. (no date – probably 2002) *Jathika Chinthanaya*. A Young Socialist Publication: Boralegamuwa: C.R.C. Press.

Narayan, K. (1989) *Storytellers, Saints, and Scoundrels: Folk Narrative in Hindu Religious Teaching*. Philadelphia: University of Pennsylvania Press.

National Peace Council (2003) *Costs of War: Challenges and Priorities for the Future*. Ratmalana, Sri Lanka: Sarvodaya Vishva Lekha Printers.

Nesiah, D. (2001) *Tamil Nationalism*. Monograph No. 6 of 19: *A History of Ethnic Conflict in Sri Lanka: Recollection, Reinterpretation and Reconciliation*. Colombo: Marga Institute.

Obeyesekere, G. (1967) *Land Tenure in Village Ceylon: A Sociological and Historical Study*. Cambridge: Cambridge University Press.

Obeyesekere, G. (1984) 'Political violence and the future of democracy in Sri Lanka,' *Internationales Asienforum, International Quarterly for Asian Studies* 15(1–2): 39–60.

Our Defense Correspondent (2004) 'Government looking for defense budget cuts that aren't there,' *Sunday Island* 9 May.

Palanithurai, G., and K. Mohanasundaram (1993) *Dynamics of Tamil Nadu Politics in Sri Lankan Ethnicity*. New Delhi: Northern Book Centre.

Pathmanathan, S. (1979) 'Historical traditions of the Batticaloa Tamils.' Paper presented at the Conference Seminar of Tamil Studies, Batticaloa, 19–21 March.

Peiris, G.H. (ed.) (1997) *Studies on the Press in Sri Lanka and South Asia*. Kandy: International Center for Ethnic Studies.

Popham, F.H. (1993) *Dambulla: A Sanctuary of Tropical Trees*. Essex, UK: Sam Popham Foundation.

Radin, P. (1963) *The Autobiography of a Winnebago Indian*. New York: Dover.

Rajanayagam, D. (1994) 'Tamils and the meaning of history. The 'groups' and the rise of militant secessionism.' In C. Manogaran and B. Pfaffenberger (eds) *Sri Lankan Tamils: Ethnicity and Identity*, pp. 54–83; 169–207. Boulder: Westview Press.

Reporters sans frontières (2004) 'Sri Lanka.' URL: htpp://www.rsf.org/article.php3?id_article=10755, accessed 18 July 2006.

Rorty, R. (1979) *Philosophy and the Mirror of Nature*. Princeton, NJ: Princeton University Press.

Russell, J. (1982) *Communal Politics under the Donoughmore Constitution, 1931–1947*. Dehiwala: Tisara Prakasakayo Ltd.

Ryle, G. (1949) *The Concept of Mind*. New York: Barnes and Noble.

Sahlins, M. (1982) 'The apotheosis of Captain Cook.' In M. Izard and P. Smith (eds) *Between Belief and Transgression: Structuralist Essays in Religion, History and Myth*. Chicago: University of Chicago Press.

Sambadan, V.S. (2005) 'The end of a dissenter,' *The Hindu* 13 June.

Scheper-Hughes, N. and P. Bourgois (2004) 'Introduction: making sense of violence.' In N. Scheper-Hughes and P. Bourgois (eds) *Violence in War and Peace: An Anthology*, pp. 1–32. Oxford: Blackwell.

Scott, D. (1994) *Formations of Ritual: Colonial and Anthropological Discourses on the Sinhala Yaktovil*. Minneapolis: University of Minnesota Press.

Selvanayagam, S.S. (2004) 'Veteran Tamil journalist killed in East,' *Daily Mirror* 1 June. URL: http://www.dailymirror.lk/2004/06/01/front/1.asp, accessed 18 July 2006.

Shanmugaratnam, N. (1993) 'Shanmugathasan – the unrepentant communist,' *Tamil Times* 12(4) (15 April): 21–2.

Shanmugaratnam, N. (2001) *Forced Migration and Changing Local Political Economies: A study from North-western Sri Lanka*. Colombo: Social Scientists Association.

Shostak, M. (1981) *Nisa, the Life and Words of a !Kung Woman*. New York: Vintage Books.

Sivaram, D. (1992) 'The weakness of an intellectual milieu.' : 1–9.

—— (1992) 'On Tamil militarism – an 11-part essay; part 1: origins and dispersion in South India and Sri Lanka,' *Lanka Guardian* 1 May. Prepared by *Sachi Sri Kantha* for electronic record, URL: http://www.tamilnation.org/forum/sivaram/920501lg.htm, accessed 19 July 2006.

—— (1993) '16 aam naaRRaaNTil maTTakkaLappu' (Batticaloa in the Sixteenth Century). In *MaTTakkaLappup pirateesas saatittiya viLaa Ninaivu malar* (Batticaloa Region Literary Celebration Commemoration Volume) maTTakkalappu: maTTakkalappu pirateesas saakittiya viLaa amaippuk kuLu, pp. 13–25 (Batticaloa Region Literary Celebration Organizing Committee).

—— (writing as 'Our Special Correspondent') (1994a) 'Govt's counter-insurgency programme and LTTE's military response,' *Tamil Times* 13(5) (15 May): 9–11.

—— (1994b) 'The Chandrika factor and the ethnic question,' *Tamil Times* 13(6) (15 June): 11–13.

—— (1995) 'Political and military objectives of the govt's Jaffna offensive,' *Tamil Times* 15 Dec.

—— (1996a) 'Devolution, the bank bomb and the dilemma of Tamil parties,' *Tamil Times* 15(2): 13–14.

—— (1996b) 'The post Operation Riversea 2 Phase,' *Tamil Times* 15(5): 12–13.

—— (2001) 'Breaking the "containment" – the options for LTTE,' MS of talk given at the Center for International Strategic Studies, Washington, DC.

—— (2003a) 'Challenges the Tigers face in the CFA,' *Northeastern Herald* 21–7 Feb. URL: www.tamilcanadian.com/pageview.php?ID=1610&SID=334, accessed 8 June 2005.

—— (2003b) 'camaataan oppantangkaLaal mTTum camaataanam vantu viTaatu' ('Peace cannot be achieved by peace agreements alone'), *Viirakeesari* 10 Aug.

—— (2003c) 'osloo pirakaTanam oru poRi; atu kiRitteRiyappaTa veeNTum' (The Oslo declaration is a trap that has to be torn up and thrown out), *Viirakeesari* 7 Dec.

—— (2003d) 'carvateeca viyuukangkaLee tamiLeeLam etirkoLLa veeNTiya cavaal' (International strategies are the challenges that Tamil Eelam has to face) *Viirakeesari* 14 Dec.

—— (2003e) 'pulikalai muTakkavaa ilangkai – intiya puutukaappu kuuTTuRavu oppantam' (Is the Lanka–India cooperative defence agreement a strategy to disable the Tigers?) *Viirakeesari* 21 Dec.

—— (2004a) 'intiya kaTaR paatukaappu valayattil ciRilangkaa' (Sri Lanka in India's ocean security zone) *Viirakeesari* 4 Jan.

—— (2004b) 'intu samuttira vallaatikka – pooTTiyil tamiLeeLam' (Tamil Eelam in the competition for domination of the Indian Ocean) *Viirakeesari* 11 Jan.

—— (2004c) 'jee. vi. pi. neeRRu, intru, naalai' (JVP yesterday, today and tomorrow ...) *Viirakeesari* 25 Jan.

—— (2004d) 'karuNaavukku oru kaTitam' (Open letter to Karuna) *Viirakeesari* 14 March.

—— (2004e) 'On the psyche of the Sinhala nation,' *Viirakeesari* 10 Oct. URL: http://www.tamilnation.org/forum/sivaram/041010.htm, accessed July 2006, English version courtesy of Tamil Canadian.

Sivathamby, K. (1995) *Sri Lankan Tamil Society and Politics*. Madras: New Century Book House Ltd.

—— (2005) 'Profile: unassuming greatness, unforgettable charm,' *Northeastern Monthly* June. URL: http://www.tamilcanadian.com/pageview.php?ID=3298&SID=514, accessed 29 May 2005.

Smith, A.D. (1986) *The Ethnic Origins of Nations*. Oxford: Blackwell.

—— (2001) *Nationalism*. Cambridge: Polity Press.

Sornarajah, M. (2000) 'Eelam and the right to secession,' text of a speech given at the International Tamil Foundation, London, 25 June.

Spencer, J. (2000) 'On not becoming a "terrorist": problems of memory, agency, and community in the Sri Lankan conflict.' In V. Das, A. Kleinman, M. Ramphale, and P. Reynolds (eds) *Violence and Subjectivity*, pp. 120–40. Berkeley: University of California Press.

Stein, B. (1980) *Peasant State and Society in Medieval South India*. Delhi: Oxford University Press.

Stubbs, R. (1989) *Hearts and Minds in Guerrilla Warfare: The Malayan Emergency 1948–1960*. Oxford: Oxford University Press.

Swamy, M.R.N. (2003) Inside the Elusive Mind: Prabhakaran – The First Profile of the World's Most Ruthless Guerrilla Leader. Colombo: Vijitha Yapa Publications.

Tambiah, S. (1976) *World Conqueror and World Renouncer: A Study of Buddhism and Polity in Thailand against a Historical Background*. New York: Cambridge University Press.

Tambiah, S. (1986) *Sri Lanka: Ethnic Fratricide and the Dismantling of Democracy*. Chicago: The University of Chicago Press.

Tambiah, S. (1992) *Buddhism Betrayed? Religion, Politics, and Violence in Sri Lanka*. Chicago: University of Chicago Press.

TamilNet.com (1999) 'Tiger manoeuvres trouble gateway garrison,' 16 Dec. URL: http://www.tamilnet.com/art.html?catid=79&artid=7406, accessed July 2006.

—— (2000) 'Senior Jaffna journalist shot dead,' 19 Oct. URL: http://www.tamilnet.com/art.html?catid=13&artid=5512, accessed July 2006.

—— (2001) 'SLTMA slams military harassment of Thinakathir,' 30 Dec. URL: http://www.tamilnet.com/art.html?catid=13&artid=6588, accessed 10 Jan. 2005

—— (2002) 'Commandos camp in hospital despite peace promise,' 25 Jan. URL: http://www.tamilnet.com/art.html?catid=13&artid=6653, accessed 29 Oct. 2005.

—— (2003) 'News Feature: Sustaining strategic parity and beyond,' 30 April. URL: http://www.tamilnet.com/art.html?catid=79&=8880, accessed 29 Oct. 2005.

—— (2005a) 'Media watchdog says JVP inciting violence against journalists', 12 April. URL: http://www.tamilnet.com/art.html?catid=13&artid=14662, accessed 29 Oct. 2005.

—— (2005b) 'Sivaram's loss, a true tragedy – Teresita Schaffer,' 29 April. URL: http://www.tamilnet.com/art.html?catid=13&artid=14776, accessed 16 May 2005.

—— (2005c) 'Media colleagues pay tribute to Sivaram,' 29 May. URL: http://www.tamilnet.com/art.html?catid=13&artid=15014, accessed 1 Jan. 2006.

—— (2005d) 'Sivaram murder vehicle, SIM card recovered – police,' 13 June. URL: http://www.tamilnet.com/art.html?catid=13&artid=15142, accessed 29 Dec. 2005.

—— (2005e) 'Sivaram murder suspect remanded till 20 June,' 14 June. URL: http://www.tamilnet.com/art.html?catid=13&artid=15152, accessed 13 Jan. 2006.

—— (2005f) 'Witnesses fail to identify Sivaram murder suspect,' 5 July. URL: http://www.tamilnet.com/art.html?catid=13&artid=15322, accessed 13 Jan. 2006.

—— (2005g) 'Joseph Pararajasingham MP shot dead in Batticaloa church,' 24 Dec. URL: http://www.tamilnet.com/art.html?catid=13&artid=16629, accessed 9 Jan. 2006.

Tamil Times (1995) 'Mass exodus as army enters Jaffna,' *Tamil Times* 14(11) (15 Nov.): 4–5.

—— (1996) 'News review: the bomb that rocked Colombo,' *Tamil Times* 15(2): 3–5.

—— (2001) 'Daring suicide attack on airport,' *Tamil Times* 20(7): 4–5.

Taraki (1991) *The Eluding Peace (An Insider's Political Analysis of the Ethnic Conflict in Sri Lanka)*. Sarcelles, France: ASSEAY.

—— (1993a) 'Whither the Tamil question? After Premadasa,' *The Island* 1 May.

—— (1993b) 'Pacifying the east?' *The Island* 21 Nov.

—— (1993c) 'LTTE consolidates its sea power,' *The Island* 12 Dec.

—— (1994a) 'Grads of Tigers' defense college,' *The Island* 3 April.

—— (1994b) 'TULF rethinks strategy,' *The Island* 24 April.

—— (1994c) 'The exclusive right to Eelam history,' *The Island* 8 May.

—— (1994d) 'Re-opening of the Pooneryn causeway,' *The Island* 23 Aug.

—— (1994e) 'LTTE's response to peace overtures' *The Island* 4 Sept.

—— (1994f) 'Pirabhakaran – family and society,' *The Island* 18 Dec.

—— (1994g) 'Ceasefire – the LTTE's concern,' *The Island* 25 Dec.

—— (1995a) 'Govt. confusion on LTTE,' *The Island* 1 Jan.

—— (1995b) 'Confederation: Mr Thamil Selvan should know better,' *The Island* 29 Jan.

—— (1996a) 'Game plan for a grand slam,' *Midweek Mirror* 3 March. URL: http://www.forum/Sivaram/960303.htm, accessed 9 June 2005.

—— (1996b) 'Riversea II and opening up of the front,' *Midweek Mirror* 21 April.

—— (1997a) 'The cat, a bell and a few strategists,' *Midweek Mirror* May. URL: http:www.tamilnation.org/forum/Sivaram/970500.htm, accessed 9 June 2006.

—— (1997b) 'Surprise in Prabha's strategy,' *Sunday Times* 8 June.

—— (1997c) 'Creeping advantage: can the government hold on to it?' *Midweek Mirror* 23 Nov.

—— (1997d) 'Troops in Tiger trap: electronic intelligence gathering can be useless if not matched and confirmed by ground intelligence,' *Midweek Mirror* 10 Dec.

—— (1997e) 'Blinded in the Wanni,' *Sunday Times* 29 June.

—— (1997f) 'Sojourn to Vanni tells all,' *Sunday Times* 4 May.

—— (1997g) 'Is there a future for the moderates?' *Midweek Mirror* 14 Dec.

—— (1998a) 'Tamil suffering on the rise under PA,' *Sunday Times* 5 April.

—— (1998b) 'In political wilderness, ex-militants go berserk,' *Sunday Times* 6 Dec.

—— (1999) 'Those who wear the Tiger mask,' *Sunday Times* 17 Jan.

—— (2004a) 'LTTE will negotiate only with parity of military status,' *Daily Mirror* 28 Jan.

—— (2004b) 'Money, power and the rebellion in the LTTE,' *Daily Mirror* 17 March.

—— (2004c) 'Contending with the Karuna factor after polls,' *Daily Mirror* 25 March.

—— (2004d) 'Tamils see rejection of Ranil as rejection of peace process,' *Daily Mirror* 7 April.

—— (2004e) 'Karuna affair: the military connection,' *Daily Mirror* 7 July.

—— (2004f) 'ISGA entails concepts and structures of final solution,' *Daily Mirror* 4 Aug.

—— (2004g) 'Tigers dominate decades of Tamil militancy,' *Daily Mirror* 18 Aug.

—— (2004h) 'A second look at US assistance to Lanka against terrorism,' *Daily Mirror* 15 Sept. URL: http://www.daily mirror.IK/2004/9/15/opinion/1.asp, accessed 15 Sept. 2004.

—— (2004i) 'Are the LTTE efforts to communicate with the south becoming futile?' *Daily Mirror* 13 Oct.

Taraki (2004j) 'Velupillai Pirapaharan [Pirabakaran] turns fifty today,' *Daily Mirror* 26 Nov. URL: http://www.dailymirror.lk/2004/11/26/opinion/1.asp, accessed 18 July 2006.

—— (2005a) 'Six months after the tsunami, will the displaced remain in tents?' *Daily Mirror* 2 Feb.

—— (2005b) 'Can the Govt. shirk red tape to become a responsible state?' *Daily Mirror* 16 Feb.

—— (2005c) 'LTTE's "hearts and minds" op. in east,' *Daily Mirror* 2 March.

—— (2005d) 'What is the larger picture in Pirapakaran's mind?' *Daily Mirror* 9 March.

—— (2005e) 'Are the Tigers militarily weak?' *Daily Mirror* 23 March.

—— (2005f) 'TV images: LTTE's next strategic dimension?' *Daily News* 30 March.

—— (2005g) 'The writing is on the wall, and it is in red,' *Daily Mirror* 13 April.

—— (2005h) 'Sleeping Tigers and hidden agendas,' *Daily Mirror* 20 April.

—— (2005i) 'JVP's war on NGOs and fears of neo colonialism,' *Daily Mirror* 27 April. URL: http://www.dailymirror.lk/2005/04/27/opinion/2.asp, accessed 18 July 2005.

Tennent, Sir James E. (1993 [1861]) *Sketches of the Natural History of Ceylon.* New Delhi: Navrang.

Tilly, C. (ed.) (1975) *The Formation of National States in Western Europe.* Princeton, NJ: Princeton University Press.

Tillyard, E.M.W (1966) *Milton.* Middlesex: Penguin.

Thangavelu, V. (2005) 'Let us resolve to carry on Sivaram's unfinished task!' 8 May. URL: www.tamilnation.org/forum/thangavelu/sivaram.htm, accessed July 2006.

Tissainayagam, J.S. (2005) 'Issues: Sivaram, his murderers and his mourners.' *Northeastern Monthly* June. URL: http://tamilcanadian.com/pageview.php?ID=3300&SID=514, accessed 29 May 2005.

Trawick, M. (1992) *Notes on Love in a Tamil Family.* Berkeley: University of California Press.

—— (1999) 'Reasons for violence: a preliminary ethnographic account of the LTTE.' In S. Gamage and I.B. Watson (eds) *Conflict and Community in Contemporary Sri Lanka; 'Pearl of the East' or the 'Island of Tears'*, pp. 139–64. New Delhi: Sage Publications.

UN (1970) 'Declaration on principles of international law concerning friendly relations and co-operation among states.' URL: http://www.tamilnation.org/selfdetermination/instruments/2625GAdeclarationofprinciplesofinternationallaw.htm, accessed 17 July 2006.

Uyangoda, J. (2005) 'Defend the middle ground: new trend disturbing,' *Daily Mirror* 5 Jan. URL: http://www/dailymirror.IK/2005/05/13/opinion/1.asp, accessed 13 May 2005.

Vaddukoddai Resolution (1976) URL: http://www.eelamweb.com/history/document/vaddu, accessed on 7 January 2003.

Van Creveld, M. (1977) *Supplying War: Logistics from Wallenstein to Patton.* Cambridge: Cambridge University Press.

Vidanage, H.R. (2005) 'Sivaram: alive and well in cyber space.' URL: http:www.tamilcandian.com/pageview/php?ID=3265&SID=512, accessed 5/4/05.

Whitaker, M. (1986) 'Divinity and legitimacy in a temple of the Lord Kantan.' Unpublished PhD thesis, Princeton University.

—— (1990) 'A compound of many histories: the many pasts of an east coast Sri Lankan community.' In J. Spencer (ed.) *The Power of the Past*, pp. 145–63. London: Routledge and Kegan Paul.

—— (1997) 'Tigers and temples: the politics of nationalist and non-modern violence in Sri Lanka,' *South Asia* 20(Special Issue): 201–14.

—— (1999) 'Learning politics from Taraki: a biographical fragment.' In Michael Roberts (ed.) *Collected Identities, Vol. II*, pp. 247–70. Colombo: Marga Institute.

—— (2004) 'Tamilnet.com: some reflections on popular anthropology,' *Anthropological Quarterly* 77(3): 469–98.

—— (forthcoming) 'Internet *counter* counter-insurgency: TamilNet.com and ethnic conflict in Sri Lanka.' In K. Landzelius (ed.) *Native on the Net: Indigenous and Diasporic Peoples in the Virtual Age.* London: Routledge.

The White House (n.d.) 'The Millennium Challenge Account.' URL: http://www.whitehouse.gov/infocus/developingnations/millennium.html, accessed 29 Dec. 2005.

Wijesinha, R. (ed.) (2000) *Richard de Zoysa: His Life, Some Work ... A Death.* Sabaragamuwa: Sabaragamuwa University Press.

Wilson, A.J. (2000) *Sri Lankan Tamil Nationalism: Its Origins and Development in the 19th and 20th Centuries.* Vancouver: UBC Press.

Wittgenstein, L. (1958) *Philosophical Investigations*, trans. G.E.M. Anscombe. New York: Macmillan.

Wittgenstein, L. (1974 [1921]) *Tractatus Logico-Philosophicus.* Atlantic Highlands, NJ: Humanities Press.

Wittgenstein, L. (1969) *On Certainty*, edited by G.E.M. Anscombe and G.H. von Wright. New York: Basic Books.

Yalman, N. (1967) *Under the Bo Tree: Studies in Caste, Kinship and Marriage in the Interior of Ceylon.* Berkeley: University of California Press.

Zulaika, J. (1988) *Basque Violence: Metaphor and Sacrament.* Reno: University of Nevada Press.

INDEX